D1553704

Between Muslim and Jew

Between Muslim and Jew

THE PROBLEM OF SYMBIOSIS

UNDER EARLY ISLAM

STEVEN M. WASSERSTROM

PRINCETON UNIVERSITY PRESS

PRINCETON, NEW JERSEY

Library of Congress Cataloging-in-Publication Data

Wasserstrom, Steven M.
Between Muslim and Jew : the problem of symbiosis under early
Islam / Steven M. Wasserstrom.
p.   cm.
Includes bibliographical references (p.   ) and index.
ISBN 0-691-03455-9
1. Islam—Relations—Judaism.   2. Judaism—Relations—Islam.
3. Jews—Islamic Empire—Intellectual life.   4. Judaism—Islamic
Empire—History.   I. Title.
BP173.J8W38   1995
296.3'872—dc20   94-43430

This book has been composed in Galliard

Princeton University Press books are printed on acid-free paper and meet the guidelines for
permanence and durability of the Committee on Production Guidelines for Book
Longevity of the Council on Library Resources

Printed in the United States of America by Princeton Academic Press

1   2   3   4   5   6   7   8   9   10

CONTENTS

PREFACE

AN AUTHOR is of course responsible for the flaws of his or her text. Still, scholarship largely remains a collective exercise, necessarily meaningless in isolation and usually enhanced by collegial interaction. The present work is no exception to these rules. Marilyn Waldman, my first teacher in the study of Islam, a true friend and revered colleague, read, heard, or responded to much that found its way into this book. She has encouraged me in more ways than I could count, all the while providing for me a model of humane, creative, engaged scholarship. *Ad meah ve-esrim.* I remain thankful that Michael Wickens, my master in all aspects of the Arabic language, and Mahmoud Ayoub, who guided me into the study of Shi'a Islam, were patient with their pupil. The help of Fred M. Donner came at a crucial time during my stay in Chicago. Over the years, Gordon Darnell Newby, Ze'ev Brinner, and David J. Halperin consistently have given support and counsel. Invitations from Martin Jaffee, Richard Martin, and Jacques Waardenburg provided forums for the early venting of ideas. Camilla Adang, Juan Campo, Reuven Firestone, Rawley Grau, Sidney Griffith, Joel Kraemer, Azim Nanji, John Reeves, Kevin Reinhart, Aziz Sachedina, Sarah Stroumsa, and Elliot Wolfson have helped in various ways, all of which mean much to me. May I be forgiven for the inadvertent omission of anyone else who deserves to be named here.

At Reed College, I am grateful for the support of Provosts Marsh Cronyn and Doug Bennett, as well as Dean Linda Mantel. For electronic aid, I thank Marianne Colgrove, Chris Lasell, and Johanna Turner. Heroic labors were provided by the Interlibrary Loan staff, who tolerated a sustained barrage of arcane requests. I particularly appreciate the considerable efforts of Sam Sayre, Michael Gaunt, Wendy Falconer, and Kristine Hunter.

I thank the editors and publishers of the following publications for their permission to use materials originally printed by them: "Jewish Pseudepigrapha in Muslim Literature: A Bibliographical and Methodological Sketch," in *Tracing the Threads: The Vitality of Jewish Pseudepigrapha*, edited by John Reeves (Scholars Press: Atlanta, 1994), 87–115; "The Shi'is Are the Jews of Our Community," *Israel Oriental Studies* 14:297–325; "The 'Isawiyya Revisited," *Studia Islamica* 75 (1992): 57–80; "Recent Works on the 'Creative Symbiosis' of Judaism and Islam," *Religious Studies Review* 16 (1990): 42–47; "The Magical Texts in the Cairo Genizah," in *After Ninety Years of Genizah Research (1897–1987)*, ed. Stefan Reif and Joshua Blau (Cambridge University Press: Cambridge, 1992), 160–66; "The Delay of Maghrib: A Study in Comparative Polemics," in *Logos Islamikos: Studia Islamica in Honorem Georgii Michaelis Wickens*, ed. Roger M. Savory and Dionisius A. Agius, Papers in Mediaeval Studies, vol. 6 (Pontifical Institute of Mediaeval Studies: Toronto, 1984): 269–86.

Material support that made this work possible came from the Social Science and Humanities Research Council of Canada; the Vollum Junior Fellowship at Reed College; and the American Council of Learned Societies. I thank Steven Gardiner and Lainie Reich for bringing some order to a disheveled manuscript. Cathie Brettschneider originally showed confidence in this book at a very early stage in its development. I thank her, my subsequent editors at Princeton University Press, Ann Wald and Sara Mullen, and my assiduous copyeditor, Cindy Crumrine, for all their help, encouragement, and hard work.

Pesha Rose and Shulamit Reba have never known a time when their father was not working on "the book." I hope that some day, on reading it, they will find the wait worthwhile. "The book" is dedicated to their mother, Judith Lynn Margles, who knows why.

Between Muslim and Jew

> How one religion behaves toward other religions, how and what it thinks
> about the "other"—the whole *theologia religionum*, in other words—is an
> essential part of the self-understanding of every religion and what it says
> about itself.
>
> —R. J. Zwi Werblowsky, "Common Roots"

THE LATE Shlomo Dov (Fritz) Goitein (1900–1985) characterized the central relationship of Jews with Muslims in the first centuries of Islam as one of
"creative symbiosis." This usage has been institutionalized in the study of
Judeo-Arabica, and shows no immediate signs of being dislodged from its
preeminence.[1] The concept *symbiosis* was first transposed from biology to the
study of Jewish history by German Jewish intellectuals. Its most salient usage
was in reference to their own cultural situation.[2] Alex Bein's influential study,
"Discourse on the Term 'German-Jewish Symbiosis,'" appeared at that time,
as an appendix to his essay (revealingly enough) on a related biological borrowing, "The Jewish Parasite."[3] After the destruction of the German Jewish
community in World War II, the brunt of this debate came to concern the
extent to which this vaunted German Jewish symbiosis was simply a Jewish
delusion. This position is eloquently, if acerbically, argued by Gershom
Scholem.[4] Nonetheless, the term continued to mount in popularity among

[1] I have dealt more fully with some of the recent literature in "Recent Works on the
'Creative Symbiosis' of Judaism and Islam," 43–47, parts of which are used herein.
[2] In the phrase given currency by H. Cohen, these Jews were torn between "Germanism and Judaism" (Deutschtum und Judentum),—a notion S. Schwarszchild ex-
plores in "Hermann Cohen's Normative Paradigm of the German-Jewish Symbiosis,"
129–72. Martin Buber and others already occasionally borrowed this scientistic metaphor within the lifetime of Cohen (Bein, "Jewish Parasite," 3–40; E. Simon, "Martin
Buber and German Jewry," 15 n. 46). Employed sporadically and vaguely until the
mid-1960s, the use of *symbiosis* was then both increased and modified. By 1976, Bronsen could publish an anthology with the encompassing title *Jews and Germans, from
1860 to 1933: The Problematic Symbiosis*
[3] Bein, "Jewish Parasite," 3–40. For the meaning of *symbiosis* in the context of para-
sitology and in the study of religion, see Smith, "What a Difference"; and Serres,
Hermes and *Le Parasite*.
[4] Scholem, "Jews and Germans," 71–93. Scholem angrily rebuts all those who suggest that any such phenomenon was anything more than the wish structure of certain
German Jews: "To whom, then, did the Jews speak in that much-talked-about
German-Jewish dialogue? They talked to themselves" (83). For Scholem, there was no

historians of Judaism operating both inside and outside the German context.[5]

The general success of the historical usage of *symbiosis* in application to Jewish history, and the concurrent polarization of the Germanism and Judaism debate, casts a retrospective shadow over Goitein's influential concept of creative symbiosis. I have therefore necessarily noted the use of *symbiosis* in general Jewish historiography, and especially German Jewish historiography, as background for its use in the Jewish-Muslim context.

CREATIVE SYMBIOSIS: FROM COINAGE TO CONSENSUS

A parallel, if comparatively more muted, debate has taken place among scholars of the Jews of Islam concerning the general characterization of Jewish life under Islam. Was it a genuine symbiosis, a Golden Age—or was it a Vale of Tears?[6] No generalization in this debate has approached the success of Goitein's irenic creative symbiosis.

Goitein is undisputably responsible for the popularization of the concept of creative symbiosis in the historiography of Jewish-Muslim relations. His standard work, *Jews and Arabs*, has introduced students to this subject for an entire generation.[7] In this work, Goitein employs the concept expansively, even enthusiastically. He even organizes the first centuries of Jewish-Muslim relations around this idea, asserting at the outset that "never has Judaism encountered such a close and fructuous symbiosis as that with the medieval civilization of Arab Islam" (130). Creative symbiosis marks Goitein's second stage of Jewish-Arab relations. Following a protracted early period, characterized by intermittant contacts,

> *then came the second* and, in the past, most important, period of creative Jewish-Arab symbiosis, lasting 800 years [from 500 to 1300], during the first half of which Muslim religion and Arab nationhood took form under Jewish impact, while in the second half traditional Judaism received its final shape under Muslim-Arab influence. (10)

This usage, moreover, would become ubiquitous in Goitein's later work. In the second volume of his subsequent magnum opus, *A Mediterannean Society*,

---

such thing as a German Jewish symbiosis—only the bathetic delusion of Jews who hungered to believe so.

[5] By 1973, C. Roth could describe a Hebrew Bible in the Renaissance "depicting on the first page God the Father, the Son and the Holy Ghost, with opposite Hebrew wording. Here is a striking exemplification of the generous Judaeo-Christian symbiosis of this period" ("Jewish Society in the Renaissance Environment," 245).

[6] Udovitch, "The Jews and Islam in the High Middle Ages"; M. R. Cohen, "Islam and the Jews," 125–37.

[7] Goitein, *Jews and Arabs*.

one finds a chapter entitled "Interfaith Symbiosis and Cooperation."[8] And in his concluding volume 5, Goitein continues to employ it (5:9).

It is no exaggeration to say that nearly every leading scholar in Jewish-Muslim studies has adopted Goitein's usage, with its popularity continuing to increase in the 1980s. Vajda, who after Goldziher could arguably rank alongside Goitein as the leader in this field, spoke of "une symbiose positive" (a positive symbiosis).[9] And Bernard Lewis, whose *Jews of Islam* has now superseded Goitein's *Jews and Arabs* as an introductory text, fully retains this terminology. He proclaims "a kind of symbiosis between Jews and their [Muslim] neighbors that has no parallel in the Western world between the Hellenistic and modern ages."[10]

Among other scholars of Judeo-Arabica, the symbiosis routinely is characterized in equally extravagent terms.[11] Thus we read about "the particular harmony, or symbiosis, in which they usually lived"; "the remarkable symbiosis of Islam and Judaism"; "the most intimate symbiosis of Judaism and Islam"; and "a sort of necessary symbiosis." Indeed, by 1984, the Institute of Islamic-Judaic Studies announced its institution for "those involved in the study of the symbiosis of Islam and Judaism."[12]

This implacably peaceable institutionalization of symbiosis among students of the Jews of Islam is all the more remarkable in light of the violent controversy over this term among students of the Jews of Germany. Some dissent, finally, has been registered in recent years. Reviewing Lewis's *Jews of Islam*, Nemoy expresses his concern. "The simple fact is that symbiosis (in Webster's definition as living together to the mutual advantage of both parties) is probably not exactly the right term . . . nor indeed is tolerance." And most recently, Brinner urges that "any approach to the question of what has been called the symbiosis, or mutual influence . . . must make its way with extreme caution."[13]

Now that Goitein's magisterial *Mediterranean Society* is complete, we can examine a mountain of Geniza evidence, most of it uncovered, translated, and synthesized for the first time by Goitein. This achievement surely deserves the

[8] Goitein, *A Mediterranean Society* 2:289–99.
[9] Vajda, "Mystique juive et mystique musulmane," 37.
[10] Lewis, *Jews of Islam*, 88.
[11] Zafrani, "Maïmonide, pèlerin de monde judéo-arabe," 260. More recently, Zafrani has spoken of an "une symbiose interconfessionelle," in "Judaisme d'occident musulman," 145.
[12] Sadan, "Genizah and Genizah-Like Practices in Islamic and Jewish Traditions," 42; Wansborough, Review of *Jews of Islam*, 28; Fenton, *Treatise*, ix; De Felice, *Jews in an Arab Land*, 5; Rippin, *Institute for Islamic-Judaic Studies Newsletter*, 5. The senior Tunisian scholar Mohammed Talbi has cast this concept in wider terms: "It is a perfectly obvious and well-known fact that Islam and the West have a long history of symbiosis and exchange" ("Possibilities and Conditions," 185). Stroumsa, Review of *Creazione*, 37–39.
[13] Nemoy, Review of *Jews of Islam*, 186; Brinner and Ricks, *Studies*, ix.

nearly unanimous acclamation it has continuously received since its first volume was published in 1967. But what is its relevance to the critical study of religions?

Goitein reserved his study of Geniza-era daily life—including religion—to this final volume. Still, of the ten massive chapters of his masterwork, only one section of this final volume deals with religion as such (323–415). Throughout his pentalogy, to be sure, he does consider relevant topics, as in his extended study of sacred time and sacred space, which opens his final volume (5–45). Indeed, now, in volume 5 of *A Mediterranean Society*, Goitein provides some generalizing, concluding assessments.

These final observations may be compared instructively to those he expressed earlier, in his propaedeutic essay "Religion in Everyday Life as Reflected in the Documents of the Cairo Geniza":

> The religion of the Geniza people was a stern, straightforward, Talmudic type of piety, concerned with the strict fulfillment of the commandments and with the pursuit of the study required for their knowldege. This somewhat jejune character of their religiosity was enhanced by the rigorous rationalism embraced by Jewish orthodoxy in the wake of centuries of sectarian and theological controversies.[14]

Goitein never changed his judgment in this regard. In a summary statement on "the religion of the Geniza people," he provides similarly provocative generalizations, final words that reconfirm his previous judgment on:[15] the sociability of these people (5); "the openness of Mediterranean society during the good years of the High Middle Ages" (6); the inclination of the Geniza man to "[leave] too much to God and [do] too little himself—especially to alleviate human suffering or work to perfect himself" (8); "the physical and educational symbiosis between Muslims and Jews, experienced during the preceding centuries, which eased the transition to the dominant faith [i.e., Jewish conversion to Islam]" (9).

On the very last page of *A Mediterranean Society*, Goitein concludes, "With the exception of the few really pious and God-possessed, religion formed the frame, rather than the content, of the daily existence" (502). In short, Goitein's concern with the content of daily existence resulted in the "thick description" of his magnum opus, which "sociographically" depicts the Jewish world of the Geniza documents. Only rarely did he examine their religion as such. Perhaps this neglect may be explained by Goitein's conviction that this society's religiosity was primarily "jejune" and "bourgeois."

In any case, the glaring fact remains that *A Mediterranean Society*—and Jewish-Islamic scholarship in general—infrequently deals directly with fundamental questions in the critical study of religion. This is not to deny that any subsequent work on the religion of the Jews of the Geniza period must now follow from the "sociography" so assiduously crafted by Goitein.

[14] Goitein, "Religion in Everyday Life," 8.
[15] Goitein, *Mediterranean Society* 5:5–10.

Bernard Lewis, like Goitein, is not a religionist. But his *Jews of Islam* has become a standard text in the field of Judeo-Arabic studies and has, in this capacity, sustained the institutionalization of symbiosis. However, like *A Mediterranean Society*, *The Jews of Islam* only indirectly considers the issues that are central to religious studies. His long first chapter, "Islam and Other Religions," fortunately provides a signal contribution to this rich, neglected area.[16] Even so, Lewis does not analyze the problems and phenomena that religionists routinely investigate. Still, the critical student of religion must turn to his fourth chapter, "The End of the Tradition," for a model study of a model breakdown in interreligious relations.[17] No fuller synthetic study of the horrific disintegration of the Jewish-Muslim symbiosis exists.[18]

SYMBIOSIS IN THE CRITICAL STUDY OF RELIGION

From the standard text of Goitein, *Jews and Arabs*, to that of Lewis, *The Jews of Islam*, the study of religion has barely begun to integrate the extraordinary phenomenon of Jewish-Muslim symbiosis, much less rethink the paradigm itself. The sizable volume of research in this area incorporates new assessments, some of considerable importance, but they rarely shake any overarching consensus. Creative symbiosis remains in place, yet to be properly assessed from the perspective of the critical study of religion.

What would such an assessment entail? What, precisely, is the character of this sharing? Is it a sharing of the *sancta* posited by Mordechai Kaplan in his architectonic constructions toward an American Judaism? Kaplan, for example, states that "religions are not necessarily mutually exclusive; they are so only when their *sancta* are interpreted as implying contradictory doctrines."[19] Or is this symbiosis to be construed as those shared civilizational components in an area demarcated as "Islamicate" by Marshall G. S. Hodgson?[20] Or is it in fact a form of civil religion?[21] Again, one wonders whether some other metaphor from the natural sciences—say, co-evolution—might not be more appropriate. Gregory Bateson calls co-evolution a "stochastic system of evolutionary change in which two or more species interact in such a way that changes in species A set the stage for the natural selection of changes in species B. Later changes in species B, in turn, set the stage for the selecting of

[16] Lewis, *Jews of Islam*, 3–67.
[17] Ibid., 154–91. This study has already been substantially amplified by Lewis himself, in his recent *Semites and Anti-Semites*.
[18] Norman Stillman, however, has now completed his ample anthologies, *Jews of Arab Lands* and the *Jews of Arab Lands in Modern Times*.
[19] Kaplan, "Reconstructionism," 437.
[20] Hodgson, *Venture of Islam*.
[21] See Robert Bellah's influential formulation in "Civil Religion in America." For a provocative exploration of the sociological interaction of Jews in American society, see John Murray Cuddihy's *No Offense: Civil Religion and Protestant Taste*.

more similiar changes in species A."[22] Perhaps it would be helpful to consider the notion of social henotheism.[23]

It may also be useful to recall that symbiosis has entered the study of Judaism along with its shadow, parasite.[24] Fortunately, as a means of rethinking its applicability to the study of interreligious relations, two approaches have emerged recently that reconsider symbiosis in its parasitological sense. First, the French interdisciplinary thinker Michel Serres has developed a theory of communication that concentrates not on the Other, but on the third party: "To hold a dialogue is to suppose a third man and to seek to exclude him; a successful communication is the exclusion of the third man. The most profound dialectical problem is not the problem of the Other, who is only a variety of—or a variation—of the Same, it is the problem of the third man."[25] This third man Serres calls the "demon," the "noise," or the "parasite".[26] Like Serres, Jonathan Z. Smith has begun a serious reflection on the problem of otherness by means of a reconsideration of the category of parasite.

> While at one level the taxonomy of parasites (and, hence, of otherness) appears to be reducible to the ancient legal question, *Cui bono?* at another level the distinctions between "parasitism," "symbiosis," "mutualism," "commensalism," "epiphytism" and the like are distinctions between types of exchange. A "theory of the other" must take the form of a relational theory of reciprocity. "Otherness," whether of Scotsmen or lice, is a preeminently political category.[27]

In my own way, I have chosen to interrogate the central construct in the study of early Jewish-Muslim relations, creative symbiosis.[28] If, minimally,

[22] Bateson, *Angels Fear*, 207.
[23] "Henotheism: a stage in religious development antedating radical monotheism, in which one believes in one supreme god for one's own particular region, race or nation, without denying the existence of other gods for other regions, races or nations. The tolerant message of henotheism is: to each his own" (Cuddihy, *No Offense*, 44). Cuddihy also cites H. Richard Niebuhr to the effect that the history of Israel "is marked by an almost continuous struggle between social henotheism and radical monotheism" (Niebuhr, *Radical Monotheism*, 57). The concept of social henotheism seems especially apt in regard to the 'Isawiyya, studied in chapter 2 below.
[24] Bein, "Jewish Parasite," 3–40.
[25] Serres, *Hermes*, 67.
[26] Serres, *Le parasite*.
[27] Smith, "What a Difference," 10.
[28] I shall not offer a definition of this term. For the reader who needs such a thing, consult Goitein's characterization cited above. "But it seems to me that people who have as many things to investigate as we have do not dispute about a name" (Plato, *Republic*, 185). "The refusal, for reasons of scientific integrity, to work with any concepts other than clear and unambiguous ones, becomes a pretext for putting the interests of a self-legitimizing research industry before those of the subject-matter itself. With an arrogance born of ignorance the objections of classical philosophers to the practice of definition are consigned to oblivion; that philosophy banished as a rem-

symbiosis suggests mutual benefit, what then is meant by *mutual*, and what by *benefit*? At a minimum, the notion of *benefit*, as employed by the religionist, should remain properly problematic, for symbiosis, ultimately, will remain a fruitful problem, a problem of genuine mutuality and authentic benefit both, only if it is allowed its delusions and its dominations, its manipulations and exploitations, its half-baked altruisms and its full-blown fusions. Symbiosis, as a thinly happy and monovalently positive benefit, did not happen. Its complexity is reduced to *mere* benefit only by a tendentious dilution. It does suggest, however, a view of real relations sufficiently capacious to include the means by which harm helps. A. R. Ammons articulates this painful paradox with poetic insight as he evokes it in "Negative Symbiosis":

even the
rattler,
his neck
gagged with
fur,

trims up
the world so
something
tiny can
come
through.[29]

For Muslims and for Jews today, it may seem that something tiny indeed has come through. For the historian of religions, however, "the living God lurks in detail."[30] Scholem believed, in fact, that Revelation itself precisely is found within the scintilla and iota of history. "Today [1937], as at the very beginning, my work lives in this paradox, in the hope of a true communication from the mountain, of that most invisible, smallest fluctuation in history which causes truth to break forth from the illusions of 'development.'"[31] Without resorting to a definition of symbiosis, then, I will employ the notion of symbiosis insofar as it arises from the *imaginaries* of development, for symbiosis unfurls out of that most invisible, smallest fluctuation for which subtle historical change I find the notion of the imaginary to be the most apposite.[32]

---

nant of scholasticism is still being perpetuated by unreflecting individual sciences in the name of scientific exactitude" (Adorno, "Sociology," 242–43).

[29] Ammons, *Sumerian Vistas*, 125–26.

[30] This was the motto of Aby Warburg, subsequently taken up by Scholem. See also the final philosophical statement of Alexander Altmann, where he cites John Locke to the effect that in religion there are no *adiaphora*, "things indifferent and insignificant." Altmann explains that "every single detail in prayer and ritual held some significance for the believer. One may add that in other language-games, too, minutiae are of the essence" (Altmann, "God of Religion," 295–96).

[31] Scholem, "Candid Word," 32.

[32] For the concept of *imaginary*, see chapter 5 below.

And, insofar as such historical change bespeaks the capacity to change as such, I adhere to the dictum of Isaiah Berlin. The human capacity to change history, he observes, "is all that the sense of history, in the end, comes to; that upon this capacity all historical (as well as legal) justice depends; that it alone makes it possible to speak of criticism, of praise or blame, as just or deserved or absurd or unfair."[33] The study of symbiosis, in this sense, necessarily is a study of historical change.

Modes of Accommodation

Granted, then, that *benefit* may remain a slippery notion, and *mutual* must be understood dialectically. Still, the issue remains: into what arena of enlightening analysis can one logistically frame—so best to still see, and not dispel— the penumbral sharing known as symbiosis? If there is little dispute concerning the general significance of the Jewish-Muslim symbiosis, there is enormous uncertainty concerning its specific anatomy. The obscure history informing this apparently hyperbolic assertion, that is, is both too well known and too little known: too well known, I believe, because its status as a rarely disputed historiographic assumption allows us to forget that the symbiosis was creative, indeed, that it created us.[34] And, on the other hand, it is too little known, insofar as the details of this creative symbiosis remain obscure almost beyond exaggeration.

In my study of the Jewish group known (to the Muslim heresiographers) as the 'Isawiyya, I note that the militant uprising of this group represented a breakdown in its otherwise accommodationist approach to the prophethood of Muhammad.[35] But Muslims, as well, needed to accommodate themselves to Jews and Judaism, despite the obvious disparity in raw power. It has been helpful, therefore, to sketch the modes of accommodation that both Jews and Muslims developed in response to one another. In this way I have tried to develop a model according to which Jews and Muslims operated as necessary components in the respective self-definitions of the other.

From the Muslim side, I discriminate between discourse directed toward Jews and a discourse that was inner directed, so to speak. The Muslim discourse directed toward Jews established a set of inviolable criteria into which all Jews had to fit. Jews were located, on this scheme, by the respective criteria of Ahl al-Kitab (People of the Book); Ahl al-Dhimma (People of the Pact of Toleration; Tributaries); Banu Isra'il (Children of Israel); and Yahud (Jews). They could also be depicted, less juridically and more culturally, as secret agents of foreign heresies. The Muslim inner-directed treatment of Jews and Judaism likewise followed several fairly well defined pathways. They charac-

[33] Berlin, "Historical Inevitability," 250.
[34] See the chapter 6 below.
[35] See chapter 2 below.

terized the other as the Jews *had been* (in the time of the prophets); as the Jews *did* (they prayed the evening prayer when the stars shone brightly and picked their leader according to the length of his arms, for example); as the Jews *were* (they *were* anthropomorphizers); and even as the Jews *would be* (they will be activists on behalf of the Antimessiah, Dajjal).

From the Jewish side, the response toward Islam could take the form of revolt ('Isawiyya); rejection (polemics);[36] debate (in salons, homes, and marketplaces); or conversion ('Abdallah ibn Salam). Inner-directed Jewish accommodations to the coming of Islam included new forms of authority structures (a shake-up in the exilarchate); new movements (the Karaites and others); Messianism (apocalyptic movements and writings); and halakhic retrenchment (culminating in Saadia Gaon).

Jew, then, served as an essential and necessary catalyst in the self-definition of Islam; and *Muslim*, likewise, operated in synergy with a Jewish effort at self-legitimation. The other—whether as myth or as history, image or enemy, precursor or opponent—had its uses. The uses of the other, in the end, produced a kind of symbiotic interdefinition.

What does this pattern of interactions imply? I would suggest a few tentative approaches toward an answer. First of all, in terms of historiography, the use of Muslim sources is simply vital for the student of this period.[37] There is much Jewish history to be written with the use of Muslim sources; obviously, this is most especially true with regard to the question of Jewish-Muslim symbiosis. Moreover, the symbiosis can be understood only in terms of mutual self-definition, insofar as these traditions (so I will argue) operated in synergy with one another.[38] Finally, I would emphasize that the debtor-creditor model of influence and borrowing must be abandoned in favor of the dialectical analysis of intercivilizational and interreligious processes.[39]

As for historical generalizations, only a few can be rendered responsibly. First, the first three centuries of Islam were a time of extraordinary Jewish mobility: all manner of change—social, economic, political, and religious— overtook the old ways. As Goitein put it: "Every aspect of what we regard today as Judaism—the synagogue service and the Siddur, law and ritual, theology and ethics, the text of the Bible, the grammar and vocabulary of the Hebrew language—was consolidated, formulated and canonized during that

---

[36] See especially Perlmann's "Medieval Polemics betweeen Islam and Judaism" for the definitive overview of Jewish-Muslim polemics.

[37] Many of the finest scholars of Judeo-Islamica—Goldziher, Vajda, Goitein, Nemoy, Lewis, Brinner, Lassner, Lazarus-Yafeh—were trained as Islamicists.

[38] Sanders, Baumgarten, and Mendelson, *Jewish and Christian Self-Definition*.

[39] Ultimately this inquiry should be undertaken in the context of world history, as Marshall G. S. Hodgson properly urged ("Hemispheric Interregional History," 715–23). For a later period, we now have the makings of a serious world-historical approach to periodization developing. See especially the signal contribution of Janet Abu-Lughod, *Before European Hegemony*. I have found helpful the review of this work by Andre Gunder Frank, "Thirteenth-Century World System," 249–58.

age." Or, in the words of Lazarus-Yafeh: "Medieval Judaism in the Arab East was not only arabicized, but in almost every sphere of life—and not only in philosophy and theology—it bore the stamp of Islam. . . . The fact of Islamic influence on medieval Oriental Judaism is today acknowledged almost unanimously among students of Jewish history."[40]

But Goitein went even further: "It was Islam which saved the Jewish People."[41] My work here necessarily is restricted to probing the dimensions of Goitein's declarative claim. Naturally, it is not my intention to "prove" such unprovable assertions. Rather, I hope to produce evidence that is persuasive in variously appropriate degrees of intensity and extent.

OVERVIEW OF THE PRESENT VOLUME

> In our attempt to present developmental aspects of Judaic religious history relevant to our problem, we entertain but modest hopes of contributing anything especially new to the discussion, apart from the fact that, here and there, some source data may be grouped in a manner to emphasize some things differently than usual.
>
> —Weber, *Ancient Judaism*

As I have said, the book in hand will not be a study of Muslim "borrowing" from Judaism, nor will it attempt to analyze Jewish "influence" on Islam. The present volume, moreover, will not provide a history of the Jews under early Islam, nor is it a survey of the attitudes of Muslims toward Jews in this period, or vice versa. Other topics that I will not cover (except in passing) include gender relations, philosophy, law, literature, and linguistics.[42] I should also note that this study will provide background for understanding the so-called Golden Age of Jewish history, in Spain (tenth–twelfth centuries), but will not study that Golden Age as such.

Rather, the present volume comprises interconnected studies devoted to rethinking the meaning of the construct creative symbiosis, with special emphasis on the period from the eighth through the tenth centuries. Occasional forays a century or two later than that, when necessary, have not been quashed. My intention is neither to refute nor to defend the idea of creative symbiosis. I hope, instead, to investigate its nuances, its implications, its depth, and its extent. In so doing, I cannot hope to be comprehensive. As is well

[40] Goitein, "Political Conflict," 169; Lazarus-Yafeh, "Judeo-Arabic Culture," 104, 109 n. 16.
[41] Goitein, "Muhammad's Inspiration," 162.
[42] For a recent survey, see J. Maier, "Jüdische Literatur," 524–45.

known, the constraints of research in this area dictate severe limitations on any such study. I hope merely to approach the problem from a helpful variety of angles, using a range of sources, to examine three (interpenetrated) dimensions of the symbiosis. These dimensions I call *trajectories*, *constructions*, and *intimacies*.

Trajectories of Judaism into early Islam remain a vexed area of research. We know very little in any detail concerning the varieties of Judaism from the destruction of the Second Temple in 70 C.E. until the efflorescence of datable Jewish sources in the ninth and tenth centuries. Until we know more concerning the physiognomy of Judaism during the rise and development of Islam, we can draw few serious conclusions concerning the relation between the two communities. We know precious little concerning the kinds of Jews that Muhammad may have known, the kinds of sources available to the Jewish converts who transmitted them to the Muslim community, and the processes and scale of that transmission.

In the face of this imposing darkness, I have tried to reconsider certain aspects of early Jewish-Muslim interaction. In the first chapter, I will look at professions, structures of authority, pluralism, and sectarianism in the Jewish community. This survey solves no problems. In it, I attempt to deepen, in fact, the problem of social differentiation in this period of Jewish history. In the second chapter, I will presume a (similarly problematic) variation on the part of the Jewish community as I review the impact of apocalypticism on the Jewish and Muslim communities. Here I begin to enter the dynamics of historical symbiosis as such, for Muslims and Jews sometimes shared the imageries of the Messiah and jointly were activating the endtime; in some cases their interaction profoundly determined the tenor and clarity of the endtime vision, as well as the means of manifesting it in social action. This was so most especially in the milieu that gave rise at once to the "'Alid loyalists"— Hodgson's characterization of the proto-Shi'ite parties—and to such important Jewish sects as the 'Isawiyya. The earliest formidable counterformations to the emerging hegemony of an eventually institutionalized Sunna were these apocalyptic and "pseudo"-Messianic movements.

Constructions of the other Muslim or other Jew obviously were as varied as there were interactions. But at least one feature stands out as important to explore in regard to symbiosis. In chapter 3, accordingly, I look at the mark left by Judaism on the mind of the developing Shi'ite community, as well as at the dialectical perception of that "Jewish Shi'ism" in its Sunni reception. The Shi'ite community employed "Judaic" paradigms, prefigurations, and confirmations of their own community. Eventually, the Sunni opposition characterized the Shi'a as the "Jews of our community (*umma*)." This construction of "the Jew" on the part of the Shi'a, and the subsequent construction of the "Jewish" Shi'ite on the part of the Sunni majority, suggests a subtler symbiosis lying far beyond any modern (Jewish or Muslim) caricature of inexorable enmity between the two communities. No subsection of the Jewish-

Muslim symbiosis, perhaps, was more complex and profound that than of the Judeo-Ismaʿili interchange. Chapter 3, therefore, concludes with the esoteric symbiosis of Ismaʿilis and Jews.

The reality of "the Jew" as such, moreover, became one component of the remarkable development of Muslim studies of other religions. Chapter 4 is devoted to the growth of this Muslim comparative religion. The classification of Jews and Judaism in that discourse suggests that a fairly elaborate array of Jewish information was utilized by Muslim intellectuals as they located Judaism to the universe of communities.

Chapter 5 addresses the full-circle effect of Israʾiliyyat. The appropriation of Jewish lore as prophetic prefigurations of the coming of the Last Prophet was a literary reception that occurred, of course, after the lifetime of Muhammad. The old is made to testify to the new; this reshaping of ancient figures implies more than an intimacy with the past. It also is a performative acknowledgment operating in the present, a living recognition of still-animating vitality on the part of an ostensibly superseded sister tradition. Muslims dialectically retained the attributed Jewishness of traditions being used to legitimate the prophethood of Muhammad. The narrative cycles associated with a historical Jew (ʿAbdallah ibn Salam) and a legendary Israelite (Buluqiyya) are examples of this instructive dialectic. I conclude, finally, with a vivid instance of this intimacy of implied acknowledgment. The angel Metatron, by the time of the prophet Muhammad, was the Jewish high angel, the chief agent of the One God. That he was reimagined in a variety of Muslim works implies not only the interreligious character of the *l'autre monde*, but the tenacity of imagination in the configuration of symbiosis.

In chapter 6, I shall reflect on the history and philosophy of symbiosis. In considering the history of the symbiosis between Muslim and Jew, I shall attempt to understand the role of intellectuals, especially writers of apocalypses, in the imaginative worldmaking that figured as a fundamental feature of that symbiosis. Finally, a joint philosophical creation often has been said to be the ultimate intellectual product of Jewish-Muslim intimacy in this period. I will therefore conclude with observations on this philosophical symbiosis.

PART I

Trajectories

But it is beyond the human mind to fathom the designs of the Creator; for our ways are not His ways, neither are our thoughts His thoughts. All these matters relating to Jesus of Nazareth and the Ismaelites who came after him, only served to clear the way for King Messiah, to prepare the whole world to worship God with one accord, as it is written, "For then will I turn to the peoples a pure language, that they may all call upon the name of the Lord to serve Him with one consent" (Zeph. 3:9).
—Maimonides

CHAPTER ONE

Who Were the Jews?

PROBLEMS IN PROFILING THE JEWISH COMMUNITY
UNDER EARLY ISLAM

THE END OF LATE ANTIQUITY is a period of Jewish history best known for being unknown. Salo Baron emphasizes the darkness of this terra incognita: "In the first three and one half dark and inarticulate centuries after the conclusion of the Talmud (500–850), Jewish intellectual leadership laid the foundations upon which the vocal and creative generations of the following three and one half centuries (850–1200) erected the magnificent structure of medieval Jewish biblical learning."[1] S. D. Goitein likewise states unequivocally that "the centuries both preceding and following the rise of Islam are the most obscure in Jewish history."[2] Not long ago, a leading specialist in this period presumed this problem once again: "We all know that the two hundred years that preceded the Arab conquest and the two hundred years that followed are among the most obscure in the history of the Jewish community in Palestine; very few historical documents of that period have reached us."[3] And Leon Nemoy, the leading student of Islamicate Karaism, recently reiterated a point he has emphasized throughout his career: "This whole period of Jewish history [remains] dark and puzzling."[4]

This darkest of all periods of postbiblical Jewish history occurred, however, at a turning point in the history of the Middle East. Henri Pirenne says: "The Middle Ages were . . . beginning. The transitional phase was protracted. One may say that it lasted a whole century—from 650 to 750. It was during this period . . . that the tradition of antiquity disappeared, while the new elements came to the surface." And Peter Brown adds, "The late seventh and early eighth century . . . are the true turning points in the history of Europe and the Middle East."[5]

---

[1] Baron, *Social and Religious History*, 6:312. For the beginnings of a social and economic history of the Jews in this period and later, see E. Ashtor, "Prolegomena to the Medieval History," 55–68, 145–66. With regard to Palestine, we also now possess an overview in English: Moshe Gil's *History of Palestine*.

[2] Goitein, *Jews and Arabs*, 95.

[3] Grossman, "Aliyah," 74.

[4] Personal correspondence, October 22, 1981. Very recently, Nemoy has reiterated that most of Karaite history "(including, alas, the intitial—medieval and most productive—period of it) is wrapped in almost total darkness" (Nemoy, "Stroumsa's Edition," 233).

[5] Pirenne, *Mohammed and Charlemagne*, 285; Brown, *World of Late Antiquity*, 200. I

At this extraordinarily important moment, blackout overcomes the history of the Jews. This fact is all the more remarkable when one recalls Jane Gerber's estimate that "between 85 and 90% of world Jewry lived in the Muslim world in the period from the eighth through the tenth century."[6] To the extent, then, that so few datable Jewish sources survive from this period, the status of the Jews at this point remains perhaps the best-kept secret of Jewish history. What can we really know concerning the Jewish community at the end of antiquity?

I shall start with Jewish professions in the first two centuries of Islamic rule, working toward a profile of the Jewish community at the end of antiquity by first surveying the kinds of work undertaken by Jews of that time. After this rough assessment of the class structure of eighth-century Judaism, I shall then describe what may be called the crisis of mobility on the part of the Jewish leadership. My conclusions will concern the ways in which the end of Jewish antiquity was brought about by a "third power," beyond the Jewish laity and Jewish leadership. This power from outside was a Muslim caliph, whose manipulation of power struggles among the Jews ironically turned out to be something of a boon to the Jews.

The Jewish Professions

"Upper" Professions

Perhaps the most salient of the "upper" Jewish professions was long-distance trade. In part because the Jews were neither Muslims, Christians, Indians, Chinese, nor Slavs, they were particularly well suited to moving goods among these various peoples.[7] Accordingly, Jewish merchants by the eighth century specialized in plying the trade routes between China, India, Russia, Persia, Western Europe, and their home bases in the Muslim world.[8] The goods they traded included slaves, spices, and other luxury items. The skilled, capital-intensive, and lucrative nature of this vastly dispersed entreprise placed long-distance traders among the highest levels of the Jewish economic elite. Indeed, the traveling merchant eventually helped pave the way for the subsequent creation of an international banking system, for such a trader was uniquely situated to convey letters of credit (*suftaja*) from country to country.[9]

---

have explored some of the implications of this turning point in my article "The Moving Finger," 1–29.

[6] Gerber, "Judaism in the Middle East," 158.

[7] For a still useful overview of Jewish occupations in the Middle Ages, see Abrahams, *Jewish Life*, 211–51.

[8] See Verlinden, "Les Radaniya," 105–32, with reference to the previous literature.

[9] Goitein, *Mediterranean Society* 1:242–45. This practice developed fully only in subsequent centuries, however.

But long-distance trade was not the only route to Jewish wealth. The Jews of the Banu Nadhir tribe, for example, controlled a palm-growing oasis in central Arabia, which was conquered by the Prophet Muhammad in the year 625. When Muhammad drove them from their home oasis, the Banu Nadhir Jews proudly paraded "their women decked out in litters wearing silk, brocade, velvet, and fine red and green silk. People lined up to gape at them. They passed by in a train one after the other, borne by 600 camels. . . . They went off beating tambourines and playing on pipes."[10] The Jews of the Arabian oases also earned their livelihoods by selling wine and importing silk. One pre-Islamic Arabic poet evoked his desert landscape as multicolored, "just as if the Jews had extended their cloth of silk, their shimmering sashes."[11] These and other Jews of central Arabia were economically powerful enough that Muhammad's earliest political maneuvers were at least in part designed to come to terms with these entrenched Jewish merchants and agriculturalists.[12]

Jews in the seventh and eighth centuries also were active in the precious and not-so-precious metal businesses. When one of the Seven Wonders of the Ancient World, the Great Colossus of Rhodes, was scrapped in the eighth century, the remains were sold to a Jewish scrap-metal dealer.[13] The Jews in the oases around Muhammad's Mecca not only raised date palms but were celebrated goldsmiths.[14] And at the turn of the eighth century a Jew was named to be the head of an Ummayad general's mint. This Jew, one Sumayr, was successful enough in this position of head minter that his coins were named *sumariyya* after him.[15]

In the earliest years of new Islam, upper Jewish professionals gravitated to the caliphal centers of power, which provided pivotal points from which to further pursue their scattered economic interests. Jewish physicians, astrologers, poets, and, eventually, viziers attended the affairs at court, if not to the caliph himself.[16] Perspicacious caliphs naturally took advantage of these readily available Jewish skills. For example, when the ʿAbbasid dynasty overtook the Umayyads in 750, the new ʿAbbasid regime decided to establish its capital city at Baghdad. The man appointed to plot out the city plan for this ideal city was a Jew, the celebrated physician and astrologer Mashal-

[10] Al-Waqidi, *Kitab al-Maghazi* 1:136, cited in Goldziher, "Mélanges Judeo-Arabes," 273.
[11] Goldziher, "Mélanges Judeo-Arabes," 273
[12] Stillman, *Jews of Arab Lands*, 3–22.
[13] In the year 627, according to the *Chronographia* of Theophanes. See Baron, *Social and Religious History* 3:235 n. 16.
[14] Newby, *History of the Jews of Arabia*, 49–78.
[15] Dietrich, "al-Hadjdjaj b. Yusuf," 41, citing Ibn al-Athir; Fischel, *Economic and Political Life*, xvii, n. 9; Gil, *History of Palestine*, 110 n. 34.
[16] I provide a number of additional examples of Jewish scientists and astrologers in "*Sefer Yesira.*"

lah.[17] This Jewish scientist calculated that the day of the historic ground-breaking should be July 30, 762. Thus, from its vary inception, the 'Abbasid dynasty, who ruled from this capital of Baghdad for the succeeding five centuries, utilized Jews in positions of technical and cultural authority.

For the ambitious young Jew already in the eighth century, then, a position of influence at the center of the Muslim world-empire was not entirely an unrealistic aspiration. And, indeed, Jewish skills continuously were co-opted in the interests of the Islamic state. By the tenth century the role of the Jews in international banking and commerce, often at the behest of the caliph, expanded considerably. The tenth century, in the phrase of Goitein, constituted "the golden age of the high bourgeoisie" for Jews as well as for Muslims.[18]

The Jewish community eventually prospered, along with its neighbors, in what Goitein termed the "bourgeois revolution," engendered by the economic boom following in the wake of the Arab conquests.[19] Certainly by the tenth century Jewish middle classes of Egypt and Mesopotamia enjoyed the pivotal advantage of powerful friends at court. But beneath these well-documented and overemphasized few success stories were squeezed a silent and apparently degraded Jewish majority.

Reviled Occupations

By the tenth century, the Jewish community had become a "religious democracy," with wealthy classes caring for the poor through efficient social services, as Goitein has shown from Geniza documents.[20] My concern at this point, however, lies with the earlier, less organized situation. I therefore now turn to the neglected "lower" levels of Jewish life, with special reference to what (little) we know of the eighth and ninth centuries. Jewish court poets, town planners, caliphal astrologers, ambassadors, and monied courtiers of that day, I suggest, did not represent their people. Indeed, for however much evidence there may be concerning court Jews and their apparent influence, there is that much more proof that the Jewish masses were in a generally miserable condition.[21]

This grim situation can best be illustrated by a look at the most frequently mentioned of all Jewish professions in the first centuries of Islamic rule. I refer to cloth-making—mere manual labor, which almost universally was considered to comprise the lowest level of society.[22] It was assumed that mer-

[17] Pingree, "Some Sassanian and Syriac Sources," 5–13; *Astrological History*; and "Masha'allah"; Fakhry, *Islamic Philosophy*, 8–9.
[18] Goitein, "Near Eastern Bourgeoisie," 583–604.
[19] Ibid., 603; Abitol, "Juifs Maghrébins," 561–77.
[20] Goitein, *Mediterranean Society*, vol. 2.
[21] See the subtle and useful observations on this question made by Sadan, "Some Literary Problems," 356. See more generally Mahler, *Karaimer*.
[22] Brunschvig, "Métiers vils en Islam," 41–60.

cantile activity possessed social status, while manual labor did not. Moreover, the social status of those engaged in laboring on cloth and fur—tanners, fullers, carders, weavers—was that of a despised underclass.[23] And of workers engaged in the manufacture of cloth, the weavers were derogated as the lowest of them all.[24]

This was an ancient prejudice. As early as the first century, Flavius Josephus describes the general Roman loathing for weavers.[25] Rabbinic Jewish views were much the same: a passage from *Tosefta* designates weaving as "the lowest trade in the world."[26] No wonder weaving has been deemed by one scholar as "the most despised profession in the East."[27] And the prejudice against weavers common in other traditional societies seems particularly acute in the medieval Muslim social world.

It is striking, then, that garment work, with its derogatory implications, was associated widely with Jews in the first centuries of Islam. An Arabic essayist tells us that the Jews of the ninth century were dyers, tanners, cuppers, butchers, and tinkers. About the same time, a geographer notes that many of the Jews of Egypt and Syria were dyers and tanners. The most striking castigation derives from a source dated between the eighth and tenth centuries: In this source, an Arabic-speaking Christian reviles a Jew in this way: "As for you, God has replaced the status of his Son and his delight with malediction, wrath and exile; instead of Royalty, the job of weaver; instead of Prophet, the profession of tanner; instead of Priest, that of barber, potter, glassblower and other vile professions." And we find this image corroborated by another Eastern Christian, who asserted that "no Jew has been raised to a position of exalted honour . . . [and] the humbler among them are engaged as tanners or dyers or tailors."[28]

This depressing background should be kept in mind in order to comprehend the full pathos of the Jewish rebellions of the eighth century, for rebellious Jews are repeatedly associated with various kinds of cloth work. It is interesting to note that garment workers in particular have been perennially associated with something more than their low class standing. They were also—not inaccurately—held responsible for social agitations. The conjunc-

---

[23] As Mez put it, "the lowest class of tax-payers were the Jewish money-changers, tanners, shoe-makers and particularly dyers" (*Renaissance of Islam*, 39, with reference to various sources).

[24] I. Friedlaender, "Heterodoxies," 29:96.

[25] I. Friedlaender, "Jewish-Arabic Studies" 3:282 n. 346.

[26] I. Friedlaender, "Heterodoxies," 29:96, citing Tosefta Eduyot 1:2.

[27] I. Friedlaender, "Jewish-Arabic Studies" 3:282 n. 346, provides numerous Jewish, Muslim, and Christian sources. In his section "Social Position" (281–85), he surveys the literature on this question.

[28] Jahiz, in an often-cited essay translated by Stillman, in *Jews of Arab Lands*, 170; Fischel, *Jews in the Economic and Political Life*, 7, citing Muqaddasi; Vajda, "Un traité de polemique," 147; my translation from the French of Vajda; Fischel, *Jews in the Economic and Political Life*, 106, citing Bar Hebraeus.

tion of cloth workers and rebellion is known outside the Muslim world. Jewish women working in the imperial Roman weaving establishment converted Christian women to Judaism. The Jewish women weavers accomplished this in such numbers that the disturbance required a special proviso in the Theodosian Code (398 c.e.) in order to allow converted women back into Christianity.[29] Even in the Europe of the High Middle Ages, several millenarian peasant uprisings were instigated by semiskilled weavers and fullers.[30]

Furthermore, more than one of the widely vilified eighth-century proto-Shiʿi prophets was said to be a weaver. The medieval Muslim historian who reports this fact dryly comments "that this claim [to prophecy] should have been raised by them in favor of a weaver is strange indeed!"[31] And, certainly, these eighth-century Shiʿi rebels propagandized on the effectively populist appeal of their own lower-class origins.[32]

We should therefore not be surprised to find that contemporaneous Jewish rebels, closely associated with these originators of Shiʿi Islam, seem to have appealed similarly to their underclass status in their uprisings. One of these Jewish rebels arose in Mesopotamia around the year 720. Around him gathered Jews who were "weavers, carpetmakers and launderers."[33] Though his rebellion was quickly put down, others were soon to follow.

The greatest of all these Jewish cloth-worker revolutionaries—indeed, the most significant Jewish Messianic figure from Bar Cochba in the second century to Shabbetai Zevi in the seventeenth century—was Abu ʿIsa al-Isfahani.[34] A reliable source says that Abu ʿIsa was "an ignorant tailor who could neither read nor write"—another lowly, illiterate cloth worker.[35] Despite—or because of—his humble origins, his movement apparently was a mass movement. Indeed, Goitein argued that Abu ʿIsa's movement, the ʿIsawiyya, was at least symbolically responsible for the decline of Jewish village life starting in the second century of Muslim rule.[36]

The way Maimonides tells this tragic story is instructive. He refers to "an exodus of a multitude of Jews, from the East beyond Isphahan, led by an

[29] Brooten, *Women Leaders*, 146.
[30] Cohn, *Pursuit of the Millennium*, 58–60, 101–2. On the twelfth-century edicts against certain heretics known as "Piphili . . . those vilest of people, the weavers," see Russell, *Dissent and Reform*, 218–21. One might note that the cultural abhorrence of weavers can be found even in India. The great Sakhi poet Kabir is despised for his origins in the Julaha weaving class. See Vaudeville, *Kabir* 1:83.
[31] I. Friedlaender, "Heterodoxies" 1:64.
[32] They are denigrated variously as *safala* ("lowlife": see Kashshi, *Rijal*, 250); ʿ*amma* ("common folk": see Kashshi, *Rijal*, 249); and *ghauga'* ("riffraff": see Halm, "Schatten II," 17). For a list of the professions of the *ghulat*, see Halm, "Schatten II," 85. See especially I. Friedlaender, "Jewish-Arabic Studies" 3:281–85.
[33] Baron, *Social and Religious History* 5:184.
[34] See chapter 2 below.
[35] Qirqisani, *Jewish Sects and Christianity*, 103.
[36] Goitein, *Jews and Arabs*, 169.

individual who pretended to be the Messiah. They were accoutered with military equipment and drawn swords, and slew all those that encountered them." The caliph stops them by proving their leader to be a phoney and then bribing his followers to return home. When pacified, the "Caliph ordered them to make a special mark on their garments, the writing of the word 'cursed' and to attach one iron bar in the back and one in the front. Ever since then the communities of Khorasan and Ispahan have experienced the tribulations of the Diaspora."[37] Goitein may have been correct to extrapolate that "it may well be that the disappearance of Jewish village population in the Arab East was partly caused by the negative outcome of such Messianic upheavals."[38]

Goitein's suggestion may be corroborated by two further indications of the serious extent of these movements. First, classical Muslim traditions have it that the Dajjal, the monstrous Antimessiah who will oppose the Messiah, "will emerge from Isfahan followed by 70,000 Jews wearing Persian shawls."[39] Note the motif of Jewish cloth—but more importantly, note that this mythical terrible uprising of Jewish peasants is permanantly embodied in Muslim tradition as a sign of the end of time.

Christian tradition provides a second indication of the impact of the weaver rebels. Their widespread appeal made their way into a later Eastern Christian report: "A weaver wanted to be a prophet. The people told him, Never has there been a prophet who was a weaver. He, however, replied to them: Shepherds with all their simplicity have been employed as prophets, why should not weavers be fit for it?"[40]

It is no surprise, of course, to find that underclasses revolt—all the more so, to be sure, in a society in which reviled occupations were so isolated and stigmatized. Nevertheless, it still seems extraordinary to realize that, in the first centuries of Islam, Jews filled so many of the occupations conveniently named by a Muslim author listing "professions that damn": blacksmith, butcher, conjurer, policeman, highwayman, police informer, night watchman, tanner, maker of wooden and leather pails, maker of women's shoes, burier of excrement, well digger, stoker of baths, felt maker, masseur, horse trader, weaver, ironsmith, pigeon racer, and chess player.[41]

Extraordinarily, there were Jewish occupations even more reviled and undesirable than any of these. It was common enough, in fact, from ancient times through the decline of Muslim power, to use Jews for dirty work—not only the smelly and offensive work of tanning or fulling, but even more repul-

---

[37] Maimonides, *Iggeret Teiman*, 458–59.

[38] Goitein, *Jews and Arabs*, 169.

[39] Siddiqi, *Sahih Muslim* 4:1525. The bad reputation of Isfahani Jews was reflected in their association with "low" occupations. See for example Abu Nuʿaim, who says that the Jews of Isfahan were workers in cupping, tanning, fulling, and butchering (Mez, *Renaissance of Islam*, 39 n. 8).

[40] Bar Hebraeus, cited in I. Friedlaender, "Jewish-Arabic Studies" 3:282 n. 398.

[41] Massignon, *Al-Hallaj* 1:267.

sive occupations. One of the worst of these was the universally loathed jailer. We already hear of Jewish jailers in sixth- and seventh-century Persia.[42] Moreover, in the Babylonian Talmud (Taanit 22a) the prophet Elijah appears in a contemporary marketplace and declares that a man there has a share in the world to come. That man was a Jewish jailer.

Jews were used not only as jailers, but even as executioners. Middle Eastern rulers, in other words, utilized Jews for the very worst jobs for well over a millennium. In illustration, I have translated a description of such activities deriving from events in fifteenth-century Lebanon. On Wednesday night, the twenty-ninth day of the month of Shawwal, in the year 1462,

> a slave and a black bondswoman conspired against their mistress at Tripoli. Her husband was away at the time and they murdered her. . . A Jew was put in charge of their execution, as was their custom in that land, for whenever such a thing occurred they would call upon a Jew at random, whoever it might be. The Jew was then ordered to execute by whatever manner of punishment the criminal deserved, out of the apprehension that one of [the Muslim community] should have to do [that undesirable deed].[43]

There was, then, a full spectrum of Jewish professions. Beyond legal occupations, Jews operated outside the law as outlaws.[44] Indeed, we possess a precious account of a Jewish highwayman at the turn of the ninth century. Because of its rarity and intrinsic interest, I translate it here (from *The History of the Rulers of Damascus and the Biography of Ibrahim ibn al-Mahdi*) in its entirety:

> 'Ali ibn al-Mughira al-Athram said: "Ibrahim ibn al-Mahdi [a professional singer, uncle of the caliphs al-Amin and al-Ma'mun] told me that he ruled the emirate of Damascus for two years, after which for a period of four years no one was waylaid in his province. I was told that disaster eventually did occur in the form of highway robbery, by Diama and Nu'man, two *mawali* [client-tribesmen] of the Umayyads, and by Yahya ibn Yirmia of the Balqa' Jews. They refused to submit to the authority of a governor, so when I came to office I wrote letters to them. Nu'man wrote to him with a solemn oath that he would not despoil his district so long as he was governor. Diama came to me 'hearing and obeying.' He told me that Nu'man had been true and had kept his promise. He told me that the Jew had written to him, 'I am going out to dispute you. So write me a note of assurance swearing to me in it that you won't do anything to me until I return to my place of safety.' I acceded to this request.

---

[42] Segal, "Jews of North Mesopotamia," 55.

[43] Zayyat, "Jews in the 'Abbasid Caliphate," 172–73, reproducing the text of 'Abd al-Basit al-Hanafi's *Al-Rauda al-Basam*, 55.

[44] Perhaps "lowest" of all were the Jewish criminals. Jewish travelers (Eldad ha-Dani and Benjamin of Tudela) in the Middle Ages noted the presence of Jewish robbers. See, for example, Ginzberg, *Unknown Jewish Sect*, 387 n. 140. For a portrayal of later Jewish weavers, see Goitein, "Portrait of a Yemenite," 3–26.

"A youth with scant hair, wearing an ornamented outer garment, a girdle, and a Mahalla sword, approached me. He entered the House of Mu'awiyya while I was in its courtyard. He greeted me off the carpet. So I said to him, 'Get on the carpet.' He said, 'O Amir! The carpet carries with it an obligation which frightens me from staying seated on it. For I don't know what on earth you will impose on me.' So I replied, 'Convert! Hear and Obey!' He said, 'As for obedience, I hope to do so. But as for Islam, there's no way. Let me know what is in it for me if I don't convert to Islam.' I said, 'There is no way for you to avoid rendering the *jizya* [(head tax)] to me.' To which the Jew replied, 'No way to do that.' [The Jew] then answered back, 'I am leaving in accordance with my pledge of safe conduct,' and I permitted that. And I ordered them to water his horse as he went out to it. When he saw that, he called for a hired horse, mounted it, and abandoned his own steed. He said, 'I'm not in a position to take anything with me which I received from you for mere convenience, for I will wage war on you upon it.' I appreciated that coming from him, and I requested that he come back inside.

"And when he entered, I said, 'Praise God, who made me victorious over you without a contract or a pact.' He asked, 'How is that?' I answered, 'Because you turned away from me and then returned to me.' He said, 'You imposed as condition that you should send me away to my sanctuary. If your abode is my sanctuary, then I shouldn't be scared. But if my sanctuary is my own abode, then return me to Balqa.' I tried hard to have him comply with my request to pay the jizya, [even] on condition that I grant him two hundred dinars a year, but he wouldn't do it. He returned and stirred up mischief in his area.

"Sometime thereafter, monies were transported to 'Ubaidallah ibn al-Mahdi in Egypt. The Jew went out to intercept this [shipment]. I wrote back to him, commanding him to war against the Jew if he interfered with the money. When ['Ubaidallah ibn al-Mahdi] encountered the Jew, both knights were escorted militarily. Al-Nu'man asked the Jew to leave the field, but he refused. He said, 'You wish me to come out to you all alone while you come out in your escort. If you so desire, we should meet in single combat. If I vanquish you, your companions will revert to me, and they will share booty with me. And if you beat me, my companions will revert to you.' Al-Nu'man said to him, 'O Yahya! Woe unto you, you youth! You have been inflated with conceit—even if you were one of the Quraysh, your hostility to the government wouldn't be possible. This amir is the caliph's brother, and I, even though we are of different religions, would prefer not to have the murder of a knight on my hands. If you wish what I wish of security, then he will not be afflicted by you and by me.'

"They both went out together at the time of the Asr [late afternoon] prayer, remaining in duel till dusk. Each stayed on his horse, supporting his weight on his lance. Al-Nu'man had his eyes poked out. The Jew thrust at him, and the spearhead of his lance got caught in al-Nu'man's girdle. The girdle revolved and the spearhead started to turn in the girdle toward the rear. At this point al-Nu'man grabbed him and said to him, 'Double-cross, O son of a Jewish woman!' Yahya replied, 'O the fighter sleeps, O son of a handmaid!' Al-Nu'man then leaned his full weight on him in his embrace and fell on top of him. Al-Nu'man was a huge man, and so, immobilizing the Jew, he cut his throat. He thereupon dispatched his head to the caliph. None after him opposed me."[45]

By the tenth century, then, Jews worked in virtually every known profession. From the documentary evidence of the Cairo Geniza, Goitein counted over 250 manual occupations and 170 types of activities in commerce, the professions, education, and administration.[46] I want to emphasize that there was a smaller but still quite considerable range of professions already occupied by Jews by the eighth century, from the highest merchant ranks to the most reviled, including those operating outside the law.

Finally, I must add that there were un-Jewish Jewish successes: ironically, one of the most spectacularly influential of all "Jewish" social roles was that of the professional Jewish convert. These converts were learned Jewish men who converted to Islam and then proceeded to spend a lifetime Islamicizing Jewish traditions. These "professional Jewish converts" partly were responsible for the Islamic assimilation of reams of Halakha and Aggada.[47]

The best known of the these professional converts, Wahb b. Munnabih, was flogged to death in the early 720s.[48] It is strange to hear that he was executed, for he spent a long life as a Muslim loyally transposing Jewish traditions into Islamic guise, in which garb they were rapidly recognized as being Muslim traditions. Wahb and other Jewish converts thereby played an invaluable role of enormous consequence in the self-definition of new Islam. But they seem to have been rather unwelcome in either of their religious communities: otherwise respectable works of Jewish history of this period do not even mention these converts. But Wahb cannot be shrugged out of Jewish history. That the professional Jewish convert posed a certain threat to the Jewish community is obvious on the face of it. Jacob Katz argues persuasively, however, that such apostates do still belong to Jewish history. In discussing two nineteenth-century French Jewish brothers who converted to Catholicism and subsequently became celebrated Catholic thinkers, Katz argues that "their lives were given much attention by Catholics but entirely ignored by Jews—wrongly so, in my opinion, for failures, no less than successes of Jewish society, belong to Jewish history."[49]

Clearly, we possess insufficient data upon which to draw defensible specifi-

---

[45] Zayyat, "Jews in the ʿAbbasid Caliphate," 155–57. This report comes from *The History of the Rulers of Damascus and the Biography of Ibrahim ibn al-Mahdi* and dates to the reign of al-Rashid (786–809). See also Kraemer, "Apostates," 34–74.

[46] Goitein, "Jewish Society," 175.

[47] I discuss some of these figures, as well as the general phenomenon of Isra'iliyyat, more fully in chapter 6 below, with special reference to ʿAbdallah ibn Salam.

[48] Faruqi, *Early Muslim Historiography*, 92–110; Horowitz, "Earliest Biographies," 530–55; Abbott, "Wahb b. Munabbih," 103–12.

[49] Katz, "Religion as a Force," 6. In this regard, it is striking that Ahroni does not discuss Wahb or ʿAbdallah ibn Saba' in his *Yemenite Jewry*.

cations concerning class conflict among the Jews of the eighth century. That being said, it seems clear enough, in general, that classes of Jews were in conflict. We know, at the broadest level, that Jews were heavily represented in the lower classes and that they participated in conflicts, even military rebellions, in which class difference played a part. To the extent that the majority of Jews at this time apparently suffered from the ugly reputation associated with those classes, it is reasonable to conclude that they also suffered the consequences of such a reputation.[50]

LEADERSHIP AND THE CRISIS OF MOBILITY

Although I began by bemoaning the absence of sources, we clearly do possess sufficient sources to assemble a roughly accurate picture—a moving picture, for whatever sources survive are marked by an inescapably vivid sense of motion. There were Jewish conversions and Jewish revolutions, inspiring Jewish rises and catastrophic Jewish falls. Things were in flux and reflux. The end of antiquity conveys such a sense of motion, in fact, that I would argue that this period of Jewish history constituted an epochal crisis of mobility for the Jewish community.

Thus far I have tried to show that some few Jews at the mid-eighth-century end of antiquity wielded power and influence, while the majority were variously alienated enough to convert, rebel, and even form new sects. These were the two obvious poles of Jewish experience, though neither of these were obviously *the* Jewish experience. There were, after all, non-Jewish courtiers and non-Jewish peasants, so neither the Jewish courtiers nor the Jewish peasants represents the essentially Jewish Zeitgeist, the characteristic Jewish spirit of the age. Who, then, did? Who led the Jewish commmunity? The answer to that question is that Jewish authority—then, as now—was made up of an interlocking and sometimes internally contested network of leadership. I have to this point described the socioeconomic pluralism of the Jewish community because that complexity provides the bases for these rival parties struggling for the center of Judaism.

Under early Islam, the very definitions of Jewish authority and legitimacy were being reconstituted. What, in fact, comprised Jewish constitutional authority in the eighth century? Who was the properly constituted leader of the commmunity? Who could legitimately lead? These questions, which we ask today of our own community, were being aggressively pursued then. Then as now, Jewish authority was being anxiously reassessed.[51]

[50] On accusations against one's enemies as belonging to the ʿamma, see Cook and Crone, *Hagarism*, 230 n. 24. For the relationship of this label to the rebellions in the early period, see Blichfeldt, "*Khassa* and *ʿamma*," 14–20.
[51] For the best overview of the political history of Jewry in this age, see Baron, *Social and Religious History* 5:3–82.

This critical reassessment was brought to a head at a brief but pivotal moment of Jewish history. I refer now to the twenty-one years of the reign of the second ʿAbbasid caliph, Abu Jaʿfar al-Mansur (754–75).[52] It is precisely then that I would locate the climactic confrontation of powerless Jews with newly empowered Muslims, as they converged around the center of real political power. During the two decades of the reign of al-Mansur, major challenges for supreme Jewish leadership emanated from three distinct Jewish parties: the Gaons, the exilarchs, and the laity. I shall discuss each in turn and try to show how al-Mansur apparently manipulated each of these Jewish challenges.

The shattering peoples' uprising of Abu ʿIsa in Isfahan, as described by Maimonides, may be the best example of the politics of the Jewish underclass.[53] Maimonides refers to a unnamed caliph who cleverly halts the dangerously spreading movement. Other sources specify that this caliph was none other than al-Mansur.[54] Here is Maimonides' account of how al-Mansur dealt with this Jewish revolution:

> [Al-Mansur] said to all the Jews of his kingdom: "Let your Rabbis go out to meet this multitude and ascertain whether their pretension is true and he is unmistakably your Expected One. If so, we shall conclude peace with you under any conditions you may prefer. But if it is dissimulation, then I shall wage war against them." When the Rabbis met these Jews . . . they asked them: "Who instigated you to make this uprising?" Whereupon they replied: "This man here . . . whom we know to be a leper at night, arose the following morning healthy and sound." They believed that leprosy was one of the characteristics of the Messiah. . . .
>
> Whereupon the Rabbis explained to them that their interpretation was incorrect, and that he lacked even one of the characteristics of the Messiah, let alone all of them. Furthermore the Rabbis advised them: "O fellow Jews, you are still near your native country, and have the possibility of returning there. If you remain in this land, you will not only perish but also undermine the teachings of Moses by misleading people to believe that the Messiah has appeared and has been vanquished. . . ." [The rebels] were persuaded by the Rabbis' arguments. [Al-Mansur] then turned over to them so many thousands of *denars* by way of hospitality in order that they should leave his country.[55]

Then, once the rebels had been bribed to depart, al-Mansur turned around and punished the Jews of his own realm![56] Al-Mansur indeed operated as a

[52] Noldeke's essay, "Caliph Mansur," in *Sketches*, is still a valuable introduction.

[53] There was a rebellion against al-Mansur in Isfahan, in the year 755–56. In 767, Mansur thought of making Isfahan his capital, though it was mere rubble at the time (Browne, "Account of a Rare Manuscript," 419). See also Fischel, "Yahudiyya," 523–26.

[54] That is the dating of Shahrastani, which I follow.

[55] Maimonides, *Iggeret Teiman*, 458–59.

[56] Ibid. Al-Mansur was hereby reinforcing the "counterrevolution," which he had already initiated against other insurgents. See Daniel, *Political and Social History*, 157, on the "striking revival of Caliphal power"; and the profile of his power relations in Hodgson, *Venture of Islam* 1:284–89.

textbook Machiavellian. In fact, a full analysis of his relations with religions, ethnic groups, and minorities would reveal, it would seem, the genius that leads Dunlop to consider al-Mansur "the virtual founder of the ʿAbbasid dynasty."[57] In short, fundamental religiopolitical reorganizations were affected by al-Mansur, including such major parties as the Manicheans and the Imamiyya (Twelver Shiʿites).[58]

He certainly knew how to get Jews to work for him. As noted above, he employed a Jewish tax collector and a Jewish town planner, who plotted his capital city of Baghdad in 762. In addition to his adroit manipulation of both the Jewish peasantry and Jewish administrators, al-Mansur was equally effective in handling the Jewish scholarly elite. He certainly used rabbis for his own ends, according to the above report of Maimonides. But the most telling of al-Mansur's meddling in the affairs of the rabbis took place in his brilliant manipulation of Gaons and exilarchs.

Gaons (Geonim), as the heads of the Babylonian Jewish academies, along with their Palestinian counterparts, constituted the supreme court of the Jewish world.[59] Indeed, their academies constituted, at once, the high court, university, and parliament of all Jewries under their jurisdiction.[60] Vying for power with the Gaons were the exilarchs. The exilarch, Leader of the Exile, (Hebrew, *rosh golah*; Aramaic, *resh galuta*; Arabic, *raʾs jalut*), were Jewish civil leaders who derived their authority from a claim of direct descent from King David.[61] The exilarchs under the caliphs served as "ministers of Jewish affairs": the Jewish commmunity paid taxes to them, who in turn passed them on to the caliph (after taking a cut). The exilarchs, in short, were wealthy courtiers who literally dwelled at the court in Baghdad. They were also, it seems, cozy with the caliphs: a ninth-century Gaon inveighs against an exilarch "who cannot control Bible or Talmud nor make practical decisions but is powerful through money and closeness to the throne."[62]

It may be instructive that we possess numerous Muslim tales of the Jewish exilarchs but no Muslim tale of the Gaons.[63] This disparity may be due to the

---

[57] Dunlop, *Arab Civilization*, 257.

[58] On an anti-*dhimmi* decree generally, see the older account concerning al-Mansur in Arnold, *Preaching of Islam*, 75. On the Manicheans, see the account of the Miqlasiyya in Ibn al-Nadim, *Fihrist of Ibn al-Nadim* 2:793–94. And on the Imamis, see al-Mansur's relations with Jaʿfar al-Sadiq. The Ithna ʿAshariyya believe that Mansur killed Jaʿfar: see Donaldson, *Shiʿite Religion*, 131–32.

[59] Gerson Cohen impressively surveyed the historiography in "Reconstruction of Gaonic History." See also I. Friedlaender, "Jews of Arabia," 249–52.

[60] Goitein repeats this characterization in various places, for example, in "Minority Self-Rule," 114.

[61] The sources on the exilarchate in this period have now been conveniently and thoroughly collected by Grossman, *Babylonian Exilarchate*.

[62] Silver, *Maimonidean Criticism*, 61.

[63] See chap. 3 below for numerous Shiʿi tales of the rosh golah. The role and function of the Gaon seem to have been almost unknown to Muslim letters.

fact that exilarchs were creatures of the courts, where they were openly and regularly observed by Muslims, who unavoidably noted their presence. This fact also implies that exilarchs were not "of the people." That the Geonim, on the other hand, must have been socially rather closer to the people than to the caliphal court we know from a variety of evidence. For example, in the late-ninth century, a certain Yom Tov Kohen became a Gaon, as a later Gaon put it, *"even though he was a weaver."*[64]

Between them, the Gaons and the exilarchs purported to represent the totality of Jewry—Catholic Israel, as Solomon Schechter translated "Kelal Yisrael"—in other words, all classes of Jews. However, during the mid-eighth-century regime of al-Mansur, the high-class exilarchs and the relatively declassé Gaons were together bitterly engaged in the "age-old drive of the scholarly class for supreme control of the Jewish community."[65] Their rivalry became, at this moment, a pointed struggle of contending legitimacies. The specific situation was the following: Already for several decades of the early-eighth century, Gaons and exilarchs had been vigorously deposing each other, attempting to impose their choices on the others and generally jockeying for that "supreme control of the Jewish commmunity." Then the Muslim dynasties changed hands at the century's midpoint, in the year 750. By the time al-Mansur ascended to the throne in 754, the Jewish commmunity would appear to be in almost unparalleled disarray. The last caliph they needed was what they got with al-Mansur: a single-mindedly calculating political genius all too inclined to widen the already gaping divisions in the Jewish leadership.

Al-Mansur insinuated himself into these shaky Jewish affairs, and his ploys were to have a sustained impact on Jewish life for centuries to follow. The story has two parts. These were the two times that we know of in which al-Mansur directly intervened in the Gaon-exilarch struggle. Both incidents involved ancient conflicts and resulted in substantial and permanant changes in the Jewish structure of authority. The first of these interventions came with al-Mansur's decision to personally resolve the dispute between two lineages over the exilarchate.[66] Al-Mansur chose "the Persian lineage," which already owed a century of obligations to the Muslim caliphs. It must surely have been due to this debt that the grateful exilarch, probably at al-Mansur's behest, moved the seat of the exilarchs to al-Mansur's new capital of Baghdad.

Meanwhile, as Baron puts its, "even more portentous was the conflict between 'Anan, the founder of the Karaite schism, and his brother Hananiah, which resulted in the permanent schism of the Karaite sect from the main body of Rabbanites."[67] 'Anan ben David was the son of the exilarch and a

---

[64] Baron, *Social and Religious History*, 5:74–5, citing Sherira Gaon.
[65] Baron, *Social and Religious History*, 5:13. It can hardly be a coincidence that the first attempt to bring Palestinian Jewry under Babylonian sway was under Yehudai Gaon, ca. 760.
[66] Ibid.
[67] Ibid., 221.

disciple of the greatest scholar of the generation. Perhaps because ʿAnan seemed too arrogant, the Gaons, who elected the exilarchs, chose ʿAnan's younger brother over him. ʿAnan refused to recognize the decision and was consequently thrown into the dungeon by al-Mansur. According to this (apocryphal) account, ʿAnan then successfully freed himself by convincing al-Mansur that he would not contest the decision but rather would start his own religion. Al-Mansur gladly freed ʿAnan, perhaps because the Muslim ruler was content to let the new sectarian leader of the "disgruntled intellectuals of Baghdad" further divide the Jewish community.[68]

Thus a crisis of mobility paradoxically paralyzed the Jewish leadership of the mid-eighth century. This gridlock of multiple leaders, I assert, was consciously encouraged by the deftly manipulative al-Mansur, a conniving master of the technique of divide and conquer. Al-Mansur used Jewish leaders against Jewish leaders to his own exquisite advantage. The canny al-Mansur knew what he was doing; just as he had pitted the Gaons against the rebels of Abu ʿIsa, so he pitted the exilarchs against the Gaons. As a result there sprang from the time of his rule the two most significant Jewish sects—the *only* important Jewish sects after the destruction of the Second Temple—the ʿIsawiyya and the Karaites. In dealing with al-Mansur, the Jewish community would seem to have played a politics of catastrophe. Or did it? To be sure, the world history of the Jews at this moment made it appear ripe for a rebirth of a Jewish commonwealth: about 740 a Jewish kingdom was established by the Turkish Khazars of Central Asia; in 768 a Jewish princedom was (said to have been) established in southern France; and the Persian Jewish rebel Abu ʿIsa tried to do the same in Persia at roughly the same historical moment.[69] Did the Babylonian Gaons and exilarchs, so strategically situated at the center of the Muslim empire, fail to seize that moment?

They did not seize the day, because al-Mansur did that for them. However, while the Khazar and the French and Persian Jewish attempts at political power ultimately did fail, we are not entitled to speak of the Jewish political catastrophe under al-Mansur—for the devious caliph in fact left the Jewish community with a legacy he himself desired: stability. And with the coming of this stability, after the end of a rather chaotic late antiquity, the darkness of our sources finally lifts. With this added information we know that the crisis of mobility of the Jewish leadership in the eighth century, culminating in the reign of al-Mansur, eventually resulted in a dialectically positive effect on the

[68] This tale is reviewed by Nemoy in "ʿAnan ben David," 309–18. See also Martin Cohen, "ʿAnan ben David and Karaite Origins"; the most important recent work on ʿAnan has been done by Haggai Ben-Shammai. See his "Between Ananites and Karaites."

[69] On the Judaization of the Khazars see Dunlop, *Jewish Khazars*; Golden, *Khazar Studies*; Golb and Pritsak, *Khazar Hebrew Documents*. On the purported "Jewish princedom" in southern France see Zuckerman, *Jewish Princedom in Feudal France*, to be used with caution; and for the rebellion of Abu ʿIsa see below, chapter 2, on the history of the ʿIsawiyya.

Jewish community. When the dust settled, the rabbinical and Karaite communities had reconciled themselves to being complementary if contending Jewish parties; the smaller Jewish sects were scattered and ineffectual, their power neutralized; the Jewish court bankers, like the Jewish weavers and tanners, went about their business. And the great caliphs residing in Baghdad rested properly comfortably with this quiescent state of affairs. Jewish antiquity was at its end, and its long medieval creativity, stimulated by new stability and new plurality, was underway.

Thus through disorientation new forms of authority were instituted. Through this novel complexity, the Jewish community grew plural without actually breaking apart entirely.[70] Did the caliph al-Mansur in fact do Judaism a favor? Is that how the Jews of his day understood him? Remarkably, we can read contemporaneous Jewish responses to al-Mansur. Of the surviving handful of Jewish texts from this time, we luckily have two or three sources arguably dating from the reign of al-Mansur. These Jewish texts include apocalypses, books of revelation revealed by an angel. The most significant of these apocalypses, *The Secrets of Shimon bar Yochai*, describes the landmark reign of al-Mansur in euphorically Messianic terms. *The Secrets of Shimon bar Yochai* seems to consider its own days as the last days of history; it even describes Muslim rule as a sign of the final redemption of the Jews.[71] The eighth-century end of Jewish antiquity was, then, immediately perceived by some Jews as being momentous: the Jewish community perceived itself to be verging on a new age.

Of course, in the absence of accurately prognosticating prophets, they could not actually know just how much was about to change. The transformative events of the mid-eighth century did reconstitute Jewish leadership. After al-Mansur's meddling, new structures of Jewish authority grew secure enough that the now more broadly based Jewish community could rest relatively more securely on them in that challenging new era. In this new age, however, the old social structures remained, however realigned. Thus a Muslim poet sang,

> Fear of God alone gives standing and nobility—to love the world makes you poor and destitute. As long as he keeps his fear of God unimpaired, it is no shortcoming for the servant of God even to be a weaver or a cupper.[72]

---

[70] Credit certainly must be given to the rabbinic leadership on this score, for example, their generous embrace of the former followers of the pseudo-prophet Serene. See the conciliatory responsum of Gaon Natronai Gaon, translated in Kobler, *Letters of Jews through the Ages* 1:69–70.

[71] As translated and annotated in Lewis, "Apocalyptic Vision," 305–38. Remarkably, Muslim sources would seem to corroborate this great hope that some placed in al-Mansur. A sect known as the Rawendiyya, in the Persian province of Khorasan (ca. 758) believed that al-Mansur was the Mahdi. See Freidlaender, "Jewish-Arabic Studies" 2:503–7.

[72] Abu 'l-Atahiya, citing from the *Kitab al-Aghani*, in Von Grunebaum, *Medieval Islam*, 124.

Moses Maimonides, (1135–1204) in so many ways, marks the end of the creative symbiosis between Jews and Muslims. To what extent this shift in relations reflects internal breakdowns in Jewish leadership remains to be seen. But Maimonides rejected the preceding Jewish establishment, and with telling phrases: "It is better for you to earn a drachma as wages for the work of a weaver, tailor or carpenter, rather than to be dependent on the licence of the Exilarch."[73]

Though few solid conclusions can be established concerning the precise profile of the Jewish community in the eighth century, its occupational and class-differentiated pluralism seems beyond dispute. I leave aside (as beyond my purview) the consolidation of rabbinic leadership in this period. But the evidence points to an "ascendency of Babylonian ritual," as Urbach puts it.[74] In any event, my concern to this point is not to write a fully rounded history of the Jews nor to study rabbinic developments. Rather, I have been concerned to show that the Jewish community, divided against itself geographically, "sectually," and between classes, could hardly have been expected to present a unified front to the Muslims around them. Thus the symbiosis did not take place on the part of some spuriously reified "Jewry," but rather on the part of many different Jews.

THE QUESTION OF JEWISH SECTARIANISM

A certain consensus of scholars prevails concerning Jewish sectarianism in the pre-Gaonic period. On this hypothesis, there had been extant several identifiable Jewish groups in Mishnaic times, but none of these survived the Roman destruction of Jerusalem or of the Temple and its cult. This watershed disaster is therefore considered a certain terminus ad quem for Jewish sectarianism: no Jewish sects have been proven to exist during the long talmudic period, roughly 200–600. The title of a recent article expresses this consensus succinctly: "The Significance of Yavneh: Pharisees, Rabbis, and the End of Jewish Sectarianism."[75]

And yet, to be sure, with the coming of Islam, Jewish sectarianism dramatically reemerged from its long night of (purported) seclusion.[76] The problem

---

[73] Letter to Joseph ibn 'Aqnin, cited in Kobler, *Letters of Jews through the Ages* 1:207.
[74] Urbach, "Center and Periphery" 233–37. Yehudai Gaon, ca. 760, attempted this regularization under al-Mansur. See Kahle, *The Cairo Geniza*, 40.
[75] S. Cohen, "Significance of Yavneh," 27–53.
[76] A history of the smaller Jewish sects under Islam remains a desideratum. Aside from the Samaritans and Karaites, who have received continuous scholarly attention over the last two hundred years, the smaller sects have not yet been studied using the full battery of available historical sources.
    The best history of the smaller sects under Islam is in Baron, "Messianism and Sectarian Trends," in *Social and Religious History of the Jews* 5:138–209. Somewhat out of date, but still extremely useful is I. Friedlaender's "Jewish-Arabic Studies." Perhaps

is simple yet intractable: What, if any, are the continuities between the Jewish groupings under the early Muslim Church and the Jewish groupings under the early *umma* (Muslim community)? How do we account for similarities such as those between the Qumran Jews and the Karaites?[77]

Primordial Karaism, while still obscure in detail, remains a pointedly salient—if still relatively little explored—promontory on the contours of Jewish historiography. Indeed, even though a "pan-Karaite" theory held sway for some years, we still do not understand even such rudiments as, for example, the social setting of the origins of Karaism.[78] Our map of Jews and Judaism after Muhammad, to be sure, will remain a pastiche of speculations and extrapolations until such questions have been thoroughly reinvestigated. Only after such studies will the light generated by Jewish internal proliferations illumine our dim understanding of Muslim-Jewish relations under the Geonim.

This imperative seems more pressing in the case of extra-Karaite Jewish

---

the fullest collections of texts and general discussions continue to be written in Hebrew, as they have been since Simhah Pinsker's *Likkute Kadmoniot* of 1860. Of more recent Hebrew-language collections, two are essential: Aeshcoly, *Messianic Movements in Israel*, 117–32; Dinur, *Judaism in the Israel*, 207–34, and the notes thereon, 268–75.

Two other points concerning the history of the Jewish sects under Islam should be made at this point. First, it is instructive to note that next to no direct information concerning medieval non-Karaite Jewish sectarianism came out of the otherwise rich Cairo Geniza. One may hope that the Firkovitch collection of Leningrad may well contain much information on this subject, since it contains numerous Karaite works. The second point, which helps us understand the first, is that medieval Jews, like medieval Muslims, were largely unconcerned with postbiblical Jewish history. The Jewish disregard for its own historiography is well reported by Yerushalmi in *Zakhor*. Likewise, there exists a vast Muslim literature pertaining to figures and events of the Banu Isra'il, but very little historical (or legendary) discussion of postbiblical Jews and Judaism.

[77] Solomon Zeitlin lead the charge of an Anglo-American revisionist argument, which asserted that the scrolls found at Qumran were to be assigned to the Karaites (*Zadokite Fragments*)

Golb explored this argument for a time ("Literary and Doctrinal Aspects," 354–74; "Dietary Laws," 51–69; "Qumran Covenanters," 38–50). Hoenig also worked this vein in "Qumran Rules," 559–67 and "Pre-Karaism," 71–93.

The fullest statement of this position is articulated impressively by Weider, *Judean Scrolls*. The consensual position of scholarship rejected this hypothesis: "The Karaite hypothesis . . . is simply untenable in the light of the combined evidence of archeology, paleography, and literary contents" (Vermes, "Essenes and History," 23). But the numerous indisputably striking parallels between the Qumran and Karaite systems have yet to be explained in historical terms. Some scholars still hold for a genetic relationship. This position is summarized by Dupuy, "Les karaites?" 139–51.

[78] The best attempts thus far have been Mahler's Marxian reading, *Karaimer*, and Ben-Sasson's Zionist "First of the Karaites," 42–55.

sectarianism. How, after all, does one sensibly go about streaming these obscure Jewish groups under early Islam? One largely obsolete method has been to follow uncritically the rubrics concocted by heresiographers. These doxographies are Muslim, Christian, and Karaite; rabbis themselves never listed their dissident groups under the umbrella rubric of "Judaism." Still, despite rabbinic silence, no one suggests that organized subgroupings of Jews did not exist; no one, that is, believes that rabbinic abstinence from naming sectarian names betokens anything more than "the silent treatment." In short, given the amplitude of the evidence, there is simply no reason to believe that Jews were monolithically "unified" at the end of antiquity. But, of course, this supposition merely leads to the more serious question: How, then, was this Jewish diversity organized?

Obviously, a historical rethinking of Jewish group organization is required. In order to transcend its confounding of folklore and philology and miscellaneously precious data, I analyzed (elsewhere) the literary-critical questions involved in interpreting Muslim heresiography of the Jews. Such source analysis is propaedeutic to a systematic reassessment of the historicity of such groups.

I should reiterate that the present work is not that study of Jewish history as such—though I did find it necessary to sketch a social description of Jews under early Islam in the preceding section of this chapter. The present work, however, is an effort to comprehend the diversity of interreligious systems of meanings as they were exchanged and transformed in the first centuries of Islamic culture. Since there exists no serious objection to the proposition that extrarabbinic, extra-Karaite groups did exist, and since I present a history of the largest of them, the 'Isawiyya, in the following chapter, my concern at this point lies more generally with the dynamics of Jewish pluralism.

After all, the history of Jews and Judaism in the first centuries after Muhammad will remain dark until the pluralism of the Gaonic period has been thoroughly reinvestigated. In short, a rethinking of Jewish group organization at the end of antiquity is required. It was with this desideratum in mind that I therefore undertook a systematic analysis of Muslim heresiography (that literature devoted to the classification and description of religious groups) of the Jews. In that work, I analyzed the surprisingly rich range of classical Arabic sources concerning Jewish sectarianism.[79] Here I present some of the results of that research, supplemented by subsequent discovery and analysis of texts.

The first problem one encounters in this field of research is the paucity of datable Jewish sources. We possess almost no Rabbanite sources that specify the identities of non-Rabbanite Jewish groups. The Geonim were famously disciplined in giving the silent treatment to their opposition and rivals; they did not "name names." Thus, aside from a few responsa and indirect state-

---

[79] Wasserstrom, "Species of Misbelief."

ments as well as some allusions in *piyyutim* and other poems, no Jewish sectarians are specified by name by the Geonim. Some rabbis do refer to contemporaneous *minim*; Saadia cryptically criticized a group of "people who are
called Jews" (anashim she-nikraim Yehudim); and, occasionally, a polemicist
referred to *apikorsim* or, in Arabic, Khawarij.[80] These derogations often simply referred to Karaites or to dissident Rabbanites.[81] Rarely can any other
firm sectarian identity be teased from these oblique clues.

A second point with regard to Jewish sources is in order. The Cairo Geniza, which one might expect to be as rich a source on this subject as it is on
so many other realms of Judaica, seems almost as silent as do the Geonim
with reference to sectarians. Exceptions from the Geniza include the few texts
(such as the Damascus Document) associated with the Qumran Jews;[82] a
fascinating tenth-century polemical text of unknown origin studied only, and
incompletely, by Jacob Mann;[83] some miscellaneous hints gleaned from documents;[84] and some works claimed by Shlomo Pines and his students to be
Jewish Christian.[85] This apparent paucity of Geniza evidence, however, may
be misleading. We have reason to believe that important texts relevant to the
study of Jewish sects under Islam exist in the Firkovitch collection in
Leningrad.

The following, then, represents an attempt based largely on Muslim
sources—as well as on Karaite, Christian, and Rabbanite sources, though
only secondarily—to survey the state of the question concerning the smaller
Jewish sects under early Islam. I have searched for groups who are called or
call themselves Jews; were considered to be or considered themselves to be
somehow Jewish; and/or were neither Rabbanite, Karaite, or Samaritan.
Thus, this search particularly concerns Jewish groups possessing a distinctive
body of doctrine and practice, whose organization and whose self-definition
set them apart from being Rabbanites, Karaites, and Samaritans but not necessarily apart from being "Jews."

Given these general criteria, one could argue repectably for the existence of
a handful of non-Karaite Jewish sects. On my reading of the sources, however, sufficient evidence exists to assert seriously the historicity of only three
of these: the 'Isawiyya, the Jewish Gnostics, and the Jewish Christians.[86] Inasmuch as I will study the 'Isawiyya and the Jewish Gnostics in chapters to
follow, I shall now look at one sectarian trajectory, that of the so-called Jewish
Christians, and one geographic region, the Persianate orbit. I have chosen

[80] Mann, "Early Theologico-Polemical Work," 411–59.
[81] Chiesa, "Il Guidaismo Caraita," 163–69.
[82] Ginzberg, *Unknown Jewish Sect*.
[83] Mann, "Early Theologico-Polemical Work."
[84] Friedman, "Menstrual Impurity."
[85] See the works of Pines on Jewish Christians listed in the Bibliography below, as
well as Crone, "Byzantine Iconoclasm"; Liebes, "Who Makes the Horn?"; and Menahem Kister, "Plucking the Grain."
[86] I deal with the 'Isawiyya in chapter 2 below.

these two areas because, in both areas, burgeoning research reveals substantial internal differentiation in these locations. Rather than review acceptably consensual reconstructions, however, I have therefore chosen to be suggestive and to try to evoke the possibilities apparent in these two identifiable areas of Jewish extrarabbinic, extra-Karaite activity.

The So-Called Jewish-Christians

Not all scholars have yet transcended the old dictum of Harnack: "Islam is a transformation on Arab soil of a Jewish religion which itself had been transformed by Gnostic Judeo-Christianity."[87] For example, not so long ago, Danielou was still saying much the same, though without the emphasis on Gnosticism: "[Jewish Christian] survival in the East can be traced from the third and fourth centuries. . . . Some were absorbed by Islam, which is itself in some ways an heir of Judaeo-Christianity." Schoeps, in the final lines of his major study of Jewish Christianity, Hegelianizes the old argument: "And thus we have a paradox of world-historical proportions, the fact that Jewish-Christianity indeed disappeared in the Christian Church, but was preserved in Islam and thereby extended some of its basic ideas even to our own day." Finally, and not accidentally, such theosophically oriented writers as Henry Corbin and N. O. Brown have returned to Harnack's original Gnostic emphasis: "Islam picks up and extends the notion, already present in Jewish (Ebionite) Christianity, of the unity of the prophetic spirit."[88]

These sweeping historiosophic assertions concerning so-called Jewish Christians and their purportedly profound impact on original Islam are to be contrasted with a remarkable series of closely argued, erudite researches. That is, the question of the survival of Jewish Christians after the Muslim conquests has been extensively surveyed and substantially extended in recent years in the brilliant, if ultimately problematic, studies undertaken by the late Israeli historian of philosophy, Shlomo Pines. In the late 1960s, Pines captured headlines in the popular press when he published his initial study of what he interpreted to be an anti-Pauline Jewish Christian tract, preserved verbatim, so he argued, in the theological encyclopedia of the tenth-century Mu'tazilite 'Abd al-Jabbar.[89] While several early Church historians eagerly embraced his reading, Pines's former coworker on this subject, S. M. Stern, forcefully responded that this sensationalist discovery merely represented another surviving apocryphal gospel, a species of text quite well known in Muslim letters.[90]

[87] Harnack, "Der Islam," 537.
[88] Danielou, "Christianity as a Jewish Sect," 282; Schoeps, *Jewish Christianity*; N. O. Brown, "Prophetic Tradition," 371.
[89] Pines's voluminous work in this area includes: "'Israel, My Firstborn,'" 177–90; "Judaeo-Christian Materials," 187–217; "Jewish Christians"; "Notes on Islam," 135–52.
[90] S. Stern, "New Light on Judaeo-Christianity?" 53–57.

While the book remains open on the identification of ʿAbd al-Jabbar's source, Pines's corollary research has turned up numerous data suggesting the presence of Jewish Christians—of one kind or another—in the first centuries of Islam. From my point of view, it is therefore all the more remarkable to see that Pines, after two decades of strenuous effort devoted to his Jewish Christians, came to rest on the ʿIsawiyya as the sole identifiable group of such sectarians.[91] This is yet another reason to write the history of this unusual group; I attempt to do so in the following chapter.

For the moment, I restrict my concern to the sheer presence of Christianizing and Christianized Jews. I conclude, along with some of the aforementioned scholars, that sufficiently manifold evidence demonstrates, within a reasonable margin of doubt, the existence of some such phenomenon. And, with Pines, I have found only one distinguishable and identifiable Jewish Christian group in this period—the ʿIsawiyya.

The varieties of evidence for so-called Jewish Christian groups has been all-too-often muddled. These currents of evidence include: preachments of an interconfessional revelation; theological sympathies for various aspects of Christian doctrine; ostensible "remnants" of groups descending from the primordial Christian Church; and miscellaneous syncretists with an uncertain relationship to these broad currents. Similar confusions plague the issue of Judaizing Christians—as opposed to Christianizing Jews, under consideration here—confusions that contaminate much of the scholarship on this benighted subject. For example, the laws and councils of the seventh-century Visigoths Recceswinth and Erwig do reveal that these authorities were exercised by what Parkes calls "Hebrew Christians."[92] A parallel problem apparently existed in Syria. A seventh-century Syriac disputation between a stylite and a Jew, in the opinion of its editor, Hayman, was authored to combat real Judaizing.[93] Marcel Simon even argues that such Judaizing among the Christians of Syria continued from the first through the thirteenth centuries.[94]

Clearly, then, the distinction between Christianizing Jews and Judaizing Christians must be maintained wherever possible. With this caveat in mind, I shall review some of the (considerably varied) literature evincing the presence of Christianizing Jews in the centuries just before and after the rise of Islam.

There would appear to have been some diffuse attraction to Christianity in these years. During the lifetime of Muhammad in the seventh century a "rabbi" was heard to say, "I fear lest the Christ, who came first, whom the

[91] Pines, "Preliminary Note," 145–53.
[92] Parkes, *Church and the Synagogue*, 358–66.
[93] Hayman, *Disputation of Sergius*, 75. For example, "I am amazed how there are among you some Christians who associate with us in the synagogue and who bring offerings and at the time of the Passover send unleavened bread" (75). More generally, see Hayman, "Image of the Jew," 423–43.
[94] On the case of Syria, as well as Africa, Spain, Anatolia, and others, see Simon, *Verus Israel*, 306–38. See more generally Dagron, "Judaïser."

Christians worship, was himself he that sent by God."[95] Many Jews were attracted to Christianity in the Byzantine period.[96] Early in the eighth century, under divergent circustances, a Syrian monk and a Mesopotamian monk independently pronounced themselves to be Jewish prophets. Both garnered Jewish followers.[97]

Even as the institutionalization of Islam progressed, some Christianizing of Jews seems to have continued. In the year 796, the Nestorian patriarch of Elam, Timotheos, wrote his now-famous letter. The patriarch stated that, ten years earlier, he had learned from trustworthy Jews, who had just recently been instructed as converts to Christianity, "that some old Hebrew manuscripts had been discovered in a cave in Jericho." He has Jewish scholars confirm that these documents included "texts of our New Testament which are not even mentioned in the Old Testament, neither in our Christian texts or in their Jewish text."[98]

This discovery, so closely parallel in circumstance to the Dead Sea Scrolls find, seems to have uncovered texts belonging to that very same ancient sect dwelling at Qumran.[99] A Jewish sect with curious, quasi-Jewish demiurgic beliefs, the Maghariyya, seem to have received this apellation, "cave people," by virtue of their utilization of these speleologically retrieved texts.[100] More-

---

[95] Neusner, *History of the Jews* 5:130, citing *Doctrina Jacobi Nuper Baptizati*. On this text see Griffith, "Jews and Muslims," 86–87. I thank Professor Griffith for sharing this article with me prior to its publication. See now the definitive work of Dagron and Déroche, "Juifs et Chrétiens"; and the edition of Déroche, *Doctrina Jacobi Nuper Baptizati*.

[96] Wilken, "The Restoration of Israel."

[97] These cases are discussed more fully below in chapter 2, in the section titled "The Jewish Messiahs of Early Islam."

[98] Braun, "Ein Brief," 299–313, first edited and translated this letter.

[99] Golb, "Who were the Magariya?" 347–59; Bammel, "Hohlenmenschen," 77–88; Wolfson, "Pre-Existent Angel," 89–106.

   Much of the subsequent literature on this sect has come from scholars of Gnosticism, who believe that this sect has much to tell them—negatively or positively—on this subject. Grant, "Les êtres," 159, for example: "Among the Maghariya we find then realized the possibility for Jewish heterodoxy, that an angel created the world, but we also find confirmed there the impossibility—for Jewish thought—that he was evil" (my translation from the French of Grant).

   Quispel found, contrarily, a "Jewish Gnostic" origin of the Maghariya demiurge: "Origins of the Gnostic Demiurge," 271–76; "Jewish Gnosis," 121. The argument for a Gnostic Maghariya has been rebutted by G. Stroumsa, "Le Couple de l'ange de de l'esprit," 42–61, esp. 49–52, where he argues that this sect was in fact antianthropomorphic. Fossum has now achieved the fullest treatment on this question in his "Magharians." Two recent contributions are of interest: Beckwith, "Essene Calendar and the Moon," 462–66; and Szyzsman, "Compte rendu," 105–6, where he reports a tantalizing (if far-fetched) possibility of modern remnants of the Maghariyya.

[100] That is, they found texts in caves—not that they were cave dwellers.

over, it is now widely recognized that five apocryphal psalms, three of which were rediscovered in 1948 at Qumran as well, were translated into Syriac subsequent to the eighth-century discovery of them.[101] In other words: Christians, Jews, Jewish converts to Christianity, and perhaps a Christianized Jewish sect all apparently read and translated these eight-hundred-year-old sectarian documents subsequent to their rediscovery in the eighth century.

Other Christianized Jews seem to have been in the environs. Ibn al-Nadim, a reporter celebrated for his reliability, describes several such Mesopotamian groups, including the so-called Ashuriyyin: "In some things they agree with the Jews and about other things they disagree with them. They seem to be a sect of Jesus." In all, Ibn al-Nadim cites five groups that bear both explicitly Jewish and explicitly Christian features.[102]

Perhaps the best known of these Christianizing Jews, aside from the 'Isawiyya, are the eighth-century Athinganoi, Byzantine Samaritan Gnostics. This group, on the argument of Crone and Jeffrey, certainly appears to be "fully" Jewish Christian: "The Athinganoi . . . accepted Christ as a mere man, replaced circumcision by baptism or had neither one nor the other, observed the Sabbath, at least when with Jews, and also Levitical purity and Mosaic law in general: [they also had] Jewish preceptors."[103]

A rivulet of Christianizing Jews also trickled through early Karaism. Qirqisani cites several Karaites with varying degrees of sympathy for Jesus as prophet.[104] Perhaps the most striking of these is one Meswi al-'Ukbari. Baron even suggests that Meswi "not only professed Christainty—[a Karaite opponent] chides him by comparing him with Matthew, John, Paul and Luke—but also 'served three deities simultaneously in his old age,' that is, he simultaneously professed belief in the God of Israel, Jesus, and Muhammad."[105]

It has not been my intention to review comprehensively the question of so-called Jewish Christians. Rather, I have sketched out the variety of some fairly clear evidence, leaving aside the highly complex literary analyses underway in

---

[101] Other texts found in Qumran also were channeled into the Islamicate (Jewish, Christian, and Muslim) world, perhaps through the Timotheos find. Among those texts were several which found their way into the Cairo Geniza. These include the Damascus Document, Hebrew Sirach, and Aramaic Testament of Levi.

A particularly interesting discussion has arisen around the apocryphal psalms found at Qumran, which find their close parallels in the later Syriac and Arabic psalms. See Philonenko, "L'origine," 35–48; Dupont-Summer, "Le psaume," 25–62; Strugnell, "Notes on the Text," 258; Goshen-Gottstein, "Psalms Scroll," 32 n. 45; Magne, "Recherches sur les psaumes," 503–8.

[102] Ibn al-Nadim, *Fihrist*, 2:813, 810–13.

[103] Crone, "Islam, Judeo-Christianity and Byzantine Iconoclasm," 75. The definitive study of the Athinganoi remains Starr, "Athinganoi," 93–106. Griffith vigorously rejects the interpretation of Crone concerning the Athinganoi ("Bashir/Beser," 311).

[104] Nemoy, "Early Karaites," 697–715.

[105] Baron, *Social and Religious History*, 5:196–97. Zvi Ankori announced the publication of a study of this sectarian, but it has never appeared.

the Pines circle. In this "darkest of all periods in post-Biblical Jewish history," it is instructive, even striking, to see such vividly vague patterns emerging. Just what were the implications of such attractively live options? And how were they activated—put into play—within the limits of Jewish life? The following chapters comprise exploratory investigations of these concerns.

The Question of the East: Persia and Beyond

It may not be accidental that the 'Isawiyya developed as a nonrabbinic force east of Babylonia. The Persian and eastern geographic sphere, even more than the Arabian Peninsula of the seventh century, constituted a veritable crucible of Jewish heterodoxy in the early years of Islam. This vast area sheltered, in addition to Abu 'Isa of Isfahan, such prominant figures of nonrabbinic Judaism such as Hiwi of Balkh and Benjamin of Nehawend. Evidence for Jewish life in this area is sparse, but it is worth reviewing, for this was a notorious arena of Jewish pluralism.

The portrait of the miscellaneously nonrabbinical character of the Jewry of the eastern provinces of early Islamicate Persia is only just now being drawn.[106] Certainly, a high percentage of the mixed reports that survive suggest this extrarabbinic profile. Already in the eighth century, for example, a Jew of Khurasan, Marwan ibn Abi Hafsa, can be found serving the 'Abbasid court as a poet.[107] In distant Bukhara, this extrarabbinism resulted in a certain marranism.[108] According to the tenth-century Karaite Salmon b. Yeruhim, "[when the Jews of Samraqand] say 'God is One' (*allah wahid*) [people who hear this] testify that by [saying] this they have become Muslims."[109]

The town of Hamadan serves as an instructive locus for such phenomena. The great disturbances initiated by Abu 'Isa of Isfahan in the eighth century were to extend, in the following two centuries, to Rayy, Qumm, Arrajan, and Hamadan.[110] In 1163, R. Benjamin of Tudela reports that there were four Jewish communities living between Susa and Hamadan and that they joined the side of the Isma'ilis in battle.[111] Heterodox teachings also emanated from Hamadan. The obscure Joseph of Hamadan was a purveyor of early proto-Kabbalistic teachings; his works were to influence the earliest European Kabbalists.[112]

---

[106] There is no adequate study devoted to this subject. But see Fischel, "Jews of Central Asia," 29–49; and Zand, "Jewish Settlements" 4–23.

[107] Fischel, "Jews of Central Asia," 34 n. 22, citing Ibn 'Abd Rabbihi, *Kitab al-Aghani* 9:36–78, and secondary literature. His family is listed in Ibn al-Nadim *Fihrist* 1:352–53.

[108] For the survival of this phenomenon, see Zand, "Bukhara," 183–92.

[109] Cited by Ben-Shammai, "Attitudes of Some Early Karaites," 10.

[110] See my full discussion of the sources in chapter 2 below.

[111] See chapter 3 below.

[112] Idel, *Kabbalah New Perspectives*, s.v. "Joseph of Hamadan."

Some relation between the Jews of Persia and various Gnostic communities is suggested by the sources. Interreligious relationships are not uncharacteristic of eastern Islamicate provinces in general. As Daniel puts it, the "profusion of religions in one area necessitated a measure of religious tolerance and contributed to much syncretism among the different groups. Thus Central Asia had a traditional role as a refuge for religious non-conformists of all persuasions."[113]

We know of at least one specific instance of this common Gnosticizing milieu, that of the Mazdakiyya. It remains unclear whether Mazdak's initial revolt garnered Jewish support, as some of the (contradictory) evidence suggests.[114] It does seem, at least, rather clearer that Mazdak's teachings on the cosmogonic potency of the alphabet are somehow related to similar Isma'ili and Jewish teachings. The *raza rabba*, "great mystery," which was apparently Mazdak's central mystery, was also a key term in what Scholem posits as being the urtext of *Sefer ha-Bahir*.[115]

Moreover, Khurasan, in Central Asia, was the home of extensive Gnosticizing revolutions in the eighth and ninth centuries, including that of Ishaq Turk, who Daniel suggests may have been a Jew.[116] Khurasan still housed Marcionists and Manicheans in the tenth and eleventh centuries.[117] Some of the earliest documentary—as opposed to literary—evidence suggests that the Jews of early Islamicate Persia inhabited communities contiguous with those of the Manicheans. The earliest surviving inscriptions in the Persian language are in a dialect of Judeo-Persian. These were discovered in the great Central Asian silk-route entrepôts of Tang-i-Azao and Dandan Uiliq, crossroads communities that also have yielded substantial evidence of Manichean habitation from the same period.[118] And some fascinating, if spotty, literary evidence linking Jews and "Manicheans" remains as well. Theodore bar-Khonai, eighth-century Nestorian bishop of Central Asian Kashgar, reports on a number of quasi-Jewish, quasi-Manichean groups, whose teachings he appar-

---

[113] Daniel, *Political and Social History*, 139.
[114] Klima, "Mazdak," 420–31; Solodukho, "Mazdak Movement," 67–86; Baron, *Social and Religious History*, 2:399 n. 15; Sundermann, "Neue Erkenntnisse," 183–88.
[115] Peterson, "Urchristentum," 81; Müller, "Mazdak and the Alphabet," 72–82; Halm, "Die Sieben und de Zwolf," 172–77; and the citation in the fully annotated French translation of Shahrastani, *Livre des religions*, 663–65. The "great mystery" of Mazdak, the *"raza rabba"* of the Mandeans, and the *"raza rabba"* of Jewish mysticism appear to have been technical terms in a common late-antique Mesopotamian cosmic semiotics.
[116] Daniel, *Political and Social History*, 132.
[117] Madelung, "Abu 'Isa al-Warraq," 220.
[118] Henning, "Inscriptions," 335–42; Utas, "Jewish-Persian Fragment," 123–37; Asmussen, *Judeo-Persian Literature*, 4; Lazard, "La Dialectologie," 79. For the publication of some remarkable inscriptions, see Jettmar, "Hebrew Inscriptions," 667–70.

ently knew firsthand.[119] This evidence points to the existence of organized Jewish Gnostic sects.[120]

Other indications also point toward the far eastern provinces as liminally Jewish. Natan ha-Bavli reports that R. Judah b. Mar Samuel (906–18) persuaded the Khurasani Jews to conform to Babylonian Halakha, which would imply their nonconformity through the ninth century.[121] This implication is corroborated by other sources. The best known of these concerns the infamous ninth-century "heretic" Hiwi al-Balkhi.[122] Hiwi elicits numerous unmistakable parallels with the contemporaneous Gnosticizing critiques of the Bible. Abu Hatim al-Razi, in refuting the Bible critique of Muhammad Zakariyya al-Razi—who may have been Hiwi's teacher and whose Bible critique asks many of the same questions—explicitly reports that his opponent sought the aid of Manichean anti-Jewish teachings.[123] Ninth-century Central Asian Jews could thus be close enough to some kind of "Manichean"-style thought virtually to the point of apostasy.

Central Asian Jews, then, possessed some access, from their vantage point at the center of Eurasia, to heterodoxies. This very geographic centrality, indeed, may itself have played a role in such syncretizings. The convergence of long-distance trade and religious liminality evident, for example, in the Persian Karaite Tustari family, was not accidental but rather seems to have been in fact characteristic of Central Asian socioreligious patterns.

What were these patterns? Karaism may provide a useful example. Karaism itself, the most profoundly far-reaching heterodoxy of the Jews under early Islam, founded several of its strongest early communities in Persia.[124] While Friedlaender oppposed the idea, Baron, Nemoy, and, most recently, Shaked, have listed reasonable parallels between the origins of Shi'ism and the origins of Karaism.[125] But Persia, it appears, was the home of the development of these two preeminent groups, rather than of their origins. The Persian communities, situated at the easternmost edges of Islamicate civilization, far from cultural and political centers, were ill suited to the creativity required to initi-

---

[119] Bar-Khonai, *Livre des scholies*, 255–61. This eighth-century bishop was in possession of many rare sources; research into the sources the eleventh book of scholia is surely very desirable. Drijvers, "Quq and the Ouqites," 112.

[120] I argue this point more fully in chapter 3 below.

[121] Mann, "Responsa of the Babylonian Gaonim," 471; see further Fischel, "Beginnings of Judeo-Persian Literature," 141–51; Shaked, "On the Early Heritage," 22–37.

[122] Davidson, *Saadia's Polemic*; Rosenthal, "Heresy in the Era of Saadia," 21–37; Rosenthal, *Hiwi al-Balkhi*; Guttmann, "Sources of Hiwi al-Balkhi," 95–103; Plessner, "Heresy and Rationalism," 3–10; Fleischer, "Fragment from Hivi al-Balkhi's," 49–57. For more on Hiwi, see chapter 4 below.

[123] See a discussion of this encounter in chapter 4.

[124] Shaked, "Origins of the Karaite," 7–9.

[125] Ibid.

ate sects of sustained conception, especially those possessing seriously threatening power. These communities however, were well suited to serve as ref-
uges far from the Mesopotamian centers of authority. Indeed, recent
researches tend to converge on Mesopotamia as the source of earliest Karaism
and of earliest Shiʿism, whence these Jewish and Muslim groups shifted some
of their subsequent bases of power to the east.[126]

The free development of ideas operated in the open markets of Central
Asia. The pre-eleventh-century Persian Karaites not only experienced considerable religious variation but some noticable economic success as well. Persian Karaite merchants are well documented in the Cairo Geniza.[127] Indeed,
the earliest known documents in the Judeo-Persian dialect are Karaite. These
two characteristics could merge in a family of Persian Karaites such as the
Tustaris. Both a business empire and (to a certain extent) a religious sub-
group, the Tustaris are both well known from literary sources and from Geniza sources.[128] That some of them apparently acknowledged Muhammad as
prophet may be only another indication of the extent to which a weakening
of "Jewish" self-consiousness could dovetail with economic expedience.

In the hypothesis of Pritsak, Central Asian Jews were noted for a distinctive social organization typified by "the harmonious co-existence of religious,
commercial and scholarly interests. . . . The long-distance traders, residing in
the oases and towns, who knew several languages and had a keen interest in
philosophical matters . . . should be credited with the alleged religious tolerance of the nomads."[129] The Jews of Persia and Central Asia, in this hypothesis, may have been among the most amenable of all the early Islamicate
Jewish communities to a certain syncretism because they represented a larger
Central Asia religioeconomic complex. Pritsak extends this hypothesis to
make the Radhaniyya responsible for the Judaization of the Khazar kingdom.[130] This amalgamating was not infrequently associated with a certain
degree of intermediate Gnosticization. This milieu, in particular, was the
same cultural sphere out of which the Central Asian school of Ismaʿilism also
emerged, under analogous circumstances.

The Jewish communities from Fars to the Central Persian provinces of
Khuzistan and Mazanderan, then, were apparently not firmly under the control of the Babylonian Geonim. They lived in a milieu of "traditional syncretism," whose comminglings were not only Jewish. Fischel notes that at least
three instances under early Islam of Muslim Hebraism where quotations
"presuppose direct contact and cooperation with Jewish scholars in
Khorasan."[131] Major heterodoxies of both Judaism and Islam emerge from

---

[126] See chapter 3 below for more on the role of Shiʿa-Jewish relation, inside Persia and
without.
[127] See Gil, *History of Palestine.*
[128] Gil, *Tustaris* and *History of Palestine.*
[129] Pritsak, "Role of the Bosporus Kingdom," 13.
[130] Pritsak, "Khazar Kingdom's Conversion," 280.
[131] Discussed more fully below in chapter 3, in regard to the Ismaʿili al-Kirmani.

CHAPTER TWO

The Jewish Messiahs of Early Islam

MUHAMMAD PROCLAIMED himself the last Apostle of God, and not a Messiah. He thus did not impose a conclusion on history. His Islam, to be sure, did end antiquity—and in so doing, initiated something epochally new. The lawfulness, the continuity, and the grand sweep of this new dispensation proved overwhelmingly persuasive while remaining irrefutably within recognizably human history.

The victory of Muhammad's "human" apostolicity—as opposed to a "divine" Messiahship—was particularly disorienting to Jews and Christians expecting a Messiah. The successful prophethood of Muhammad thereby forced rival Jewish and Christian redeemer figures into taking up unprecedented guises. The transformations of the Messiah complex after Muhammad, in other words, are inexplicable without recognition of the implicit reference to Muhammad. Muhammad himself, however, simply could not be made into a Messiah. The polymorphous Jewish Messiah complex, meanwhile, was surviving the death of antiquity, adapting itself, as ever, to the sharp turns of human events. Unable to stop and incarnate itself in Muhammad himself, the Messiah transposed, as a consequence, onto a figure as close to him as possible—his shadow, as it were. I refer to Muhammad's son-in-law, cousin, and erstwhile successor, ʿAli ibn Abi Talib.

The argument of the present chapter is that the major Messianic movements of Jews and of Muslims that responded to the advent of the Qurʾan consciously played on Judaic salvational paradigms, and both did so within the arena of original Shiʿism. On the one hand, the early Shiʿa utilized typology of the Jews to argue their own Islamic ascendancy. Concurrently, Jewish expectations eventuated in a sect, the ʿIsawiyya, which burst forth amid proto-Shiʿi movements. These contemporaneous trajectories of the mobile Messiah complex in both Judaism and Islam are most comprehensible if understood as interpenetrated in the origins of the Shiʿa (party) of ʿAli.

For a brief moment at the end of antiquity, the dialectic between Messianic myth and Messianic social movements, between apocalypse and apocalypticism, developed along patterns that were structurally parallel within Judaism and Islam.[1] Jewish Messianic anticipations could become Muslim myths, and even movements, but not by "influence" or by "borrowing." Rather, the family resemblance of idea and organization was due to a shared inheritance. And this common cultural milieu encompassed more than the expected econ-

---

[1] The fundamental study in this regard remains I. Friedlaender, "Jewish-Arabic Studies."

omies, cuisines, architecture, head gear, and jurisprudence. Jewish and Muslim Messianic movements shared, as well, fundamentally generative systems of meaning, systems explaining how the universe ran, how it began, and how, apocalyptically, it would find its end. And so the venerable system of common meaning personified as Messiah could be sometimes Jewish, sometimes Muslim.

THE JEWISH MESSIAHS OF EARLY ISLAM

The Palestinian Jewish communities, conquered by the Persians in the early-seventh century, had been praying for just such a savior to relieve them.[2] Within two decades, they received quite another answer to their prayers, in the form of the Muslim conquests. Unable adequately to address these tumultuous events in the present, Jews from the Nile to the Oxus turned ever more to the future, near or far, a future that would bring to them neither Persian nor Arab, but rather a final redeemer from God.

This may have been the most dramatic, complex, and sustained Messianic *metanoia* in Jewish history. For the first century and a half after the coming of the Prophet Muhammad, from the first decades of the 600s until approximately 750, various parts of the Jewish world were seized with immediacy, caught up in the ecstasy of hope come home, for he had arrived—so it seemed.

We may best get a sense of the Jewish Messiahs of early Islam by starting back a century or so. The Jewish communities of the sixth century were already beginning to feel this immediacy, or at least to demonstrate their drive for independence. A Jew of the late-fifth century on the island of Crete proclaimed himself the Second Moses. He led his susceptible disciples over a cliff to their demise on the rocks below, having promised them miraculous transport to the Promised Land.[3] In the years 484, 529, and 556, Samaritan Jews in Palestine rebelled against their Byzantine overlords. In May 529, "Samaritans rose up in revolt, sacking and burning churches and villages of the Christians, murdering the Bishop of Neopolis and many priests and others, and proclaiming an emperor of their own race."[4] These revolu-

---

[2] Hirschberg, "Footsteps of the Messiah," 112–24. Some of this material is also treated by Rabin in *Qumran Studies*, 123–24.

[3] On this "Moses of Crete" see the text reproduced in Marcus, *Jew in the Medieval World*, 225–26. The Mosaic claim of the new prophet was not unusual. A Jew of Pallughta claimed to be a Moses Redivivus: see n. 30 below. That Messianic pretensions attached themselves to the figure of Moses was known in Jewish and Christian experience. See, for example, Bentzen, *King and Messiah*. For the expectation of the Mosaic Ta'eb, or expected redeemer of the Samaritans, see now Dexinger, "'Prophet wie Mose,'" 97–113; and idem, "Der Taheb," 1–173.

[4] Chitty, *The Desert a City*, 115. See also Parkes, *Church and the Synagogue*; and S. Winkler, "Die Samariter in den Jahren, 520–530," 435–57.

tionary Samaritan Jews attempted to establish their own state but were crushed.

There were, then, rumblings throughout the two superpower empires of Persia and Byzantium, Jewish rumblings that were taking on a Messianic form. Two further episodes suggest the degree to which this Jewish Messianic intensity may have affected non-Jews. In the early-fifth century, a Mesopotamian monk "in a dream saw an army of Jews vanquish an army of Christians in battle. Therefore he had himself circumcised and became a Jew."[5] Two centuries later, but also under Byzantine rule, in the first years of the seventh century, a monk at the monastary of St. Catherine's on Mt. Sinai had a dream. He left his monastery and descended to the Jordan Valley, where he converted to Judaism and preached to the Jews living there. He was "greatly venerated by the Jews as a second Abraham, not more than a year or two before the Persian invasion."[6] We do not know what became of these monk-converts, but their dreams and subsequent conversions do at least reveal the potent attractiveness of Jewish Messianic ideas in the years immediately preceding Muhammad's arrival.

These manifest expectations convulsed the farthest corners of the Jewish world. Such agitations could reach out to non-Jews, sometimes in the form of military confrontation. It was, indeed, these aggressively outward-oriented postures that characterized the Jewish Messianism of the particularly out-of-the-way Arabian Peninsula, where Jews had lived for many years. We know of Arabian Jewish Messianic leaders by name, we know of predictions of a savior current among Arabian Jews just before the time of Muhammad, and we know of powers coming from outside to change all that.

There had even been a Jewish king of Arabia. This remarkable monarch, Dhu Nuwas, reigned in South Arabian Yemen until his demise in 525.[7] He was seen by some to be a real savior, by some even to be the Messiah of the house of Joseph.[8] But he was just another tyrant who persecuted his Christian neighbors and whose kingdom soon fell to invaders. His example does show us the potential power of the Jews of Arabia in his day. The last we see of Dhu Nuwas, he was fleeing an Abyssinian attack. As the enemy approached, "he directed his horse towards the sea, then, spurring it on, rode though shallow water until he reached the depth and finally threw himself with his horse into it; this is the last that was known of him."[9] Dhu Nuwas was the first of the Messiahs of the Jews of Arabia.

At least two early-seventh-century Arabian Jews apparently, if not apocryphally, spoke of themselves in Messianic terms. One of these, Umayya, was

[5] Wasserstrom, "The Jewish Messiahs of Early Islam" (the Resler Lecture, Ohio State University, April 1986).
[6] Chitty, *The Desert a City*, 154, citing the Sabaite Antiochus.
[7] The most recent overview of this subject has been made by Newby, *History of the Jew of Arabia*, 33–49.
[8] See Hirschberg, "Footsteps of the Messiah," 113–14.
[9] I. Friedlaender, "Jewish-Arabic Studies" 2:501 n. 101, citing Tabari.

tempted by a demon coming from his left side who asked him to wear a black robe. It was said that if it had come from the right, and if Umayya had liked white robes, he would have become the prophet of Islam.[10] And the Jewish Arabian poet Samuel just before the time of the Prophet Muhammad sang his own claim to rule the people of Israel: "There will come to me the prophet-hood of the kingship of David."[11]

These were mere anticipations. Of such hopes, we possess yet another and rather more tantalizing (if not equally apocryphal) account. Found in the classical Arabic biography of ʿAntar, it is an epic tale of the battles, loves, and songs of Arabian tribal heros in the years just before the arrival of Muhammad.[12] One of the Jewish warriors depicted as an antagonist in this epic was ʿAntar's great opponent, Jabbar. Jabbar proclaims the coming of the Messiah to the Jews of Arabia in this way:

> There will appear from across the river Sambatyon in that year the Great Savior; he will appear on a white ass; he will possess a powerful body; he will make all religions of all countries disappear, renewing the Law of Moses which God spoke to Moses on Mt. Sinai, so that the glory of the Law of Moses should become more dazzling than it had been before. "Prepare!" thus announced Jabbar to the Jews of central Arabia—"prepare for this Savior . . ." The poet goes on to say, "This prediction was just as the sages of the Jews had predicted in their day, and as they continue to propagate, believing that their religion is perfect. The Jews of that era ruled fortresses, colonies, and armies. Their force had not yet been broken, their religion had not yet been suppressed by the Prophet Muhammad. . . . Jabbar announced that in that year there would appear in the East from across the Sambatyon [the legendary river of sand] the Savior, followed by numberless warriors, many of whom would be seated on lions; every fortress besieged by them would collapse, every army attacked by them would be annihilated.[13]

The foregoing semilegendary tales suggest that a sustained expectation of imminent redemption seems to have swept the Jewish communities of Arabia around the time of Muhammad. Early Muslim traditions explicitly corroborate the portrait of seventh-century Jews actively awaiting a prophet to come and save them,[14] and a Christian chronicler explicitly tells us the same.[15]

Many such traditions survive which suggest that Muhammad himself was directly affected by these expectations. On the other hand, such stories in

[10] Meier, "Aspects of Inspiration by Demons," 427. According to Tor Andrae, Umayya "aspired to become the Messiah to the Arabs": see *Ursprung*, 198–206.
[11] Goren, "As-Samauʾal b. Adiya," 55–66.
[12] The fullest studies of ʿAntar have been undertaken by Bernhard Heller. For a survey of these works see Scheiber, "Bernhard Heller," 198–200, and nn. 44–52.
[13] The original text was not accessible to me. I have therefore translated from the French translation of Heller, "Youschaʿ Al-Akbar."
[14] See n. 2 above.
[15] *Doctrina Jacobi Nuper Baptizati*, discussed by Griffith, "Jews and Muslims in Christian and Arabic Texts," 86–87.

Jewish sources are designed to show that Muhammad was merely taught by Jews. We must therefore read these accounts of Jewish teachers and Jewish companions of Muhammad with great care, especially the tales concerning Jewish companions first predicting a prophet and then embracing Muhammad as that predicted prophet.[16]

Many such traditions were designed to demonstrate retrospectively that Muhammad's prophethood itself had been anticipated. However, other evidence militates against writing off all these stories preemptively. For example, an early Christian account tells us that Muhammad was impressed by the Jews of Palestine. Acccording to this Christian chronicle, Muhammad believed that Palestine "had been given to the Jews as a result of their belief in a single God." Muhammad therefore declared that for Jews accepting his revelation, "God would give them a fine land flowing with milk and honey."[17]

With the eventual coming of Muhammad and his revelation from God, the Qur'an, those Jews were directly faced with a terrible decision—whether to publicly acknowledge that this prophet was indeed the promised one. What seems to have been the predominant Jewish reaction to Muhammad is recorded in the Qur'an: "And when there come to [the Jews] a Book from God, confirming what is with them—although from of old they had prayed for victory against those without faith—when there comes to them that which they should recognize, they refuse to believe it" (2:89).

To be sure, large numbers of Jews surely did recognize the Qur'an and did believe in the new prophet. Muhammad accepted companions who had converted from Judaism; he even took a Jewish wife, said to be descended from Moses' brother, the high priest Aaron.[18] Within ten years of his epochal emigration to the city of Medina in 622, Muhammad had conquered all the Jewish communities of Arabia. This rapidly shifting situation necessarily provoked a rich variety of Jewish responses.

Various Jewish compromises with the new dispensation were attempted. Some Jews who had nominally converted to Islam asked that they be allowed to continue observing the Jewish Sabbath and studying the Torah at night. A verse of the Qur'an denied them this privilege. Other Jews used their Jewish learning to inform the shaping of the new tradition. Thus we read that "the Jews used to read the Torah in Hebrew and to interpret it to the people of Islam in Arabic." The Prophet Muhammad recognized the value of such compromises and declared to his community: "Believe in the Torah, in the Psalms and in the Gospel, but the Qur'an should suffice you."[19]

As the great conquests of the first Islamic century progressed, this still-fluid

[16] I deal with the quasi-legendary companion of Muhammad, ʿAbdallah ibn Salam, and the folkloristic precursor of the prophet, Buluqiyya, in chapter 5 below.

[17] Dionysios of Tellmahre, cited in Brock, "Syriac Views of Emergent Islam," 12.

[18] Saffiya. See Gil, "Origin of the Jews of Yathrib," 208; Goitein, "Banu Israʾil," citing Ibn Saʿd, viii, 85, to the effect that she was from "pure Jewish stock, a descendent of the high priest Aaron."

[19] Kister, "Haddithu," 215–39.

situation continued to evolve in unpredictable ways. In 614, just before the coming of the Prophet Muhammad, Jews aided Persian armies in conquering the city of Jerusalem.[20] This event reactivated the Jewish hope of final redemption at hand, for the restitution of Israel was a sign of the end. This hope also spread throughout the Jewish world as Persia and Byzantium, the two great superpowers within whose boundaries most of the world's Jews lived, continued to battle for imperial supremacy.

The sudden Arab conquest of *both* these superpowers was seen by some as a sign from God. This perception would seem to have been held even more acutely after the Arab siege of the world city of Constantinople in the 717. A new world-era was seen as emerging;[21] It should, therefore, have been joyously received. And indeed, we do possess several provocative accounts of Jewish communities responding to the Muslim conquests by welcoming the arriving Muslim armies as saviors. We read that the large and ancient Jewish community of Isfahan, in Persia, danced and sang as they welcomed the conquerors.[22] This strange event may have become imprinted on the imagination of those Muslims who were simultaneously composing their own Messianic prophecies. Muslim tradition relates that one of the signs of the end of time will be seventy thousand Jews of Isfahan wearing green Persian shawls (*taylasan*) and following the monstrous Antimessiah (Dajjal).[23] A traditional Jewish source claims when the Arabs conquered the Persian town of Piruz-Shapur, the Jewish leader came out to meet the Muslim leader 'Ali "and received him in a friendly manner, and in Piruz-Shapur at that time were 90,000 Jews, and 'Ali likewise received them in a friendly manner."[24]

Through the early-eighth century, we continue to hear of Jews reading Messianic implications into the acts of the Muslim conquerors. Many of these readings naturally were focused on the land of Palestine itself. Thus when the caliph 'Umar visited the site of the Holy Temple in Jerusalem, some Jews asumed that this act foreshadowed the Messianically promised rebuilding of the Holy Temple.[25] 'Umar's visit may indeed have been intended to corroborate just such perceptions.

[20] Gil, *History of Palestine*, 4–8. See esp. p. 6: "There seems to be considerable exaggeration, however, in the accounts of those who describe the Persian conquest of Palestine as if it were an era of squaring accounts for the Jews; a sort of Messianic era."
[21] On the apocalyptic expectations excited by the siege of Constantinople, see Canard, "Les Expéditions des arabes," 61–121. Note also the skepticism of Gil, cited in the previous note.
[22] Abu Nu'aim, *Dhikr Akhbar Isfahan*, 22–23.
[23] See below on these traditions with reference to the Isfahani prophet Abu 'Isa.
[24] *Iggeret Sherira Gaon*, cited in Neusner, *Jews of Babylonia*, 130.
[25] Goitein, "Jerusalem in the Arab Period," 168–96, esp. 172–73, that 'Umar's purifying of the Temple Mount was welcomed by Jews, who "saw the renewed use of the Temple site as the beginning of the Redemption." Expectations of the rebuilding of the Temple had been brewing for several centuries at the end of antiquity. See Brock, "Letter Attributed to Cyril," 267–86, esp. the appendix on 283–86, where Brock

Jewish reactions to the rise of the new civilization continued to express the Messianic stresses of the first century of Islam. Various kinds of Jewish writings gave voice to these anxieties. One vivid form was the apocalypse, a scenario of the events of the endtimes as revealed by an angel. Most Jewish apocalypses bemoaned the new conquests as terrible signs of the end of history. This agony was also expressed in such midrashic collections as the *Pirke de Rebbe Eliezer* and also in the majestic, Messianic synagogue hymns of the *payyetan* (hymn composer) Eliezer Kallir, who we now know was an exact contemporary of Muhammad's.[26]

In the eighth-century Jewish apocalypse, *The Secrets of Shimon bar Yochai*, Muslim success is viewed as God's will. The Jewish sage Shimon asks his recording angel,

> "Is it not sufficient that we had to suffer so much at the hands of Rome? Must we now undergo persecution also under the rule of the Muslims?" [To this impassioned query the angel responds,] "Fear not O son of man for the Holy One, blessed be He, established the kingdom of Ishmael [the Muslims] for the sole purpose of redeeming you from the wicked kingdom of the Romans. God gave the Muslims a prophet according to His Will, and this Prophet conquered Palestine, and the Muslims will return it to Israel with glory."[27]

Finally, a substantial number of Jews responded to these disturbing events by moving to Palestine, such immigration being itself a Messianic gesture. Pietist Jews called the Avele Tzion, the Mourners of Zion, devoted themselves to a life of asceticism in the Holy Land, practicing voluntary poverty and pious devotions in anticipation of the promised coming of the Messiah to that Land.[28] And most importantly, the Jewish sect of Karaites were born in the mid-eighth century, very much in the midst of such pietism. From early Karaite hymns and prayers we are familiar with the ardent Messianic hope of these sectarians.[29]

To recapitulate: Jewish Messianic reactions to the rise of Islam are varied and difficult to categorize. These responses may have included midrashim, new sects, prophecies, conversions, calculated compromises, and emotional upheavals. But perhaps the most dramatic reactions where the particularly striking cases of those individual Jews who responded by themselves claiming to be the very prophesied savior of the Jews.

One of these leaders, ironically, was originally a Christian. The following is

---

translates the main accounts. For a full review of the "episode of the Temple Mount and the return of the Jews to Jerusalem," see now Gil, *History of Palestine*, 65–74.

[26] Fleischer, "Qaliri Riddle" 383–429.

[27] Lewis, "Apocalyptic Vision," 321. Gil has submitted this midrash to his typically searching analysis: *History of Palestine*, 62–63, esp. n. 65.

[28] See Grossman, "Aliya," 176–87, for an important review of the evidence. This evidence was already used to make such historical arguments by Bamberger, "Messianic Document," 425–31.

[29] Ben-Sasson, "First of the Karaites," 44–55.

an abbreviated verison of the longest account concerning this unnamed charismatic who arose in Syro-Mesopotamia in the year 720: This individual had
acccess to the house of an important Jew, but he secretly entered it and corrupted the daughter of the house. Since he was a Christian, the Jews inflicted
long and cruel tortures on him, during which time he escaped from their
hands. "From that moment he dreamt of submitting [those Jews] to all sorts
of foul treatments." He mastered black magic as a means of revenge. Then he
said to the Jews: "I am Moses, the same Moses who brought Israel to Egypt,
who sent them through sea and desert for 40 years. I am sent anew for the
redemption of Israel and to guide you into the desert, and to finally to return
you to the Promised Land which you will possess as you did in days of old."
By means of such oratory, accompanied by incantations, he convinced large
numbers of Jews. They went out to the mountains, where they leaped off
cliffs to their deaths or were shut up in caves. They also gave him much gold
and other goods, which he took (from them) and fled. The disillusioned Jews
caught up with him and brought him before the authorities. According to
this Christian account, the Jews were granted permission to torture and eventually to crucify this charlatan. It was said that he had successfully gathered
followers as far away as Spain.[30]

As we can see in this story, and as we have seen in earlier accounts, the
Jewish communities of the seventh and eighth centuries were capable of displays of power. All the more striking are the diverse displays of Jewish militarism in the eighth century. In Central Asia, an enormous tribal confederation
converted to Judaism: these Judaized Khazars effectively halted the spread of
Islam eastward.[31] And in North Africa a Jewish queen of the Berbers, the so-
called Kahina, was said to have led Berber armies against the Arabs.[32]

From Messiah to Imam: The Remaking of an Image

The image *Messiah* expresses a complex of fundamental ambivalence: a
worldly longing for another world; expectation and inevitable frustration.

[30] Dionysius of Tellmahre, cited by Chabot in "Trois épisodes," 291–94. This move-
ment is subsequently and more fully studied by Starr in "Le Mouvement messianique," 81–92. See also I. Friedlaender, "Jewish-Arabic Studies," 210–11 n. 104; S.
Kraus, *Byzantinischen-jüdischen Geschichte*, 37–39; Mann, "Early Theologico-
Polemical Work," 411–59, at appendix, 454–59; Barnard, *Graeco-Roman and Oriental Background*, 36–38; the reviews of the literature by Baron, *Social and Religious
History*, 380–82, n. 58, the sources translated into Hebrew by Dinur, *Israel in the
Diaspora*, 225–28.
[31] See my comments on the Khazars above, Chapter 1. More fully, see Barthold and
Golden, "Khazar"; Dunlop, *Jewish Khazars*; Golb and Pritsak, *Khazar Hebrew Documents*; Golden, *Khazar Studies*; Szyszman, "La Question des Khazars," 189–202;
and, most recently, Huxley, "Byzantinochazarika," 69–87.
[32] Hirschberg, *History of the Jews*, 65–66. See also Mohammad Talbi, "al-Kahina";
idem, "Un nouveau fragment de l'histoire"; Déjeux, "La Kahina," 1–42.

The foregoing Jewish expectations and their accompanying frustrations simultaneously reerupted within Judaism and within Islam. This was not a "borrowing"; rather, a common culture shared a common telos, a longing for a figure of the ultimate, under the impact of common circumstances.

The party, or Shi'a, of 'Ali—the son-in-law and cousin of the Prophet Muhammad—was the major alternative force contending for legitimate authority over the new Muslim community. The foundational myths of this Shi'i party, which was loyal to the family and to the cause of 'Ali, were initially and partially typologized upon Judaic paradigms. Sunni and Shi'i sources themselves explicitly linked this Jewish connection with the Shi'i notion of the Mahdi, the so-called Muslim Messiah. The Mahdi was conceived as "the Rightly Guided One," who would return at the end of time to cover the world with justice as it was then covered with injustice.

Both Shi'i and Sunni sources moreover relate that a Yemenite Jew named 'Abdallah b. Saba' was the first to publicly proclaim that Muhammad himself was indeed this Messiah.[33] But after Muhammad's death, 'Abdallah was said to have switched his allegiance to 'Ali. The Jewish convert subsequently announced that 'Ali was the Messiah who would return at the end of time, riding on the clouds. Whether or not 'Abdallah was an apocryphal figure, it is striking to note that recent research suggests that the earliest Shi'ite groups, largely made up of Yemeites, were sometimes known as Saba'iyya, presumably named after this Jewish convert.[34]

These early proto-Shi'i groups of the late first Islamic century were imbued with a keen Messianic longing, so familiar from our Jewish examples. Their poets (in Friedlaender's felicitous summary) "picture the Mahdi as dwelling in a glen of the Radwa mountains, surrounded by beasts of prey on which eternal peace has descended, holding intercourse with angels and sustained from overflowing fountains of milk and honey, and with genuine religious fervor do they call on [the Mahdi] to emerge from his retreat and, preceded by noble steeds and flying banners, return to his believers in order to inaugurate the Messianic age of justice and peace."[35]

But, as seen in the Jewish imagery from which these groups seem to have partially drawn their not entirely pastoral inspiration, armed rebellion was claimed capable of bringing this Mahdi. These groups revolted, asserting that their Mahdi was living among them as a descendant of 'Ali's, and their rebellion consequently posed a serious threat to the ruling Umayyad dynasty.[36]

That this Shi'i military Messianism resembled that of the Jews was soon argued by Sunni polemicists. Thus we read in an early, popularly reproduced Sunni tradition: "The Jews say, 'There shall be no fighting for the sake of God

---

[33] See I. Friedlaender, "'Abdallah b. Saba," 296–327.
[34] Van Ess, "Das Kitab al-irğa'" whose analysis of this group is further discussed below, in this chapter.
[35] I. Friedlaender, "Jewish-Arabic Studies" 2:488.
[36] Madelung, "Al-Mahdi," 1230–38. See also Blichfeldt, *Early Mahdism*.

until the Messiah, the Expected One, goes forth and a herald from heaven proclaims his arrival.' The Rafida [Shi'a] say, 'There is no fighting for the sake of God until the Mahdi goes forth and a herald descends from heaven.'"[37]

The Mahdi, then, could be understood by both Sunnis and Shi'is to have been patterned in some sense on Jewish antecedents. Stories of the Mahdi, like all such stories deriving from pre-Islamic times, were taken from Isra'iliyyat, stories and traditions pertaining to biblical figures. Many of these Isra'iliyyat were recorded on the authority of Yemenite Jewish converts such as Ka'b al-Ahbar, "Ka'b of the rabbis." Thus an early Shi'i poet could sing of the Mahdi, that "he was the one whom Ka'b told us in days of old."[38]

Distinctively Shi'i imagery of the final redeemer prophesied that the Mahdi would emerge at the end of time from the house of 'Ali. This image of the future also had a certain Jewish inspiration in the form of traditions concerning a future plurality of Messiahs. The Qumran Scrolls speak of two Messiahs, the Messiah of Aaron and the Messiah of Israel.[39] This doubling is important to note in light of Shi'i traditions that relate 'Ali's status to Muhammad as being like Aaron's status was to Moses. Indeed, another tradition has it that the two celebrated martyr-sons of 'Ali, Muhammads's only two grandsons, received their names, Hasan and Husayn, as translations of the names of the sons of Aaron.[40] In other words, for the early Shi'a, as with the Jewish sectarians of Qumran, a future redeemer would emerge from the house of the sons of Aaron.

'Ali's close relationship to Muhammad stood "like Aaron to Moses." Such was 'Ali's preeminence that Shi'i traditions relate that 'Ali inherited key secret teachings in addition to communal authority from Muhammad. This secret and public legacy subsequently authorized the leadership of the imams, who descended from 'Ali, and who led the Shi'a after him. The specified contents of the inheritance were seen as having been originally bequeathed by Muhammad from the Children of Isra'il. These contents were said to include the Torah itself, the secret seventy-three-letter name of God, the known name and the hidden name of the Messianic imam, and prophesies detailing the events of the endtime. All of this legacy of 'Ali's was explicitly acknowledged to have been a heritage from the Jews.[41]

Muslim prophesies of the last days were known, among other names, as *malahim*. These malahim depicted, among other woes, wars at the end of time.[42] They bear a close family resemblance to the Jewish scenario of wars

---

[37] I treat this tradition in its context in chapter 3 below.

[38] Kuthayyir, cited by al-Mas'udi, *Muruj al-Dhahab*, 181; see Rabin, *Qumran Studies*, 118, and Goldziher, *Muslim Studies* 2:77.

[39] The theory of the dual Messiah was something of a near consensus for thirty years after the discovery of the scrolls, but in a recent review it has been called into question. See the next section, below.

[40] This tradition is treated at length in chapter 3 below.

[41] Wasserstrom, "*Sefer Yesira*," 16–20.

[42] A rich review and revisionary treatment is now provided by Bashear, "Apocalyptic and Other Materials," 173–207. See his pp. 173–74, for a survey of the literature,

(Hebrew, *milhamot*), marking the violent, preliminary era preceding the final Redemption.[43] Ironically, these Islamic reimaginings of Jewish apocalyptic prophecies ended up casting Jews in the role of Islam's ultimate enemy in these last struggles, the final irony of Islam's creative rereading of Jewish Messiahs.

The irony to which I refer was that of the Antimessiah, the mythical figure who was to emerge at the endtime to do battle with the Messiah. For Jewish tradition, the Antimessiah was called Armilos: "He will be bald, one of his eyes will be small, the other big. His right arm will be only as long as a hand, and his left arm will be two and one half cubits. And he will be leprous on his forehead. And his right ear will be stopped up and the other open."[44] The Jewish Messiah would ultimately destroy this monstrous adversary.

Muslim tradition relates that this Antimessiah would be known as the Dajjal.[45] The Dajjal, according to various traditions, would be a Jew who would emerge from the Jewish quarter of Isfahan, followed by seventy thousand Jews wearing green Persian shawls. His right eye would be filmy and his left eye would hang down on his brow and glow like the morning star.[46] This Jewish Dajjal would ultimately be defeated by the Muslim Mahdi.

Thus we have a series of interlocking ironies. In Jewish apocalypses, the Muslim conquerors represent the Antimessianic agonies of the endtime. In Muslim apocalyptic traditions, the Jews represent the horrible beast of the end of history. And yet we also have Jewish apocalypses like *The Secrets of Shimon bar Yochai*, in which the advent of Muslim rule is seen as deliverance to the Jews, and Shi'i traditions that depict the Mahdi as emerging from the house of 'Ali, inheritors of the house of Aaron.

What conclusions can be drawn from these intertwined Messianic imaginings? Muhammad, 'Ali, and the early Muslims did not borrow their Messiah from Judaism, nor was Jewish Messianic imagery lent by a Jew to a Muslim in the sense that a lender lends to a debtor. Rather, Muslims consciously and creatively reimagined the Messiah. These Islamic rereadings, consonant with the decentralized pluralism of the Jewish redeemer myths, never pronounced one image of the Messiah as definitive. There were, of course, no councils of Judaism or Islam to rule on an officially proper Messiah.

Islam's Messiahs, like Judaism's, were multiple. Because these prophetic expectations were so varied, the men who claimed to be Messiahs made a variety of claims, pronouncing themselves the Second Abraham, the Second Moses, the Messiah of Israel. We cannot say why particular pretenders chose

---

with special reference to the work of Madelung, Conrad, and Cook. See also Aguadé, "'Kitab al-Fitan,'" 349–52.

[43] The portents (to be compared with the "birth pangs of the Messiah" [*hevlei ha-maschiah*] in Jewish tradition) are reiterated with expectable variations in the numerous sources listed by Bashear, "Apocalyptic and Other Materials," 175 n. 10.

[44] M. Friedlander, "L'Anti-Messie," 14–37; Rosenstiehl, "Le Portrait de l'Antichrist," 45–60; Dan, *The Hebrew Story*, 40–43.

[45] Halperin, "Ibn Sayyad Traditions," 213–25; Morabia, "L'Antéchrist," 81–99.

[46] Fischel, "Isfahan," 111–28.

certain titles and not others, but we do know that the variegated Messianic traditions of Islam and Judaism were open-ended enough to be manipulated for a variety of causes.

I do not mean to imply that this multiplicity of Messianic images somehow spread shapelessly in all directions. To be sure, Judaism gave shape to its own Messiahs out of its own internal teachings, but not only so. Judaism was alive in the midst of outside powers. When Abu 'Isa invoked Islam's vocabulary of prophethood at precisely the same moment when contemporaneous Shi'ite Mahdis invoked a Judaized vocabulary of prophethood, a circle was completed. The circle turns, as each image is returned to its maker, only to be remade again, to be once more imagined anew.

The coming of the Messiah was spectacular. The waiting had ended. Men and women ran into the street. They leapt from rooftops, believing they could fly to the Promised Land. They danced, they sang, they gave away their possessions. They ran into the lances of the government troops sent to pacify them. They had no fear, for he had come.

Jews have not waited for the Messiah for millennium without satisfaction, for he has come—too many times, some would say. He has been charismatic, a real spellbinder—too many times, some would say. Some would say, with Messiahs like these, who needs enemies?

Nor did these agonies happen only long ago. Some Jews and Christians *actively* are preparing again.[47] They are weaving large white robes for Jewish priests. They are preparing for the Messianic age when they themselves shall serve as functionaries in the Third Holy Temple. They hope it will come soon. The Messianic idea lives. We already know that this idea two thousand years ago was powerful enough to incite the early Christian community to accept Jesus of Nazareth as the Messiah. The reimagining of the imminent Messiah also moved the earliest Muslims, much as it did the Jews spontaneously responding to that new faith. But none of those Jewish, Christian, or Muslim anticipations could accurately foresee the form that history would take, as it inexorably overcame them. The Messiah always stays one step ahead of expectation. As Kafka foresaw, the Messiah will not come on the last day—but on the day after.

THE MESSIAH BEN JOSEPH IN ARABIA AND BEYOND: MESSIANIC TYPOLOGIES IN LATE ANTIQUITY AND THEIR RAMIFICATIONS UNDER EARLY ISLAM

Students of Jewish history in the early Islamic period have much to learn from historians of the Jews in the early Church period. Judeo-Arabists, alas, possess nothing comparable to the recent collection *Judaisms and Their Mes-*

---

[47] As I write this note, the international Lubavitcher community expected the coming of the Messiah to occur that week (the week preceding Passover 1992, during which time their Rebbe enjoyed his ninetieth birthday).

siahs at the Turn of the Christian Era pertaining to the turn of the Islamic era.[48] And yet the latter era may prove equally rich for the student of Jewish diversities of Messianic hope.

To understand the impact of multiple imaginings of the Messiah at the turn of the Islamic era, I have studied traditions concerning the (Jewishly imagined) Messianic end of history, up to and including the time in which such traditions penetrated the simultaneous origination of the Shiʿa. The clashing and meshing of typologies in that convergence generated heat, but also a dialectic light, which still illuminates the Messiah figures of each community.

It should be no surprise that these classificatory schemas carried obvious political valences. For centuries, typological schemas had been reflecting the tierings of social hierarchy. Scholars of the multiple Messiahs of late antiquity, in particular, emphasize the diversity of political roles that these categories traditionally played in rationally differentiating the functions of society. Burton Mack makes this point: "Thus, the [Messianic] figures are peculiarly social formations, loci for the imaginative study of the intricate nexus of social forces specifically relevant to Jewish social history. They encapsulate and faciliatate very tough thinking about the exigencies of actual social history in the light of given norms and models held to be definitive for Jewish social identity."[49]

At the turn of the Christian era, a panoply of interrelated salvational schemas thundered across the Judaic inscape. The Qumran texts are the best known: "once 4Q Testimonia was published, nearly all scholars agreed with Allegro that its selection of Biblical passages was organized around a tripartite messianic expectation: a prophet like Moses, a king like David, and a priest like Aaron."[50] The relationship of this tripartite scheme to the more celebrated dual Messiah (of the Damascus Document and other Qumran texts) remains uncertain. A certain consensus seems to have been reached, however, that "the the view in the [*Testament of the Twelve Patriarchs*] of a dual messiahship, with an anointed king from Judah and an anointed priest from Levi, parallels the (not always consistent) messianic outlook at Qumran."[51] There may have been as many as four Messianic figures imagined by the Qumran sectarians: the Messiah of Aaron, the Messiah of Israel, the Second

---

[48] Neusner, Green, and Frerichs, *Judaisms and Their Messiahs*. And see now the helpful recent review provided by VanderKam in "Jubilees and the Priestly Messiah," 353–65. Other materials are gathered by Fitzmyer, "Elijah Coming First," 295–96. For general frameworks see Bartal, "Messianic Expectations," 171–81.

[49] Mack, "Wisdom Makes a Difference,'" 15–48, at 20.

[50] Brownlee, "Anointed Ones," 37–45 at 42. In the same volume is the important article by F. Dexinger, "'Prophet wie Mose,'" 97–113; and see idem, "Der Taheb," 1–173. For an overview of Qumran Messianism see Cacquot, "Le Messianisme qumrànien," 231–49; Talmon, "Waiting for the Messiah," 111–37, esp. 135 n. 32.

[51] Kee, "Testament of the Twelve Patriarchs," 778. See also the general treatment by George W. E. Nickelsberg and Michael E. Stone, *Faith and Piety*, chap. 5, "Agents of Divine Deliverance," 161–77.

Moses, and Elijah.[52] Such Messiah figures were transmitted as a semicoherent mythic system, the constituent elements of which varied depending on their shifting historical contexts. The Samaritans, for instance, seem to have differentiated among four Messianic functions, or types: a restorer of the Tabernacle, Joseph "the King," the Taheb, and the prophet like Moses.[53] Stating the case in general terms, then, Heinemann argued influentially that the Jews of late antiquity did not believe in a dual Messiah but in a plurality of Messianic figures.[54] The mass of pseudepigrapha and midrash, which chronologically bridges the talmudic period, never systematizes its eschatological redeemers. Nor does the Talmud. It would seem that diversity and ambiguity were somehow essential to the late-antique psychosocial complex, "Messiah."

And yet, Berger has recently and properly stressed "the overwhelming impact of typology on Jewish messianic thought." Berger uses *typology* in its technical sense of "traditional prooftexts utilized as prefigurations of present or future events."[55] In its more commonplace connotation, *typology* means simply classification according to types. With regard to multiple Messiahs, it would seem that Jewish tradition generated the latter by means of the former. In the following sections, I am concerned with the latter meaning, without submitting any new hypotheses regarding the traditional processes, prooftexts, and prefigurations by means of which these classifications were generated. My concern, rather, lies in the social organization of imaginal diversity, the Jewish and Muslim reorganization of those preexisting classifications in the first Islamic centuries.

The Jews of Arabia

Such diversity and ambiguity certainly marks the Arabian situation. Hirschberg, who collected much evidence concerning the Messianic expectations of the Jews of Arabia, found a considerable plurality of beliefs and images, which he did not attempt to sort into categories.[56] While it is still premature to clarify fully the relation of these texts to one another—which ultimately cannot be accomplished without generations of patient textual criticism of the sources, so that dating may be assured—I tentatively would suggest nonetheless that certain patterns may be discernible in them. Indeed, certain patterns seem to perceptibly suggest themselves.

[52] According to the controversial interpretation of Wieder. See *Judean Scrolls and Karaism*, preceded by "'Law-Interpreter' of the Sect of the Dead Sea Scrolls," 158–75, and "Doctrine of the Two Messiahs," 14–25.
[53] Kippenberg, *Garizim und Synagogue*, 314 and 321. Isser (*Dositheans*, 124–28) supports Kippenberg and refutes Crown's "Dositheans," 70–85.
[54] Heinemann, "Messiah of Ephraim," 1–17.
[55] Berger, "Three Typological Themes," 141–65, at 149. In the specific context of Messianic typology, Berger defines the phenomenon as "the utilization of the figures, events and periods of the past to illuminate the messianic age" (142).
[56] Hirschberg, "Footsteps of the Messiah," 112–24.

The pattern that most insistently recurs concerns the military Messiah ben Joseph.[57] This option seems to have been the dominant Messianic alternative chosen by the Jews of Arabia. To argue that this is the case I shall adduce five sets of evidence: (1) traditions concerning the Himyarite king Dhu Nuwas; (2) the identification of Dhul Qarnain as Messiah ben Joseph; (3) the testimony of *The Biography of 'Antar* concerning the belief of the Jews of Arabia in the imminent coming of one Yusha' al-Akbar; (4) traditions concerning 'Abdallah ibn Saba', who proclaimed that Joshua was the *wasi* (legatee) of Moses; and (5) Shi'i traditions concerning Jonah, Joshua, and Joseph, which recur throughout the early Shi'i traditions.

The earliest evidence we possess is that of the imagery attached to the role of Dhu Nuwas, the semilegendary Jewish king of Arabia (sixth century). We cannot say much more than that he did have Messianic imagery attached to him. His name, Joseph, may have been chosen to signify the symbolic importance of the establishment of a Jewish kingdom.[58] It may be more than mere coincidence that the king of the Khazars was known as "Joseph son of Aaron the Khazar priest."[59] As is well known, political leaders concerned with manipulating Messianic expectations, such as the 'Abbasid caliphs, adopted regnal titles resonant with Messianic traditions.[60]

Further evidence indicates that the Jews of Arabia may have not only imagined but actively anticipated the Messiah ben Joseph. Such evidence includes traditions concerning Dhul Qarnain.[61] The acute arguments concerning the identification of Dhul Qarnain made by Beer in 1855 have not been followed up.[62] Beer argued that Dhul Qarnain, a legendary figure which the Qur'an (18:83) identifies as Alexander the Great, was none other than the Messiah ben Joseph:

[57] See the convenient treatment by Klausner, *The Messiah Idea*, 483–501, which concludes with the observation that "only such sanguinary events as the Arab wars of the seventh and eighth centuries and the Crusades of the twelfth century could revive the belief in a second Messiah" (501). The best recent treatment may be that of Heinemann, "Premature Exodus." For other (arguable) survivals of Jewish "bi-Messianism" in the early Islamic era, see Wieder, *Judean Scrolls*; and Paul, "Les 'deux Messies' chez Daniel al-Qumisi," 127–30.
[58] The report of Ibn Ishaq clearly associates this name with his conversion: "He adopted Judaism and Himyar followed him. He was called Joseph and reigned for a some considerable time" (*Life of Muhammad*, cited in Newby, *History of the Jews of Arabia*, 39].
[59] See my discussion of the Khazars in this chapter.
[60] Lewis, "The Regnal Titles," 13–22. Goitein notes that these titles, like those of the contemporary Geonim, may arise from "the messianic stirrings at the time of the advent of the Abbasids," though the Geonic names were given at birth and not at installation ("'Meeting in Jerusalem'" 43–57, at 51).
[61] Abel, "Dù'l Qarnayn," 1–18.
[62] Beer, "Welchen Aufschluss," 785–94. He draws special attention to *Genesis Rabbah*, 99, and *Pirke de Rebbe Eliezer*, 19. Beer, it should be said, does not seem to be aware that *Pirke de Rebbe Eliezer* is a post-Islamic work. Beer's work was noted, so far as I can tell, only by Friedlaender, in "Chadirlegende," 107 n. 4.

[The] Jews at the time of Muhammad, indeed, awaited a hero under the title "Two-Horned," by whose diverse, adventurous campaigns and great acts will conquer the peoples—especially, in the end, Gog and Magog—but will also be gifted with high moral power and dignity, so that they also associated the Last Day and Last Judgment with him.[63]

After dismissing the arguments that Dhul Qarnain referred to either Cyrus or Alexander, Beer concludes that Dhul Qarnain was the none other than the Messiah ben Joseph, "the Hero and Savior stemming from their own nation and described as 'Two-Horned.'"[64]

This suggestion would seem to carry some special weight if the *Biography of 'Antar* may be utilized responsibly as a corroborating source,[65] for *'Antar* contains another evocative passage concerning the Messianic expectations of the Arabian Jews. If we may assume that this obviously folklorized account somehow reflected contemporaneous beliefs, the following would help make sense of this passage. First, it will be recalled that Joshua, according to midrash (Genesis Rabba, chap. 29), was a descendant of Joseph. Second, the Messianic title "Yusha' al-Akbar" would seem to reflect Zecharia 3:1, "And he shewed me Joshua the High Priest standing before the angel of the Lord."[66]

Third, certain details of the *'Antar* tale conspicuously reflect antecedent Jewish traditions. To the various midrashic elements of *'Antar* elucidated by Heller, I would add the midrashic motif of the enormous physical weight of Joshua, which should be compared to the bulkiness of Yusha' al-Akbar in the *'Antar* account.[67] Another Jewish tradition source related to *'Antar* concerns

---

[63] Beer, "Welchen Aufschluss," 793, my translation.

[64] Beer's position rejects the alternative theories that Dhul Qarnain refers either to Alexander the Great or to the Persian emperor Cyrus: ("Welchen Aufschluss," 794). For these theories see Nagel, *Alexander der Grosse*.

[65] Heller, "Youscha' Al-Akbar," 113–37. Heller published this article in Hebrew in *Festschrift*, 1–14.

[66] This observation was made by Norris, *Adventures of 'Antar*, 66. That chap. 3 of the book of Zecharia repeatedly was invoked in Messianic expectations under early Islam is a fact yet to be fully analyzed. Its background in antiquity is developed by David Aune, *Prophecy in Early Christianity*, 122–23. Newsom has also indicated the importance of Zech. 3 in Qumran texts, in *Songs of the Sabbath Sacrifice*, 67. See also Wieder's *Judean Scrolls*, 108, and "'Law-Interpreter' of the Sect," 158–75, at 162, for the vision of the "Four Craftsmen" in Zech. 3, and its typological significance. I have indicated the relevance of this vision to the typological prefigurations of Abu 'Isa al-Isfahani, in "Species of Misbelief," 319. Eventually, Zech. 9:9 is cited by al-Kirmani with reference to the prophethood of al-Hakim: see van Ess, *Chiliastische Erwartungen*, 62; and S. Stern, *Studies in Early Isma'ilism*, 93. That Kirmani apparently knew Jewish sources is discussed below, in chapter 3. Note also Heller's observation that "Yusha" (Joshua) was an unusual Arabic name, which thus makes sense in light of Goitein's subsequent observation that Yeshu'ah was "a technical name for the coming of the Messiah" ("'Meeting in Jerusalem,'" 51).

[67] Heller himself adduces this motif in his glosses on Ginzberg's *Legends of the Jews*,

the "Children of Moses" (B'nai Moshe), as related by Eldad ha-Dani. The B'nai Moshe dwell beyond the Sambatyon (the legendary sandriver) and trace their traditions through Joshua: "Thus did we learn from our Rabbis, from the mouth of Joshua, son of Nun, from the mouth of our Patriarch Moses, from the mouth of the Almighty."[68] Although Eldad is not a trustworthy historical source, the fact that (the certainly historical) Abu 'Isa al-Isfahani of a century later used the motifs both of the B'nai Moshe and of the Sambatyon in his own Messianic appeals suggests their currency in the eighth century.

Finally, in addition to the legends of Dhu Nuwas, Dhul Qarnain, and Yusha' al-Akbar, a fourth consideration to be adduced in any discussion of the Messianic expectations of the Jews of Arabia is the story of 'Abdallah ibn Saba'.[69] The most familiar report on 'Abdallah, that of Shahrastani, tell us that "'Abdallah is said to have been a Jew who was converted to Islam. While still a Jew he used to say that Joshua b. Nun was the legatee [*wasi*] of Moses. He also said the same later of 'Ali whose appointment as Imam he was the first to uphold."[70] While 'Abdallah b. Saba' was in most traditions associated with this original conception of the delegation of constitutional authority, he is likewise held culpable of grossly exaggerating (*ghuluww*) the status of 'Ali—some say he was a prophet to 'Ali's Messiahship.[71] It would seem to follow that he held 'Ali to have played a kind of Joshua redivivus to Muhammad's Moses redivivus.

Friedlaender analyzed the many Shi'i traditions that patterned the role of 'Ali upon that of Joshua.[72] In the "*Hadith* [traditional report] of the Turning Back of the Sun," for example, an 'Alid loyalist exclaims, "By Allah! I do not know whether 'Ali has appeared to us and the sun turned back for him or

---

but he does not apply it in this context ("Ginzberg's *Legends of the Jews*," 393–418, at 400). Every horse upon which Joshua rode broke down under his enormous weight.
[68] I. Friedlaender lists other false Messiahs who play on the motif of the Sambatyon. See "Jewish-Arabic Studies" 3:263 n. 304. For sources on the Sambatyon in Muslim literature, see Ginzberg, *Legends of the Jews* 6:407–8; and Schwarzbaum, "Prolegomenon," 69–70, for much of interest on the Eldad haDani legends, especially those concerning the Sambatyon. Schwarzbaum adds a passage from the *1001 Nights* to the dossier. See also Loewenthal, "La storia del fiume Sambation."
[69] I. Friedlaender, "'Abdallah b. Saba'.
[70] See the important notes provided by Gimaret and Monnot in their valuable translation of Shahrastani's *Livre des religions*, 509–10.
[71] This accusation became the standard for rejection of this figure, as reflected in the early Shi'i sources of Qummi and Nawbakhti and reiterated in recent Shi'i scholarship such as that of Jafri, *Origins and Early Development of Shi'a Islam*, 300.
[72] I would note that the typological prefigurations of Joshua in the role of Messianic forerunner were well developed in the Jewish and Christian traditions. Of the Qumran texts, 4Q Testimonia cites an unpublished "Psalms of Joshua," which seems to describe a multivalent Messianic figuration. See Devorah Dimant, "Qumran Sectarian Literature," 518.

whether Joshua has been among our people!" 'Ali stops the sun, a reversal that the tradition explicitly relates as being like Joshua's cognate miracle.[73]

The proto-Shi'ite *ghulat* (extremists) also picked up on this typology of 'Ali and Joshua. The Mansuriyya, followers of Abu Mansur, are to have said: "The Imam after al-Baqir will be Abu Mansur, for al-Baqir designated it to him to the exclusion of the Banu Hashim, just as Moses did to Joshua, to the exclusion of his own progeny or the progeny of Aaron."[74] When one recalls the tradition concerning a prophet Joseph in Yemen, it seems reasonable to accept that the historical continuities at work in the Yemen led, in part, from the imaginings of a Jewish Messiah into the reimaginings of a Shi'ite imam.[75]

The Saba'iyya

The Yemenite trajectory is perhaps clearest in the origins of the proto-Shi'ite parties. The earliest proto-Shi'ite ghulat were known as Saba'iyya. After an exhaustive investigation into the historicity of original Shi'ism, Wadad al-Qadi concludes that "our first Muslim group that was labeled *ghulat* must have been, then, the remants of the old Saba'iyya living in Kufa during the days of al-Mukhtar." Similarly, basing himself on an early letter from the grandson of 'Ali, van Ess has shown that these groups at the end of the seventh century were known as Saba'iyya before they became known as Mukhtariyya or Kaysaniyya. And, finally, Rubin's contribution corroborates these arguments. Rubin provides many more early sources, none later than the mid-second Islamic century, which describe the model of Joshua's deputation in association with that of 'Abdallah b. Saba'.[76]

Both the earliest sources and the majority of scholars, then, trace the earliest Mahdi expectations back to these Saba'iyya/Kaysaniyya circles. Mukhtar is said to be the first to use the title mahdi, in reference to 'Ali's son, Muhammad b. al-Hanafiyya.[77] Mukhtar, moreover, was said to have advised his fol-

---

[73] I. Friedlaender, "Heterodoxies" 68–71, provides variants and analysis, as well as a lengthy text of the "Hadith of the Turning Back of the Sun." Friedlaender observes that this "*hadith* owes its origin to the Shiitic tendency to pattern the biography of 'Ali, the '*wasi*' of Muhammad, after Joshua, the *wasi* of Moses" (71). There are other levels of comparison that would be fruitful to pursue. For example, the Talmud observes, "The face of Moses is like the sun; that of Joshua is like the moon" (Baba Batra 75a). Like Joshua, 'Ali is associated with the moon, becoming a virtual moon-god in some traditions. See Goldziher, *Introduction*, 227–28.

[74] Tucker, "Abu Mansur."

[75] See the tradition reported by Jubair to the effect that, after the creation of Adam, there had been a prophet sent by God to the land of Yemen, whose name was Joseph. See Maqdisi, *Kitab al-Bad' wal-Ta'rikh*, 7.

[76] Al-Qadi, "The Development of the Term *Ghulat* in Muslim Literature," 300; Van Ess edits the relevent text in "Das Kitab al-irğa'" and discusses it in "Beginnings," 93–96, and again in "Early Development of Kalam," 116; Rubin, "Prophets and Progenitors," 52 nn. 60–63, for more evidence of the earliness of these traditions.

[77] Sachedina, *Islamic Messianism*, 9, with reference to the work of van Ess.

lowers not to use weapons of metal, for they were not to be used until the Messiah came.[78] It is well known, furthermore, that the followers of Mukhtar utilized various motifs from the Banu Isra'il. One of the more striking of these motifs is their veneration of the seat (*kursi*) of 'Ali. The seat was carried into battle, compared to the Ark of the Covenant, and said to contain "a remnant of things left behind by the families of Moses and Aaron."[79] Douglas Crow has suggested that this motif may be associated with the secret transmission of *jafr* (esoteric knowledge of cosmological secrets), which he associates with ancient Israelite cultic practices concerning the ephod. Crow cites Morgenstern to the effect that "their transmission in any way from one person to another determined the right of sucession to the clan authority and leadership."[80] Morony likewise notes these traditions of the Ark of the Covenant, observing that "it is natural to look for a Yamani Jewish background among those clans which accompanied the *kursi*."[81]

In short, Jewish-Arabian Messianic images apparently first entered the Shi'i imagination in association with a figure called 'Abdallah b. Saba', who is described as being an Yemenite Jewish convert to Islam. More generally, Jewish models of political delegation and Messianism seem to have been confounded—or effectively conflated—in the simultaneous self-understanding of the earliest proto-Shi'i movements.

The next question that presents itself concerns the possible political role of "rival castings" of the Messiah in the evolution of the earliest Shi'a. To anticipate my argument, I shall now try to show that the Harbiyya, one of the first (relatively) distinct groups emerging from the debacle of the Mukhtariyya, utilized a model of political delegation that reimagined paradigms of the Jewish tradition. I hope to demonstrate, within a reasonable range of probability, that these rereadings simultaneously comprised models of multiple Messiahs and typologies of constitutional authority.

The Harbiyya

The little-known figure whom I shall simply call "Harb" served as an obscure link between the first followers of 'Ali and the subsequent, mid-eighth-century Gnosticizing ghulat.[82] I concur with al-Qadi on this point: "One

---

[78] Tucker, "Abu Mansur," 66–76, at 73 n. 54.; and I. Friedlaender, "Heterodoxies," 92–95.

[79] Morony, *Iraq*, 495; and Sharon, *Black Banners from the East*, 110 n. 37, with reference to the sources.

[80] Douglas Crow, "Teaching of Ja'far al-Sadiq," 111 n. 68, with reference to Morgenstern, "The Ark, the Ephod and the 'Tent of Meeting,'" 153–266; see also Crow, 1–52, at 48. I thank Mahmoud Ayoub for guiding me to this source.

[81] Morony, *Iraq*, 495.

[82] This figure is discussed most fully by Al-Qadi, in *Kaysaniyya*, as well as in *Al-Firaq al-Islamiyya fi'l Shi'r al-Umawi*, 140–41. Brentjes, *Die ImamatsLehren im Islam*, 22; Friedlaender, "Heterodoxies," 71; and Tucker, "Rebels and Ideologues," 49–51.

member of this group, namely Abu al-Harith al-Kindi, may very well be the companion of ʿAbdallah b. Sabaʾ known variously in the sources as ʿAbdallah [b. ʾAmr] b. al-Harb al-Kindi, and ʿAbdallah b. Haras."[83] The paucity and conflicting nature of the sources precludes certainty in establishing his name, but I would suggest that at least one of his names is pertinent to the question at hand. Indeed, it is directly relevent to the effective convergence of Messianic models and political authority that I perceive.

The name "Harb," as it turns out, is insinuated into a number of early traditions concerning the sons of ʿAli. Jahiz reports that ʿAbdallah ibn Sabaʾ himself was also known as "ibn Harb."[84] But the most important of these accounts is the story of the naming of Hasan and Husain. ʿAli, it is said, originally named them "Harb." But the prophet, inspired by the angel Gabriel, intervened. He instructed ʿAli to name them with the names of the (two or three) sons of Aaron. On the instructions of Muhammad, ʿAli therefore uses the (ostensible) Arabic translation of the names Shabir and Shubbayr (and Mushabbir), that is, Hasan and Husain (and Muhassin).[85]

I would suggest that we may be dealing here with titles denoting the role of a military redeemer, titles deployed for immediate political purposes. I should now like to adduce one of the most striking texts in this regard, a passage from a relatively lengthy report of the doctrine of the Harbiyya as given by the early heresiographer Qummi.

This passage describes the argument of the Harbiyya for the division of Islamic constitutional authority on the basis of a paradigm from Jewish tradition:

> They alleged that the tribes [of the Children of Israel] are four in number, on the following prooftext: *Power, Nobility, Might*, and *Prophethood* are from the progeny of Jacob ben Isaac in four manifestations, and the rest become tribes through [these four]. They were the prophets and kings, and the rest had no power but through them. [These four] were Levi, Judah, Joseph, and Benjamin, and the rest became tribes only through the nobility of their [four] brothers, just as a man can become eminent through the eminence of his brother, or his son, or his master, or his cousin. Judah had as descendants David and Solomon, in [both of] whom is joined the incomparable kingship with prophethood; Miriam bat Amran, mother of Jesus; and the Exilarch [*raʾs al-jalut*], who is the king after the prophets and apostles. The progeny of Levi are Moses; Aaron; ʿUzair; Ezekiel; Elijah; Elisha; Jeremiah; and Khidr, all of whom are the progeny of Aaron. Descending from their stock are the kings and prophets such as Asaph b. Berachia, chancellor of the

Some of the reports (Nashshi, Nawbakhti, and Qummi) with reference to the *ghulat* are translated into German by Halm in *Die Islamische Gnosis*, 70–75.

[83] Al-Qadi, *"Ghulat in Muslim Literature,"* 295–319, at 30; and idem., *Kaysaniyya*, 154–56.

[84] Friedlaender, "ʿAbdallah ibn Saba," pt. 2, n. 6 refers to the connection between ʿAli and Harb.

[85] See my discussion of these traditions below, in Chapter 3.

Throne of Sheba. The progeny of Joseph includes Joshua b. Nun. The progeny of Benjamin includes Saul, of whom God speaks in His Book (Q. 2:247).[86]

This fourfold typology is highly relevant for the present purposes: early ʿAlids did indeed consciously pattern their own models of authority on identifiably "Jewish" tradition. The Harbiyya tradition, as given by Qummi, ostensibly classifies a quaternity of constitutional functions in Jewish and Shiʿite society, which would appear to be (1) the priesthood; (2) prophethood with kingship; (3) military service; and (4) prophethood without kingship. The report proceeds to apply this typology to the imamate, caliphate, and kingship, by means of allegorical reading of the Qurʾan.

Such typology as prefiguration was of course common to the Sunni tradition as it was to the early Church. But in the present instance, the early Shiʿis—as, indeed, did the subsequent Shiʿi tradition—appealed less to the prefigurative, "moralistic" typologizing associated with the Banu Israʾil than to the classificatory "historicist" typologizing of Jewish tradition. This assertion is strengthened not only by the inclusion of the exilarch in the Harbiyya typology; it is also made likelier by the report of one of the ghulat who asserted that they "were the children of Islam, as the Jews were the children and friends of God."[87] I emphasize that this was recourse to Yahud (Jews), and not to models from the Banu Israʾil (Children of Israel), which were prevalent among the Sunnis.

Another fourfold Shiʿi typology featuring Joseph may be considered in this regard.

> In the Lord of this Order, there will be a precedent from Moses, a precedent from Jesus, a precedent from Joseph, and a precedent from Muhammad. As for the precedent from Moses, he will be afraid and watchful; as for Jesus, it will be said about him what was said about Jesus; as for Joseph, imprisonment and concealment; as for Muhammad, his rising with the sword, following his conduct and explaining his traditions.[88]

The Sabaʾiyya, the Harbiyya, the Mansuriyya, and the Waqifiyya were early ʿAlid loyalists, to use the phrase given currency by Hodgson. Their allegorizing of the Qurʾan was facilitated by their use of preexisting models of reading a scripture. Indeed, I would argue that the *taʾwil* (hermeneutical exegesis) so distinctively Shiʿi, which these groups pioneered, was not indebted to the Judaic models.[89] Rather, it was a creative extension of those traditional tech-

---

[86] Qummi, *Maqalat* 247, my translation. Note that Masʿudi's *Ithbat*, a work with discernible Shiʿi overtones, cites the priestly families, beginning with Phineas, son of Joshua, and also the Levitical families, from Solomon to Asaph b. Berachia; see Rubin, "Prophets and Progenitors," 51.

[87] With reference to one Sari: Ivanow, *Ibn al-Qaddah*, 107, who notes that "there is a certain flavour of Judaism in the ideas of this branch."

[88] Waqifi, according to Madelung, "Al-Mahdi," 1230–38, at 1236.

[89] For a detailed comparison of Jewish and Shiʿi uses of *taʾwil*, see below, chapter 4.

niques, reread in their own distinctive terms. This is nowhere so evident as in their employment of typology, which so early formed a firm foundation both for an alternative theory of government and for an eschatologically validated charismatic leadership to guide that government.

The 'Isawiyya

One final element must be adduced in a study of the convergence of Messianic typologies from the Jews of Arabia to the earliest 'Alid loyalists: the Jewish uprisings, coterminous and geographically contiguous with the proto-Shi'i movements. These Jewish groups, centered in the Persianate provinces, have long been recognized to have been related on many levels to the Shi'i movements. These groups include several local rebellions as well as at least two major sectarian movements. Of these, certainly the most significant is that of the Karaites.

The 'Isawiyya were a sectarian formation second only to the Karaites in their geographic extension and their eventual place in Jewish history. This statement is true not only in terms of their origins in a proto-Shi'i milieu, but in absolute terms. That is to say, the 'Isawiyya and the Karaites, the two most significant Jewish sectarian movements from the time of the Second Temple until the early modern period, both were formed in the same crucible that bore Shi'ism. But it is important to adduce at least one aspect of the history of the 'Isawiyya here. The Messianic pretender Abu 'Isa, according to Shahrastani's precious account, held

> that he was a prophet [*nabi*] and apostolic messenger [*rasul*] of the awaited Messiah [*al-masih al-muntazar*]; that the Messiah has five harbingers [*rusul*] who precede him one after the other . . . that the Messiah is the best of the children of Adam; that he is of a higher status than the foregoing prophets [*anbiya'*]; and that since his is his apostle, he is the most excellent of them all likewise. He enjoined faith in the Messiah, exalting the mission [*da'wa*] of the harbinger [*da'i*]; he believed that the harbinger is also the Messiah.[90]

This passage may best be understood in the light of the contemporaneous Messianic typologies that I have already adduced. Specifically, I would suggest that this passage reveals Abu 'Isa's self-conscious systematization of those contemporaneous options. Abu 'Isa, as did his proto-Shi'i contemporaries, successfully reread these complex and contending Messianic typologies into an effectively unified ideological platform.

Abu 'Isa, in other words, wielded a variegated prophetic vocabulary that would have been comprehensible to both Jewish and Muslim ears. He employed the titles *'abd* (servant), *rasul* (apostolic messenger), and *nabi* (prophet), epithets applied to Muhammad in the daily prayers and that were

---

[90] I have published a review of the 'Isawiyya question as "'Isawiyya Revisited," 57–80. This in turn is published in modified form in this chapter, below: see these discussions for a full review of the sources and arguments.

doctrinally definitive of Muhammad's role.[91] Thus, on the one hand, Abu 'Isa was clearly attempting to play the role of the Jewish prophetic harbinger of the endtime—and not Messiah—in a still thinly Arabicized milieu. This shift may be seen in his riding a horse, like Dhul Nuwas and like an imam, as contrasted with Yusha' al-Akbar riding on an ass, like a "traditional" Jewish Messiah.[92]

Abu 'Isa's names, moreover, are quite revealing. Eved Elohim ("servant of God"; cf. Mal. 3:18) bears unmistakably Jewish Messianic denotations, while the name given by Shahrastani, Abu 'Isa Ishaq ibn Ya'qub, may represent this prophet's attempt to refer to himself as the Messiah ben Joseph. The name Abu 'Isa suggests a programmatic revaluation of tradition. And this inversion would be to the point. Reminiscent of the contemporaneous, early 'Alid title of Fatima as Umm Abiha, "Mother of Her Father," such bouleversement would have conveyed an appropriate valence for the agent provocateur of the *eschaton* (endtime).[93] Messianic figures overturn the old order of things: "When our Qa'im rises, he will bring a different order than what was before."[94] The same case, in short, may be applied concerning the name Abu 'Isa, "Father of Jesus."

Abu 'Isa also spoke of "five harbingers" and the "missionary/forerunner" (*da'i*). The latter may be explicable in its Shi'i context, where the propagation of the 'Alid program was known and continued to be known as *da'wa* (mission). The identity of the former has longer excited puzzle-infatuated scholars, who have tried their hand at identifying the cryptic "five harbingers of the awaited Messiah."[95] I shall not join those who think they have solved this little mystery, but I can offer my own reading in this regard. That he does intend to include himself in the five is made clear enough in the well-known wording of Shahrastani. The earlier report of Abul Ma'ali seems to make this reading certain. "He proclaimed to people that he was the apostle of the Messiah and that, before the Messiah, five apostles would come, among whom, it is said, he mentioned a certain 'Shepherd,' who was none other than 'Isa b. Maryam."[96]

Thus, to paraphrase these accounts (which both are likely to derive from a

---

[91] Wasserstrom, "'Isawiyya Revisited," and this chapter, below.

[92] That the "traditional" Jewish Messianic impostor rides on an ass seems to derive from the vision in Zech. 9, "lowly and riding on an ass." For the contrast between the ass-riding and horse-riding Messiahs, see Friedlaender, "Jewish-Arabic Studies," 499 n. 38, and, on Dhu Nuwas, 501 n. 101. It should be noted as well that Heinrich Graetz (*Geschichte der Juden* 5:152, n. 15) suggested that Abu 'Isa was seen as the Messiah ben Joseph: Graetz was followed in this opinion by Greenstone, in *Messiah Idea*, 319, n. 5.

[93] Apocalyptic figures are typified by their reversal of norms, a variant of the phenomenon of carnivalization. See Ivanow, "Semiotic Theory of Carnival," 11–34.

[94] Cited by Madelung, "Al-Mahdi," 1236.

[95] See I. Friedlaender's exposition of this issue from a comparative perspective: "Jewish-Arabic Studies" 3:235–46.

[96] Cited in Monnot, *Islam et religions*, 107.

common source), Abu 'Isa was the consummating fifth of five, at once a peer and primus inter pares of the Messiah's forerunning prophets. Shahrastani does not identify the other four, but Abu Maʿali does specify that one is 'Isa b. Maryam. Like the Harbiyya, then, the 'Isawiyya utilize a typology of Messiahs that lists Jesus alongside Jewish prophetic forerunners of the Messiah. The 'Isawiyya would seem to share with their "sectarian milieu" an active interest in playing upon available mythological models of social transformation.

Principium Divisionis

Finally, this sectarian milieu may have generated its Messiah complex organically out of its social psychology. In the Jewish instance, a certain political structuralism of the psyche has been suggested. Siegmund Hurwitz, in his Jungian reading of the Jewish Messiah, suggests a "Spaltung des Messiasbildes" (splitting of the Messiah image) into a "Messias-Quaternio" (fourfold Messiah): King (David)/priest (Melkizedek)/prophet (Elijah)/hero (Joseph).[97] Abu 'Isa, perhaps, intended to appropriate some such available psychosocial system. He claimed to be "of a higher status than the foregoing prophets . . . the most excellent of them."[98]

The foregoing schemas— double, triple, quadruple, and even quintuple typologies of savior-figures, deriving from diverse historical settings—should not be brutally harmonized. I have been concerned to sketch, rather, their ongoing diversity of schematizings. After all, these myths were not programatically devised, but were imaginal reflections of shifting conditions, of expectations of the future, and of rationalizations of the present. In short, they reflected the conflicting realities of contending social arguments. Rabbinic tradition did eventually systematize its constitutional theory into a tripartite theory of "three crowns": *torah/kehunah/malkhut*.[99] Some such rough division of social functions is also delineated in Jewish Messianic myth. I have tried to show that this was the case with the eschatological myths and constitutional legitimations of the Jews of Arabia.[100]

The stunning appearance of Muhammad and 'Ali provoked a spectacular crisis of legitimation for the conquered communities of Arabia. One result was an an epochal contest of myth, in which contending schemes worked against each other for dominance. The history of the origins of Shiʿism is particularly useful for studying this process, for the imamate was the con-

[97] "Some Psychological Aspects of the Messianic Idea in Judaism" in *The Well-Tended Tree*, ed. H. Kirsch, 130–42. The full, original treatment is in Hurwitz, *Die Gestalt des Sterbenden Messias*, 192–202, on "Spaltung," and 89, on the "Messias-Quaternio."
[98] Shahrastani "Kitab al-Milal," 508.
[99] S. A. Cohen, *"Three Crowns."*
[100] I. Friedlaender's apposite conclusion was that "the complicated character of the Messianic idea and the variety of Messianic forerunners, such as the prophet Elijah, the Ephraimitic Messiah, the Antichrist, gave the Messianic imposters . . . a choice of roles" ("Jewish-Arabic Studies" 3:261–62).

tender par excellance for Islamic authority. And the earliest Shi'is, in particular, stimulated a veritable poetic efflorescence of possibilities. Their groups, subgroups, groupuscules, and their myths, countermyths, and inverted myths eventually resolved themselves into the reifications deemed Imamiyya, Isma-'iliyya, Zaydiyya, and others—the heresiographers specify dozens of them.

Still, it has not been my intention to prove the "influence" of the Jews of Arabia on these proto-Shi'is, or the "borrowings" of the latter from the former. Rather, I have tried to show the awareness of and creative manipulation of socially legitimating eschatologies. The contestation of myth on the part of proto-Shi'is, proto-Sunnis, proto-Karaites, and 'Isawiyya occurred at the end of antiquity. Their working against one another worked synergistically together to construct a new world, Islamicate civilization. The eventual political design of that civilization was constructed by reference to a myriad of suggested blueprints.

That these paradigms included mythic systems, such as multiple Messianic functions, proves once again that myth serves to restate the forgotten obvious. This may be another way of saying that those depths of oceanic, psychological struggle freely revealed themselves in sacred narrative in order to conceal their surface necessity, the social conflict of group against contending group.

THE 'ISAWIYYA

In the first scholarly exposition of the subject, Heinrich Graetz suggested that the Jewish sect founder Abu 'Isa al-Isfahani (d. ca. 750) believed himself to be the Messiah ben Joseph.[101] At the turn of the century, Israel Friedlaender reassessed the state of research on this Jewish Messianic pretender, in the only sustained piece of original scholarship ever attempted on the neglected 'Isawiyya.[102] It is striking that Friedlaender's work has not been superseded, despite the fact that there has been no history written of this group as such. Abu 'Isa was by far the most significant Jewish prophet-figure of early Islam. Indeed, Abu 'Isa was the most influential Jewish "prophet" between Bar Cochba in the second century and Shabbetai Tzvi in the seventeenth century. In fact, this charismatic sectarian played on Jewish Messianic expectations in an almost-successful attempt to create a new political Judaism along the lines of Shi'ism. His political creation, the 'Isawiyya, was nothing less than the most important Jewish sect (after the Karaites) in the millennium from the rise of

---

[101] See n. 92 above. The present study is concerned exclusively with the study of the history of the 'Isawiyya: for the numerous Muslim theological refutations of the 'Isawiyya, see my "Species of Misbelief." I wrote a preliminary version of this chapter first as an appendix to "Species" (314–41). It has since appeared in another version as "'Isawiyya Revisited," 57–80. For Graetz, see *Geschichte der Juden* 5:438–41, and n. 15.

[102] I. Friedlaender, "Jewish-Arabic Studies."

Islam until the tenth/sixteenth century. And the impact of this group was registered in dozens of works of medieval Muslim literature as well as in all substantial works of modern Jewish historiography dealing with Judaism under early Islam. In these works, Abu 'Isa remains notorious for his relativization of revelations—the doctrine that Muhammad and Jesus were genuine prophets, but only to their own communities.

In this section I will review the available evidence for such a history. Toward this end, I will discuss the name and the date of the originator, Abu 'Isa. I will then assess the history of the movement that he started, from the time of Abu 'Isa himself until the apparent demise of his sect. I will compare the 'Isawiyya with a contemporaneous proto-Shi'i group, the Mansuriyya. Thus, by reassessing the full range of sources for the first time since Friedlaender, I hope to show that the impact of the 'Isawiyya both on Jews and on Muslims was broader and more sustained than it heretofore has been considered to be.

The Date of the Origin of the 'Isawiyya

Only two sources explicitly state the date of the origins of the 'Isawiyya, and they directly contradict each other. The great fourth/tenth century Karaite polymath Qirqisani locates Abu 'Isa during the reign of 'Abd al-Malik, the fifth Umayyad caliph (586/705).[103] (Maimonides' comment in his *Letter to Yemen*, that a Jewish false Messiah arose in Isfahan at the beginning of the Umayyad dynasty, probably follows Qirqisani's tradition.)[104] Shahrastani, the greatest premodern historian of religion in any language, tells us that Abu 'Isa began his mission in the reign of the last Umayyad caliph, Marwan ibn Muhammad (744–50).[105]

Several arguments may be adduced in support of the dating found in the Jewish sources (i.e., Qirqisani and Maimonides), which would place the uprising in the caliphate of 'Abd al-Malik. This dating could be corroborated by the Messianic ferment which was stirred at that time by the clash between the Umayyads and Byzantium over Constantinople.[106] Mahler argued that the earlier dating was synchronous with the rise of the Khawarij during the time of 'Abd al-Malik, which several scholars have suggested was perhaps a related movement.[107] Finally, there may be some connection with the rebellion ini-

---

[103] Nemoy, *Kitab al-Anwar wa al-Maraqib*, 12; idem, "Al-Qirqisani's Account," 317–97; Chiesa and Lockwood, *Ya'qub al-Qirqisani*, 102–3.

[104] A convenient English translation is found in Twersky, *Maimonides Reader*, 458–59.

[105] Wasserstrom, "Species of Misbelief," 184–94, text and translation 388–401. For an assessment of the new translations of Shahrastani, see my review article, "Islamicate History of Religions?" 405–11.

[106] Baron, *Social and Religious History* 5:192–93.

[107] Mahler, *Karaimer*, 106 (*HaKaraim* is the Hebrew translation of the Yiddish). Among those linking the 'Isawiyya with the Kharijites are Baron, *Social and Religious History* 5:187; Morony, "Conquerers and Conquered," n. 84; and van Ess, "Yazid b. Unaisa und Abu 'Isa al-Isfahani," 305–15.

tially led by Mukhtar (in 685–87), which controlled both Isfahan as well as Abu 'Isa's hometown of Nisibis, and which was marked by several superficially Judaic elements.[108]

However, in the only monograph devoted exclusively to a close study of the 'Isawiyya, Israel Friedlaender argues persuasively for the later dating, that provided by Shahrastani.[109] His argument is based on circumstantial evidence and on grounds of general probability. Friedlaender suggests that the fifteen similarities between the 'Isawiyya uprising and those of the proto-Shi'ite ghulat may be due to a common historical context, that of the revolts of the mid-second Islamic century. This hypothesis best accounts for all the facts as presently known. That being said, it also remains correct that, as Pines put it, "on the available evidence no definitive solution can be found" for this problem of dating the origins of the movement.[110]

Variant Appellations

In the vast majority of Muslim sources the sectarian leader is called Abu 'Isa al-Isfahani. There are only a few significant variants. The Karaites' Qirqisani and Yehudah Hadassi call him Ovadiah, but also know him as Abu 'Isa al-Isfahani.[111] Khwarizmi calls him 'Isa al-Isfahani, which may be of some evidence for the Christianizing tendencies of his schism.[112] Ibn Hazm calls him Muhammad ibn 'Isa, which sounds like the ultimate appelative for a Jew who taught that Muhammad and Jesus ('Isa) were prophets, but this may well be an error: Steinschneider, Poznanski, and Nemoy point out that no Jew could be called Muhammad, and the 'Isawiyya were indubitably seen as Jewish.[113] Finally, Mahler observes that by calling himself Abu 'Isa, "Father of Jesus," he

---

[108] Khwarizmi asserts that Abu 'Isa originated in Nisibis (*Liber Mafatih al-Olum*, 34). For Mukhtar in Isfahan, see Morony's *Iraq*, 328. For Mukhtar's control of Nisibis, see al-Qadi, "Development of the Term Ghulat," 295–319, at 297 and 301. On the possible Judaic elements of Mukhtar's movements, see the treatment of Mukhtar in Morony's *Iraq*, esp. 495–96.

[109] Wasserstrom, "'Isawiyya Revisited" 58–59. Some of the sources were collected in Dinur, *Israel in the Diaspora*, 2:228–34; and by Aescholy, *Messianic Movements in Israel*, 117–32.

[110] Pines "'Isawiyya" 4:96.

[111] For Qirqisani see n. 103 above; Hadassi, *Eshkol haKofer*, 41b.

[112] Khwarizmi, *Liber Mafatih al-Olum*, 34. That some variation on the names "'Isa" and "'Isawiyya" existed in the Arabic milieu before the eighth century may be indicated by the fact that a "monastery in South Syria, near the Christian Ghassanid Arabs, bore in A.D. 571 the name 'Isaniyah, that is to say, 'of the followers of Jesus,' i.e., of the Christians" (Mingana, "Syriac Influence," 77–99, at 84).

For background on the dynamics of naming in early Judaism, see Kippenberg, "Name and Person," 103–25; and N. G. Cohen, "Jewish Names," 97–128.

[113] This issue has been discussed by Nemoy in his study "Attitude of Early Karaites," 701 n. 14. See also Poznanski, "Le nom de 'Isâ," 276–79, at 277; and Goldziher, "Gesetzliche Bestimmungen," 256–66, on the popularity of the name Abu 'Isa among Muslims, despite theological objections.

74

placed himself in the Davidic, hence Messianic, lineage. This suggestion possibly may be corroborated by the report of Maimonides.[114]

Finally, in a report apparently derived from Abu 'Isa al-Warraq, the author of *Bayan al-Adyan* calls the sectarian leader Ishaq ibn Ya'qub.[115] Probably also drawing on Abu 'Isa al-Warraq, Shahrastani calls the heresiarch "Abu 'Isa Ishaq ibn Ya'qub al-Isfahani, known as Ufid Alluhim, that is [in Arabic], 'Abid Allah."[116] Besides demonstrating a knowledge of Hebrew (which was most likely translated and transliterated for him), Shahrastani here provides a parallel form of Ovadiah, "Servant of God." (For the sake of completeness, it should also be noted that a few late Karaites split his name into two names in their genealogical lists of Karaite leaders; they place these two—Abu Nissi and Ovadiah HaMaskil—at the head of their lists, as the bifurcated progenitor(s) of Karaism.)[117]

The full significance of Shahrastani's report on Abu 'Isa's name has not heretofore been recognized. Shahrastani clearly states that the heresiarch possessed two names (or sets of names). On the one hand, his Arabic name is given as Ishaq ibn Ya'qub al-Isfahani. Abu 'Isa may have been an honorific *kunya*, probably a Messianic title. This latter name, it seems, was Abu 'Isa's exoteric name, and it was the name by which he is known to posterity. His second name, on Shahrastani's account, Oved Elohim or Ovadiah (two Hebrew forms of the name "Servent of God"), appears to be an esoteric name. The dual naming of divine and quasi-divine beings—prophets, angels, imams, and others—was a common feature of both Jewish and Muslim traditions.[118] It was true of both Muhammad and Jesus, and was also typical of the proto-Shi'ite sectarians contemporaneous with Abu 'Isa.[119]

As for his specific esoteric name, it may be possible that it is linked to his alleged ascension to heaven.[120] Moses, who also was held to have ascended, was known as Oved Adonai (cf. Deut. 34:5; Josh. 13, 15; Exod. 14, 31), and

[114] Mahler, *HaKaraim*, 107 n. 56.

[115] Chapter 5 of Abu-l Ma'ali's *Bayan al-Adyan* was recovered and studied by Monnot, *Islam et religions*, in his chapter, "Les religions," 97–125, where the text history is discussed.

[116] Wasserstrom, "Species of Misbelief," 389 (text), 395 (translation).

[117] For the name Abu 'Isa apparently split into two as the purported Karaite progenitors, see Nemoy, "Elijah ben Abraham," 63–87, at 79.

[118] Gruenwald, *Apocalyptic and Merkabah Mysticism*, 175 n. 4; C. H. Kaplan, "Hidden Name," 181–84; Smith, *Map Is Not Territory*, 31 n. 13; van Ess, "Der Name Gottes im Islam."

[119] See, for example, Kohlberg, "From Imamiyya to Ithna-'Ashariyya," 521–34, at 522 n. 9. In the context of the study at hand, it is significant that the *ghali* (extremist) Abu Mansur was said to have been given the name *al-kisf* (the meteor): Tucker, "Abu Mansur," 66–76, at 70.

[120] Maqdisi, *Kitab al-Bad'*, 35: "The Isbahaniyya [*sic*; 'Isawiyya] are followers of Abu 'Isa al-Isbahani, who proclaimed himself a prophet. [He claimed] that he had ascended to heaven, where God anointed him on the head, and that he had seen Muhammad in heaven and believed in him. The Jews of Isbahan claim that the Dajjal is one of them and will emerge from their area."

this title was applied to Jesus by early Christians as well.[121] But, more importantly for the purposes at hands, the angel Metatron, a popular divine potency among Jews under early Islam, bore the esoteric name of Eved Elohim.[122] In this regard, it is interesting to note that the report of Abul Ma'ali on the 'Isawiyya begins, "It is said that he was an angel: God knows!"[123] The angel Metatron, it should be noted, is the revealer figure of the eighth-century Jewish apocalypse *The Secrets of Rabbi Shimon bar Yochai*, a text for which Goitein has observed that "the influence of the ['Isawiyya] is discernible."[124] In short, the dual naming of a sectarian prophet, as reported by Shahrastani, could have had some plausible basis in Jewish practice.

In conclusion, the best sense to be made of the reports concerning his name is that he was called Abu 'Isa in Arabic, and Ovadiah, or Eved Elohim, in Hebrew, and that the Arabic name Abu 'Isa was an honorific, probably prophetic, and perhaps Messianic title.[125]

[121] Apposite here may be Mal. 3:18: "Then shall ye return and discern between the righteous and the wicked, between him that served God (*oved elohim*) and him that did not serve him."

[122] The angel Metatron is called Oved Elohim in *Hekhalot Rabbati*, for which see Odeberg, *3Enoch*, 97–98.

[123] Monnot, *Islam et religions*, 107 (I translate from Monnot's French). Another report may be of some relevance here. Nashwan al-Himyari reports that the "Isfahaniyya ['Isawiyya] assert anthropomorphism, like the Jalutiyya [Rabbanites], except that they assert that 'Uzair is the Son of God *in the aspect of a child*, as God did to Abraham in calling him Friend" (*Al-Hur al-'Ayn*, 140, my emphasis). To this may be compared the well-known examples of Metatron depicted as a "youth" (*na'ar*). See, for example, the discussion by M. Cohen, "Shi'ur Qomah," 131–32. The social milieu into which I am placing Abu 'Isa in the present chapter is one that also knew examples of divinized worthies depicted as angelic youths: contemporaneous Jewish mystics knew the biblical human Enoch transformed into the demiurgic potency Metatron. For ghulat parallels, I would cite, for example, the heavenly ascension of Abu Mansur. When God gives him his celestial commission, He refers to this visionary as "my child" (*Ya buniyya* in Arabic, or *Ya pisar*, in Persian, in some versions). See I. Friedlaender, "Heterodoxies," 62, and "Jewish-Arabic Studies" 3:273 and 274 n. 357. Finally, among the Khurramiyya, the neo-Mazdakite branch of the ghulat, all meetings began with blessings to "Mahdi Firuz, son of Fatima the daughter of Abu Muslim, whom they call *The Learned Boy* (and in Arabic [al] Fata'l-'Alim)" (Nizam al-Mulk, *Book of Government*, 237). For more ramifications of the motif of the wise child, see chapter 5 below, where I also study permutations of the biography of Metatron.

[124] Goitein, *Jews and Arabs*, 170. Graetz was the first to assert this connection between the piyyut and the sect; he was widely followed in this regard, for example, by a popularizer like Greenstone, *Messiah Idea*, 122–23. For an annotated translation of the poem accompanied by another interpretation along these lines, see Lewis, "Apocalyptic Vision," 308–38. A full historical gloss on this midrash is now provided by Gil, *History of Palestine*, 62–63.

[125] This name, of course, is one of the few bits of evidence for Pines's Jewish-Christian thesis.

The Uprising

Very little is known of his uprising itself. The most detailed and, indeed, virtually the only coherent narrative of these events is that provided by Shahrastani:

> Many Jewish people followed him, and claimed signs and [unparalleled] miracles for him: they claimed that when he was embattled he made a line around his followers with a myrtle stick, saying, "Stay behind this line and no enemy will reach you with weapons." And the enemy would charge at them, but turn back upon reaching that line, fearing that he might have placed a talisman or *ʿazima* there. Then Abu ʿIsa went beyond that line, alone and on horseback, and fought and killed many Muslims. He went out to the Banu Musa b. ʿImran, who lived beyond the sandy river, to preach to them the Word of God. It is said that when he fought against the followers of Mansur at Rayy, he and his companions were killed.[126]

Some of the motifs in Shahrastani's narrative, such as the drawing with a myrtle twig of an apotropaic circle around himself and his followers (as protection in battle), can be seen as reflecting as much "Muslim" or "Arab" folk beliefs as they do "Jewish."[127]

But most of the features of Shahrastani's account are tellingly Jewish. For example, in the denouement of his account, Shahrastani tells us that the rebel "went out to the Banu Musa ibn ʿImran, who live beyond the sandy river, to preach to them the Word of God."[128] Here we seem to find reference to those Banu Musa known in Jewish tales, retold by Eldad ha-Dani in the ninth century, in which they are said to dwell beyond the legendary "sandriver" Sambatyon, which rushes with a cacophonous din during six days and rests on the Sabbath.[129] Friedlaender pointed out that, according to *Josippon*, their land is called Aretz Ovdei Elohim, the "land of the servants of the Lord."[130] It seems far-fetched, however, to extrapolate from these few scraps of information that Abu ʿIsa proceeded to proselytize the Khazars and other tribesmen of Central Asia, as Dinur asserted.[131] In short—and as I shall argue

[126] Wasserstrom, "Species of Misbelief," 389 (text), 395 (translation).

[127] On the employment of a myrtle in the magical praxis of Jewish Merkaba mysticism, see Schiffman, "Recall of Rabbi Nehuniah ben haQanah," 269–81, at 276–77; for apotropaic power of encirclement by a myrtle branch, see Lauterbach, "Origin and Development," 367–424, at 410; cf. A. Marmorstein, to the effect that "It is well known to all who have studied comparative religious history that the myrtle has a chthonic character" (*Doctrine of Merits in Old Rabbinic Literature*, 18 n. 61). In a work deriving from eighth-century Kufan ghulat (Tamir, *Kitab al-Haft wa al-Azilla*, 114) ʿAli's brother, chased by enemies, encircles his animals with an apotropaic circle.

[128] Wasserstrom, "Species of Misbelief," 389 (text), 395 (translation).

[129] Friedlaender, "Jews of Arabia," 252–57. For more on the Sambatyon, see my note 68 in this chapter.

[130] I. Friedlaender, "Jews of Arabia," 255.

[131] Dinur, *Israel in the Diaspora*, pt. 1, bk. 2, 274 n. 47.

more fully below—the peculiarities of this narrative arguably may be explained by their having been derived from the 'Isawiyya themselves.

The Three Stages of the Movement

It is his uprising again on behalf of, and not opposed to, Jews to which we shall now look to find what may be the special significance of this movement. I will now try to show how "the first Jewish Mahdi" (in the phrase of Friedlaender) and his followers can be understood in the context of early Islamic history, in order to demonstrate that they constitute a rare militant Jewish reaction to Islamicization.

I would argue more specifically that the 'Isawiyya rebellion represents a Jewish failure of accommodation to the recent Islamic conquests. This attempted adaptation to the new regime should not be seen as contradicted by their armed rebellion. The prophet-inspired uprisings of the first and second Islamic centuries were often in conflict with certain ruling houses, governors and generals, but were not, so far as the evidence allows, anti-Islamic as such. This holds true for both Muslim and non-Muslim insurgencies. The pattern of this attempted accommodation to political reality, and its failure, can be traced in the history of the 'Isawiyya in three broad phases: accommodation, apocalypticism, and reconciliation.

The first two phases may not be in fact separable. But we would assume that, as with other such movements in the history of religions about which we are better informed, there must have been a history of the group, a development, before the cathartic climax of its actual rebellion. In this phase, I would assert, their doctrine was formulated. In this phase, Abu 'Isa would have worked out his vision of himself as prophet (*nabi*) and apostolic messenger (*rasul*) of the awaited Messiah, "the most excellent of the five harbingers of the Messiah." And it would have been at this stage that this apostolic stature invested his ritual innovations with divine authorization.

This first period, then, was one of expansion and consolidation of gains. The sources agree that the eventual uprising was supported by substantial numbers of followers. A few references roughly indicate the extent of the accommodationist character of this spreading movement. There is, first of all, the background evidence of the Qur'an, which indicates that there were already some Jews who were willing to recognize Muhammad as a prophet and still retain their Judaism.[132] Traces of these conciliatory Jews also survive in hadith: The Jewish youth who is cast as a prophesying rival to Muhammad, Ibn Sayyad, is willing to recognize Muhammad as a prophet to the nations that have not received Scriptures (*rasul al-ummiyin*).[133]

This movement, then, must have been well entrenched by the second Is-

---

[132] Stillman discusses such a possible reading in *Jews of Arab Lands*, 10.
[133] Halperin, "Ibn Sayyad Traditions," 213–25, at 216. On Muhammad as prophet to the nations, see now Goldfeld, "'Illiterate Prophet,'" 58–67.

lamic century, as a variety of other sources testify. The best known of these is
the Jewish apocalpyse, *The Secrets of Rabbi Shimon bar Yochai*, in which
Muhammad is characterized as a true prophet. As I have already noted, Goitein has stated that in this text "the influence [of the ʿIsawiyya] is discernible."[134] The student of the jurist Abu Hanifa, Shaybani, writing circa
184/800, says that "today the Jews in the areas of Iraq recognize that there is
no god but God and Muhammad is the Prophet of God, but they claim that
he was sent as a prophet only to the Arabs, and not to the Jews."[135] This
passage, written within a century of Abu ʿIsa's rebellion, is more good evidence for the widespread movement among Jews to get around conversion by
such an interpretation of the Shahada.

Later writers would seem to corroborate this picture of the situation. The
mid-tenth-century Karaite Salmon ben Yeruhm, for example, states: "I have
learned that when the Jews of Samarqand and the region say "God is One" (*allah
wahid*), [people who hear this] testify that by [saying] this they have become
Muslims."[136] The early-fifth/eleventh-century Baghdadi, furthermore, devotes
several passages to this question. He tells us that this lenient interpretation of the
credo was held by several Muslim groups. In a later chapter, he discusses yet
other Muslims who considered as believers anyone "who confirmed the prophetic character of Muhammad even if he did not join his religion."[137] Ibn
Hazm tells of some Kharijites who held related doctrines.[138]

Here, then, is a situation in which both the ʿIsawiyya and several Muslim
groups share, to a certain extent, a developing doctrine of accommodation.
Thus, two groups of the Kharijites protected Peoples of the Book and allowed the aforementioned doctrine.[139] A son of ʿAli, Muhammad ibn al-
Hanafiyya, an influential proto-Shiʿite of one school, held that anyone who
said the Shahada is a *muʾmin*, "believer."[140] Perhaps most significantly, the

[134] Goitein, *Jews and Arabs*, 170.
[135] Goldziher, "Usages juifs," 75–94, at 91–92.
[136] See his *Commentary on Lamentations I*, xiii, cited and translated by Ben-Shammai,
"Attitudes of Some Early Karaites," 3–41, at 10. I have somewhat altered his
translation.
[137] In his *Al-Farq bain al-Firaq*. Baghdadi argues that the ʿIsawiyya and their congeners, the Shadhaniyya, should be considered Muslims only if one follows the erroneous argument of the Karramiyya, that anyone who enunciates the Shahada is a
Muslim (220; Halkin, *Schisms and Sects*, pt. 2, 37–38). And, against the Yazidi Kharijites, who allow the same, he adduces the case of the ʿIsawiyya and the Rayʿaniyya:
"There is nothing which can allow anyone who regards Jews as Muslims to be counted
as one of the sects of Islam." (263; Halkin, *Schisms and Sects*, pt. 2, 104).
[138] Ibn Hazm discusses Zayd ibn Abi Unaisa, who, he says, held that "even if there
were Jews and Christians who said 'There is no god but God and Muhammd is the
Apostle of God, to the Arabs and not to the Jews,' [he held] that they are still believing friends of God": *Kitab al-Fisal* 4:188.
[139] Salem, *Political Theory and Institutions*, 40; Morony, *Iraq*, 471 and 473 n. 26.
[140] Van Ess, "Early Development of Kalam," 109–25, at 117.

Murji'ites were famous for their emphasis on faith over works, some of them believing that "anyone who called himself a Muslim was saved."[141]

The 'Isawiyya were, then, playing both sides against the middle. They could be recognized as Jews by (Rabbanite and Karaite) Jews because they seemed Judaically orthoprax, and could be recognized as believers by (Kharijite and Shi'ite) Muslims because they seemed Islamically orthodox. This was, perhaps, an unwieldy if not spurious symmetry; at least, in retrospect, it proved an awkward half-step.

We are at a loss in reconstructing the next steps that the 'Isawiyya took, which were to lead to the eventual debacle of their breakaway. Why, if the machinery of accommodation was being successfully forged from both sides, was it not sustained? The reason that the 'Isawiyya were led into the second phase, the apocalyptic phase, may lie with the extremity of the times. Throughout the early-second Islamic century, the Umayyad dynasty was coming undone. Ghulat were leading uprisings among the partisans of the house of 'Ali. Anti-Umayyad uprisings wracked Isfahan at least four times during their rule.[142] These anti-Umayyad movements, on the part of the ghulat and the 'Abbasids, were ultimately orchestrated by the successful insurgent Abu Muslim, who skillfully manipulated apocalyptic imagery to stir up revolutionary sentiment.

The Jews were perhaps inevitably swept up in this situation. *The Secrets of Rabbi Shimon bar Yochai* reflects a certain ardent hope raised in the hearts of Jews in these years. I would argue that it is precisely this hope, and its disappointment, that forced Abu 'Isa into his Messianic delusion. This hope, we know, has its roots in ancient Jewish eschatology. There was, as I have already shown, a considerable resurgence of Jewish Messianism among the Jews of Arabia just before and after the rise of Islam.[143] This is also seen in the Ibn Sayyad story. And we also find this motif in the text that describes the Jews of Isfahan dancing and making music in expectation of imminent salvation at the hands of the approaching Arab conquerors.[144]

There was, then, a strong and highly ramified prophetic expectation among the Jews under early Islam. Some Jews converted under the influence of the Prophet Muhammad. Some others attempted a compromise. But as the first two Islamic centuries progressed, the Messiah did not come and the new prophet's community proved to be merely "tolerant" of the Jews. The last

[141] See the discussion, for example, in Williams, *Islam*, 160. For the tradition that "the Jews are the Murji'a of this Umma," see S. Stern, *Studies in Early Isma'ilism*, 43.
[142] "Isfahan," *Encyclopedia of Islam*, 2d ed., 4:97–105 at 97. It should also be noted that Isfahan was part of the *thaghr* (admistrative satellite) of Kufa, which may help explain the apparent preponderance of ghulat doctrine and practice among the 'Isawiyya. See Djait, "Kufa" ibid., 5:350, for a helpful discussion.
[143] Hirschberg, "Footsteps of the Messiah," 112–24.
[144] Abu Nu'aim, *Dhikr Akhbar Isfahan* 1:22–23. For the same report related concerning Nihawand, see Noth, "Isphahan-Nihawand," 274–96. I thank Fred M. Donner for suggesting this last reference.

years of the crumbling Umayyad house, then, may have evoked a *resurgence* of hope among the Jews—the hope, now, that there was a way out from under the disillusioning and unaccommodating caliphate.

We do not know precisely what precipitated the final break of Abu 'Isa. Several sources, both Jewish and Muslim, do tell us that he had an ascension experience: Maqdisi reports that he ascended to heaven, where God "stroked him on the head" (famasaha 'ala ra'isihi).[145] He was said to be an illiterate tailor who wrote books by inspiration.[146] We know that the parallel Muslim ghulat movements also drew upon the disaffected for support: the illiterate, women, weavers, and *mawali* (client tribespeople), are frequently mentioned.[147] The picture that emerges here is one of the Jews, along with other marginalized groups, made increasingly miserable by the breakdown of imperial cohesion in the mid-second/eighth century, eagerly following charismatic leaders who offered them promises of supernatural redemption. We see the same picture in the imagery of the Dajjal, or Antimessiah: his following is said to comprise Jews and mawali.[148] This imagery of the followers of Abu 'Isa, a Jew of Isfahan, and the followers of the Dajjal, moreover, seems be conflated in the famous hadith that reads "the Dajjal will be followed by 70,000 Jews of Isfahan wearing Persian shawls."[149]

It is interesting to note that accounts of Ibn Sayyad, the Jewish youth identified in some Muslim traditions as the Dajjal, share certain features in common with the reports concerning Abu 'Isa. Thus, both are said to have: (1) ascended to heaven; (2) stated that Muhammad is a prophet to the Gentiles; (3) been identified as the Dajjal, and (4) been associated with certain motifs characteristic of the Jewish mystical Merkaba traditions.[150] Since Maqdisi claims that the Jews of Isfahan thought that Abu 'Isa was the Dajjal, I suggest that there may have been, at least in the eyes of the beholders, some (coincidental) "Antimessianic" association between these two figures.

The Messianic uprising of Abu 'Isa was not only powerful enough to be echoed permanently in Muslim tradition, but also to make a substantial mark on the Jews of the day. Shahrastani speaks of large numbers of followers; Maimonides even specifies that they were ten thousand. One is reminded of

---

[145] See n. 163 below.

[146] Chiesa and Lockwood, *Ya'qub al-Qirqisani*, 144.

[147] See chapter 1, above for a study of despised professions among the Jews of the eighth century. For now, see Brunschvig, "Métiers vils," 41–60.

[148] Wasserstrom, "The Moving Finger," 129. See also Gil, *History of Palestine*, s.v. "mawla, mawali," for numerous examples of the role played by these client-converts.

[149] See, for example, Vajda, "Juifs et musulmans," 57–127, at 113, for variants. This hadith is not the only example of the notoriously low estimation of Isfahani Jews. Abu Nu'aim reports that the Jews of Isfahan worked in the "métiers vils," cupping, tanning, fulling, butchering (cited in Mez, *Renaissance of Islam*, 39). Note also the popular story of the Jew of Isfahan, as discussed in Kraemer, *Humanism in the Renaissance of Islam*, 81.

[150] Halperin, "Ibn Sayyad."

Scholem's description of the Sabbatian conflagration: "An emotional up-heaval of immense force took place among the mass of the people, and for an entire year [1665–66] men lived a new life which for many years remained their first glimpse of a deeper spiritual reality."[151] It is not surprising, then, that when Friedlaender analyzed these descriptions, he compared them to the explosive spread of the Sabbatian heresy.[152] It must, unfortunately, remain a matter of speculation whether the 'Isawiyya had had a similar impact. The report given by Maimonides, however, does emphasize that the suppression resulting from their revolt was both severe and sustained.

After the caliphal forces put down the insurrection—after the apocalypse, as it were—the movement moved into its last phase. A series of successors, notably the obscure Yudghan/Yudh'an and Mushkan/Sharikan, continued the movement in Persia. Yudghan/Yudh'an, we are told, emphasized allegori-cal interpretation (ta'wil), while his successor, Mushkan/Sharikan, is said to have renewed the military option. The several decades of agitation among the Persian Jews were registered not only in Jewish apocalypses such as *The Se-crets of Rabbi Shimon bar Yochai* but also in Christian apocalypses. Thus, in the eighth-century Christian apocalyse known as *The Apocalypse of Peter*, we read: "When you see the children of Ishmael mixing with the children of Persia, and when you see the Jews learning the art of warfare . . . know, O Peter, that the end of the Kingdom of Ishmael is at hand."[153] This may be seen as ad-ditional evidence for a substantial impact felt by observers of these developments.

The movement was strong enough to surmount several military defeats and to survive into 'Abbasid times. Under Yudghan/Yudh'an of Hamadan, Abu 'Isa's teachings rose again out of the ashes of the battlefield.[154] This reaction by Yudghan/Yudh'an parallels a development among the Muslim proto-Shi'ite extremists, who, after the executions of their prophet-leaders, contin-ued to refine theology, largely through ta'wil. The Yudghaniyya/Yudh'aniyya are said to have seen the holidays and fasts of Judaism as not binding on those in exile and to have held that they serve only as symbols.[155] The "cognitive dissonance" engendered by the disconfirmation of prophecy—the defeat of Abu 'Isa—must have accelerated the shift into esoteric interpretation.

The subsequent uprising led by Mushkan/Sharikan, in which, we are told, only nineteen men participated, may be seen in retrospect as an atavistic mo-

---

[151] Scholem, *Major Trends in Jewish Mysticism*, 288.

[152] Friedlaender, "Jewish-Arabic Studies," for comparisons with the Sabbatians. Of the initial impact of Sabbatianism, Scholem elsewhere writes: "The appearance of Sabbatai Zevi and the growth of popular faith in his mission caused [an] inner sense of freedom, of a 'world made pure again,' to become an immediate reality for thou-sands" (*Messianic Idea in Judaism*, 87–88).

[153] Mingana, *Apocalypse of Peter*, 272.

[154] See Breur, "Yudghanites," 624–25.

[155] For the sources see Dinur, *Israel in the Diaspora*, pt. 1, 2:232–34, and notes thereon.

ment of last resistance to the inevitable.[156] This subsection of the 'Isawiyya, however, was still large enough to have been noticed by several Jewish and Muslim scholars. Saadia Gaon, for example, apparently mentions a sectarian ritual innovation of theirs.[157] The Isma'ili author Abu Hatim al-Razi mentions the Jewish sectary S'dkh in connection with the ghulat.[158] And Baghdadi, in particular, discusses how many of the Muslim rituals this group could observe and yet remain Jewish.[159] These reports, however—the rationalization of collapse, the shift into symbol, the second accommodation to events—are the last we hear of the end of phase three, after their military defeat.

The Proto-Shi'i Milieu: The Mansuriyya

By contrast to the yet-inconclusive search for a Christianizing background as a key to understanding the origins of the 'Isawiyya (the thesis of Pines), a far more profitable analysis consists in contemporaneous contextualization, that is, in placing the 'Isawiyya in the context of the contemporaneous ghulat, or proto-Shi'i extremists. Fortunately, the only sustained study ever undertaken of the 'Isawiyya, that of Friedlaender, already appropriately isolated fifteen "Shi'itic elements" in the 'Isawiyya.[160] Therefore, rather than review or replicate his (still-valuable) work here, I shall refine its focus.

To be precise, in the following I shall detail the ramified and manifest relationship between the accounts concerning Abu 'Isa and those concerning one proto-Shi'i "extremist" (*ghali*), Abu Mansur al-'Ijli (d. ca. 738–44), his exact contemporary. These parallels, as a return to the insights of Friedlaender and as a specification and a focusing of his pioneering work, should leave little doubt concerning the precise formative milieu of Abu 'Isa. I want to emphasize thereby that a sustained return to Friedlaender's lapsed investigation of this proto-Shi'i milieu will be far more profitable than any other approach to the study of the 'Isawiyya, most especially by contrast to Pines's analysis of the 'Isawiyya as an "Jewish-Christian" sect.

In sum, the features shared in common between the reports conerning Abu 'Isa and those concerning Abu Mansur include: (1) the date, (2) a heavenly ascent, (3) illiteracy, (4) prophetology, (5) temporary leadership status, (6) tax raising, (7) the role of Christ, (8) the role of the desert, and (9) militarism.

1. *The Date*. The 'Isawiyya may be dated to the events devolving from what I would call "the second Purge," of 736–37. The interrelated uprisings fol-

[156] See I. Friedlaender, "Jewish-Arabic Studies" 1:207 n. 93, and 289, for the sources.
[157] Poznanski, in his bibliographic additions to Graetz, *Geschichte der Juden*, 306–12, at 311, cites Harkavy's Russian-language article to this effect.
[158] Stern, *Studies in Early Isma'ilism*, 41.
[159] Baghdadi, *Al-Farq Bain al-Firaq*, 9.
[160] I. Friedlaender, "Jewish-Arabic Studies."

lowing Muhammad al-Baqir and Muhammad ibn al-Hanafiyya—those led by
Mughira b. Saʿid, Bayan b. Samʿan, and Abu Mansur—were crushed at that
time.[161] As Friedlaender demonstrated, the ʾIsawiyya are most clearly related
to these groups.

2. *A Heavenly Ascent.* The ascension reports concerning Abu ʾIsa and Abu
Mansur are nearly identical, verbatim.[162] Such an ascension is reported of no
other ghali. In both cases God is claimed to have "patted" or "stroked" (*mas-
aha*) the visionary on the head. As Friedlaender observed, the Messianic implications of this use of the Semitic cognate *m-s-h* are manifest.[163]

3. *Illiteracy.* Both leaders claimed to author holy books even though they
were said to be illiterate.[164]

4. *Prophetology.* Both leaders speak of a sequence of prophets, including
themselves, who precede and serve as forerunners for the eventual arrival of
the final redeemer. The report apparently attributable to Abu ʾIsa al-Warraq
on Abu ʾIsa would seem to imply an identical scenario to that reported of Abu
Mansur: that five prophets, followed by himself as a sixth, would herald the
ultimate seventh, who would be the final redeemer.[165]

5. *Temporary Leadership Status.* Both leaders specify the transitional nature
of their own authority, that they are forerunners of the ultimate savior. An
important report on Abu Mansur indicates that he is perhaps the first teacher
of the doctrine of the *imam mustawdaʿ*, the temporary, or repository, imam:
significantly enough, he uses the analogy of Joshua's deputyship to argue this
delegation of authority.[166]

[161] Wasserstrom, "The Moving Finger," 129; the only sustained study of Abu Mansur
is that of Tucker, "Abu Mansur," 66–76. Note that Ibn Hazm and Baghdadi both
discuss the ʾIsawiyya in association with the ghulat.

[162] See Tucker, "Abu Mansur," for the sources and a brief analysis. See also Tahanawi's
Kashshaf fi Istilahat al-Funun 2:1385; and Widengren, *Muhammad the Prophet*, 29–
30.

[163] I. Friedlaender, "Jewish-Arabic Studies," 271–75, on "anointment." I concur
with Friedlaender that "the words *famasaha ʿala raʾsihi* originally meant to convey that
God had poured holy oil on [Abu ʾIsa's] head and by consecrating him as the Mashiah,
'the Anointed one,' empowered him to become the redeemer of Israel" (275).

[164] For a rich study of such "inspiration" in this regard see ibid., 275–80. Nawbakhti,
Kitab Firaq al-Shiʿa, 35, describes Abu Mansur as being illiterate (*ummi*); see also
Qummi, *Kitab al-Maqalat wal Firaq*, 46–47. These sources also are discussed and
translated by Halm, *Die islamische Gnosis*, 86–89.

[165] Friedlaender, "Jewish-Arabic Studies," 258–61. For more on Abu Mansur, see
Tucker, "Abu Mansur"; Nashwan al-Himyari, *al-Hur al-ʿAyn*, 168–69;
I. Friedlaender, "Heterodoxies," 89–90; Kashshi, *Rijal*, 257, where Abu Mansur is
castigated as being "Rasul Iblis," i.e., the "Apostle of Satan," and then listed among
seven "lying Satans"; and Widengren, *Muhammad the Apostle*, 35, on the chain of
seven prophets reported by Tabari.

[166] This doctrine is discussed with full reference to the sources concerning Abu Mansur in the Gimaret and Monnot annotated translation of Shahrastani, *Livre des religions*
1:443 n. 40. For this doctrine associated with the Jews, see p. 596.

6. *Tax Raising.* In both cases, a *khums* (one-fifth) tax is raised, not just for the present leader himself, but also for the future leader. According to Abul Ma'ali, Abu 'Isa "established a tax of two-fifths: one-fifth for the Community, and another fifth for the treasury of the Messiah (in such a manner that it remains in the treasury until the manifestation of the Messiah)." According to Ibn Hazm, "After the death of Abu Mansur, [his followers] used to deliver one-fifth of the goods taken from those they killed by strangling (or breaking their skulls) to al-Husayn, the son of Abu Mansur."[167]

7. *Role of Christ.* Abu Mansur's possible Christian connection may be compared to that of Abu 'Isa, as already studied above. Abu Mansur originates in the Banu 'Ijl, an Arab tribe Christianized before Islam. He swears by the "Logos" (*kalima*). And he teaches that Jesus was the firstborn of Creation.[168]

8. *Role of the Desert.* A social clue may be provided by the detail that both sectarians are associated with desert areas. Abu Mansur is said to have been raised in the desert (*sawad*); Abu 'Isa escapes to the "Banu Musa, Banu Amran, who live beyond the sandriver [Sambatyon]".[169]

9. *Militarism.* Both heresiarchs lead pathetically futile military escapades. Abu 'Isa "protects" his rebels with apotropaic magic, and then singlehandedly gallops into the caliphal troops.[170] Abu Mansur's rebel followers were armed only with sticks and stones.[171]

Doctrines of the 'Isawiyya

It remains to review the evidence concerning the doctrines of the 'Isawiyya. Of all his teachings, his prophetology earned him eternal notoriety. His most famous teaching, one that gained him centuries of calumniation in Muslim dialectical texts, was that Jesus and Muhammad were indeed true prophets, but only to their own communities, not to all peoples everywhere. In fact, this continues to be a feature of the reports concerning the 'Isawiyya

[167] I. Friedlaender, "Heterodoxies" 1:63; Sachedina, "*Al-Khums*," 39; I. Friedlaender, "Heterodoxies," 63.
[168] Donner, "Bakr b. Wa'il Tribes," 5–38, at 26, 30–32; on the Logos, see al-Ash'ari, *Maqalat* 1:74 and Tucker, "Abu Mansur", 74 n. 65; on Christ as firstborn, see Tucker, "Abu Mansur," 72 n. 47, also citing al-Ash'ari, *Maqalat* 1:74.
[169] Abu al-Ma'ali helpfully supplements Shahrastani's mention of the "sandy-river": see Monnot, *Islam et Religions*, 107, my translation from Monnot's French. See also I. Friedlaender, "Jews of Arabia," 52–57.
[170] Qirqisani, *Kitab al-Anwar* and Shahrastani *Kitab al-Milal* provide the only substantial details of the 'Isawite rebellion.
[171] Tucker, "Abu Mansur" discusses Abu Mansur as a "terrorist." The most interesting account in regard to Abu Mansur as a "strangler" (*khannaq*) is that of Jahiz, *Kitab al-Hayawan* 6:388, who describes the hideout of the group, complete with two entrances to facilitate quick getaways. See also Tritton, "Muslim Thugs," 41–44; and Rajkowski, "Early Shiism in Iraq," 186 n. 1, for a full discussion, and also 718–19.

in traditional Muslim universities (such as at al-Azhar) until quite recent days.[172]

Qirqisani and Shahrastani supply us with the only other substantial information on Abu 'Isa's doctrine. According to these writers, he was said to have forbade divorce; required either seven or ten prayers a day; retained the rabbinic forms of the Shemoneh Esre and the Shema; exalted rabbis almost as highly as prophets; and forbade the consumption of meat, fowl, and wine.[173] Shahrastani may not be mistaken when he says that Abu 'Isa "opposed the Jews in many of the precepts of the Great Law mentioned in the Torah," for Abu 'Isa may indeed have diverged programmatically from tradition on certain points of law. Hadassi calls the 'Isawiyya "the Sect of the Interpretation of the Law (*kat pesher dat*)."[174] However, as I have tried to show, the evidence suggests that exegetical variance in fact tended toward pietistic and ascetic *increases* in ritual observance.

Abu 'Isa himself apparently saw his teachings as lying within the Jewish tradition. And the rabbis agreed with him: Qirqisani reports that the 'Isawiyya were allowed to marry Rabbanites because they observed the same holidays.[175] It might also be added that Ibn Hazm and Nu'mani, both of whom may have had some personal contact with 'Isawites, seem to indicate that the 'Isawiyya used the same text of the Torah as the Rabbanites did.[176]

Still, this "Jewishness" was apparently blended with certain proto-Shi'i doctrines, as I tried to show above. In this regard, an early, important source on the doctrine of the 'Isawiyya, recently come to light, seems particularly significant. In the *Bayan al-Adyan* of Abu-l Ma'ali (written in 485/1092), two reports on Abu 'Isa are found. In the long-lost chapter 5, we read these apparently unparalleled details:

> He imposed ten ritual prayers in every twenty-four-hour period. He said, "One to whom a nocturnal emission occurs and does not perform ablutions will not be pure for seven days." He established a tax of two-fifths: one-fifth for the Community and

[172] These all concern the purported 'Isawiyya doctrine of *naskh*, "abrogation." See, for example, the discussions of Jewish sects, including the 'Isawiyya, in the following modern al-Azhar texts: al-Zurqani, *Manahil al-'Irfan fi 'Ulum al-Qur'an* 2:98–105; Zayd, *Al-Naskh fi al-Qur'an al-Karim* 1:130; and al-'Arid, *Fath al-Mannan fi Naskh al-Qur'an*, 143.

[173] Perhaps the fullest discussion of these doctrines is found in the Russian-language Jewish Encyclopedia entry on Abu 'Isa by Poznanski, 171–74. I am grateful to Rawley Grau of Toronto for a translation from the Russian.

[174] Hadassi, *Eshkol haKofer*, 41b. See the text and discussion in Dinur, *Israel in the Diaspora*, pt. 1, bk. 2, p. 229 and notes thereon. For pietistic increases in ritual practices at this time, see Wasserstrom, "Delay of *Maghrib*," 269–87, at 278, with reference to the sources.

[175] Chiesa and Lockwood, *Ya'qub Qirqisani*, 144–45.

[176] Nu'mani, *Kitab al-Ghayba*, 65; Ibn Hazm, *Kitab al-Fisal* 1:93.

another for the treasury of the Messiah (in such a manner that it remains in the treasury until the manifestation of the Messiah).[177]

The doctrine of the ʿIsawiyya, then, was hardly antinomian, though it was syncretistic. Their "prophet" enjoined the same prayers and studied the same Torah as did the Rabbanites. Even some of his divergences are paralleled in talmudic tradition. Harkavy and Poznanski, for example, suggest that although his proscription of wine and meat may have been influenced by the passage about the Rechabites in Jeremiah (25:210), these rules were more likely derived from such Rabbinic traditions as those found in Baba Batra 60b, "that meat and wine ought not be indulged in by Jews so long as they live in exile." This admonition was taken literally by the contemporaneous Avele Tzion, "Mourners of Zion," traces of whose practice, these scholars suggest, can be found in earliest Karaism, a contemporaneous movement.[178]

In addition to their apparent family resemblance to the quasi-Karaitic ascetic cultus of the Avele Tzion, the ʿIsawiyya also bear at least superficial similarities to early Karaites like ʿAnan, who also proscribed consumption of meat and wine. It was largely based on these pietistic similarities that most students of this subject, including the perspicuous pioneers Schreiner and Harkavy, suggested that Abu ʿIsa's innovations influenced the origins of Karaism.[179] But all these "parallels" tell us only that Abu ʿIsa, simply put, was a pietist, a type with which contemporaneous Jewish history was replete. In addition to the Avele Sion and the Karaites, there were also other Jewish pietists under early Islam, who, Goitein suggests, may have influenced the origins of Sufism.[180] In short, there is no evidence and no reason to believe that Karaism "subsumed" the ʿIsawiyya.

It is possible to trace lingering vestiges of the ʿIsawiyya, their destiny, and some late echoes of their beliefs for several centuries. We first hear of them again in the fourth/tenth century. Our sources lived mostly in the fourth/tenth and the fifth/eleventh centuries, and several of them indicate that the ʿIsawiyya were still alive in their day. It is well known that Qirqisani, in the 930s, says that there were some twenty of the ʿIsawiyya still surviving in Damascus (a report which led some scholars to suggest that the ʿIsawiyya

[177] Monnot, *Islam et Religions*, 107 (my translation from the French).
[178] See the sources collected in Dinur, *Israel in the Diaspora*, pt. 1, bk. 2, pp. 215–18; Zucker, "Responses to the Karaite Movement," 378–401; Grossman, "Aliya," 174–87.
[179] Thus, Martin Schreiner: "Abu ʿIsa and his disciple Yudghan greatly influenced the founder of the Karaites, Anan" ("Ishak ben Yaʿkub Obadiah Abu ʿIsa al-Isfahani," *Jewish Encyclopedia* [1904], 6:646); and Harkavy: Anan "succeeded in uniting all heterogeneous elements under his standard, and in forming a powerful sect out of them" ("Anan ben David," 553–56, at 553). This position was followed subsequently by Nemoy, *Karaite Anthology*, xvi–xviii; and Wieder, *Judean Scrolls*, 254–55. But see now Cook, "ʿAnan and Islam," 161–83, at 181, who cites these precedents but supports against them, as I do, the arguments of I. Friedlaender, "Jewish-Arabic Studies," 214.
[180] Goitein, *Jews and Arabs*, 148–51.

expected the return of their awaited savior in that city, and which led others to suggest a connection with the Zadokites of the Damascus Document) and a few more in Isfahan.[181]

But there is another interesting piece of fourth/tenth-century evidence. I refer to the (heretofore unnoticed) text of Nu'mani (mid-fourth/tenth century). His *Kitab al-Ghayba* is representative of the Twelver Shi'ite appproach to the doctrine of occultation. In his discussion of biblical prefigurations of the twelve imams in that work, he "quotes" from the genealogy of Ishmael in Genesis.[182] After authenticating his understanding of the Hebrew text with a Samaritan and with another Jewish scholar, he also checks with an 'Isawite scholar, Ishaq ibn Ibrahim ibn Bahsun, who lived in Arrajan in the Persian cultural sphere. He is, so far as I know, the only member of the 'Isawiyya whose name has survived, other than the initial leaders.

A generation after Nu'mani, Baqillani, one of the founding fathers of Kalam, polemicizes at some length against the 'Isawiyya. He not only refers to them as one of the sects still alive in his day, but he also calls them a "great community" (*umma 'azima*).[183] Baqillani's younger contemporary Baghdadi also describes the continuators of the 'Isawiyya, the Sharikaniyya, as alive in his day. He says that they profess the full Shahada, hold that Islam is a true religion, perform some of the Five Pillars, and yet are not considered to belong to the Community of Islam.[184] If this report is accurate, then by the turn of the fifth/eleventh century, they would seem to a Muslim observer to have been largely Islamicized. They were, at that time, certainly still active: In the 1020s (ca. 411–420), the Spanish scholar Ibn Hazm testifies to the presence of 'Isawiyya by stating that he had met "many distinguished Jews who follow this same school of opinion."[185]

The most impressive of all such testimonies comes from the sixth/twelfth-century Shahrastani. This fine medieval scholar may have relied on an informant from the 'Isawiyya in formulating his report on Jewish sects. This hypothesis would help explain the presence of several unique features in his

[181] See Nemoy's edition of Qirqisani, *Kitab al-Anwar* 3:283. An assertion that belongs in the realm of speculation is Massignon's "Distribution of Religions" in Baghdad, including "Jews 14% (including 0.5% Karaites, 'isawiyya)" (*Passion of al-Hallaj* 1:241)

[182] Nu'mani, *Kitab al-Ghayba*, 64–65. I thank Mahmoud Ayoub for first guiding me to this source.

[183] Baqillani, *Tamhid*, 170, par. 289: "It should furthermore be said to [the Jews]: it is necessary to accept the truthfulness of the evidentiary signs of Muhammad's prophethood because of the corroborative witness of the 'Isawiyya, and they are a great nation, for they were not coerced into this position."

[184] Al-Baghdadi, *Usul al-Din*, 325–26, and *al-Farq bain al-Firaq*, 9.

[185] Ibn Hazm, *Kitab al-Fisal*, 1:93: "Concerning the first page of the Torah of the Jews which is used by their Rabbaniyya, 'Ananiyya and 'Isawiyya, whether they inhabit the Eastern parts of the Earth or the Western parts, they do not disagree on that text, not even in one respect . . . (la yukhtalifuna fiha 'ala sifa wahida . . .)"

report: why neither Rabbanites nor Karaites are adequately represented; why he reports at length on Abu ʿIsa, the ʿIsawiyya, and the two major continuators; why his report on the group utilizes (transliterated) Hebrew names, as well as unmistakably Jewish terms and images, with no critique of them; why Shahrastani's sole detailed report on any of the Jewish sects, that on Abu ʿIsa, is not only a self-contained narrative unit, with a beginning, middle, and end, but also dispassionately refers to the ʿIsawiyya depiction of Abu ʿIsa as *ʿabd, rasul, and nabi*, epithets reverently applied to Muhammad in the daily Muslim prayer.[186] As I pointed out above, Shahrastani was also informed of both the exoteric and the esoteric names of the pietistic prophet of the ʿIsawiyya. Nor is it unthinkable that Shahrastani may have had an ʿIsawite informant: the ʿIsawiyya did meet with Muslim scholars, as we are told that they did with Ibn Hazm and Nuʿmani.

A few later sources, of uncertain reliability, seem to indicate an ongoing ʿIsawiyya presence. In the first half of the seventh/thirteenth century a little-known author, in his Persian-language heresiography, mentions the doctrine of the ʿIsawiyya and discusses the group in the present tense, saying that they are "but a few."[187] In the early-tenth/sixteenth century, Abu al-Fadl al-Maliki al-Suʿudi says that four Jewish sects are still extant in his day: Karaites, Rabbanites, Samaritans, and ʿIsawiyya.[188] But these reports may represent only the scholastic repetition of heresiographic motifs.

Finally, it is requisite to briefly summarize the geography of the ʿIsawiyya (on the basis of the evidence cited above), to show that they were widely (if sparsely) distributed over the lands as well as through the centuries of classical Islamicate civilization. I shall limit myself to sites that are specified in our sources. Thus, from his hometown of Nisibis, Abu ʿIsa took his movement to Isfahan. Subsequently, in the Persian orbit, we find these sectaries in Rayy, Hamadan, Qumm, and Arrajan, whence they may have spread as far as Transoxania. In the central Islamicate lands, they may have settled in Palestine (if that is where the Palestinian rabbi Jacob ibn Ephraim encountered them), as well as in Damascus, where Qirqisani knew of a group of them. Remarks made by Shaybani and Maimonides suggest their possible presence in Mesopotamia. And, finally, that presence may have extended to Andalusia: Ibn Hazm tells us that he met many Jews who held such doctrines.

---

[186] See my discussion in "Species of Misbelief," 190–92.

[187] Abu al-Maʿali, *Bayan al-Adyan*, 22–23: "Know that those which are in the Persian lands today are two fairly prominent sects: one is called the Qaraan and one is called Rabbanan. . . . And a third group is called ʿIsawi. They say that abrogating revealed law is not allowable on rational grounds nor in legal fact, and that Muhammad is an Apostle, but that he was sent to the Arabs and was not a prophet to the Children of Israel. This group comprises only a few."

[188] Abu al-Fadi al-Maliki al-Suʿudi, *Disputatio pro religione*, 190: "Well-known today [al-maʿ aruf al-an] are four sects: The Qarraʾun, the Rabbaniyun, the ʿIsawiyya and the Samira."

The 'Isawiyya: A Summation

We have evidence of the 'Isawiyya surviving through the fifth/eleventh and sixth/twelfth centuries, with some possibility that they survived even later than that. Spread throughout the Islamicate world, this group survived at least three hundred years. This evidence militates against the consensus of modern scholarship, that this sect was merely an ephemeral aberration. There has indeed been little historiographic progress in this connection, from the time, eighty years ago, that Poznanski asserted that the pre-Karaite Jewish sects under Islam sprang up and died away "like mushrooms," to the *Encyclopaedia Britannica* entry by Gerson Cohen, in which he claims that such groups were "by and large quickly and forcefully suppressed."[189]

The 'Isawiyya were not a mere flash in the crucible within which Islam was forged and Judaism was transmuted. They were, rather, a comparatively long-lived Jewish reaction to Islamicization. They may have had their roots in the heterodox pietism of late-antique Judaism; they may have survived until the tenth/sixteenth century: there is no question that they existed as a far-flung, discrete Jewish sect for at least three centuries, perhaps for four or five. Both their doctrine and the memory that they once stood beside the Rabbanites and Karaites as a substantial school within Judaism persist to the present: Abu 'Isa is enshrined in Karaite traditional texts as a progenitor, while the 'Isawiyya are still thought to be a major Jewish sect in Muslim scholarly traditions within living memory.[190] The 'Isawiyya survive even today, but only as a kind of scholastic spectre, a shadowy reminder of their ultimate failure.[191]

---

[189] Poznanski, "Philon dans l'ancienne litterature," 10–31, at 22; G. Cohen, "Rabbinic Judaism," 316–22.

[190] For Abu 'Isa as Karaite progenitor, see Nemoy "Elijah ben Abraham," 63–87, at 79. For some modern Muslim scholars of al-Azhar who mention the 'Isawiyya, see n. 172 above.

[191] With regard to the absence of Rabbanite evidence for the very existence of the 'Isawiyya, the researcher is left with *argumentum ad silentio*. The silent treatment to which Rabbanites subjected schismatics was based on the talmudic precepts to the effect that heretics within the community are worse than idolaters (Babylonian Talmud Shabbat 13 [14] 5).

PART II

Constructions

> When the quick victories had created a vast imperium, the external spaciousness allowed room for an internal spaciousness to arise. There was a readiness to consider the thoughts of the others who dwelt in the land and to grant them their place. There was an openness to other directions of thought and teaching. . . . To the children of the Jewish people who lived in the lands of the descendents of the Prophet there was vouchsafed, in all these developments, something great, something historical.
>
> —Leo Baeck, *This People Israel*

CHAPTER THREE

Shiʿite and Jew between History and Myth

SHIʿITE AND JEW IN SYMBIOSIS

The "symbiosis" of Jew and Shiʿite does not appear in the famous pages of Ignaz Goldziher's *Introduction to Islamic Theology and Law*. Rather, the "doctor maximus" of turn-of-the-century Islamic Studies observed merely that on "examining the legal documents, we find that the Shiʿi legal position towards other faiths is much harsher and stiffer than that taken by Sunni Muslims." The pages following that observation then enumerate the precise horrors of Shiʿite purity laws. S. D. Goitein, Goldziher's successor as master Orientalist in the realm of Judeo-Arabica, also neglected the possibility of Judeo-Shiʿite symbiosis. Thus, after his memorable firsthand account of the terrors of Jewish life under Shiʿite rule in the Yemen, Goitein concludes that, "[again,] it was sectarian [i.e., Shiʿite] Islam, which deviated from the practice followed by the majority of Muslims and was responsible for the mass conversion of adults." The strength of such statements on the part of leading Judeo-Islamists accordingly allowed scholarly nonspecialists like Heschel to state simply as fact that "Shiites had always been more intolerant of other faiths than the Sunnites." It would appear, in short, that most scholars agree on the unremittingly harsh attitudes of and actions taken by Shiʿites toward the Jews.[1]

In fact, by sharp contrast to this apparent consensus, a parallel track of scholarship long has recognized a rare closeness between Shiʿite and Jew. Wellhausen, for example, was willing to accept a certain veracity in the Sunni polemical linkages of Jews with Shiʿites: "Certainly many things are called Jews and Jewish by the Muslims without any reason. But in fact the dogma of Shiʿism, the founder of which is considered to be Ibn Sabaʾ, seems to stem more from the Jews than the Persians." Against the rejection of Jewish-Shiʿite symbiosis, likewise, one might juxtapose the vaunted "interconfessionalism" of the early Ismaʿili Shiʿites, as first articulated by Bernard Lewis. A few other exceptions, such as Joel Kraemer, readily can be located in the scholarly literature. He states unequivocally that a "striking socio-religious phenomenon during [the Buyid] period was a rapprochement between Jews and Shiʿis."[2]

---

[1] Goldziher, *Introduction to Islamic Theology and Law*, 217. He treats this issue on 213–17; Goitein, *Jews and Arabs*, 80; Heschel, *Maimonides*, 106–7.

[2] Rudolph, "Julius Wellhausen." Lewis, *Origins of Ismailism*; Kraemer, *Humanism in the Renaissance of Islam*, 79. See also p. 29: "In the medieval period Shiʿism (more than Sunnism) opened windows to foreign currents of influence . . . . in the medieval pe-

Unlike so many other historiographic disputes in the study of Jewish history the question of Shiʿite-Jewish symbiosis has not been debated by proponents of those opposing positions. The historiographic *problem* is not there. A comprehensive review of Jewish-Shiʿite relations in the period under consideration, therefore, has not seemed urgent and so remains to be written. And, of course, until numerous detailed studies are undertaken, all generalizations in this regard will be left ultimately unsubstantiated. My goal in this chapter, nonetheless, will not be that substantiation. Rather, I intend to lay some groundwork for such an eventually fuller reconsideration.

Even so, it is impossible to review modern historiography of Jewish-Shiʿite relations until the full range of original sources serving as the basis for that analysis are rethought. In this chapter, therefore, I will begin by looking at the ways in which both Shiʿites and Sunnis perceived Shiʿite-Jewish symbiosis. After a review of that classical stereotyping, I will reassess the scholarship pertaining to the history of Jewish-Shiʿite relations in the first centuries of Islam, with special reference to the case of Ismaʿili Shiʿism.

SONS OF AARON: TYPOLOGY AND PERCEPTION

The relative terra incognita of the Shiʿite uses of typological precursors has yet to be reconnoitered adequately. Fortunately, the recent work of such Israeli scholars as Kister, Rubin, Schwarzbaum, and Kohlberg has now provided some reliable guideposts for further exploration.[3] Their work fully confirms earlier observations concerning the mythic riches of Shiʿite Islam in this regard. Indeed, it would not be inaccurate to say that both Twelver and Sevener Shiʿism were considerably "biblicizing" in their attitude toward the past.

The fundamental statement of Shiʿite biblicism, as noted in the previous chapter, is expressed in the celebrated equation, "ʿAli is to Muhammad as Aaron is to Moses." I have already examined some of the implications of this statement above, in connection with the Harbiyya. In this point, I shall argue that the Shiʿite propensity for such linkages with the Banu Israʾil was so extensive that Sunni anti-Shiʿite propagandists could eventually develop lengthy lists of Shiʿite-Jewish equations. These polemical lists may have been fabricated to be (at least a distantly echoed) mockery of Shiʿites' own self-associations with the Banu Israʾil.

The way these Shiʿite equations continued to build up over time can be seen in the accretions of equations concerning the sons of ʿAli. The primary extension of the fundamental "Muhammad = Moses/ʿAli = Aaron" equation

---

riod Shiʿism exhibited greater intellectual openness than did Sunnism." In addition to such important connections with the Shiʿite sect of Islam, Savage has recently pointed to the parallels with the Ibadi sect: "Ibadi-Jewish Parallels," 1–15.
[3] See the many works by these authors listed in the bibliography below.

was the legend that the angel Gabriel named 'Ali's two sons Hasan and Husain, after Aaron's two sons, Shabbar and Shubbayr.[4]

This linkage may have been essayed as a typological echo. Rabbinic tradition portrays the two sons of Aaron—Nadab and Abihu—as martyrs par
excellence, "who died in order to sanctify God's name."[5] Nevertheless, however much a historicist quest for such "sources" may succeed, it will be of only
severely restricted utility in our understanding of the ultimately political
point being made in the context in which it was being asserted.

That context may best be clarified by the range of variations of this tradition. Just as the basic equation made a political point, so did the variations on
it. The versions that mention three sons—Shabbar/Hasan, Shubbayr/
Husayn, and Mushbir/Muhsin (Mushabbir/Muhassin)—were apparently
contributed by ghulat circles.[6] More specifically, as I have already argued
above, these ghulat may have been the Kaysani Harbiyya. I would argue that
this Muhassin mytheme represents an attempt to infiltrate the status accruing
to the 'Alid lineage descending through Fatima, on the part of ghulat descending from Muhammad ibn al-Hanafiyya. Muhassin, in other words,
comprises a trope for this extension of the 'Alid lineage, all the more so since
Muhassin seems surely to be an apocryphal figure.[7]

The figure of Muhassin may be argued to be tendentiously apocryphal for
several reasons. First, his brothers, Hasan and Husayn, are so vastly significant it would have made no mythic sense for him to be mentioned in relation
to these Imams unless a certain point were being made. Moreover, this stillborn cipher not only was not an imam, but was revered only in ghulat circles

[4] Massignon gathered many sources on this problem. See for example, "Muhassin,"
585 n. 3 and 599; "Origines shi'ites de la famille," 484–85. See also the discussions of
Goldziher, "Ueber die Eulogien," 119. Rubin, "Prophets and Progenitors," 52, notes
that this tradition was already cited by al-Baladhuri and Ahmad, suggesting its considerable antiquity. Note also that a Jew of Arabia at the time of Muhammad apparently
had a son named Husain. See Lecker, "Note on Early Marriage Links," 17–40, at 20–
21.

[5] Flusser and Safrai, "Nadab and Abihu," 79–84.

[6] It will be noted that Jewish sectarians also emphasized the importance of Aaron and
his *three* sons. See Yadin, *Temple Scroll*, 78–81, on the consecration of Aaron and his
three sons in an annual eight-day ritual, occuring on 1–8 Nissan (cols. 15–17 of the
scroll). For the three sons in later Muslim letters, see the sources gathered by
I. Friedlaender, "'Abdallah b. Saba,'" 13 n. 8.

[7] It is important to observe that the ghulat chiliastic expectations may be yet another
factor implicated in their adoption of this motif—that is, the Messianic overtones of
the Aaronid line, well established in Jewish tradition, seem to have been revitalized by
the ghulat and symbolized by them in the "Muhassin" mytheme. Aaron and his sons
were the original "anointed ones" (*mashiah*) (Exod. 28:41). See Segal, "Descent of
the King Messiah", 133–36 on the Messiah as a descendant of Aaron. See above,
chapter 2, on the Messiah of Aaron in the texts of Qumran. The first Mahdi of Islam
was in fact Muhammad ibn al-Hanafiyyah, the half-brother of Hasan and Husain and
the hero of the ghulat.

such as the Nusairis.[8] It seems likely, therefore, that ghulat mythmakers played on the permutations of word roots to extend the point of this tradition beyond the moderate ʿAlid line to their own group. This third group was represented by the third son, Muhassin, whom the Nusairis call "the mystery of obscurity."[9] Finally, ʿAli was said to have twenty-seven children, twenty-eight if one counts the stillborn Muhassin: twenty-eight is the number of letters of the Arabic alphabet. Since this tradition explicitly builds on numerology (*jafr*), this enumeration is not likely to be coincidental.[10] Finally, it is a remarkable fact that ʿAli and his sons recur in Jewish literature, sometimes in a context of positive valuation, for several centuries.[11]

Subgroups, in other words, could manipulate biblicizing differences for political purposes. This was true as well of the Imamis and the Ismaʿilis, both of whom had recourse to manifold biblical typologies for their own purposes. Not only did both these traditions develop elaborate myths based on Isra'iliyyat materials; not only did they both use biblical citations to make their propagandistic points; but they also both used Hebrew quotations to do so. Similar observations can be made concerning the general biblicizing approach to salvation history common to both the Sunni and the Shiʿa. One may legitimately state that the biblicizing hiero-history of Islam shares a world with Judaism and seems designed to live in a common universe. This is most strikingly the case with the early Ismaʿiliyya.

SHIʿIS ARE THE JEWS OF OUR COMMUNITY: AN INTERRELIGIOUS
COMPARISON WITHIN SUNNI THOUGHT

> The anthropologist can never assume that the chosen symbols of religious
> controversy are arbitrary.
>
> —Mary Douglas, *Natural Symbols*

[8] See the sources cited by Strothmann in *Festkalendar*, esp. at 4–5.
[9] Salisbury, "Notice of the Book," at 240, 246. See p. 240 for "Muhsin, Mystery of Obscurity, at daybreak." See also the more recent discussion of these texts in Halm, *Die Islamische Gnosis*, 341, 344, 387 n. 698, 389 n. 707.
[10] Mufid, *Kitab al-Irshad*, 268–69. On *jafr* and the Jewish-Shiʿi symbiosis, see my "*Sefer Yesira.*"
[11] The rosh golah Bustanai, like the imam Husain, is said to have married a Persian princess. For extensive bibliographies of sources and studies on Bustanai, see Cutler and Cutler, *Jew as Ally of the Muslim*, 421 (this book is otherwise not recommended). An ethical will of ʿAli to his son Husain is preserved in Hebrew in the Cairo Geniza. See Goitein, 'Meeting in Jerusalem.' See also the Yemenite "writs of Protection" ostensibly dictated by Muhammad to ʿAli, preserved in Judeo-Arabic. See the texts and analysis gathered by Ahroni, "From *Bustan al-ʿuqul* to *Qisat al-batul*, 311–60, at 329. To Ahroni's list may be added the work of Nini, "A Writ of Protection." And see below, this chapter, on the uses of the parallelism between the imamate and the exilarchate, in the self-legitimation of the Shiʿis.

The Jewish-Shi'i relationship is perhaps the least studied and almost certainly the most poorly understood aspect of early Jewish-Muslim relations. I take up a salient case in point, the lists appended to the widely repeated maxim that "the Shi'is are the Jews of our Commmunity." To see how this is so I shall now analyze this tradition in two ways: First I consider the formula "The X are the Y of our umma [community]"; then I examine the list of equations and its implications.

It was of course only with a sufficient development of heresiographical information and classification that such internal cross-referencing of religious groups became possible. But the cross-referencing formula "the X are the Y of our umma" was more than a device for the indexing of sectarians[12]—for it is one of the most striking features of Muslim scholarship on religious pluralism that it classifies Muslim and non-Muslim groups according to the same criteria. This categorical formula thus implies *a view of religion*, the implications of which may be derived from the following facts.

First of all, it is reasonable to assert that the Shi'a-Jew equation is the most significant variation on this equation. The other variations are much less frequently found. These include "the Murji'a are the Jews of our umma" and the "Mushabbiha are the Jews of our umma."[13] This latter variant, like the fairly popular "Qadariyya are the Majus of our umma," do become clichés of the Kalam presentation of foreign religions.[14] However many variants one could adduce—and there are many—the Shi'a-Jew comparison is not only quantitatively but, I believe, qualitatively different from all others.

The Sunni scholars who used this axiom certainly *were* familiar with the well-established "facts" of Shi'i self-understanding: that the Shi'i imamate was patterned after the rabbinic exilarchate; that "Ali was to Muhamamad as Moses was to Aaron"; that the names of Hasan and Husayn were translated from the names of Aaron's sons; that the twelve imams were like the twelve tribes, and so forth. Moreover, the Sunni researcher was well acquainted with several foundational assertions concerning the purported historicity of this identification: that a Jew ('Abdallah ibn Saba') originated the heresy of deifying 'Ali; that another Jew (Maymun ibn Qaddah) initiated the Isma'ili sect; that Jews and Shi'i were familiar minorities who made the exclusivist claim that, as al-Qazwini put it, "the Shi'a resemble the Jews, who say, we will go to paradise and others won't."[15]

Aside from matters of content, the issue of context is also apposite to note at this point, for these equations tended to arise *not* within Sunni discussions concerning Jews, but in the context of Sunni discussions with regard to Shi'is. The problem, in other words, was one of interior differentiation, of

---

[12] See below, chapter 4, for the techniques used in the generation of such equations.

[13] For another early Shi'i source on this equation, see Ibn Shadhan, *Kitab al-Idah*, 47; for Mushabbiha, see the modern work of Ahmad Mahmud al-Subhi, *Fi 'Ilm al-Kalam*, 20, citing al-Iji.

[14] The Druze assert that "the Sunnis are the Jews of our *umma*." See Bryer, "Origins of the Druze Religion" 5–28, at 10–11.

[15] Calmard, "Le chiisme imamite en iran," 43–67, at 51 n. 32.

differences within *our umma*. Our umma is not totally other, a unique species, sui generis. Rather, it is a *religion*—the ultimate such entity, to be sure,
but nonetheless recognizable as such. And, as such, the umma is congenitally
susceptible to the same structural weaknesses as other religions are. In this
regard I am reminded of the following citation by the great historian of religions, Shahrastani, in the introduction to his masterwork:

> The Prophet compared each of the misguided sects of his community with a
> misguided people of former times. Thus he said, "the Qadarites are the Majus of
> this umma, the Mushabbiha are the Jews of this umma and the Shi'ite are its Chris-
> tians." Speaking in general terms he said, "You walk along the path of former
> peoples in exactly the same way, so much so that if they have entered the hole of a
> lizard you will enter it too".[16]

Equation Lists

I begin with a Sunni list that identifies Jewish and Shi'ite doctrine and practice. Repeated and amplified for several centuries, this collection of equations
came to summarize the authoritative Sunni perception of a damning linkage:
the paradigmatic others within the umma were in essence the same as the
paradigmatic others without. Shi'ism was seen as a threatening extension of
Judaism into the world of Islam, the evidence for which aspersion was gathered starkly into a list. Nowhere else, perhaps, has *Listenwissenschaft*, the ancient literary technique of ordering knowledge, been more polemically
effective.[17] This "scientific" summation of guilt by association "proved"
its underlying assumption, that heretics are heretics. The power of this tautol-
ogy generated, eventually, an entire range of Muslim polemic and
heresiography.

Lists of kinds of Jews, with more or less of a description of their respective
originators, beliefs, and rituals, constitute the bulk of Muslim heresiography
of the Jews. The list as a distinct subgenre has been studied at some length in
recent years, provocatively so by J. Z. Smith in his paper "Sacred Persistence."
In this self-described effort "toward a redescription of canon," Smith medi-
tates on Listenwissenschaft and its three primary constituent elements: list,
catalog, and canon. In these terms of Smith's, I believe that the materials with
which we are working could be termed *canons,* insofar as they are lists dis-
playing a demonstrable effort at closure, or "exegetical totalization," as
he describes canon.[18] However, since these are canons of the *other*—
countercanons, a kind of normative domestication of all (mis)belief—I have
tried to be explicit here at the outset about its presuppositions. The list as I

[16] Shahrastani, *Kitab al-Milal*; see Gimaret and Monnot, *Livre des religions*, 121–22.
In general on Shahrastani see my "Islamicate History of Religions?" 405–11.
[17] Goody, *Domestication of the Savage Mind*, esp. chap. 5, "What's in a List?" 74–112;
see pp. 80 and 94 for some of the background to the use of the term *Listenwissenschaft*.
[18] J. Z. Smith, *Imagining Religion*, 48.

use it is an admixture of (proto-)science of religions and imperial co-option of all known belief.

In practical terms, either for the Muslim legist or the modern historian, these lists are of limited utility for penetration beyond them to actual groups. The listers were only occasionally competent in compiling an accurate taxonomy. This was only partially their fault: the scholarly tradition within which they worked mandated the list genre, which was simply too Procrustean to be of serious scientific value. What William Scott Green has observed about the list in the Mishnah holds true here as well: "The identification of the Mishnah's literary genre (i.e., list) makes it hard to be sanguine about extracting its social world, for it is hard to imagine a literary form more removed from social reality and less able to capture anything of it than the list."[19]

An additional difficulty in studying the Muslim *religionsgeschichtlich* lists is that of what might be termed *taxonomachia*, the conflict of taxonomies. I resort to a partial neologism because of the novelty of the observation. I would suggest that the many Muslim scholars who tried their hands at this genre typically came up with many conflicting lists, not one definitive list. One perceives a parallel phenomenon in the Islamicate "divisions of the sciences": many schemata were devised, virtually none of which coincided precisely with any other. This taxonomachic propensity would seem to be due to a desire for completeness converging with a kind of ambitious, if not combative, instinct to "make one's name" by producing one's own, revised, complete system. Taxonomachia, then, may be seen as a sign of scholarly health: so long as ongoing revision takes place, ossification is delayed.[20]

Thus, as the anthropologist of religion Mary Douglas suggests, "the more coherent and all-embracing the classification, the more the pressure to sustain its general credibility against rival systems."[21] Intersystem conflict is built in. Constructed on an assumption of schematic pluralism, this classificatory system of the list builds itself against other schemata. The "exegetical totalization" of J. Z. Smith implies that authors of lists must strive against each other.

Smith, like the anthropologist Jack Goody, employs the term Listen-wissenschaft, which is borrowed from scholars of ancient Near Eastern literatures.[22] Green is a scholar of rabbinic Judaism, Douglas an anthropologist of ever-widening interests. All these scholars are emphasizing, from a variety of

---

[19] Green, "Reading the Writing of Rabbinism," 191–207, at 200.

[20] Makdisi in his *Rise of Colleges* treats in some detail the educational system of the Muslim colleges. Progress in that system was dependent upon one's prowess in the disputation (*munazara*); students collected notes on the masters' lectures, which lecture notes (*ta'liq*) were modified so that the student, in part through disputation and in part through the employment of an "improved" version of the lecture notes, himself ascended to master status (*riyasa*). It may be that the taxonomachic propensity to generate schemata of essentially the same materials but with varying classifications may be a function of this educational system.

[21] Douglas, *Implicit Meanings*.

[22] See n. 17 above.

perspectives, the primary role of a classificatory system in imposing shape on purportedly *raw* information; data are not merely found and listed, but are in some sense generated by the list.

This characteristic would seem to have also been a feature of the pre-Islamic Christian scholarly tradition. In the words of Kurt Rudolph, this tradition "which can be traced right down to the heresiological literature of Islam, made the catalogues of heresies not only a fixed and increasingly unrealistic constituent of apologetic and theological writing, but also a means of coming to grips with new heresies and of combating them by referring back to the 'classic' constituent of the heresy of bygone history, and to some extent by identifying them with names familiar from it."[23] In these terms, the combative element of the list was aimed outward, as indeed it often was in the Muslim tradition.

I have attempted to demonstrate that the list genre is central to my argument not only because the lists comprise the bulk of the texts under review, but also because the list genre was of critical importance in explicitly formulating the worldview implicit in all the texts studied. Therefore, some attention must now be given to the propositions that generated the lists.

In the religions list, the political power to dominate is crystallized into the synthesizing capacity to identify. The oneness of the umma is strengthened by contrast to the singularity of enmity to the umma. This domination by identification governs Sunni imagining of Jews and Shi'ites in the "classical" centuries of Sunni power. As such, this domination must be the starting point for any study of the shaping of Jewish-Shi'ite relations, for these archetypal non-Muslim and Muslim minorities were conflated relentlessly by the opinion makers of the Sunni majority.

In his *'Iqd al-Farid*, Ibn 'Abd Rabbihi (d. 328/939), the earliest great Arabic-language belle-lettrist of al-Andalus, relates the first lists of parallels between the Rafida and the Jews.[24] The list is cited in a quotation attributed to the Kufan 'Amir ibn Sharahbil ibn 'Abd al-Sha'bi (103/721–722), a well-respected hadith transmitter.[25] The discussion of these parallels by al-Sha'bi is almost certainly spuriously placed in the mouth of this reliable transmitter of traditions. The issues involved and the neatly symmetrical equations indicate an authorship dating from at least several decades after Sha'bi's death. Only at such a later date were these "heretical" positions and the polemics against them at all well defined. That being said, most if not all of the purportedly shared features of Shi'ism and Judaism can be found to possess some basis in observable practice and doctrine. Polemic gains potency by such "verisimilitude." Sha'bi prefaces his catalog of damning linkages with a caveat: "Beware

[23] Rudolph, *Gnosis*, 20–21.
[24] The lists are repeated in Amin, *Duha' al-Islam* 1:334–35.
[25] For the role of al-Sha'bi in hadith transmission, see Azmi, *Early Hadith Literature*, 63–64. For his philosophical orientation, see Watt, *Islamic Thought*, 73–74.

of these misleading beliefs! The worst of them are those of the Rafida's, for they are the Jews of this community, and they loathe Islam, as Jews despise Christianity."[26] There then follows a succinct list of nine reprehensible beliefs and practices ostensibly shared by the Jews and the Rafida.

The device of linking the Jews and the Rafida was to become a standard feature of subsequent Sunni polemic. That this device was disseminated throughout Ash'ari *kalam* (scholastic theology), for example, can be seen by its inclusion of this list of equations in a series of classical Kalam treatises.[27]

The list ascribed to Sha'bi, after the classical Kalam, is then considerably amplified in Ibn Taymiyya's *Minhaj al-Sunna*.[28] While the list in *Minhaj al-Sunna* incorporates later accretions, it does retain the early motifs, while amplifying their number and clarifying their meaning. I translate it here in extenso (with my own added enumeration):

> Al-Sha'bi said: Beware of the people of these misleading beliefs, the worst of them being the Rafida. They did not enter Islam of their own desire, nor out of fear [of God], but rather out of hatred of the people of Islam, to commit outrages against them. 'Ali burnt them and banished them to the far countries. Of them was 'Abdallah ibn Saba', a Jew from among the Jews of Sana' [who was] banished to Sabit, and 'Abdallah b. Yasar [who was] banished to Khazar, which events support the claim that the rebellion [*mihna*] of the Rafida is the rebellion of the Jews.
>
> 1. The Jews say sovereignty is only valid when in the House of David; the Rafida say: The imamate rightly belongs only to the descendants of 'Ali.
>
> 2. The Jews postpone prayer till the stars shine, as do the Rafida, who postpone *maghrib* [evening prayer] till the stars shine. There is a hadith that the prophet said: "My people will continue in their proper state so long as they do not postpone the evening prayer till the stars shine brightly."
>
> 3. The Jews turn slightly away from the *qibla* [traditional direction of prayers, toward Mecca for Muslims, toward Jerusalem for Jews], as do the Rafida.
>
> 4. The Jews sway in prayer; so do the Rafida.
>
> 5. The Jews let down their garments in prayer; so do the Rafida.
>
> 6. The Jews don't hold for the remarriage cooling-off period, nor do the Rafida.
>
> 7. The Jews falsified the Torah, as the Rafida did to the Qur'an.

---

[26] For other examples of the Shi'i-Jew equation see the sources cited by Kohlberg, "Views on the *Sahaba*," 143–75, at 143 n. 1. One such tradition is traced back to Ibn Hanbal. See Abul-Husain al-Farra', *Tabaqat al-Hanabila* 2:267 (cited by Laoust, *Profession de Foi d'Ibn Batta*, 49 n. 1). As I indicate below, these equation traditions and their variants require an extensive structural analysis.

[27] Abu Ya'la, *Kitab al-Mu'tamad fi 'Usul al-Din*, 260, no. 466; Isfara'ini, *Al-Tabsir*, 43–44.

[28] Tritton noticed this citation and quotes part of it but gives no indication of its background or context. See "Islam and Protected Religions," 330–31.

8. The Jews say: God enjoined fifty prayers on us. So do the Rafida.

9. The Jews don't say sincere greetings to Believers without Death on you (*Sam* means death); so do the Rafida.

10. The Jews don't eat eels or *marmahi* [a bitter-tasting eel] or tails, nor do the Rafida.

11. The Jews don't [observe the regulations regarding] wiping the shoes [at the point where the shoes fit], nor do the Rafida.

12. The Jews regard as lawful the taking of another's property, as do the Rafida. God has told us about them concerning this in the Qur'an, where they say, "There is not a way obligatory for us among the Prophet's people."

13. The Jews prostrate to their foreheads in prayer, as do the Rafida.

14. The Jews don't prostrate till their heads are bowed several times in a similar manner to genuflection, as do the Rafida.

15. The Jews belittle [the angel] Gabriel, saying, "He is our enemy among the angels," as the Rafida claim, saying "Gabriel erred in inspiring Muhammad."

(The Jews and Christians are better than the Rafida in regard to two traits: When the Jews are asked who are the best people of their religion, they say the people of Moses. When the Christians are asked who are the best people of their religion, they say the Apostles of Christ. [But] when the Rafida are asked who the worst people of their religion are, they say the companions of Muhammad. . . .)

16. The Jews do not consider divorce anything at all except during the menstrual period, like the Rafida.

17. The Jews do not hold by dismissing concubines, nor do the Rafida.

18. The Jews proscribe eels and *marmahi* as do the Rafida.

19. The Jews proscribe [the consumption of] rabbits and of spleen, as do the Rafida.

20. The Jews do not apostasize, nor do the Rafida—after having apostasized from our prophet!

21. The Jews place a palm leaf on the stomachs of their dead, as do the Rafida. . . .

22. [Some of the Rafida] proscribe [the consumption] of the flesh of goose and of camel, in similarity to the Jews.

23. Likewise, they always conflate the prayers, for they pray only at the three set times of prayer, in similarity to the Jews.

24. Likewise they say divorce does not take but the production of witnesses against the spouse, in similarity to the Jews.

25. Likewise, they make the accusation of pollution against the bodies of non-Rafidite Muslims and Peoples of the Book

26. And they forbid sacrifices.

27. And they accuse of pollution that which is touched by the drinking of their water and fluids.

28. And they wash the vessels from which non-Rafida eat, like the Samaritans, who are the worst of the Jews. For that reason people place the Rafida among the Muslims as they do the Samaritans among the Jews.

29. And they employ *taqiyya* [doctrinally enjoined dissembling] and dissimula-

tion, their outward expression being the opposite of what they really do, out of enmity, as do the Jews.

[To which may be added] many similar parallels.[29]

A full study of the Jewish and Muslim sources lying behind each of these accusations would require a sustantial monograph in itself. Cook's lengthy analysis of early Islamic dietary law, for example, demonstrates the complexity of such an study, were it to be extended to all the parallels on Ibn Taymiyya's list.[30] The assertions concerning ritual purity, to take another example, derive from a vast range of legal and legendary traditions, not only Shi'ite and Rabbanite, but Samaritan, Pharisee, and others.[31] The references to prayer practices, on the other hand, plausibly may reflect some actual changes of Jewish practice in Fatimid Egypt, if they do in fact reflect Ibn Taymiyya's observation of the Muslim influences on Jewish worship rituals, such as those studied by Weider.[32]

These points being noted, I want to reiterate that any such strictly historicist quest for a "basis in fact," while of proper interest to historians, is likely not to yield—at least in this case—a complete solution to the problem of symbiosis. The model of "influence and borrowing," by means of its overemphasis on genetic origination, may in fact obscure insight into a mature interreligious sharing. In the case under consideration now, a dangerously full-blown Jewish-Muslim symbiosis, accepted by Sunnis as "fact," was perceived to have developed insidiously within the precincts of the Muslim world. Indeed, this case shows that such a fully developed interreligious relationship was seen as a paradigmatic "threat from within." The purported factuality of this Judeo-Shi'ism, then, was posited, not argued. Its historical development simply was assumed.

When one probes this "factuality," then, one finds that the problem is, as it were, loaded from the outset. That this is so can be seen, for example, in the

---

[29] My translation from Ibn Taymiyya, *Kitab Minhaj*, 6–9. Note that elsewhere in this polemic, Ibn Taymiyya demonstrates some familiarity with the work of Moses Maimonides. See Pines, "Ibn Khaldun and Maimonides," 265–74, at 271–73. See also, more generally, Morabia, "Ibn Taymiyya," 91–123 and 77–109. Ibn Taymiyya's *al-Jawab al-Sahih* deals with critiques of Christianity and, to a much lesser extent, Judaism. See Lazarus-Yafeh, *Intertwined Worlds*, esp. 127, where she cites this work (2:17) on Ibn Taymiyya's consultation with a man who knew Hebrew.

[30] Cook, "Early Islamic Dietary Law," 217–77. For example, on the proscription of the consumption of eel, see 240–43 and 266. For recent reviews of the relationship between Jewish and Muslim law, see Brunschvig, "Voeu ou serment?" 125–34; Goitein, "Interplay of Jewish and Islamic Laws," 61–78; Meron, "Points de contact," 83–119.

[31] Goldziher, "La Misasa." See also Lazarus-Yafeh, "Some Halakhic Differences," 207–26, esp. her second section on purity laws. See also Noja, "La question se pose encore une fois," 83–195.

[32] Wieder, "Islamic Influences," 37–120; on genuflections see 75–93; on kneeling, see 93–96.

case of 'Abdallah ibn Saba', with the invocation of whom Ibn Taymiyya be-gins his list.[33] Even more striking, however, is the characteristic confounding of practice, borrowing, and accusation in early Shi'ite sources.

A close study of the first two accusations—respectively concerning the linkages of exilarchate and imamate, and of evening prayer practices—demonstrates this confounding interpenetration of traditions. In the follow-ing, then, I will look at some of the historical background that lies behind these two accusations. I will first examine two modes—the past and the present—by which Shi'ites utilized Judaic models as analogies to the ima-mate. The past mode utilizes the Aaronid priestly line as a typological precur-sor to the 'Alid lineage of charismatic authority; the present mode employs the Jewish exilarch as a "present" witness to the legitimacy of the imamate. I will then look at the second accusation, concerning the delay of the evening prayer. My analysis throughout will emphasize the means by which purport-edly Jewish doctrine and practice were, from the earliest origins of Shi'ism, deployed as polemical pawns in Sunni-Shi'ite rivalries over authority and le-gitimacy. The tracing of actual borrowing and influence—although still largely uninvestigated—is not my task at this point.

The equations of Jewish and Shi'i practice are asserted as fact but are not argued out as such. This lack of argument is of course not due to an absence of a critical sense, as Orientalists were once wont to assume. Indeed, at the risk of sounding patronizing, I note that medieval Muslim scholarship dem-onstrates a subtle, if naturally selective, historical consciousness concerning religous difference. For example, Jahiz (776/7–868/9) questions the Qu'ra-nic statement that the Jews believe that 'Uzair is the son of God: instead, he tells his readers that only *some* Jews believe this, and he then proceeds to specify which ones.[34] Now, one may complain that this remains an incredu-lous attitude, but it does represent a historical criticism of religious attitudes. Similarly, al-Khatib al-Baghdadi (d. 1071) proved that the celebrated "ex-emptions" from the *dhimma* (pact of toleration) purportedly granted to the Jews of Khaybar were in fact forgeries; in this he was followed generally.[35] In any event, a posture of omniscience was not a general conceit of serious Mus-lim scholarship. Rather, the more popular pose was that of publically admit-ted fallibility, to proclaim *la adri*, "I don't know." Thus, al-Sha'bi, the earliest known transmitter of the axiom in question here, was once asked for what work he was paid by the government. He answered, "For saying, '*I don't know*,' with regard to matters which I actually do not know."[36]

[33] I. Friedlaender, "'Abdallah b. Saba'."
[34] Finkel, "Risala fi radd 'ala al-Nasara," 35. See also Starr, *Jews in the Byzantine Em-pire*, 113–14. Lazarus-Yafeh, *Intertwined Worlds*, 52, discusses this point. She adds that the ninth-century Zaydi, al-Qasim ibn Ibrahim, said that he never met a Jew who worshiped 'Uzair (52 n. 6, citing Madelung, *Der Imam al-Qasim*, 90).
[35] Rosenthal, *Technique and Approach*, 47 n. 2; Gil, "Religion and Realities in Islamic Taxation," 21–33, at 28 n. 22.
[36] F. Rosenthal, *Technique and Approach*.

In other words, the function of gathering these equations was not, strictly speaking, historical or even critical. Clearly, these scholars could have dealt with the interreligious comparison in a critical fashion had they wished to. So what, then, was its function?

Legal Implications

To put the question differently: What are the implications of this comparison for the study of comparative law? After all, this is a list of legal comparisons. First, this axiom and its list of equations carried no jurisprudential weight; it had no discernible bearing on *fiqh* (Islamic jurisprudence).

The reason for this was not that heresiography and related forms of historical or quasi-historical understanding of religious difference played no role in legal decisions. Some examples of the ways that religious difference played a part in religious decisions may make this point clearer. An early tradition of al-Auza'i, reported by al-Tabari, forms the basis for the important legal ruling that there can be no inheritance between members of different religious communities, by which the *fuqaha'* (specialists in jurisprudence) specified certain Jewish sects as well as mainline denominations.[37] Other rulings also indicated that the *shari'ah* (Islamic religious law) was concerned with sectarian delimitation.[38] So too were some Muslim rulers. Al-Ma'mun is said to have issued a proclamation that all members of sects with more than ten members could legally have their own leaders.[39] Later, the son of Maimonides, Abraham Maimonides, was brought up on charges before the sultan for potentially sectarian innovations that he sponsored in Jewish liturgy.[40]

In other words, the practice of Jews and the practice of Muslim sectarians like the Shi'is could indeed both be matters for concern for fuqaha' and rulers alike. But the comparison between them, even when it explicitly concerned matters of practice, had no particular bearing on decision making. The reason, then, seems clear enough: this axiom was a matter of legal theory, of metatheory, as it were, but not of practice.

I would pursue this point a bit further, for historicity in matters of denominational legal status seems to have been at once crucial and immaterial. A good example of this point is that of the Jewry oath, the oath to be sworn by

[37] Yaqut, *Irshad al-Arib* 6:454.
[38] Ibn Qayyim al-Jauziyya, discussed in my "Species of Misbelief," 227–31. Especially see his *Ahkam Ahl al Dhimma* 2:90–92, where he discusses the problem of including Samaritans in the purview of the *jizya* (head tax). For this problem addressed in the seventeenth century, see Mittwoch, "Muslimische," 845–49.
[39] See the dicussion of the sources and their impact on the *geonim* in Baron, *Social and Religious History* 5:295 n. 6.
[40] See now the touching tribute to Abraham Maimonides with which Goitein concludes his final volume of *A Mediterranean Society*. The controversy over the ruling is treated in detail by Wieder, "Islamic Influences."

Jews at court.[41] This oath, whether in its early form under the ʿAbbasids or its fullest formulation in the courts of the Mamluks, was packed with ostensibly Judaic details.[42] The court, moreover, knew enough to devise different oaths for Rabbanite, Karaite, and Samaritan Jews.[43] But these were of course neither authored by nor sanctioned by the Jewish community. They were administered to them. The Jew was a Muslim object. The Jew's existence and difference from others mattered, and that point needed to be conveyed with verisimilitude. But the verification or falsification of particular difference beyond that assertion was simply unnecessary.

Monitory and Imaginary

The comparison, in this case, was theoretical. It answered a kind of cartographic necessity: How do we locate ourselves? The answer was the classificatory abstraction, "The X are the Y of our umma."

It is perhaps misleading that I have termed these comparisons *equations*, for these are perhaps less equations than correspondences. In this case, the principle of identification *seems* straightforwardly historical: both Shiʿite and Jew proscribe goose. But how does this apparently realistic comparison actually operate? It operates by means of a reduction to familiarity. This familiarization technique sets out to prove that these recent enemies are just like the familiar old enemies. As such, this is an analogy made by conventionalizing. The role played by correspondences here, then, is less lyric and more occult,

[41] See the oaths reported by al-ʿUmari and al-Qalqashandi in my "Species of Misbelief," 223–26, 235–40.

[42] Goitein, "Caliph's Decree," 118–25; S. Stern, *Fatimid Decrees*. Other translations and discussions of the oath can be found in Starr, *Jews in the Byzantine Empire*, 173–81; Parkes, *Conflict*, 398–400; Baron, *Social and Religious History* 3:195, 322 n. 28. Other materials can be found in Marcus, *Jew in the Medieval World*, 49–50; Baron, *Social and Religious History* 11:106ff., 334ff., nn. 40–43; 17:191–92, 384–85 n. 81. Of related interest is Kisch's *Jews of Medieval Germany*, "Brief History of the Medieval Jewry Oath," 275–79.

I would emphasize that the Jewry Oath is to be distinguished from the charges to office. The oath given by ʿUmari has had a long history in scholarship. It was translated by Goldziher into French in "Les Serments des Juifs" *Revue des études juives* 45 (1902), 1–8, on 3–5. Another French version was made by Fagnan, although he did not attribute it to ʿUmari, in "Arabo-Judaica," 225–30, on 225–29. A Hebrew translation was made by Mayer in his "Status of the Jews." Baron translated Mayer's Hebrew version into English in *Social and Religious History* 17:191–92. Stillman produced another English translation in his *Jews of Arab Lands*, 267–68. Qalqashandi used ʿUmari's texts verbatim.

[43] The Jewry Oath given by ʿUmari sheds light on the oaths of office given by ʿUmari (and copied by Qalqashandi), which do specify the leaders of the various communities. In this regard it should be noted that the Jewry Oath presumably was designed for Jews of all sectarian persuasions, while the charges to office are two: for the Head of the Jews (Rabbanite and Karaite) and for the Head of the Samaritans.

that is, less like poetic metaphor and more like the mechanistic chains of identity found in contemporaneous systems of magic and hermeticism.[44] This familiarizing, conventionalizing use of correspondences is indeed quite the converse of the technique of defamiliarization, which Viktor Shklovsky argues to be at the essence of literary art.[45]

I have already noted how this cartographic and familiarizing use of correspondences was monitory: it warned members of the Sunna against those who rejected their path. This legal comparison, one might say, was therefore imaginary, in the sense that certain philosophers give to the term *l'imaginaire*.[46] It is more concerned with practice on the map than with practice in the act. As such, it is an imaginary comparison, serving more an ideological than an immediately effective function—but effective nonetheless.

The political power to dominate was thus crystallized in the synthesizing capacity to identify. The oneness of the umma is strengthened by contrast to the singularity of enmity to the umma. This domination by identification governs Sunni imagining of Jews and Shi'is in the "classical" centuries of Sunni power. As such, this domination must be the starting point for any study of the shaping of Jewish-Shi'i relations, for the opinion makers of the Sunni majority relentlessly conflated these archetypal non-Muslim and Muslim minorities. Their strategy was inspired: to show that the non-Muslim and Muslim groups respectively possessing the strongest claims to primordial authority were so close to the Sunna of Muhammad precisely because they were so far from it, being the ultimate rejecters of it. Kohlberg has shown how the very imagining of the Rafida, "Rejecters," in the mind of the Sunnis was retrojected to biblical times, even into antediluvian times.[47] Their rejecting of Islam was intimately rooted, as it were, in the dialectic of salvation history.

A final word from the other end of history. The Sunni comparison list is not a conspiracy theory, though some who used such correspondences may have verged on such thinking.[48] Conspiracy theory is the totalization of such correspondences. Thus, this Sunni treatment of Jews was not anti-Semitic in the modern sense. Modern Muslim anti-Semites, borrowing from European Jew haters, do totalize such correspondences: Jews = Communists = Satan, and so forth.[49] The Sunni scholars I have discussed here, however far they

[44] On the mechanisms of corresponences in the occult sciences, see the important studies of Vickers, especially "On the Function of Analogy in the Occult," 265–92.
[45] Shklovsky "Art as Technique."
[46] See chapter 5 below.
[47] Kohlberg, "Term 'Rafida,'" 677–79.
[48] Conspiracy theory may be understood as the totalization of such correspondences. See the penetrating work of Umberto Eco on this dangerous tendency toward a paranoiac totalization. See "Intepretation and Overinterpretation," 141–203, especially 162–82. For a vivid dramatization of the tendency, see Eco, *Foucault's Pendulum*.
[49] See, for example, the paper "Know Your Enemy," published by the Muslim Brothers in 1979 in *al-Da'wa*. Here the Crusaders, Jews, Marxists, and Secularists are conflated into one enemy (Lewis, *Semite and Anti-Semite*).

went, did not totalize in this way, for at least one reason. They were more concerned with piously locating themselves in the universe of religions than they were in fabricating totalitarian pseudo-sciences of hatred. Here, as so often, the difference makes a real difference. These classic Sunni lists of practices were theoretical: today's Jew-hating lists of theoretical correspondences, alas, are all too practical.

TALES OF THE ROSH GOLAH

> Those among our legal scholars [*'ulama'*] who have gone wrong have
> ended up resembling the Jews, and those among our ascetics [*'ubbad*] who
> have gone wrong became like the Christians.
>
> —*Abu 'Uyayna*

Neither Sunnis nor Shi'ites dwelt with any particular degree of concern on postbiblical Jews and Judaism. This observation holds true with certain significant exceptions. Heresiographers, for example, did exhibit a limited interest in the presence of extant Jewish sects.[50] And both Shi'ites and Sunnis also elaborated numerous tales concerning the leaders of the Jewish community. Of these, Shi'ite tales of the rosh golah were developed for the purpose (among others) of legitimation.

In the equations of parallels between Jews and Shi'ites most elaborately provided by Ibn Taymiyya, the first parallel reads: "The Jews say sovereignty is only valid when in the House of David; the Rafida say: The imamate rightly belongs only to the descendants of 'Ali."[51] Thus the metaphoric identification of the imamate and the exilarchate propounded by the Imamiyya themselves became famous enough to have been included as the first entry in this widely copied Sunni catalog of opprobria aimed at the Imamiyya. The Shi'ite propensity for Judaic typological symbolism was recognized as such by their Sunni opponents.

These opponents also—properly—recognized that the ultimate symbolic linkage asserted by the Imamiyya was precisely this homology between their 'Alid hereditary line of communal authority and the Davidic royal lineage of the Jews. Out of this early recognition grew numerous tales starring the (usually unnamed) rosh golah (Arabic: al-ra's al-jalut or ra's jalut). While these Shi'ite legends must be understood in the light of stories of the rosh golah in Muslim letters at large, the majority of these accounts were not only of Shi'ite

[50] See Wasserstrom "Species of Misbelief," and chapter 4 below.
[51] The history of this report and an annotated translated are provided above, in the present chapter. A rich treatment of the exilarchate is now provided by Grossman, *Babylonian Exilarchate*.

authorship but were, moreover, obviously concerned with the legitimation of the imamate.

The fact that much of the nonheresiographical Muslim literature concerning the rosh golah is legendary may indicate that most Muslim writers would have known only the title of the leader of this Jewish community. This knowledge could then be applied, for the appearance of verisimilitude, to all manner of legitimizing myth. Stories that place the rosh golah at the time of Jesus or that indicate various fabulously accurate prognostications on the part of some unnamed rosh golah are such examples. Even these Shi'ite legitimation myths were parodied by Sunnis.

A good example of this Shi'ite-Sunni dynamic of legends of the rosh golah can be found in the tale told by Tabari, which would seem to implicitly mock the Shi'ite claims to have inherited the esoteric *jafr* (cosmological secrets) from the Banu Isra'il.[52] God bestows on Adam, the first man, a magic mirror that allows Adam to apprehend all things. Despite the periodic efforts of demons to subvert this plan, the mirror passes through successive Jewish leaders down to King Solomon and, eventually, to a rosh golah at the end of the Umayyad dynasty, who gives it to the caliph Marwan. Although the caliph destroys it and the rosh golah with it, the second 'Abbasid caliph, Abu Ja'far al-Mansur, eventually finds it in the possession of a Shi'ite usurper, whom he likewise punishes.[53]

In this fable the final retrieval of the mirror by the Shi'ite rebel after the death of the rosh golah serves as an exact structural parallel to the earlier retrievals of the mirror by demons after the deaths of Adam and of King Solomon. Thus the intervention of the 'Alid is portrayed as a demonic subversion of history. Insofar as this portrayal is mockingly aware of the Shi'ite tales of the rosh golah, it can also be considered a narrative counterpart to the Sunni polemic lists of equations.

The genre of 'Alid tales being mocked are those explicit and repeated Shi'ite associations of the exilarchate and the imamate. These tales effect this linkage primarily through the fictive device of encounters between the rosh golah and various members of the 'Alid lineage. Thus, the rosh golah asks 'Ali leading questions that allow the Prince of the Faithful to give the Jewish leader lengthy theological lessons. This form of the encounter, in its turn, is apparently calqued on the Masa'il genre common to both Sunni and Shi'i traditions.[54] The Shi'i genre of Ihtijaj (argumentation), which were widely reproduced and eventually gathered together at length by Majlisi, recount

---

[52] Tabari, *Annales*, 165–66, cited by Goldziher, "Notes et mélanges," 123–24; also cited by Stillman in *Jews of Arab Lands*, 39. After Goldziher, the only review of the subject has been Fischel, "'Resch-Galuta,'" 181–87.

[53] Tabari, *Annales*.

[54] Daiber, "Masa'il wal-Adjwiba." For more on the Masa'il literature, especially in connection with the traditions associated with 'Abdallah ibn Salam, see chapter 5 below.

numerous such dialogues between Muhammad, ʿAli, or the imams and various non-Muslim interrogators.[55]

A number of the Shiʿite tales of the rosh golah concern the number one son of ʿAli, the great martyr Husain. Husain and his brother, Hasan, it will be recalled, were said to have been named after the sons of Aaron. Moshe Gil has exhaustively investigated the complex of history and legend surrounding a curious parallel involved with Husain: like his contemporary, the rosh golah Bustanai, Husain is said to have been given a Persian princess to marry.[56] Here, again, the paralleling of the imamate and the exilarchate is highlighted. Bustanai is also recounted to be the interlocutor of the prophet in a widely distributed question-and-answer account.[57]

In another tale a rosh golah claims that ancient Jewish predictions concerning a martyrdom of a prophet at Karbalaʾ caused him anxiety each time he passed that place, lest he be that martyr.[58] He expresses relief when these prophesies turn out to refer to Husain. And yet another legend has it that a rosh golah chides ʿAli's protégé, Abu al-Aswad al-Duʾali.[59] Though seventy generations have passed since King David, the Jews still honor the rosh golah, he says, while but a single generation after ʿAli, his son Husain is murdered.

A quite early legendary account of the rosh golah with yet another son of ʿAli is found in the recently edited *Akhbar al-Daula al-ʿAbbasiyya*.[60] Because it comes from this early source; because this account is a particularly interesting variation on the theme; and because it stars the imam manqué Muhammad ibn al-Hanafiyya, it is worth translating here in full:

> ʿUmar ibn Shibbah said, "ʿAbdallah ibn Muhammad told me that Shaikh Yukna Abu ʿAbdallah said Muhammad b. ʿAli came to Hisham b. ʿAbd al-Malik, along with his two sons, Abu Jaʿfar and Abu al-ʿAbbas. Another day, he entered the pres-

---

[55] Many of these texts were gathered by the indefatigable al-Majlisi. For the only utilization of these texts from the point of view of Jewish-Muslim symbiosis, see Schwarzbaum, *Biblical and Extra-Biblical Legends*. See also Tabarsi, *Al-Ihtijaj*, on the imam al-Rida meeting with the rosh golah at the salon of the caliph al-Maʾmun. Vajda notes that the *Ihtijaj* closely resemble the "biblical difficulties" posed by Hiwi al-Balkhi. For more regarding these questions, see chapter 5 below.

[56] Gil, "Babylonian Encounter," 35–74. For more on Bustanai, see Gil, *History of Palestine*, s.v. "Bustanai, exilarch."

[57] Gil, "Babylonian Encounter," 56 n. 48 provides the references. See, more generally, Holmberg, "Public Debate as a Literary Genre," 45–53; Yassif, "Pseudo Ben Sira," 48–63.

[58] Goldziher, "Notes et mélanges," 123, citing Tabari.

[59] Ibid., 123–24, citing the *ʿIqd al-Farid* of Ibn ʿAbd Rabbihi, 309. Another report has Abul-Aswad quoting a rosh golah, to the effect that Kaʿb al-Ahbar was in fact citing not the Torah but the Book of Prophets. See Ibn Hajar, *Isaba* 5:324, cited by M. J. Kister, "Haddithu," 229.

[60] Duri and al-Muttalibi, *Akhbar al-Daula al-ʿAbbasiyya*, 171–72.

ence of Hisham b. ʿAbd al-Malik, coinciding with the visit of the son of the Rosh Golah, who was a Jew.

"Muhammad was the most beautiful of men, and Hisham was not one to over-look beauty [*wa-kana Hisham sabihan ma aghda*], and when he lifted his head [and looked at Muhammad], his eyes crossed [in pleasure], and Hisham looked at the son of the Rosh Golah, who was darting sharp glances toward Muhammad, and said, 'What's with you that you gaze at him [that way]?' Hisham replied, '[I have] good [intentions]; who is that person?' The son of the Rosh Golah said, 'That is one of the members of the Family of the Prophet. Is that one the closest relative to the Prophet?' Then Hisham became embarassed, which he did not like, and he did not admit it to himself.

"So Hisham replied, '[No, the closest to the Prophet is] My [fore]father.' The son of the Rosh Golah then said, "But if you are correct, then he should be in the center of your *majlis* [i.e., instead of you]; between me and my forefather, on whose account the Jews honor me, is forty forefathers.'

"Hisham got furious at this. He had the son of the Rosh Golah brought forward, and the chamberlain came to him and evicted him. The chamberlain said [to the son of the Rosh Golah], 'I'm not sure that the Prince of the Faithful [Caliph Hisham] won't order me to behead you.' The son of the Rosh Golah then said, 'What on earth is more [egregious] than that people say, "a Jew came with a a word of truth to the Caliph, and he killed him!?"' Hisham then affected to be hostile to Muhammad and Muhammad said, 'By God O Prince of the Faithful, I did not address nor did I respond: but you addressed him and he responded to you.' Hisham then ordered that [the son of the Rosh Golah] be given one thousand dinars, and he departed from his presence."[61]

In this Shiʿi history, the son of ʿAli, Muhammad ibn al-Hanafiyya, is por-trayed as having common cause with the son of the rosh golah against their jointly defied opponent, the Umayyad caliph Hisham. These homologous heirs support each other: the Jewish heir defends the ʿAlid claim to the rightful leadership of the community, and the ʿAlid heir defends the right of the Jew to speak the truth to the caliph. As in the tale of the magic mirror, "the truth" attested by the Jewish heir and denied by the caliph is that the ʿAlid claim is just.

A related Shiʿi tale of Jewish legitimatizing was noticed by H. H. Milman, who reproduced it in his landmark *History of the Jews* in 1831:

> The Jew came boldly forward, while the throne was encircled by the splendid retinue of courtiers and people, and asked in marriage the daughter of the caliph. Omar calmly answered, "How can I give my daughter in marriage to a man of another faith?" "Did not Mahomet," rejoined the Jew, "give his daughter in mar-riage to ʿAli?" "That was another case," said the caliph, "for ʿAli was a Moslemite, and the Commander of the Faithful." "Why, then," rejoined the Jew, "if ʿAli was

---

[61] Pages 171–72. This account came to my attention through the notice in Gil, "Bab-ylonian Encounter," 55 n. 47.

one of the faithful, do ye curse him in your mosques?" The caliph turned to the courtiers and said "Answer ye the Jew!"

[The caliph then substitutes the following prayer for the "Curse of ʿAli"]: "Forgive us, Lord, our sins, and forgive all who have the same faith with us."[62]

Finally, another motif of uncertain provenance that became a popular feature of this homologization was the ʿAlid assertion that the imam and the rosh golah shared certain physical characteristics. As Stillman has pointed out, this notion may have some basis in Jewish belief.[63] The characteristic specified in the version of the Zaydi Imam al-Qasim ibn Ibrahim, that the hands of the rosh golah "are longer that those of ordinary men so that they reach their knees when standing up straight. This is a deceitful lie!"[64] This description is repeated, without the condemnation, a century later by Khwarizmi.[65] Biruni, a tenth-century contemporary of Khwarizmi, repeats this description with the additional telling remarks that this is just as "the generality of people relate concerning the Prince of the True Believers, ʿAli b. Abi Talib, and of those of his descendents who are qualified for the *Imama* and the rule of the community."[66]

All these ʿAlid tales of the rosh golah were generated on the cusp between observable fact and historical cliché. On the one hand, the exilarch was a prominent feature of cultural life in the ʿAbbasid capital of Baghdad during the Geonic period. Benjamin of Tudela's familiar descriptions of the "pomp and circumstance" attending the public appearance of the rosh golah, even if exaggerated, at least indicate a substantial standing of that figure.[67] The importance of the exilarchate, perhaps hypertrophied in Muslim accounts because the exilarch served as a prominent and official liaison with the ʿAbbasid caliph, is already seen in Maqdisi's tenth-century listing of the Jalutiyya as a separate Jewish sect.[68]

---

[62] This story is related in an undocumented prose version by Milman, *History of the Jews* 3:221.
[63] "There may be a kernel of truth to this obviously legendary account" (Stillman, *Jews of Arab Lands*, 39 n. 42).
[64] Pines, "Une Notice," 71–73. This notice is translated into English by Stillman in *Jews of Arab Lands*, 176–77.
[65] Khwarizmi, *Mafatih al-ʿUlum*, analyzed at some length in my "Species of Misbelief," 119–26.
[66] Biruni, *Kitab al-Athar*, 68–69.
[67] See the texts printed in Grossman, *Babylonian Exilarchate*, along with others attesting to the role of the rosh golah: (pt. 2, 45–75). This may be amplified by the report of Natan haBabli that the exilarch wore the "Seal of Muhammad." On Natan, see the translation in Stillman, *Jews of Arab Lands*. Compare the remarks of Bickerman, "Symbolism in the Dura Synagogue," 127–51, at 146–47: "In the synagogue of Istanbul, I saw old scrolls of the Torah crowned by the Mohammadan crescent. This was not a sign of some mystical attraction to Islam, as a reader of Goodenough would be led to believe, but an expression of loyalty to the Ottoman Empire."
[68] *Kitab al-Badʾ wal-Taʾrikh* 4:34–36.

Maqdisi's report highlights the bleeding into heresiographical sterotype that lies at the opposite end of the spectrum of Muslim uses of these tales.[69] While it is still uncertain to what extent the historical encounters resulted in the heresiographical reports, there almost certainly was a channel there, especially in the eighth through the tenth centuries. The ninth-century Dirar b. ʿAmr is also said to have debated with a rosh golah.[70]

The fullest "recorded" encounter of a later imam is that of an unnamed rosh golah with the imam al-Rida at the court of al-Maʾmun.[71] Reported by Ibn Babuya less than a century after the (ostensible) event, this long debate is copied by Tabarsi and Majlisi and is also included in an autonomous volume of *Akhbar al-Rida*.[72] I translate the version given in Ibn Babuya's *Kitab al-Tauhid*:

> The Exilarch said, "Whence is established the prophethood of Muhammad?" Al-Rida replied, "Moses, Jesus, and David (his Caliph on Earth) testified to this prophethood." The Exilarch said, "Prove to me the discourse of Moses." Al-Rida said, "Are you aware, O Jew, that Moses charged the Children of Israel in saying to them: 'There will come to you a prophet from among your brethren—acknowledge him, hearken to him!' Are you aware that the Children of Israel have brothers other

[69] Thus subsequent heresiographers reify Rabbanite Jews as the Jalutiyya. See, for example, Nashwan al-Himyari, *Al-Hur al-ʿAyn*, 144–45.

[70] Van Ess, "Dirar b. ʿAmr und de Cahmiya," 241–79, 1–70, 318–20: see 7; Watt, *Formative Period*, 190; Al-Kashshi, *Rijal al-Kashshi*, 223.

[71] In 1853, Dozy, in a review of Renan's *Averroës et l'Averroïsme*, quoted from an Oxford manuscript an account of an eleventh-century Spanish Muslim (see now al-Humaydi, *Jadwa al-Muqtabas*, 101–2), who was scandalized by a Parliament of Religions held in Baghdad between various representatives of religions, in which only arguments founded on reason could be adduced. This was apparently the earliest modern mention of this motif, which became a conventional prooftext in modern scholarship for demonstrating the extent of open debate in the classical Muslim world. Thus, for example, is it found in MacDonald, *Development of Muslim Theology*, 194; Altmann's introduction to a selection from Saadia, in "Saadia Gaon," 13; and Baron, *Social and Religious History* 5:83. That such events did take place thus becomes a conventional element in the historiography of the symbiosis. See for example Guttmann, *Philosophies of Judaism*, 416 n. 7.

There is no reason to doubt that such meetings did take place, in a variety of settings. For such a meeting of ten disputants in Basra under the late Umayyads, see Vajda, "Les Zindiqs," 173–229, at p. 204. For accounts of assemblies held at the court of Maʾmun, run on the rules of reason, see Masʿudi, *Muruj al-Dhahab*, 38–43; Suyuti, *Taʾrikh al-Khulafaʾ*, 310; and Fischel, "'Resch Galuta,'" 186 n. 42. See the discussion in van Ess, "Disputationspraxis," 23–60. The conventional wisdom continues to be that these disputations provided the material for the written controversial literature. Thus, in "Islamic Theology and Philosophy," in the new *Encyclopaedia Britannica*, Mahdi writes, "From such oral and written disputations, writers on religions and sects collected much of their information about non-Muslim sects," 1012–13. See also the important article by Zayyat, "Sects. Innovation," 37–40. For more on interreligious meetings, see chapter 4 below.

[72] Thomas, "Two Muslim-Christian Debates" provides the relevant literature.

than the progeny of Ishmael, since you had known the relationship of Israel to Ishmael, and the descent which they both share back to Abraham?" The Exilarch answered, "That is the speech of Moses—we don't deny it." Al-Rida said, "Did there come to you from the brothers of the Children of Israel a prophet other than Muhammad?" The Exilarch answered, "No." Al-Rida then said, "Has this [speech] not been recognized as true among your people?" The Exilarch said, "Yes, but I would like it if you would prove its truth to me from the Torah [itself]." So al-Rida said to him, "Do you deny that the Torah says to you, 'The light came from Mt. Sinai [Jabal Tur Sina] and shone on us from Mt. Seir [Jabal Saʿir] and became clear to us from Mt. Paran [Jabal Faran]'?" The Exilarch said, "I know these words but I do not know their interpretation." Al-Rida said, "I shall tell you [its interpretation]: as for its saying, 'The light came from Mt. Sinai,' that refers to the revelation of God, who sent the revelation to Moses on Mt. Sinai. As for its saying, 'And shone on us from Mt. Seir,' that saying refers to the mountain on which God revealed himself to Jesus, and Jesus was on that mountain. As for its saying, 'And beame clear to us from Mount Paran,' that refers to one of the mountains of Mecca, a day's distance from Mecca.

"Shaya [Isaiah?] the Prophet said in Torah (concerning what you and your companions are saying), 'I saw two riders. [God] illuminated the earth for them, one of them riding an ass and the other on a camel.' Who is the one riding the ass? Who is the one riding the camel?" The Exilarch said, "I do not know these two, so you tell me who they are." Al-Rida said, "As for the rider on the ass, he is Jesus; as for the rider on the camel, he is Muhammad. Can you deny that that is from the Torah?" The Exilarch said, "No, I cannot deny it."

Then the Imam said, "Do you know Habakuk the Prophet?" The Exilarch said, "Yes, I am knowledgable concerning him." Then al-Rida said, "[Habakuk] said— and your Book says this: 'God brought an explanation from Mt. Paran, and the skies were filled with the praising of Ahmad and his community, and He bears aloft His host on the sea as He bears them aloft on the land. He shall bring us a new book after the Destruction of the Temple'—that is, the Book, the Qur'an: Do you recognize it and have faith in it?" The Exilarch said, "Habakuk has said that, and we cannot deny his words."

The Imam said, "David has said in his Psalms which you recite, 'O God, send one to raise up the tradition after an interval!' And do you know a prophet who raised up the tradition after an interval other than Muhammad?" The Exilarch said, "We give assent to these words of David and cannot deny them, but he means by this [saying to refer to] Jesus, and his days are the interval." Al-Rida said, "You are ignorant, for Jesus did not oppose the Sunna but had confirmed the Sunna of the Torah until God raised him up to Him, and in the Gospel it is written, 'The Son of Man goes out and the Paraclete comes after him, and his is the one who shall weaken the bonds, and he shall explain everything for you, and he shall testify to me as I testified to him. I came to you with metaphors, and he shall come to you with their interpretations.' Don't you believe that that is in the Gospel?" The Exilarch said, "Yes, I cannot deny it."

Al-Rida said, "O Exilarch, can I ask you about your prophet, Moses b. ʿAmran?" The Exilarch said, "Ask." Al-Rida said, "What is the proof by which Moses' prophethood was established?" The Jew said, "He brought what no prophet before him brought." Al-Rida said, "Like what?" The Exilarch said, "Like the splitting of the [Red] Sea; and the transforming of his staff into a snake which moved; and striking the rock from which springs burst forth; and drawing forth his hand white for all to see; and signs the likes of which men are not capable of." The Imam said, "You are correct. If the reason for his prophethood is that he brought the likes of which men are not capable, and if you do not deny that everyone who claims that he is a prophet and then brings the likes of which men are not capable, then [mustn't that person] necessarily receive your assent [as to his authenticity]?" The Exilarch said, "No, because Moses possessed no equal in his relationship to his Lord and his closeness to Him, and it is not necessary for us to confirm the prophethood of one who claims it until he brings such signs [of prophethood] as he brought." Al-Rida said, "And how do you confirm the prophets who had come before Moses who did not divide the sea; and did not split the rock with twelve springs; and whose hand was not drawn out white like the drawing out of the white hand of Moses; and did not transform the staff to a moving serpent?" The Exilarch replied, "I have already related that when they brought forward the claim of their prophethoods in the way of signs the likes of which mankind is not capable, and even if they brought what Moses did not bring or were different [signs] than what Moses brought, then we must affirm their veracity." Al-Rida said, "O Exilarch, what stops you from affirming Jesus, who had revived the dead; and who cured the blind and the leper; and who created from clay something of the form of a bird and then breathed into it and it became a bird by the permission of God?" The Exilarch said, "They say that he did it, but we did not eyewitness it." Al-Rida said, "Are you trying to tell me that [regarding] the signs which Moses brought, you did personally eyewitness it? Were they not simply recounted in the traditions from the authoritative transmitters of the companions of Moses that he performed thus?" The Exilarch said, "Indeed [yes]." Al-Rida said, "Similarly, the unbrokenly transmitted have come down to you concerning what Jesus did, so how can you confirm the veracity of Moses but not that of Jesus?" The Exilarch could not give an answer. Al-Rida said "Likewise is the case with Muhammad, and what he brought, and the case with every prophet which God sent, and among His signs is that he is Orphan, Poor, Shepherd, Day Laborer, who did not study any written document and who did not have recourse to a teacher, and then who came with Qur'an which contains tales of the prophets and their traditions letter by letter, and tales of prominent figures who were and who will subsist till the Day of Resurrection, and he would tell them their secret thoughts and what was done in their houses and would come with many signs without number." The Exilarch said, "To our way of thinking, the account of Jesus and that of Muhammad are not sound, nor is it permitted us to confirm the way in which they are not true." Al-Rida said, "The eyewitness who witnessed Jesus and Muhammad was a false witness?" The Exilarch could bring no reply.[73]

It seems reasonable to suggest that the sheer presence of exilarchs at the early Imami salons, depicted in this account, and especially their participa-

---

[73] Ibn Babuya, *Kitab al-Tauhid*, 417–41, for the full debate; 427–30, for the text of the rosh golah debate.

tion in some such interreligious disputations, could have lent itself to the forging of a certain common cause with the ʿAlid imams. This was apparently the case, I shall argue, at the Fatimid instance. ʿAbbasid and Fatimid dignitaries would have had reason for comparing themselves with each other favorably, at the expense of the caliph. Certainly for the anxious imams, who were striving for legitimacy, the presence of the Exilarchs, long settled into their official status, lent further impetus to the imams' long-standing inclination to analogize the two religious leaderships.

The Delay of Maghrib

The reiterated lists of parallels between Rafida and the Jews show that the Sunni community's well-known initial efforts to disengage itself from Jewish practices—the primordiality of the concern is reflected in the choice of early-first-century Shaʿbi as hadith transmitter—becomes conflated with criticisms of the reprehensible Shiʿite practices with which Jewish customs are literally equated. Leaving aside the precise extent to which any of the other positions on the list ascribed to either group has any historical basis, the accusation of the delay of the evening prayers is not inaccurate in connection with Jews and Shiʿites.

Jewish tradition has commemorated its own conflict over the time of the reiteration of the Shema in the evening with a certain pride of place. The first line of the first tractate (Berakhot) of the first order (Zeraʿim) of the Mishnah reads: "From what time do they begin to recite the Shema in the evening?"[74] The various disagreements over the mandating of the time of this recitation are then recorded in rabbinic tradition.[75] After centuries of debate over the content of the evening service—evidence from the Cairo Geniza shows that a variety of texts were still in use in the twelfth century—the rabbinic traditions concerning its timing were consolidated to confirm a specified, binding practice (with continuing variations according to exigence and national custom).[76] This canonization is recorded in the first great liturgical manual, the mid-ninth-century *Seder Rab Amran*.[77] After stating that the Shema of the evening service is to be recited only after the appearance of the stars—"[if] any man recites [the *Shema*] before the prescribed time, he has not fulfilled his

[74] *Berakhot* 1:1. See Blackman, *Mishnayoth*.
[75] This resulted in the deposal of Rabban Gamaliel II: see *Berakhot* (*Bavli*) 27b–28a. The Karaites, who pray two times daily, also varied in the setting of the times of prayer; see Goldberg, *Karaite Liturgy*, 1–5; he notes that "from the time of Aaron ben Joseph (second half of the thirteenth century), however, the Karaites held that the evening prayer (*arav*) can only be recited between sunset and darkness" (4 n. 3).
[76] Stefan Reif describes some of the textual variations in the evening service in "Liturgical Difficulties," esp. 116–17. And see Mann, "Genizah Fragments."
[77] Hedegard, *Seder Rav Amran*.

obligation"—the *siddur* [Jewish prayer book] adduces the talmudic proof-texts for the exact time:

> And how many stars should appear for it to be night? There is a Baraita: R. Nathan says: [As long as only] one star [is visible] it is daytime, [as long as only] two [are visible] it is twilight, (when there are) three it is night. And R. Jose ben Abin said: Not the great stars which appear by day nor the small stars which appear in the night, but the average stars.[78]

We can assume that from the earliest years of Islam their proximity to Jewish communities, Jewish conversion to Islam, and their direct consultation with Jewish scholars must all have sustained the Iraqi Muslim scholar's awareness that the Jewish practice was to wait till the stars were out before beginning the evening service. Perhaps it is due to this awareness that the Prophet's prognosticating the right path, the norm (*fitra*) for Muslim practice become modified in some collections with a phrase specifying the wrong path: the Jewish practice. "The Prophet said, 'My people will stay on the right path only so long as they do not postpone the *maghrib* in waiting for the advent of darkness, as do the Jews"; "My people will remain adhering [to Islam] so long as they do not . . . postpone the *maghrib* prayer till darkness, as in Judaism."[79]

As we have seen, Sunni tradition explicitly condemns the delay of the maghrib as a kind of Judaizing practice, and also condemns certain leaders who allegedly tried to lead the community in such a practice. In lists of linkages with other practices, this practice was later also condemned as a Rafidi observance. Imami fiqh, in fact, also establishes the same timing of the evening prayer as the Sunnis do.[80] It is therefore not entirely surprising to discover that Shi'ite sources also consider this practice unacceptable and curse those held responsible for proposing it. But these culprits, according to the imamis, are neither Jews nor Umayyad leaders, but rather certain "extremists" (ghulat) from the "proto-Shi'ite activist period" (the periodization is that of Watt).

According to authoritative imami traditions, the delay of the evening prayer was enjoined upon the people of Kufa by Abu 'l-Khattab (d. ca. 143/760), eponymous "founder" of the Khattabiyya, sometimes listed in the heresiographies as among the ghulat, sometimes among the Rafida.[81] The

---

[78] Ibid., 162. See also L. Levi, "Astronomical Aspects," 251–63.

[79] Al-Zurqani, *Sharh Muwatta'* 1:32. For more on the development of the prayer periods in Islamic tradition, see Rubin, "Morning and Evening Prayers," 40–65. Rubin's work on the *salat al-ʿasr* (esp. 53–56), for example, is complementary to mine on the *maghrib* prayer period.

[80] Ibn al-Hasan al-Tusi, *Tahdhib al-Ahkam* 2:27–35. More generally, see Kister, "Do Not Assimilate," 321–71.

[81] Ibn Qutayba lists the Ghaliya and the Khattabiya among the Rafida: see Watt, *Formative Period*, 61–62. Al-Nawbakhti includes the Khattabiyya as among the ghulat: see al-Nawbakhti, *Firaq al-Shi'ah*, 73–78, 148–50.

bulk of the reports on Abu 'l-Khattab in the biographical dictionaries deal
with his falling-out with and excommunication by Jaʿfar al-Sadiq (ca. 700–
756), the sixth imam, but one of his practices is always singled out for stric-
ture: the delay of the evening prayer. The Fatimid Ismaʿili jurist Qadi
al-Nuʿman (d. 974) gives the most complete single report on the conflict
between these two over this issue:

> It is related that the Prophet said, "When night comes from this side, and he
> pointed with this hand toward the East (then is the time to begin the prayer)." Abu
> 'l-Khattab, God's curse be upon him, was listening to Jaʿfar as he was saying "If the
> redness has fallen below this point—and pointed with his hand to the East—then is
> the time of sunset prayer." Whereas Abu 'l-Khattab said to this companions, when
> he brought the major deviation which he brought [i.e., his deification of Jaʿfar],
> "The time of the prayer at sunset is the disappearance of the redness from the
> *western* horizon; therefore, do not pray maghrib till the stars shine brightly." They
> brought this to Jaʿfar's attention, at which he cursed Abu 'l-Khattab for it, and
> cursed Abu 'l-Khattab saying, "He who intentionally leaves off saying the evening
> prayer till the stars shine brightly, I will have nothing to do with him."[82]

This is clearly an attempt to portray Abu 'l-Khattab as slavishly extending
Jaʿfar's refinement of Muhammad's practice.

It is perhaps after Jaʿfar had been informed of Abu 'l-Khattab's heretical
teaching that the imam was forced personally to direct the extremist in the
proper procedure. "Jaʿfar ordered Abu 'l-Khattab to pray maghrib only at the
time of the disappearance of the redness at the time of the sun's beginning to
set, for he thus located (in the western horizon) the redness which is before
the actual sunset, and would accordingly pray so at the time of the disappearance of that twilight."[83] But just as the extremist claimed a divinity for
the sixth imam, which Jaʿfar repudiated, so did Abu 'l-Khattab—according to
the "official" version—claim that Jaʿfar had commanded this innovative practice. "Jaʿfar said, 'As for Abu 'l-Khattab, he lied about me, saying that I commanded him and his followers not to pray maghrib till they see stars in the
sky."[84]

As believers came to the imam perplexed over the variations in practice, he
gave them reasons for his own teaching. "A man said to Jaʿfar, 'Shall I postpone the maghrib till the stars shine?' He replied, 'Are you one of the Khattabiyya? For Gabriel came down to the Prophet at the time when the disc of
the sun was sinking below the horizon [i.e., that time was good enough for
Gabriel].'"[85]

There must have been many such ʿAlid loyalists in the Kufa of the 750s. Ibn

[82] My translation, from Al-Nuʿman ibn Muhammad Abu Hanifa, *Daaʾim al-Islam*
1:168; repeated in al-Majlisi, *Bihar al-Anwar* 83:70 n. 44.
[83] Al-Majlisi, *Bihar al-Anwar* 83:56 no. 8.
[84] Al-Tustari, *Qamus al-Rijal* 8:402.
[85] One of the most frequently cited traditions on this conflict: see al-Kashshi, *Rijal al-Kashshi*, 247; al-Tusi, *Tahdhib* 2:32 no. 98, 49; al-Majlisi, *Bihar al-Anwar*, 83:65, no.
29. See also "Djabraʾil," in *Encyclopedia of Islam*, 2d ed.

Hazm places the number of Khattabiyya in the thousands, while Twelver traditions record an apprently wide acceptance among the Kufans: "Abu 'l-Khattab corrupted the ʿamma [not the "common folk" here, but the Sunni majority] so that they began not praying the maghrib till the disappearance of twilight. . . . A man asked Imam al-Rida, 'How could Jaʿfar say what he said about Abu 'l-Khattab [i.e., his earlier disapproval of him] and then proclaim his disavowal of him?' He replied, 'Is it for Jaʿfar to install someone and not to displace him?'"[86]

Once Jaʿfar had deposed Abu 'l-Khattab, for reasons of theology as well as ritual, the breakaway leader and his low-status followers were summarily dismissed by the imam: "Beware of these lowlife [safala] and watch out for these lowlife, for I have proscribed Abu 'l-Khattab because he did not submit to my command."[87] Imamite tradition has forever vilified Abu 'l-Khattab for his divergence from the example of the sixth imam. In a canonical Twelver collection from the tenth century, Jaʿfar apodictically pronounces his position against the schismatic: "Jaʿfar al-Sadiq said, 'Accursed, accursed is the one who postpones the evening prayer in seeking to accrue credit for doing so.' It was said to him that the people of Iraq postpone the evening prayer till the shining of the stars, to which he replied, 'This is the practice of Abu'l-Khattab, the enemy of God.'"[88]

IMAMI SHIʿISM AND RABBINIC JUDAISM IN COMPARISON

It lies outside the scope of the present work to undertake a comparison of Muslim and Jewish law. Such a comparison, fortunately, has been accomplished in accessible locations.[89] It is worthwhile, however, to note that a synchronic comparison between the system of imami (Twelver) jurisprudence and that of rabbinic Judaism could yield some significant results.

Both understand themselves as ultimately transitional systems, predicated, as Scholem puts it, on "a life lived in deferment."[90] On the one hand, the imami concept of occultation (*ghayba*) and, on the other, the rabbinic doc-

[86] Al-Kashshi, *Rijal*, 249; repeated with slight variations in al-Tusi, *Tahdhib*; and al-Majlisi, *Bihar al-Anwar*, which repeats Kashshi's version.
[87] Al-Kashshi, *Rijal*, 250.
[88] Babuya, *Man la Yahduruh al-Faqih*, 1:142 no. 660, no. 15.
[89] Standard works and specialized studies address this complex comparison in greater or lesser detail. For a sampling, see Rosenthal, *Judaism and Islam*, pt. 1, "Judaism in Islam," 1–49; Goitein, *Jews and Arabs*, chap. 4, "The Jewish Tradition," 46–62; Lazarus-Yafeh, "Judeo-Arabic Culture," 101–10, at 102–6; Lazarus-Yafeh, "Some Differences," 175–91; Brinner and Ricks, *Studies in Islamic and Judaic Traditions*, pt. 2, "Religion and Law," 65–151; Brunschvig, "Voeu ou serment?"; Goitein, "Interplay of Jewish and Islamic Laws," 61–78; and Meron, "Points de contact," 83–119. A book-length bibliography of specialized studies on this subject could and should be compiled.
[90] Scholem, *Messianic Idea*, 35.

trine of exile (*galut*) undergird the fabrication of law during a tentative cosmic dispensation, a world always verging on dissolution. Abdulaziz Sachedina uses the term *Messianism* to refer to the protracted Twelver Shiʿi anticipation of the coming Qaʾim and the Expected Imam.[91] One would like to learn more concerning the fructifying legal role of parallel notions of pre-Messianic stewardship in the respective development of Jewish and Twelver Shiʿism as religions of law.

Specific elements of the rabbinic and Twelver systems of jurisprudence, indeed, could be compared usefully. Explicit designation (*nass*), so well analyzed by Sachedina, may bear close comparison with rabbinic ordination (*semikha*).[92] Respective crises of designation/ordination would be particularly instructive to compare. Furthermore, Sachedina calls the Twelver rite of pilgrimage (*ziyara*) "covenant renewal."[93] Twelver Shiʿism and rabbinism may both be considered systems of covenant renewal. Significantly, Twelver tradition itself asserts that the Children of Israel (Banu Israʾil) were rightly guided by their own legists,[94] demonstrating that Twelver leadership was aware of analogies with rabbinic Judaism.

Finally, I shall compare the authority vested in the institutions of the imamate and the rabbinate. Like the authority of the rabbis, the notion of jurisprudential *saltana* (power) was forged under intermittent but often seemingly interminable conditions of oppression. What we do not yet have, it seems to me, is an application of political and social thought concerning the respective development of these persistently oppressed communities, especially in relation to the notion of power.[95] With regard to Shiʿism, a tradition in which power and its deleterious consequences generated theory so primally, the absence of reflection by social theorists does a disservice to that long-oppressed tradition. We need critical social theory, that is, to fully understand Twelver Shiʿites' massively muffled dissimulation (*taqiyya*) and their soteriologically validated "life lived in deferment" as being in part methodical expressions of built-in millennialist frustration.

Sachedina has shown, as perhaps no scholar before him, that the theory of authority in Twelver jurisprudence evolved not in the vacuum of rarified scholasticism but in muscular interaction with other social forces. As this developing system encountered ghulat, Zaydis, Ismaʿilis, Buyids, Safavids, and Qajars, it was progressively modified. Its theoretical self-modifications were

---

[91] Sachedina, *Islamic Messianism*.
[92] Sachedina, *Just Ruler*, 83–83, 98–99, 173. For a collection of papers (from a Reform perspective) relative to *semikha*, see Elliot Stevens, *Rabbinic Authority*.
[93] Sachedina, *Just Ruler*, 79.
[94] For a ruling of Najafi and commentary by Sachedina, see Sachedina, *Just Ruler*, 208–9. Najafi concludes that "if a *faqih* who is appointed by the Imam on the basis of general permission is appointed a *sultan* or *hakim* for the people of Islam, there will be no unjust rulers, as was the case with the Children of Israel" (208).
[95] An exception is Biale, *Power and Powerlessness*. Dabashi, *Authority in Islam* is not recommended.

constructed, heroically and intractably, by a social group. This persistent encroachment of legal scholars into the center of the imami power structure, an intellectual elite gradually enacting the self-legitimation of its own class by means of its characteristic control of authoritative exegesis, extended their reach into the center of imami practice as such. This success bears the closest comparison with the history of the rabbinate, especially that of early modern times. In both cases, this process was preceded by a glacially patient seizure of power—a regularly extended and self-perpetuating discourse on rightly guided authority, which led to the seat of practical hegemony: a cathedra, in fact, that they created for themselves.

These reflections particularly are apt for the present juncture in the study of religion. A fundamental rethinking of religiopolitical authority is characteristic of the present stage of social thought, a time in which both imams and rabbis have retaken the stage of history. This unanticipated development, of course, itself directly catalyzed the present perplexity of social theory, for the return of religion has caused untold consternation for social theorists. Until very recently, social scientists almost wholly had subscribed to variants of Weberian modernization theory, which predicated the progressive disestablishment of religious authority. It is worth recalling that in the early post–World War II period, the leading historian of "enthusiasm" reasonably could speculate that emotional appeals in religion would soon become a thing of the past:

> Account for it how we will, by the less general diffusion of religious sentiment, by the decline in fundamentalism, by the modern educational outlook, by the influence of radio's oratorical technique, it is clear that our fellow countrymen are less susceptible, in these days, to the emotional appeal. Perhaps it is a closed chapter, this chapter in the history of religions.[96]

By 1980, barely a generation later, such speculation was obsolete. In the now-famed observations of Mary Douglas, "Events have taken religious studies by surprise. . . . None credited the traditional religions with enough vitality to inspire large-scale political revolt. . . . Thus no one foretold the resurgence of Islam. . . . Religious studies were taken unaware because of the rigid structure of their assumptions." Nor was religious studies alone caught unaware. "In no case was the success of fundamentalist groups, Jewish or non-Jewish, anticipated by social scientists. On the contrary, the revival of rigorous religious belief and practice has challenged reigning notions of 'modernity' prevalant until the last decade." The sudden and wholesale collapse of such thinking has led Robert Wuthnow to conclude that "modernization theory is, on the whole, a lot like late Ptolemaic conceptions of the solar system."[97]

---

[96] Knox, *Enthusiasm*, 578.
[97] Douglas, "Effects of Modernization," 1–21, at 1; Leibman, *Deceptive Images*, 45; Wuthnow, "Understanding Religion and Politics" (1–21), and the citation is drawn from a section titled "Modernization Theory and Its Collapse" (2–5).

In short, social reality has reminded social thinkers that a coming world, a telos, hangs over the rationalization process. We should not have been shocked, for Messianic foreshadowing always has hovered like a harbinger angel over historical change. Revelations' promise of a perfected end has always required historical development to be understood by believers as necessary fore-appearance, as preparation. Authority in both Twelver Shiʿism and rabbinism thus must remain (fictively) provisional, and concomitantly must operate as a trajectory to the Messianic. History becomes apocalypse—in both senses, as an end and as a revelation—in slow motion. All the while, as legal authority arrogates practical rationality into its jurisdiction, it slows down the anabasis past the clouds to the mountain itself, where truth "breaks forth from the 'illusions of development.'"[98] History becomes apocalypse means, more ex-actly, that history is utilized to co-opt apocalypse, to slow its coming, to ward it off; history is used as a deferral of apocalypse. Northrop Frye thus notes the outlook of the Book of Revelation: "Man creates what he calls history as a screen to conceal the workings of the apocalypse from himself." The provi-sional law interpreter can never replace the omniscient *angelus interpretes*: "The coincidentia oppositorum, which Cusa in *De visione Dei* called 'the wall of paradise behind which dwells God,' does not materialize this side of the screen."[99] The deferral of eschatological finality, in short, accompanies the practical reason that won jurists their center of power inside history.

But now that their effective power is recognized (albeit belatedly) by theo-rists of society, and precisely at a time when practical reason would seem to have eclipsed other spheres of reason, an apocalyptic irony obtrudes. For in a temporal lag—which led previous generations of social scientists to count them out—imami and rabbinic legists all along were interiorizing rationaliza-tion, just one step removed from the pace of the social sphere at large. Their "return" is, then, not a relic of another time but a product of our own. The present Twelver reappropriation of Iranian society itself, an appropriation not for mere postmodern ends but for fully posthistorical ends, toward the ulti-mately just rule of the Mahdi himself, reflects developments akin to those also occurring within Judaism. The extent to which these apparently parallel de-velopments were determined by an original symbiosis remains a question for scholarship fully to investigate.

JEWS AND THE ORIGINS OF ISMAʿILI SHIʿISM

Bernard Lewis set the tone for further analyses of Ismaʿili interconfessional-ism in his groundbreaking dissertation of 1940, *The Origins of Ismailism*. In-sofar as his assertion of Ismaʿili interconfessionalism was based primarily on

[98] See the introduction for this phrase in Scholem, "Candid Word," 32.
[99] Frye, *Great Code*. 136; Kracauer, *History*, 202.

the evidence of the *Rasa'il Ikhwan al-Safa'*, this hypothesis has not been challenged. A consensus remains in place that the Ikhwan al-Safa' "did in fact profess a philosophy of religious toleration and tried to demonstrate the harmony of all the different religious doctrines and practices."[100] However, S. M. Stern, the author of this observation, has challenged Lewis's supposition of an early Isma'ili "interconfessionalism." Stern charges that more detailed studies now show that "while the society of the Ikhwan grew, no doubt, out of Isma'ilism, they far outgrew it [with regard to an initial interconfessionalism]."[101]

Stern, then, attempted to refute Lewis's reading of the early Isma'ili movement as being essentially irenic in orientation. Stern contended, by contrast, that there was absolutely no sign of an [Isma'ili] attitude toward other religion which could be characterized as deviating in principle from the common opinion of Islam." Stern, in support of his case, points out texts which do indeed demonstrate that Isma'ili missionaries utilized the scriptures of targeted communities in their propaganda—but with the modifying caveat that "in this matter Isma'ilism added nothing to that which was practised by orthodox Islam."[102]

I believe that Stern has rather missed the mark, if we are to judge from the widest available range of evidence concerning what, justifiably, may be termed "Judeo-Isma'ilism." The Isma'ili appeal to Jews went deeper than a merely sophisticated wielding of chapter and verse in public *majalis* (audiences). This is not to vindicate "official Isma'ilism," whose attitude toward foreign religions Stern has adequately characterized. However—and without attempting to establish an even more problematic dichotomy between "official" and "unofficial" Isma'ilism—I follow a growing body of scholarship which demonstrates that a certain interconfessional convergence of Judaism and Isma'ilism did indeed occur. I shall now sketch the main outlines of this scholarship.

This "convergence of two oceans" (*majmu' al-bahrain*) may be most lucidly perceived with—to vary the metaphor—the binocular vision of the comparativist. The two counterposed and, and I would argue, interactive aspects of this convergence may be crudely termed "Judaizing Isma'ilism" and "Isma'ilizing Judaism." To be sure, the analysis of such a phenomenon—bearing, as it does, instructive analogies to the notoriously difficult problems concerning "Judaizing Christians" and "Jewish Christians"—is nevertheless warranted by the phenomenon. I shall therefore briefly discuss both in sequence. Before I can do so, however, I must review the evidence for the Jewish role played in the origins of Isma'ilism.

---

[100] Lewis, *Origins of Ismailism*. And see also "Legend of the Jewish Origin" on the origins of the Fatimid dynasty.
[101] S. Stern, *Early Isma'ilism*, 85–86.
[102] Ibid, 86, 95.

The Yemen and Kufa in Shiʿite Origins

The role of Jews in the origins of Shiʿism may be located as a subset of the role played by Yemenites in the boomtown of Kufa. The "South Arabian" hypothesis first put forth by Watt holds that "the core of the early Shiʿa was in south Arabian or Yemenite tribes."[103] Most recently, Rubin has attempted to show that of those "who tried to establish the veneration for the Shiʿi heroes on Judaeo-Christian models, the ʿIraqi Arabs of southern (Yemenite) descent [were] some of the earliest among them."[104] Baron's survey of the the evidence lead him to conclude, "the Jewish community [of early Kufa], growing by leaps and bounds, contributed greatly to the city's intellectual and economic life."[105] The presence of Israʾiliyyat traditions in early imami traditions, much of it stemming from heavily ʿAlid-loyalist Kufa, has been discussed in several recent studies.[106] Thus, Rubin similarly concludes that "the Shiʿa seems to be responsible for the main flow of Judaeo-Christian motifs into the Muslim literature already since the first century A.H."[107]

Three waves of early Shiʿism, in particular, bear what appear to be marks of some kind of "Judaizing" at some uncertain point in their respective developments. In each case, these movements—if they can sensibly be termed "movements"—can be linked to the formative wave of Yemenites who participated in the construction of ʿAlid loyalism based, primarily, at Umayyad Kufa. I refer, then, to (1) the Sabaʾiyya, (2) the Mukhtariyya, and (3) the ghulat proper.

The findings of recent scholarship concerning the Sabaʾiyya make clear that, whether or not we link the Sabaʾiyya with Jews, they were certainly the first proto-Shiʿite ghulat group; did indeed derive from the Yemen; were instrumental in ʿAlid activism centered in Kufa; and were early accused of Judaizing.[108] This tells us that a genuinely early Yemenite impact on the self-definition of Shiʿism was also perceived as having some Judaic connection.

Other evidence supports the postulation of a noticeable Jewish presence in early Kufa. I have already dealt with the relation between the Mansuriyya and the ʿIsawiyya. I would note that this connection might be explained in part by the fact that Isfahan served as an administrative satellite (*thagr*) of Kufa.[109] Other ghulat also betray some possible Jewish traces. Some of the sectarian continuators of Abu ʾl-Khattab betray some apparent Judaizing tendencies.

---

[103]Watt, "Shiʿism under the Umayyads," 158–72. See also Morony's characterization of the "South Arabian explanation" in *Iraq*, 652. What would seem to be important corroborating data is gathered by Djaït, "Les Yamanites," 148–81.
[104] Rubin, "Prophets and Progenitors," 63.
[105] Baron, *Social and Religious History* 3:89.
[106] See above, chapter 2.
[107] Rubin, "Prophets and Progenitors."
[108] See abover, chapter 2.
[109] Djaït, "Kufa."

One group followed al-Sari, who his followers alleged was called "Moses, the Strong and the Trustworthy" by Ja'far al-Sadiq. The same group also claimed to be the Children of Islam "as the Jews were the Children of God." In the opinion of Ivanow, "there is a certain flavour of Judaism in the ideas of this branch."[110]

Another argument for the possibility of Jewish activity in Kufa concerns the great legist Abu Hanifah. According to Rabbanite sources, the Karaite heresiarch 'Anan b. David reconciled himself with the caliph who had jailed him by changing his mensal calculation to direct observation of the moon.[111] Here a mid-eighth-century sectarian from the Jazirah adopts the majority Muslim practice of waiting till direct celestial confirmation. This constitutes a striking inversion of the case of Abu 'l-Khattab, a mid-eighth-century sectarian from the Jazirah who adopted the Jewish practice of direct celestial confirmation.[112]

'Anan was reportedly advised to thus change his practice by his jailmate, Abu Hanifah (80–150).[113] Founder of the Hanafite line of jurisprudence and a Kufan student of Sha'bi, Abu Hanifah may have had some impact on the jurisprudence of 'Anan. Indeed, Goitein and Lewis have noted a possible Jewish background of Abu Hanifah himself.[114] In this light, Abu Hanifah's unusually lenient attitude to Jews and Christians seems all the more provocative. Of the four great jurists, he alone ruled that failure to pay the poll tax did not deprive the *dhimmi* (member of a tolerated minority, i.e., either a Jew or a Christian) of protection; that the dhimmi could enter the *haram* (sanctuary); that a dhimmi could enter the mosque without special permission; and that a Muslim must be executed for murdering a dhimmi.[115]

All this admittedly circumstantial evidence would seem to suggest, at least, a milieu in the Kufa of Abu Hanifah, al-Sha'bi, and Abu 'l-Khattab in which Jewish practice might have been accessible to some sectarians. To this evidence I would add a last conjectural connection, that of esoteric traditions. Perhaps the most compelling such evidence concerns the apparent impact of Jewish mystical and mythic imagery and practice in Umayyad Kufa. The evidence was originally submitted by Friedlaender. Tucker, Halm, van Ess, and I have subsequently amplified this material, which, evocative as it is, remains murky.[116] Thus, for example allegedly original Jewish texts, such as *Shi'ur*

---

[110] Ivanow, *Ibn al-Qaddah*, 107.

[111] Nemoy ensconced a consensus of skepticism concerning this report; see "'Anan."

[112] See my study of the delay of the maghrib prayer in this chapter.

[113] Harkavy, "Anan, der Stifter," 107–22, for a summary of arguments for Hanfaite influences. Poznanski, "Anan et ses écrits," 161–87, at 167 n. 2, and 168. Zucker, in *Saadia Gaon's Translation of the Torah*, supports the story's veracity (149). So too does Baron (*Social and Religious History* 5:388 n. 1).

[114] Goitein, "Jewish Society and Institutions," 171. See Lewis's footnote to Goldziher, *Introduction of Islamic Theology and Law*, 53, note f.

[115] Tritton, *The Caliphs and Their Non-Muslim Subjects*, 16, 17, 176, 177, and 179.

[116] See van Ess, "Youthful God," 12–13, where he cites my materials on the Khattabiyya and the Jews in Kufa.

Qomah, are cited as "sources" for ghulat anthropomorphic myth.[117] But these works are neither certainly dated nor subtly differentiated by formal criteria. The "Jewishness" of ghulat Gnosis, in short, remains to be demonstrated definitively. The evidence that does exist, however, is sufficient for me to agree, at least tentatively, with the recent conclusion of van Ess: "Was Islam, then, the continuation of Judaism, as has been suggested anew in recent studies? Perhaps in Kufa, but only there; in other places the constellation was different."[118]

ORIGINS OF ISMAʿILIS AND FATIMIDS

The arguments for the Judaic role in the origins of Ismaʿilism and the Fatimids have been successfully dismissed by Lewis and Ivanow.[119] This "Jewish legend" laid blame for the establishment of the heterodox empire at the feet of one Maimun al-Qaddah. If Jews are not "to blame" for the origins of the Ismaʿilis or of the Fatimids, we are still left with a historiographic dilemma. The problem is that, as I have tried to show, Jews were indeed (somehow) present, as converts, models, or paradigms, in the original imagination of Shiʿites, as the ʿAlid loyalists were constructing their tradition in Kufa. Likewise, as I shall now show, subsequent Shiʿite tradition retained a living link with Jews, through the mediation of the Sevener Shiʿites, the Ismaʿili tradition.

The question, then, that presents itself concerns the precise role of Ismaʿilism in Judaizing, while other forms of Shiʿism quickly cast off any connections whatsoever with Jews.

HERMETICISM AND NEOPLATONISM

Hermeticism and Neoplatonism were popular among Jewish philosophers and mystics. Some years ago Kraus demonstrated the relationship between the alchemy of Jabir ibn Hayyan and *Sefer Yesira*. Another important hermetic work on which Kraus fruitfully worked was the *Secret of Creation*.[120] It now turns out that this hermetic apocryphon was translated into Hebrew.[121] Yet another Neoplatonic pseudepigraph, *Pseudo-Empedocles*, was widely read by Jews. David Kaufmann showed its impact on ibn Gabirol.[122]

Of all Neoplatonic and hermetic works that were studied by Jews, *The*

[117] See my "The Moving Finger."
[118] Van Ess, "Youthful God," 12–13.
[119] Lewis, *Origins of Ismailism* on the "Jewish Legend" of the origins of the Fatimid dynasty, 67–69.
[120] See my detailed treatment in *"Sefer Yesira."*
[121] Plessner, "Balinus," 994–95 (see p. 994 for a Hebrew translation of this work).
[122] Kaufmann, "Pseudo-Empedokles."

Theology of Aristotle may have had the biggest impact.[123] In a recent study, Paul Fenton has argued that the long recension of *The Theology of Aristotle* may have been made by a "Jewish Neoplatonic circle" in Fatimid Egypt.[124] It is also relevant to note that this work may have played some role in the Kabbalism of Azriel of Gerona and of the related early Kabbalah circles.[125]

RASA'IL IKHWAN AL-SAFA'

Having briefly surveyed the available evidence for the common milieu in which Jews may have played some role in formative Isma'ilism, I shall now complete this overview with what little we know of Jewish Isma'ilism. In other words, having glanced at Judaizing Isma'ilism, I would now like to touch on Isma'ilizing Judaism. Like so much of this material, the evidence for Isma'ilizing Judaism is tantalizingly suggestive and frustratingly fragmentary. I have already mentioned the (somewhat problematic) evidence of (sometimes apocryphal) Jewish converts active in formation of Isma'ilism. These include the (probably apocryphal) Maimun ibn al-Qaddah, the Fatimid vizier Ibn Killis, and perhaps even the Central Asian *da'i* (missionary) al-Kirmani. Goldziher even suggested that one or more Jewish converts cooperated with the Ikhwan al-Safa'—a group closely associated with early Isma'ilism—in the authorship of that collective work.[126]

Aside from these possibly Isma'ilized Jews, the evidence for the Isma'ilizing of Jews largely concerns influence in matters of philosophical theology. In this connection it is appropriate to begin with the Ikhwan al-Safa', the Sincere Brethren.[127] Their esoteric Isma'ilism encouraged a broadly eclectic brand of what may be deemed "Gnostic ecumenicism." If they had a clandestine ax to grind, it was one of many edges. They seem sincerely to have held not that some unspecified creed was "the best," but rather that the divergences between religious believers was an "evidence of divine wisdom, a providential dispensation (*hikma*)."[128]

As with their approach to phenomena in general, the *Rasa'il Ikhwan al-Safa'* (*RIS*) addressed the topic of "world religions" by a systematic review of them.[129] This "comprehensivist" or "encyclopedist" reflex can be found in

---

[123] Wasserstrom, "Social and Cultural."

[124] Fenton, "Arabic and Hebrew Versions"

[125] Heller-Wilensky, "The 'First Crafted Thing.'"

[126] Goldziher, "Le Moutakallim," 414–15.

[127] Netton, *Muslim Neoplatonists*; Marquet, *La Philosophie des Ihwan al-Safa'*; Diwald-Wilzer, *Arabische Philosophie*; Bausani, *L'Enciclopedia dei Fratelli*.

[128] Netton, *Muslim Neoplatonists*, 95.

[129] Marquet, "Les Ikhwan al-Safa'," 129–58, at 129: "tous les objets de connaissance de l'époque y sont passés en revue méthodiquement" (all the objects of knowledge of the epoch are methodically passed on review). On encyclopedism in Muslim scholarship, see Shboul, *Al-Mas'udi*, 92 n. 180, and the discussions in Paret, "Contribution à

most branches of Islamicate literature (discussed in chapter 4 below). The *RIS*'s Judaism, however, was not that of the Jewish tradition, but that of the Muslim; the *RIS* address not Jews, but the Qur'anic and traditional imagery of an Abrahamic cousin. The Brethren could thus espouse the notion that theirs was the *milla* (religion) of Abraham, without ever encountering Judaism. Christianity, Hermeticism, science, and magic were all, if one may so put it, ideologies holding a considerable attraction for the "comprehensive" *RIS*. Judaism was not. Consequently, their treatment of the kinds of Jews simply further distorts the already polemical portrait of a merely notionally consanguinary family relation.

The *RIS* stand out among Muslim heresiological depictions of Judaism for their unusual portrayal of the diversity of religions not merely as occasions to exercise the ingenuity of their dialectics, but as *preparatio* for their own consummative system. Less interested in refutation than in a useful subordination to their own ends, the *RIS* could do little more than merely name the Jewish sects in their discussion of intra-Judaic pluralism. Ostensibly more "sympathetic" to the manifold expressions of communal diversity, in practice they saw these different religions, much as did their overtly polemical colleagues, as mere names to be manipulated when appropriate to their own purposes.[130]

It would seem, therefore, all the more extraordinary that *RIS* proved popular among Jews. But one need only glance at the introduction to Husik's (outmoded) *History of Mediaeval Jewish Philosophy* to see how long this popularity has been well known: "In turn such Jewish writers as Ibn Gabirol, Bahya, Ibn Zaddik, Judah Halevi, Moses and Abraham Ibn Ezra, were much indebted to the Brethren of Purity."[131] However, Husik's list represents a specifically Andalusian tradition of Jewish philosophy, which was indeed philosophical. The Gnosticizing elements of the *RIS* appealed less in the West. These more explicitly mythical materials were, however, picked up by those Eastern Jewish authors who wrote philosophical theology.[132]

> However we evaluate the Jewish influences on Shi'ites or Isma'ilis under Islam, Nestorians or iconoclasts in Byzantium and Albigensians or Passagi in the West, the very fact that [Jews] persisted in their different beliefs and interpretations of the Bible, as well as in their diverse rituals and modes of living, served as a stimulant to religious-minded individuals to rethink their own positions.[133]

---

l'étude," 47–100; Pellat "Les encyclopédies dans le monde arabe," 631–58. Von Grunebaum devoted much energy to this question; See, for example, "Sources of Islamic Civilization," 1–54; and "Muslim World-View," 111–26.

[130] See my discussion in "Species of Misbelief," 115–19.

[131] Husik, *Mediaeval Jewish Philosophy*, xxxix. Subsequent research tends to support the argument that Jews participated in the circles around the formation of *RIS*: F. Rosenthal, "A Jewish Philosopher of the Tenth Century," 162 n. 16, that the Jewish philosopher Wahb ibn Ya'ish took part in these circles.

[132] For example, Hoter ben Shelomo. See David Blumenthal, *Commentary*.

[133] Baron, *Social and Religious History*, 5:136.

ISMAʿILI MISSIONARIES AND JUDAIZING ISMAʿILISM

Early Ismaʿili missionaries utilized Jewish materials sometimes which could have been transmitted only by willing Jews. Such limited Judaizing is evident in the works of such tenth-century missionaries as Abu Hatim al-Razi, al-Kirmani, and Jaʿfar ibn Mansur al-Yamani. It must first be admitted that this Judaizing was not the only receptivity to foreign religions apparent in these somewhat syncretistic thinkers. However, the fact that it was not so provides a key to the specific phenomenon of Judaizing. As Halm has demonstrated, the earliest Ismaʿilis somehow came to learn, orally or textually, the teachings of various Gnostic groups whose identities have yet to be established.[134] Shiʿi revolutionary thinkers, indeed, largely were responsible for what I have called the re-Abrahamization of Gnosis. Thus rescripturalized, Gnosis could then more acceptably burrow back into the teachings of other Peoples of the Book (ahl al-Kitab). Gnosticizing Shiʿis provided a halfway house, so to speak, for Gnostic teachings in their peregrinations back to a kind of reconcilation with revealed religion. I have tried to show that that it was by means of such Shiʿitizing intermediaries that a re-Abrahamized Gnosis was readmitted into rabbinic Judaism, in *Sefer Yesira* and *Sefer ha-Bahir*.[135]

The Judaizing of the early Ismaʿili missionaries must therefore be set into a generally Gnosticizing framework. Unfortunately, while we know something of the Gnosis of these missionaries, through the efforts of Ivanow, Corbin, Stern, Halm and others, we know very little of their lives.[136] Therefore, neither Poonawala's otherwise extensive *Biobibliography of Ismaʿili Literature* nor the *Encyclopedia of Islam* are able even to summarize much concerning the details of their biographies. Accordingly, almost nothing concrete is known of their relations with Jews.

This lacuna is all the more striking when juxtaposed to the remarkable Judaic "interests" evinced by some of the earliest Ismaʿili missionaries. The best-known example is that of Hamid al-Din al-Kirmani (d. ca. 1021), who quotes from and transliterates both Syriac and Hebrew.[137] These passages have garnered some sustained scholarly attention for the reason that Kirmani apparently either utilized willing Jews (and Christians) to write his works or else himself knew these languages. Kirmani's citations from the Bible concerning Messianic "expectations" were sufficiently au courant for van Ess to question whether Kirmani or his Jewish informant translated them. To this observation Goitein responds that he "should not be surprised at all if it were discovered some day that Kirmani, who hailed from northeastern Iran, was

---

[134] Halm, *Die islamische Gnosis*. See also my "The Moving Finger" for more on the earliest continuities with ancient Gnosis.

[135] For now, see my *"Sefer Yesira."*

[136] The little that we know about the major figure of Kirmani is now gathered by Walker in "Metempsychosis in Islam," 236 n. 42.

[137] See P. Kraus, "Hebräische"; and Pines, "Shiʿite Terms," 243–44.

himself a Jewish convert to Islam, or a son of one. His excessive use of *gematria*, although not unknown in Islam before him, makes him suspect." Pines draws this conclusion forcefully: "A conclusion which may, I think, be legitimately drawn from Kirmani's text is that, at the beginning of the 11th century at the latest, there were scholars of Jewish origin who were associated in some capacity in the elaboration of the Isma'ili doctrine, which they may have influenced."[138]

These opinions are based primarily on Kirmani's utilization of Hebrew sources. Most importantly, Kirmani cites a phrase from Pirke Avot (5:1), linked with a line from Isaiah (60:19), in a form unknown to Jewish literature. This citation reads "By ten dicta [*ma'amarot*] was the world created, and through ten commandments [*dabarot*] the world subsists, for the Lord shall be thy everlasting light."[139] Paul Kraus first brought this tantalizing text to the attention of the scholarly world.[140] Blumenthal and Pines, independently of each other, cited a number of related Jewish texts that similarly relate the Ten Words of Creation and the Ten Commandments.[141] Blumenthal is, however, constrained to observe that "the problem is that, in all these sources, the actual text does not correspond to that of Kirmani."[142] Nor could Pines identify a single source.[143] Other recent reappraisals of this citation have fortunately moved closer toward an appreciation of the full significance of Kirmani's originally Jewish text in the history of Jewish thought. These concern, first of all, a possible connection with *Sefer ha-Bahir*, pointed out to Pines by Yehuda Liebes and shortly thereafter investigated more fully by Moshe Idel.[144] Idel also proceeded to make a signal contribution, utilizing this connection, toward writing a history of the idea of ten sefirot.[145]

Another early Isma'ili missionary who was aware of Jewish traditions is Abu Hatim al-Razi (d. 322/934).[146] In three of his works, *Kitab al-Islah*, *Kitab al-Zina*, and *A'lam al-Nubuwwa*, Abu Hatim adduces a varied familiarity not only with Muslim heresiography polemics and concerning the Jews, but also with the philosophy, scriptures, and even the esoteric teachings

---

[138] Van Ess, *Chiliastische Erwartungen*, 62; Goitein, "'Meeting in Jerusalem,'" 43–57 at 54; Pines, "Shi'ite Terms," 244.

[139] Translation of Shlomo Pines. The full passage in which this appears is translated by Pines, "Shi'ite Terms," 243.

[140] The foundational work was Kraus, "Hebräische," 243–63.

[141] Blumenthal, "Isma'ili Influence," 155–74, at 157–58; Pines, "Shi'ite Terms," 244.

[142] Blumenthal, "Isma'ili Influence," 157–58.

[143] Pines, "Shi'ite Terms," 244.

[144] Ibid. Idel, "The Sefirot," 270, nn. 168–69.

[145] He gathered his arguments in this connection into *Kabbalah: New Perspectives*, 112–22. He notes that "no doubt the quotation found in the Isma'ili source and its parallel in the Jewish Isma'ili source reflects an older Jewish view" (p. 362, n. 128, where he provides two midrashic near parallels).

[146] I have dealt with Razi below, in chapter 4; see the sources gathered there.

of the Jews themselves. Many of these references, to be sure, are merely fleeting mentions or allusions. Abu Hatim, for example, knows of a Jewish false prophet called S'dkh; of the rosh golah; of the tradition that the "Jews are the Murji'a of this Community"; and of the Khazars as an archetypal Jewish nation.[147] But these particular bits of information would indicate only a broad education, for all these phenomena were generally well known in Arabic letters. Nor do these passages suggest any particular leaning toward Judaism.

He does, however, know the Jewish scriptures intimately and quotes them copiously and with understanding. In his situation, as an active controversialist, polemicist, and disputant, one necessarily needed to first learn the errors of others in order to subsequently refute them. Even though knowledge of the scriptures of one's opponents served essentially as polemical weaponry, to some extent Razi and his counterparts among the proponents of revealed religions in this period shared a common cause against absolute enemies of the scriptural traditions. Thus could Abu Hatim quote copiously from the Hebrew Bible and New Testament against the attacks of Muhammad ibn Zakariyya al-Razi, just as Saadia was counterattacking Hiwi al-Balkhi, whose antiscriptural positions were closely related to those of Muhammad b. Zakariyya.[148] Abu Hatim's relative support of Jewish scriptural tradition, in this context, can not be construed as Judaizing, but only as common cause.

However, the case of common esoteric traditions is rather different. Georges Vajda has studied in detail the cosmic semiotics of the *Kitab al-Zina* of Abu Hatim. In Vajda's words: "Abu Hatim completes his linguistic observations with a tradition of the Imam Ja'far al-Sadiq . . . [comprising] a cosmological myth in which letters play a role astonishingly similar [*étonnament semblable*] to those of the *Sefer Yesira* of Jewish gnosis." Although it is not possible to establish Abu Hatim's dependence on the *Sefer Yesira*, or vice versa, there can be little doubt that these works derive from what is (inadequately) termed "a common milieu."[149]

Abu Hatim al-Razi, like his fellow missionaries al-Kirmani, al-Sijistani (d. ca. 996), and al-Nasafi (d. 943), were natives of the Persian cultural milieu. Halm has already shown the extent to which Ja'far ibn al-Mansur (d. 914), another early Central Asian Isma'ili missionary, exhibits a cosmic semiotics parallel to that of *Sefer Yesira*.[150] Moreover, the Isma'ili dialogue form used by Ja'far should be compared to the dialogue written by the later Jewish Isma'ili, Judah ben Nissim ibn Malkah (thirteenth century).[151] The recognizable schools of earliest Isma'ilism were to a certain extent a function of geography.

---

[147] On S'dkh, see Stern, *Early Isma'ilism*, 41 n. 27; on the Khazars see A. Razi, *A'lam al-Nubuwwa*, 266. See also Ivanow, "Notes sur le Umm al-Kitab," 3–4.

[148] On these relationships see my discussion in chapter 4 below.

[149] Vajda, "Les Lettres," 119, my translation; 125, with which I concur.

[150] Halm, *Kosmologie*, 48–50.

[151] Vajda, *Judah*. Compare Judah ben Nissim's dialogue, *Uns al-Gharib* (Consolation to the stranger) with Ja'far's dialogue of the *rajul al-gharib* (stranger). See Vajda, *Judah*, 5–6 for *Uns al-Gharib*; and Ja'far's dialogue, *Kitab al-'Alim wal-Ghulam*, 49.

These Central Asian Isma'ilis shared certain theological similarities with others seen as representative of this school, such as the earlier Ikhwan al-Safa' and the slightly later Nasir-i-Khusraw (1004–ca. 1088).

THE APPEAL TO JEWS

This Eastern Isma'ilism seems to have been the form that held a particular attraction for Jews. It is clear now that the early Isma'ili movement did aggressively proselytize unbelievers, and that this mission enjoyed some success. Their missionizing technique is detailed in a spurious letter that has, according to Stern, "some foundation in reality":

> If you have a chance to meet a Jew, hold his attention by speaking to him about the Messiah; tell him that it is the same as the Mahdi; that the knowldege of him procures rest from the duties imposed by religion and its troublesome obligations, in the same way as his law enjoins him to rest on the Sabbath-day. You will gain his sympathy by speaking disparagingly of the ignorant Christians and Muslims with their assertions concerning Jesus; that he has not been born and that he had no father. Tell them that Joseph the carpenter was his father and Mary his mother; and that Joseph was her husband. By this and similar speech you will soon make them your followers.

Utilizing the Bible interpretation of the tenth-century Karaite Yefet b. 'Ali, Stern also showed that this "Judeo-Isma'ili ta'wil" succeeded to some considerable extent. Stern's cautious conclusion seems sound. There was, indeed, "a large-scale movement of conversion among the Jews in the second half of the tenth century, the hey-day of the Fatimid empire. . . . A very substantial number of Jews have accepted the religion of the State 'for sundry worldly reasons.'"[152] But there clearly seem to have been otherworldly reasons as well. One worldly result was that Jews rose to the very top of the Fatimid administrative hierarchy.[153] The best known of these successes was Ya'qub b. Killis. Recent work on this apostate emphasizes that this Jewish convert seemed to embrace both the Fatimid political cause as well as its Isma'ili theology.[154]

In the following sections I shall review the evidence that Isma'ilism remained a tenaciously attractive temptation for Jews from the tenth through the twelfth centuries, with instances of Jewish Isma'ilis being found as late as the fifteenth century. Isolated Jewish testimonies remain to be coordinated with the evidence gathered from surviving Jewish texts betraying Isma'ili theology. Thus we do not know what to make of reports such as that of Benjamin of Tudela, who reports that, around the year 1163, four Jewish congregations near Sus and Hamadan joined Isma'ilis in making war.[155] For-

[152] Stern, *Early Isma'ilism*, 65, 91.
[153] Lewis, "Legend," 3–4; Fischel, *Jews in Economic and Political Life*, 45–90.
[154] M. Cohen and S. Somekh, "In the Court," 283–314.
[155] *The Itinerary of R. Benjamin of Tudela*, 120.

tunately, we are much better informed about Jewish thinkers who make use of Isma'ilism in formulating a syncretistic theology.

THE PHILOSOPHICAL TRADITION

Three of the greatest Jewish thinkers of the period of creative symbiosis— Saadia Gaon, Judah Halevi, and Maimonides—use theological motifs that seem to derive from Isma'ili teachings. Saadia's commentary on *Sefer Yesira* is the earliest and slightest of these, while Pines's analysis indicates that the most profound impact may be found in Halevi's *Kuzari*.[156] Even Maimonides seems to have utilized some Isma'ili thinking. In fact, Ivry speaks of "an entire pattern of sympathy which Maimonides harbors towards Isma'ili methodology and even doctrine."[157] His followers in the practice of "philosophical mysticism" did so undeniably.[158]

Scholem, Pines, and Ivry have all suggested ways in which Maimonides himself may be understood as having possibly appropriated certain notions from Isma'ilism. Scholem, for example, stated that "there is no essential difference between so radically spiritualistic a doctrine as the prophetology of the the Isma'ili and a rationalistic theory like that of Maimonides." More recently, Pines and Ivry have sketched out other aspects of this hypothesis. Ivry lists these parallels as (1) the dichotomy of *zahir/batin* (exoteric/esoteric); (2) "the negation of attributes" (also discussed by Pines); (3) the doctrine of Creation both by emanation and ex nihilo; and (4) certain parallels with the *Rasa'il Ikhwan al-Safa'*.[159]

It lies beyond my competence to assess this hypothesis in detail. It is interesting to note, however, that a series of Jewish philosophical mystics who follow Maimonides closely also seem to bear some possiblity of Isma'ili theology. Heller-Wilensky, for example, has made such a suggestion recently in regard to Ibn Latif.[160] The most significant instances of the coincidence of Jewish philosphical mysticism conflated with Isma'ilism, however, are to be found over a period of years in the Yemen.

BUSTAN AL-'UQUL

Perhaps the earliest known instance of this Eastern Jewish Isma'ilizing tradition is that of the *Bustan al-'Uqul*, the philosophical masterwork of the

---

[156] Vajda, "Les Lettres"; Pines, "Shi'ite Terms."
[157] Ivry, "Islamic and Greek Influences," 139–56, at 144.
[158] Wasserstrom, "Social and Cultural" and "Jewish-Muslim Relations."
[159] Scholem, *Kabbalah and Its Symbolism*, 10; Ivry, "Islamic and Greek Influences," summarizes this material on pp. 141–43; Pines, "Shi'ite Terms."
[160] Heller-Wilensky, "Guide and Gate," 266–78; and "'First Created Thing.'"

twelfth-century Yemeni R. Nethanel Ben al-Fayyumi.[161] While there is no serious doubt that this work is inspired by the model of *RIS* and of later Ismaʿili works, a debate has recently emerged concerning its essential "Islam-icization." Insofar as this debate concerns the question most fundamentally at issue here—the solidity of the cultural common ground—it is worthwhile to examine this argument more closely.

Abraham Halkin, Ronald Kiener, and Paul Fenton have suggested that al-Fayyumi deviates from Jewish tradition in his acknowledgment of the proph-ethood of Muhammad. Kiener states this position most forcefully: "In R. Nathanel's relativism Muhammad is a prophet of the God of Israel and the Qur'an is indeed His prophetic communication." This argument has now been challenged by Joseph Qafih and, more fully, by Reuben Ahroni, who suggests that "Ibn Fayyumi's 'concession' with regard to the role of Muham-mad is no more than a tongue-in-cheek acquiescence . . . dictated by the spe-cific condition of the Jews of Yemen who were socially oppressed and constantly subjected to religious persecution."[162]

The crux of this disagreement appears to rest, alas, on sincerity. It is there-fore necessary to shift the focus of the question in order to work toward at least larger contextualization of this problem. This can be done by establish-ing that there was a long, if scattered, tradition, stretching before and after al-Fayyumi, of Yemeni Jews acknowledging the Prophethood of Muhammad. I would suggest that al-Fayyumi's "concession" was neither "in the very spirit of Ismaʿili interconfessionalism" (Kiener) nor was it "mere lip service, condi-tioned by the desperate need of Yemenite Jewry" (Ahroni). Rather, it was, at least in part, an expression of those many Jews under Islam who, while re-maining fully Jewish, still believed that Muhammad was indeed a prophet to the Arabs—but not to the Jews.[163]

Having assessed this question, I must agree with Sirat. Her conclusion is that Nethanel did indeed recognize the prophethood of Muhammad: "His text does not represent an oratorical precaution only. In fact, not only in his constant citing from Islamic writing but also in the decidedly universalistic tendency of his own writing, Nethanel adopts as his own an entirely natu-ralistic conception of revelation."[164]

[161] The work was submitted to exemplary analysis by Pines, "Nathanaël ben al-Fayyûmî," 5–22. He refers there to the little scholarship done before him on this subject. The work was edited and translated by Levine as *The Bustan al-Ukul*. It was reedited and translated into Hebrew by Qafih.
[162] Kiener, "Jewish Ismaʿilism in Twelfth-Century Yemen," 265; Ahroni, "From *Bustan al-ʿUqul* to *Qisat al-batul*," 328–29.
[163] Kiener, "Jewish Ismaʿilism in Twelfth-Century Yemen"; Ahroni, "From *Bustan al-ʿUqul* to *Qisat al-batul*." I refer to the study of the ʿIsawiyya in chapter 2 above and to the material on Jewish acknowledgments of Muhammad in Chapter 5 below. My point is simply that the historiographic vision of multiple revelations, once firmly ensconced as a Jewish worldview (by way of Muslim intermediation) resulted in a conveniently accommodating theological capaciousness.
[164] Sirat, *Jewish Philosophy in the Middle Ages*, 92.

Finally, the survival of Isma'ilized Judaism in the Yemen for several centuries after Nethanel would also suggest that this form of interconfessionalism was not some freak occurrence but was, at least to some extent, incorporated into a certain strain of Yemeni Jewish Isma'ili syncretism. Georges Vajda and Franz Rosenthal have filled in some of the looming gaps in our history of this tradition. They have authored short but altogether reliable studies of works of twelfth- and fifteenth-century Yemeni Jewish Isma'ilism.[165] Far more fully, the work of the fifteenth-century Hoter ben Shelomo has now been extensively examined by David Blumenthal, who emphatically and persuasively argues for its Isma'ili content.[166]

What little we know about this curiously penumbral tradition has been summarized with just proportion by Rosenthal: "Jewish scholars in the medieval Yemen [became] so strongly assimilated to their Muslim, and largely Shi'ah, environment and imbued with its persuasive philosophical ideology that they provoked disapproval from their more traditional coreligionists and created an intellectual atmosphere as lively as their generally restricted circumstances would allow."[167] The Yemen, in particular, has yielded just enough examples of this Isma'ilized Jewish tradition for us to reasonably plot a rough trajectory of Jewish Isma'ilism. However, it would at this stage still be foolhardy to depend too completely on this one still-tenuous trail in our attempt to plot the general direction of Jewish-Muslim symbiosis. But it does, at least, corroborate our understanding of an underestimated Shi'i participation in the sharing of theologies.

[165] Vajda, "Un Opuscule ismaélien," 459–66; F. Rosenthal, "'Unorthodox' Judaism," 279–90.
[166] Blumenthal, *Commentary*.
[167] F. Rosenthal, "'Unorthodox' Judaism," 280.

CHAPTER FOUR

Jewish Studies and Comparative Religion in the Islamicate Renaissance

THE THINKERS of early Islam faced extraordinary intellectual challenges. They routinely confronted a bewildering array of serious opponents whose doctrines were well established and carefully defended. Among these, Jews and Shiʿis were the closest in theory and in practice to the defenders of Sunni Islam. Indeed, the very closeness of these groups presented the gravest danger to the self-understanding of the people of the Sunna of Muhammad. And intimate intellectual intercourse between these three groups persisted despite doctrinal and social obstacles. In part because Jews, Shiʿis, and Sunnis were themselves not monolithic units, individuals from among various subgroups could find those of other subgroups occasionally to be congenial, if not receptive, to personal and intellectual overtures. In this way, the "vast imperium" of Islamic civilization engendered pluralistic contacts, which in turn stimulated pluralistic approaches to the study of religion. Out of oppositional relations a certain comparativism arose. Eventually, comparative research on religions included a historical and (occasionally) critical study of Judaism.

In the following chapter, I shall describe and interpret the shift on the part of Muslim scholars from a polemical comparative exegesis of foreign scriptures to the critical study of other religions. To do so I will trace some varieties of allegorical interpretation, of interreligious contacts, and of heresiographical classifications. Once Muslim scholars of other religions thus had the data and the devices to understand comparative religion, they successfully proceeded to create the best-informed and most theoretically sophisticated premodern history of religions.

THE ORIGINS OF TAʾWIL

The deployment of allegory as an explanation for obscure figures of speech in the Qurʾan was neither a mystical nor a rationalist device, as is conventionally asserted. Rather, I shall argue that *taʾwil* originated as a mode of comparison. Allegorical interpretation, in this sense, was a revisionary technique deriving from and responding to interreligious conflict. I hope to show that taʾwil, in the context of Jewish-Muslim interactions, was less a defensive apology for figuration in scripture than it was an offensive mode of community assertion.

It would be no innovation for me to announce that the Kufan ghulat originated the Muslim exegetical technique of pneumatic allegorizing known as *ta'wil*. But this consensus represents a misleading accuracy.[1] The so-called extremists, or ghulat, were proto-Shi'ite Gnostics who flourished in an eighth-century boomtown, the new Arab settlement of Kufa (in present-day Iraq). It is to their magnificent failure that we can attribute the first recourse to the esoteric interpretation of the Qur'an. Why did these Gnostics use this technique, and why did it fail? To get at these concerns I would first note the dynamics of Gnosis as it recurred in early Islam.

These ghulat, in effect, were functionaries without a function. Neither the mainstream Shi'ite imams to whom they were initially loyal nor the emerging 'Abbasid caliphs who betrayed them needed them.[2] It is here, in the mid-second Islamic century, at the cusp of disinheritance and ongoing prophetic inspiration, that we can perceive the first glimmerings of taw'il. Constructed as typical Gnostic myth, their ta'wil proceeded by the apparent paradox of pneumatically derived but rationally applied "inspiration."[3] It reflected on immediate needs and reread a sacred narrative accordingly. In the case of the ghulat, ta'wil was first fabricated in the calculated interests of their increasingly desperate *da'wa*, their activist political cause.

Gnosis, under the early Muslim umma as under the early Church, operated as an ideological legitimation of defeat. Utilizing (what Rudolph called) "protest exegesis," Gnostics revisioned the cognitive dissonance devolving

---

[1] Perhaps the most influential statement of this position was that of Hodgson, who asserted that the beginnings of *ta'wil* "can be traced to the Shi'i ghulat of the second/eighth century in 'Irak" ("Batiniyya" 1:1098). See also his "How Did the Shi'a Become Sectarian?" where he refers to "symbolical explanations of the Qur'anic text, introducing a type of problem that has been with Islam ever since" (7). Compare the typical assertion of Tucker, referring to Mughira ibn Sa'id's allegorical play on Q 87:1: "This is a prime example of the allegorical interpretation of the Qur'an, a practice which appears to have originated within the offshoots of the movement led by al-Mukhtar ibn Abi 'Ubayd" ("Rebels and Gnostics," 41). Similarly, Morony says, "They [the ghulat] freed themselves from the literal meaning of the Qur'anic text by finding the hidden truths behind it" (*Iraq*, 501). Rajkowski considers ta'wil as one of the "Five Principles" of the ghulat (see *Early Shi'ism*, 690–91). Massignon places this development even earlier, asserting that "Salman [Pak, al-Farisi] had assisted in the genesis of the very first *ta'wil*" (*Salman Pak*, 21). On the same page, Massignon claims that "it was among the Shi'ites that the *ta'wil* has commenced."

[2] See my analysis in "The Moving Finger." See also my analysis of the social setting of apocalypse in the final section of chapter 6 below.

[3] Claims to extraordinary exegesis were the hallmark of the Gnostics of antiquity. See Puech, "Gnosis and Time," on the *pneumatikoi*, "spiritual men," who claim "transcendent and exhaustive interpretations of Christianity and of the entire visible and invisible world" (54). See more fully Pearson, *Pneumatikos-Psychikos Terminology*. Lafargue also deals with this issue at some length in *Language and Gnosis*. One may consult now the excellent comparative study by Dawson, *Allegorical Readers*. For the survival of such techniques of reading, see Morony, *Iraq*, 427. For a general treatment, see Whitman, *Allegory*.

from failed apocalyptic.[4] Their Gnosis was thus intensely ambivalent. It parasitically fed on the host Revelation, subverting and allegorizing according to the needs of an increasingly marginalized constituency. Its weakened ideologues wielded central texts but used their readings ever more wildly against central authorities. The result of this proto-Shi'ite legitimist Gnosticism was a rereading of the Qur'an as a great code, a cipher whose secret was proclaimed to be themselves. Their leaders, their ritual, their myth, and the future consummation of their hope thus were all found to be encoded in the Qur'an. The *ghali* Abu Mansur flatly taught that Qur'anic references to heaven and hell in fact referred to men: "Hell refers to the four Caliphs [Rashidun, so-called Rightly-Guided Ones, said by Shi'i tradition to have usurped the lineage of 'Ali]; Paradise to the Imams."[5] We have extant books authored by these groups, surviving examples of this sectarian evangelistic revisionism.[6]

This ta'wil rested on the infallible authority of the imam's ultimate Gnosis. For example, in the 730s the Gnostic revolutionary Mughira b. Sa'id is to have claimed direct initiation from the imam as his legitimation; "I met one of the 'people of the house [of Muhammad, i.e., an imam]' and he slaked my thirst with a drink of water and there remained nothing but I knew it." Drinking at the source of the imam, then, could alone provide the right reading of Qur'an for all subsequent Shi'is.[7]

Already as early as the ninth century, a scholar tells us that esoteric exegesis was considered characteristic of the ghulat:

> Mughira [ibn Sa'id] published an interpretation of the Qur'an that he called "knowledge of the esoteric" and that diverged from what Muslims accept. He asserted that the Qur'an is entirely composed of symbols and cryptic hints and that mankind cannot learn anything of its mystical meanings but through him, because of the power invested in him by the Imam.[8]

---

[4] Rudolph, *Gnosis*, 54.

[5] Cited in Tucker, "Abu Mansur," 72. (For the relation between Abu Mansur and the Jewish prophet Abu 'Isa, see chapter 2 above.) Note the resemblance between this politically polemical use of Gnosticizing allegorical interpretation and that of the Gnostic heresiarch Basilides (fl. 117–38), who was to have said, "We are men, and the others are all swine and dogs. Therefore it says, 'Cast not pearls before swine nor give what is holy to the dogs'" (Grant, *Gods and the One God*, 139). Even the names adopted by these heresiarchs were said to have been derived from the Qu'ran by means of ta'wil. This is true of Bayan ibn Sam'an, Salman al-Farisi and Abu Mansur al-'Ijli, known as Al-Kisf, "the Meteor," after the Qur'an 52:44. See I. Friedlaender, "Heterodoxies" 89.

[6] *Umm al-Kitab* and *Kitab al-Haft wal-Azilla*. In addition to these works, dozens of such examples of this sort of allegorical readings are recorded by the heresiographers who studied these gnostics.

[7] Dhahabi, *Mizan al-I'tidal*, 4:161.

[8] Al-Nashshi, *Kitab al-Ausat*, 41 of the text, as found in van Ess, *Frühe mu'tazilitische Häresiographie*.

This first ta'wil, then, was self-consciously esoteric and sectarian. This was far from its only incarnation, however. To be sure, Henry Corbin spent much of his career analyzing the subsequent esoteric techniques of Shi'ite and Sufi ta'wil, emphasizing the extent to which this visionary exegesis was central to the mature programs of Shi'ism and Sufism.[9] Corbin's influence, however, has led precisely to the misapprehension that ta'wil was exclusively mystical or sectarian, restricted to its Shi'i and/or Sufi usages.

This view leads to a serious mistake in emphasis, for the full importance of early ta'wil cannot be appreciated unless the logos of ta'wil is recognized along with its mythos. I take my cue from Marshall Hodgson's study of *batini* (esotericist) ta'wil.

> What *ta'wil* did accomplish was to replace what seemed a "naive" Kur'anic world-view with a more "sophisticated" intellectual system, one which seemed to go beneath the superficial differences among the quarelling religious communities with their incompatible dogmatic claims, to reach a profounder common truth.[10]

These observations suggest that the program and practice of ta'wil may have more to do with arguing systemically for common truth than they do with mere defensive apologetics.

Mu'tazilite Ta'wil

In the ninth century, the great interreligious controversies between Muslim and Jew and Christian and Manichean—to name only the major participants—resulted in the development of a common intellectual language. These groups were already speaking and writing Arabic, but their debates generated a common discourse as well. The result was a new rationalist usage of ta'wil. This quasi-allegorical interpretation was used to compare and defend scriptures in an explicitly interreligious setting.

This comparativist exegesis climaxed in the tenth-century Islamicate Enlightenment, in a situation of live contact between a variety of believers. The content of this comparativism was in fact the very verses of the foreign scriptures. Ta'wil thus emerged as the perfect tool: a shared interpretive technique used by the disputants in these interreligious forums, which all could share and yet all could deploy against each other. I emphasize that this rationalist and offensive usage was neither Shi'ite sectarian ta'wil nor Sufi mystical ta'wil.

By contrast to those "interiorizing" hermeneutics, ta'wil, in the context of the ninth-century ordinary usage, was simply a common term for interpretation, a usage found even in the titles of the most influential early Sunni works

[9] See the characteristic treatment in Corbin, *Avicenna*, 28–35, *"Ta'wil* as Exegesis of the Soul." Corbin's sense of ta'wil is analyzed by Adams "Hermeneutics of Henry Corbin," 129–50.

[10] Hodgson, "Batiniyya," 1099b.

of Qur'an interpretation, as well as of such later works as well.[11] While *tafsir* came to be known as the dominant mode of exegesis, it was recognized that the scope of tafsir was limited: tafsir was concerned with the meaning of strange words or with the establishment of a historical "occasion" for the revelation of a given verse.[12] As a complement to this lexical and historicist function of tafsir, ta'wil, by contrast, was primarily directed to the "covert meaning" in the verse. Since this covert meaning was most commonly understood to reside in obscurities (*mutashabihat*), that is, in figures of speech, ta'wil typically presented the understanding of figuration in the scriptural text.[13]

The Mu'tazila was a school that perfected and championed this new, non-esoteric ta'wil. To be more precise, this form of ta'wil constituted less an organized school of thought than an interpretive emphasis utilized by any Muslim or non-Muslim group that found it advantageous to do so. For my purposes, I emphasize that this Mu'tazilite use of ta'wil, which flourished in the ninth and tenth centuries, in fact was important not because it was used for one sectarian cause, as it had been in its origins, but because it could now be used by many causes.

How did it do so? It was effective in answering the problem of obscurity by bringing in noncanonical materials to interpret the canon. The recourse to these nonscriptural traditions to interpret the scripture is the crucial point. Each well-established group drew upon the traditions venerably belonging to it to interpret the obscurities of scripture. The means for doing so, for the nonesoteric Mu'tazilites, then, was certainly not inner Gnosis but "reason, personal opinion, individual research or expertise."[14]

To be sure, this new Mu'tazilite interpretation was still predicated on a fundamental notion shared with the earlier Gnostics, that the scripture contained both an outer and an inner meaning. But the purpose of the Mu'tazilite reading was to defend the outer meaning as the authoritative reading for the community at large. For the Jewish Mu'tazilite allegorical reading, thus, the outer meaning was the "generally accepted [Jewish] sense."[15]

---

[11] For example, that of Ibn Qutaiba (828–89), *Kitab Ta'wil*. Lecomte notes that Ibn Qutaiba "applies the term indifferently and does not use the word *tafsir*" (454). See also Tabari, *Jami' al-Bayan*; and Maturidi, *Ta'wilat Ahl al-Sunna*, discussed by Rippin, "Sa'adya Gaon and Genesis 22," 33–46, at 34.

Perhaps the most rounded discussion of the (Mu'tazilite, Sufi, Isma'ili) varieties of ta'wil is that of Goldziher, *Introduction to Islamic Theology*, s.v. "ta'wil (allegorical exegesis)."

[12] Rippin, "Sa'adya Gaon," 34.

[13] Ibid., 35.

[14] Ibid., 35.

[15] Faur, *Golden Doves*, 12.

Jewish Ta'wil

> Against this background, systematic Jewish theology and Jewish religious
> philosophy were being shaped, paralleling much of what was going on
> in the respective Muslim circles.
>
> —Moshe Perlmann, "Medieval Polemics"

Ta'wil, then, could function both in an apologetic and in a harmonizing
mode. In its apologetic thrust it was utilized against anthropomorphism. Altmann goes so far as to call ta'wil "the Muʿtazilite answer to anthropomorphism."[16] On the other hand, the Ismaʿilis also employed their notorious,
mystically harmonistic ta'wil, which could tease a transcendent unity of world
religions out of any and all scriptural figuration.[17] Ta'wil succeeded on both
sides of the line because it could be used in almost any way the reader needed.
Ta'wil, in this sense, amounted to a *reading-in* of figures of speech.[18] This
likewise was true of Jewish ta'wil.

The earliest evidence for Jewish ta'wil is early indeed. Shahrastani gave this
important report on the Maghariyya and Yudghaniyya: "[Yudghan] used to
claim that the Torah had an exoteric [*zahir*] and an esoteric [*batin*] meaning,
a revealed textual form [*tanzil*] and an interpretation of that form [*ta'wil*], but
he differed with the majority of the Jews in his interpretations [*ta'wilat*]."[19]
Shahrastani's full, provocative account is focused on the avoidance of anthropomorphism (corporealizing; "*tashbih*") by ta'wil.[20]

Ibn ʿAbd Rabbihi, in his *ʿIqd al-Farid*, describes the ta'wilat of the Jews and
the Christians at the *majlis* [public audience Salon, meeting] of al-Ma'mun as
being without conflict among them.[21] At roughly the same time, Jahiz sneers
that the Jews were incapable of providing an adequate ta'wil of the Hebrew
Bible (*tawrat*) because they did not command *Arabic* adequate to that inter-
pretative task.[22] But ta'wil among the Jews was hardly monolithic. The fullest

[16] Altmann, "Saadya's Theory of Revelation," 140–60, at 145. And, more generally,
Altmann, "Bible: Allegorical Interpretations," 895–99. See also the still-valuable article by Ginzberg, "Allegorical Interpretation."
[17] See for example, Feki, *Les idées religieuses*, chap. 7, "Le *Ta'wil*," 267–301; Heinen,
"Notion of *Ta'wil*," 35–45; and Poonawala, "Ismaʿili *Ta'wil* of the Qur'an," 199–222.
[18] Stetkevych, "Arabic Hermeneutical Terminology," 81–97, at 92, for the theory of
"reading-in."
[19] I discuss this text in "Species of Misbelief," 261–69.
[20] See the remarks in *Jewish Encyclopedia* 12:624; in Poznanski, "Philon," 23; and in
Golb, "Magariya".
[21] Ibn ʿAbd Rabbihi, *ʿIqd al-Farid* 2:385 (wa-la yakun al-Yahud wal-Nasara ikhtilafun
fi shay'un min al-ta'wilat) (The Jews and the Christians do not differ in any way in
matters of ta'wil).
[22] Jahiz in Finkel, "Three Essays," 28–29.

evidence of the pluralistic vicissitudes of taʿwil among the Jews is in the Karaite camp. Already with ʿAnan, if Harkavy is correct, we find some influence from Abu Hanifah's theory of ta'wil.[23] Salmon ben Yeruham criticizes Benjamin al-Nehawandi's ta'wil, and yet, as Jacob Mann points out, he himself used the method in his intepretation of the Song of Songs.[24] And Daniel al-Qumisi "entirely opposed . . . the allegorical interpetation of the Commandments, since 'God did not ordain his Commandments in allegorical form.'"[25] As for Qirqisani, he rejects ta'wil in principle but not in practice:

> The other learned group claims that Muhammad is mentioned in the Torah elliptically and allusively, toward which knowledge one ascends by way of ta'wil and deduction, and that the Jews twist that wording and interpret it by another meaning. . . . Why did God propose for [such a great matter] to be mentioned by clues and allusions, so that knowledge is achieved by farfetched ta'wil and deduction, which give rise to many disagreements?[26]

Saadia Gaon, the nemesis of the Karaites, used Muʿtazilite rationalizing, nonliteral ta'wil, much as did his equally hardheaded Karaite colleague. The Gaon's formulation was definitive.[27] Already in the tenth century, an Ithna ʿAshari Shiʿi scholar approached Jewish scholars and solicited their opinion on the correctness of a biblical translation *along with its ta'wil*.[28] In the ensuing centuries between Jahiz in the ninth century and Ibn ʿAknin in the thirteenth century, Jews thus capably constructed a persuasive, Arabic-language metaphoric defense of their own.[29]

What is so striking about this form of "allegorical" interpretation is that it was actively used by established groups in their polemics against each other. So powerful was it found to be that Jewish, Muslim, and Christian leaders all used it. Indeed, there was a moment in the ninth and tenth centuries in which Rabbanite and Karaite Jews, Coptic Christians, and Zaydi and Twelver Shiʿites, along with Sunni theologians, all used Muʿtazilite ta'wil. All these

---

[23] Harkavy, "Anan," 1:555: "Abu Hanifah was accustomed in certain cases to take the words of the Kuran not in their literal but in a symbolical sense (Ta'awil); and Anan adopted the same method with the Hebrew text of the Bible."

[24] Mann, *Texts and Studies* 2:17 n. 32. Poznanski claimed that Benjamin al-Nehewandi "read an allegorical sense into many passages of Scripture" ("Karaites," 664). This argument is more fully developed in his classic article "Allegorische Gesetzauslegung," 237–59.

[25] Poznanski, "Karaites," 664, citing Yehuda Hadassi's *Eshkol ha-Kofer*.

[26] Qirqisani, *Kitab al-Anwar*, 2:296. My translation.

[27] Saadia Gaon, *The Book of Beliefs and Opinions*, 265–66. See Rippin, "Saʿadya Gaon and Genesis 22" 35, on this formulation. Note than an unnamed fifteenth-century Jewish writer of Ismaʿili leanings asserts that both Saadia and Maimonides themselves need *ta'wil*. See Rosenthal, "From the 'Unorthodox' Judaism," 279–90, at 289.

[28] Nuʿmani, *Kitab al-Ghayba*, 65.

[29] In the thirteenth century, Ibn ʿAqnin eloquently defends the Song of Songs to the Almoravide king by means of ta'wil. See the discussion by Talmadge, "Apples of Gold," 324.

establishment leaders utilized this technique to defend the rationality of their own scriptures and to attack the irrationality of their opponent's scriptures.

Perhaps the most critical concern shared by these leaders was the defense of figuration, of the figural obscurities and otherwise mythical elements of their holy books. But why was the defense of figuration crucial for interreligious comparativists, who were usually not community leaders? Because, as I try to show in the following section, the exercise of ta'wil was not restricted by a priori assumptions of the dictionary or the historical scenario, assumptions that by this period had been set firmly in place by communities. Tafsir's function, like ta'wil's, was to strengthen communal boundaries. But in ta'wil the signified of the text's obscure signifier could be found—and here lies both the strength and weakness of ta'wil—in the rational mind and emotive heart of the reader.

"Rational" ta'wil, in short, made sense of scripture for the now-doubting and potentially apostasizing adherent. Where Gnostic ta'wil had preached to the converted, Muʿtazilite ta'wil controverted the uncertain. And so, by contrast to tafsir, ta'wil, then, emerged in this period as the cutting edge, the vanguard of a more coherently interconfessional reading. Nor did it provide such an intelligible opening only to the normative Muslim or normative non-Muslim. Sectarian Jews, Christians, and Muslims also deployed it alongside and against establishment leaders.

Interreligious Ta'wil

Ta'wil, in short, provides us with an instructive paradox. It could be inspired exegesis or politically tendentious historiography; establishment or sectarian; Muslim or non-Muslim; rationalist or traditionalist. Most especially it presents us with a technique that could be equally effective in a defensive or an offensive mode. It is here that I would locate its defining characteristic. I therefore disagree with those who assert that it was really allegorical interpretation at all. Rather, as Halkin noted, it is a "device applied to a text which, there is every reason to suppose, was not originally intended to serve as an allegory."[30]

What, then, was ta'wil? Without falling prey to the fallacy of functionalism, I find it clear that ta'wil provided an opening of discourse both between religions and within religions. My conclusions concern this poorly understood discursive function. To make this point I want to conclude with three observations concerning the Jewish use of ta'wil.

First, by the tenth century, the Jews were accustomed to having the Torah read in Arabic by their Muslim opponents, who criticized it relentlessly. One of the most intensive and successful such campaigns agaiinst the Torah took the form of what S. M. Stern terms "Judeo-Ismaʿili *ta'wil*."[31] Ismaʿili syncre-

[30] Halkin, "Judeo-Islamic Age," 246.
[31] S. Stern, *Studies in Early Ismaʿilism*, 84–96. The fullest treatment now is Lazarus-Yafeh, *Intertwined Worlds*.

144 CONSTRUCTIONS

tism aimed at Jews programmatically appropriated the target population's sacred book, the better to facilitate conversion. Walter Fischel described this program:

> [Isma'ilis] in their attempt to propagate their ideas concerning the Seventh Imam among all religions and creeds and in their endeavor to bind together Arabs and Persians, Christians and Jews, and indeed, all mankind, regarded as necessary the study of the holy books of other religions, including the Old Testament.[32]

In addition to appropriating their opponent's techniques of reading, using ta'wil to defend themselves against this Isma'ili propaganda, Jews more generally defended Torah against all kinds of Muslim arguments by the same means. These surprising encounters reflect but also belie a somewhat more "official" Jewish attitude to ta'wil. Already in the ninth century, for example, the great Rabbanite leader Saadia Gaon rejected outright the ta'wil of others. Followed by subsequent rabbinical authority, his opinion was that the basis of authority of ta'wil was subjective, and so its value lay only in its communal acceptability. Because of this, it could not be imposed. According to a subsequent Gaon,

> No one has the right to formulate a ta'wil of the Torah against us contrary to our consensus because we are the authorities of its language, the transmitters of its text, and the proclaimers of its veracity. We have received it from the Prophets verbally [i.e., directly], as well as its meaning and its ta'wil.

This accepted rabbinic opinion held that ta'wil "is the exclusive perogative of the Jewish people." Muslim and Christian leaders, mutatis mutandis, said the same. The point, for my purpose, is obvious enough: opposing communities could make structurally analogous claims, understandably asserting their traditional rights to correct interpretation of their own scripture. As Faur properly observes, "the specific bond between a people and a book can only be effected through the process of . . . ta'wil. . . . Outside the perimeter of 'Book—People of the Book,' ta'wil is illegitimate."[33]

"Opponents" were making structurally analogous claims. Scripture is a group dream, a shared construction, a common well-made world. In a modernizing moment like the Islamicate tenth century, only political communication, rhetorical power, the ability to persuade and defend could save scripture from being picked apart by the explanations of others. The argument had to remain that this was *our* text, *our* group's ultimate reality.

I conclude that ta'wil was less visionary than it was revisionary—or rather, its visionary youth gave way to its revisionary maturity, as these communities in conflict struggled together for respective self-definition. Even when, in maturity, exclusivist truth claims were announced unequivocally, and ta'wil was arrogated as the preserve of the in-group, this hermeneutics still consti-

[32] Fischel, "Israel in Iran," 817–58, at 821.
[33] Faur, *Golden Doves*, 124, 13.

tuted the overlap, the debating arena, the shared space where persuasion was theoretically possible. A full study of the texts and contexts of this discourse, therefore, can help us understand the irreducible and inescapable problem of the historical study of religions: What do religions demonstrably hold in common?

The Comparativist Climate in the Tenth Century

> They foregather all, in search of a solution, they circle and tremble like an-
> gels of intoxication, and to the last one states one thing, while a second
> tells the opposite.
>
> —Anonymous author of "Bible Difficulties" (ca. tenth century)

Louis Massignon evokes the Zeitgeist of the Islamicate Renaissance of the ninth and tenth centuries with memorably stormy "individual crises of conscience." Even Josef van Ess, in more tentatively characterizing this era, ascribes its genius to "a certain spiritual uncertainty." Some soul-searching uncertainty, it is widely recognized, stimulated a quest for assurance in the ninth and tenth centuries. While the Judaist Halkin therefore enjoys some support for his apodictic conclusion that "absolute truth was their aim, and no other truth existed," the rise of relativism undoubtedly magnified the intensity of this quest. Out of this climate of dissatisfaction among the Jewish and Muslim intelligentsia residing in the Islamicate capitals of the ninth and tenth centuries, Jews and Muslims were ironically drawn together. Out of a mutual self-interest, they strove to help each other distinguish the True Religion from the False. Fortunately, Massignon also suggests a resolution to this paradox: "[The great mystic and martyr] Hallaj benefited from these [interconfesssional] contacts by learning to make use of a 'comparativist' . . . vocabulary."[34]

At an acute atmospheric shift in cultural climate, a few probing minds penetrated the boundaries of foreign religions. What led them to make their daring comparisons? This was a time when both Aristotle and the Bible were being translated and annotated in Arabic. Arabic was by the late-ninth century the lingua franca of the Islamicate empire, within which domain the vast bulk of world Jewry resided. By this time, in fact, Jewish and Muslim theologies, both written of course in Arabic, had dovetailed to a remarkable extent. I use Marshall Hodgson's term *Islamicate* to refer to this common culture, which was not restricted to the religion of Islam, but which encompassed Arabophone Jews and Christians as well. In short, Jews and Muslims

---

[34] Massignon, *Passion*, 1:197; van Ess, "Ibn al-Rewandi," 12; Halkin, "Judeo-Islamic Age," 260. On Ibn al-Muqaffaʻs "conviction that any positive religion had only relative merit," see Goitein, "A Turning Point," 151 n. 1. Massignon, *Passion*, 1:190.

were speaking a common language: linguistic, exegetical, theological, and comparativist.

This situation, of course, was deeply problematic. The first comparativists, in fact, must be seen in light of the distressingly sudden overload of foreign and ancient texts. This diffuse cultural burden presented an almost inescapable challenge to serious thinkers of all religions. Itself a result of the bourgeois revolution following in the wake of the Arab conquests, which produced this kind of cultural open market, the textual surfeit further stimulated an unsettling competition, a nervous mobility of ideas. As a result, a common quest for a new epistemological certainty was undertaken by Arabic-speaking Jews, Christians, and Muslims. With their shared Arabic language, shared Abrahamic monotheism, and shared fund of formative philosophical texts, these religious rivals undertook a firsthand comparison of the truth value of scriptural claims and of the efficacy (or absurdity) of foreign practices.

Such rival claims were disputed in interreligious meetings.[35] Of course, already from the beginning of the career of the Prophet Muhammad (and until today), Muslims had been in continual contact with Jews. But the disputation to which I now turn was a form of contact that surely climaxed in the Islamicate Renaissance. What might be termed "official" and "unofficial" interdenominational disputations both flourished at this time. As for official disputations, Jewish and Muslim leaders of their respective religious communities were depicted as officially representing their constituencies in public disputations.[36] In the early ninth-century, to take just one of dozens of such examples, the Twelver Shi'ite Imam al-Rida neatly confutes a Jewish exilarch at some considerable length: much of their discussion concerns the precise truth or falsity of specific biblical verses.[37] Likewise, perhaps the same Jewish leader debated under the auspices of the caliph al-Ma'mun, a detailed record of which is preserved as well.[38] Indeed, most of the Umayyad and early 'Abbasid caliphs (the great Sunni monarchs), as well as all of the early Shi'ite imams, are depicted as sponsering or participating in such forums. But "official" leaders defending their religions in public are not the only form interreligous meetings took.

"Unofficial" interdenominational meetings were in some ways rather more romantic affairs: their drama is certainly more relevant to the present scenario, for the finest pioneer comparativists were not official leaders but radical

---

[35] Holmberg, "The Public Debate as a Literary Genre."

[36] Zayyat, "Sects, Innovation."

[37] Ibn Babuya, *Kitab al-Tauhid*, 427–41. Concerning such meetings, Lazarus-Yafeh notes that the "literary discussion must echo, at least in part, the many personal encounters between followers of different religions and sects, in which ideas were exchanged orally" (*Intertwined Worlds*, 133). See Lazarus-Yafeh's excellent discussion of these meetings, 132–35. See also Holmberg, "The Public Debate as a Literary Genre," 45–53.

[38] Ibn 'Abd al-Rabbihi, *'Iqd al-Farid* 2:384–87.

freethinkers suspect by the offical leadership. This characterization is epito-mized by the Jews Daud al-Muqammis and Hiwi al-Balkhi and by the Mus-lims Ibn al-Rewandi, Abu 'Isa al-Warraq, and Muhammad Abu Bakr al-Razi.

We know precious little concerning the biographies of these philosophical radicals. It seems that the resemblances between these bold comparativists may be due to their frequenting some of the same social circles. So far as we can tell, these Jewish and Muslim radicals met together privately, presumably in their own homes. Thus it is suggested by Nemoy that Daud al-Muqammis, the first Jewish theologian to write in Arabic and the sole Jewish scholar of comparative religion in this era, may have been "a Jewish member of the fairly small contemporary group of 'liberal' . . . thinkers who felt an equal regard for all monotheistic religions as in their basic essence mere variants of the same divine faith."[39]

If this was the case, then these interreligiously liminal intellectuals, under-standably burdened with crises of conscience, did have common cause to join together. Espousing a dangerous philosophy, they were all derogated as be-ing "deviant." Not surprisingly, their precise allegiances remain a mystery. This oblivion can of course only be partially blamed on the typical fate of outsiders, whose writings magnetically attract suppression.

Comparative Exegesis and Scriptural Difficulties

In any case, comparative exegesis flourished in the briefly open cultural atmo-sphere in which these comparativists operated. Comparative exegesis was their originally polemical use of cross-denominational scriptural interpreta-tions. Its content, then, was the comparative interpretation of scripture, for which it drew on venerable precedents. Scriptual criticism in late antiquity took the form, among others, of the genre of "question and answer," known also as "*testimonia*" and "Bible difficulties."[40] Church Fathers by the fifth cen-tury were already collecting hundreds of examples of inner contradictions, moral difficulties, and logical absurdities in the text of the Hebrew Bible. It was such critiques that were reapplied vigorously in the interconfessional set-ting of early Islam.

Thus, by the ninth century, Hiwi al-Balkhi—an infamous Hebrew-language polemicist and perhaps the prototypical Jewish heretic of the Islam-icate period—drew upon this genre to attack rabbinism.[41] Baron colorfully described Hiwi as

> one of those smart-alecky eclectics who took his arguments wherever he could find them, without necessarily committing himself to any particular set of beliefs. In the

---

[39] Nemoy, "Attitudes of Early Karaites," 703; S. Stroumsa, "On Apostate Jewish Intellectuals."

[40] See also Daiber, "Masa'il wa'l-Adjwiba." See more on the encyclopedic question-naire in chapter 5 below.

[41] Davidson, *Saadia's Polemic*; J. Rosenthal, *Hiwi al-Balkhi*; Fleischer, "Fragment."

Arabian world at large, Hivi's was the generation which first embarked upon a scientific study of comparative religion, often in a positively heretical, even free-thinking vein.[42]

At the same time as Hiwi, then, the radical Muslim philosophers al-Razi and Ibn al-Rewandi, his close contemporaries and possible colleagues, exploited such scriptural critiques to attack traditionalist Islam.[43] The multidimensional challenges cast by this gadfly group provoked some famously authoritative rebuttals. In the process, Jews, Zoroastrians, Muslims, and unaffiliated philosophers collectively refined "scriptural criticism" in composing challenges, and responses to challenges, to the integrity of the Bible. It is this interreligious discourse of spiritual critique and defense that I am calling comparative exegesis.

The intellectually serious aspect of such scriptural debates in early Islam continues to be underestimated by scholars of the period. In this connection, I must dissent from a recent assertion that "neither [Muslim nor Jew] deemed the other's scripture worthy of serious consideration."[44] In the first place, we know that the first two centuries of Islam, the seventh and eighth centuries, already saw much Muslim reading of foreign scriptures. The result of this substantial encounter was the cumulative evidence of so-called Israelite traditions and of the Islamization of early historical traditions, especially Persian history.[45] Such evidence demonstrates that the Bible was broadly and sensitively, if sporadically, scrutinized by the first Muslim scholars. Moreover, subsequent Muslim polemicists also manifestly required, and did indeed occasionally acquire, scriptural ammunition. Nor was the famous eleventh-century scientist Biruni the only Muslim scholar of the classical period to study Hebrew. In fact, the phenomenon of Muslim Hebraism, while never widespread and rarely deep, routinely has been underestimated.[46]

The Ta'wil of Biblical Sacrifices: A Case Study

> Even a non-Jew who studies the Torah of our master Moses resembles a
> High Priest.
>
> —Maimonides

[42] Baron, *Social and Religious History* 6:301
[43] Fakhry, *Islamic Philosophy*, 97–105; van Ess, "Ibn al-Rewandi"; Plessner, "Heresy and Rationalism."
[44] Powers, "Reading/Misreading," 109.
[45] F. Rosenthal, *History of al-Tabari*; Newby, "Tafsir Isra'iliyyat." For a discussion of Isra'iliyyat, see chapter 6 below.
[46] Schreiner, "Zur Geschichte"; Baalbeki, "Early Arab Lexicographers"; Corbin, "Theologoumena Iranica," 233.

Of the five aforementioned "deviants," Muhammad Abu Bakr al-Razi produced the most lasting contribution to world thought with his distinguished
if radical philosophy. This philosopher, who claimed a status equal to that of
Socrates and Aristotle, mastered the whole of the available Greek philosophical tradition, was famed as the premier physician and alchemist of his day, and
is known by at least one historian of philosophy as "the greatest nonconfor-
mist in the whole history of Islam."[47]

Razi's notoriety, then as now, derives from his disdainful rejection of the
positive content of revealed religion. In the excerpt to which I now turn,
Razi's attack on the Torah, he unmistakably draws upon the venerable tradition of rationalist "Bible questions." Alas, the full text of his Bible critique has
survived only in the version of his enemy, the early Isma'ili missionary Abu
Hatim al-Razi.[48]

Al-Razi forthrightly attacks the Torah on the grounds that it is absurd to
believe that God *needs* burnt sacrifices.[49] Razi adduces lengthy biblical texts,
and Abu Hatim muscularly responds with much longer citations concerning
the Tabernacle, Ark, and sacrifices from the books of Exodus and Leviticus.
Razi argued that these detailed biblical descriptions could only be satanic
work, so glaringly inimical were they to the abstract purity of the true philosophers' ratiocination.

Abu Hatim responds to Razi with accusatory ripostes. The Isma'ili Abu
Hatim contends that

> [Razi] claimed that [these biblical passages] were corrupted and their use was mere
> prattle and a jest. [In these assertions Razi] relies for assistance on the assertions of
> the Manicheans, that Moses was one of the Apostles of Satan. He said: "Anyone
> who is concerned with this [question] should read the *Book of Books* of the Mani-
> cheans. Then he will become aware of the wonderful things in their statements
> concerning Judaism, from Abraham to the time of Jesus."[50]

[47] Fakhry, *Islamic Philosophies*, 97; Razi, "The Book of the Philosophic Life."
[48] Ivanow, *Guide*, 32; Halm, "Abu Hatem Razi," 315; Madelung, *Religious Trends*,
98–100. For some of his works see *A'lam al-Nubuwwa*, and parts of *Kitab al-Zina*: the
section on the sects was edited by A. S. al-Sammarra'i as an Appendix to his *Al-
Ghuluww wal-Firaq*. Another section was edited as *Kitab al-Zina*. This latter work was
analyzed by Vajda in "Les Lettres," 113–30.
[49] On the ancient critique of sacrifices in the context of this line of argumentation, see J.
Rosenthal, *Hiwi al-Balkhi*, 36 n. 154. Razi may well have followed the Manichean
rejection of sacrifice. See Pines, "Jewish-Christians," 302–5. Note that Abu Hatim
explicitly denounces what he claims to be the Manicheanism of Razi (see the next note).
[50] In his "Principles of Biblical Exegesis," Qirqisani announces that he would "mention the problems involved in Biblical passages of ambiguous and seemingly contradictory nature, which are pointed out by dissenters and deviators, such as the Man-
naniyya [Manichean] sect and others" (Nemoy, *Karaite Anthology*, 53). See also the
paragraph on the Mananniya on p. 336, citing *Kitab al-Anwar* 2:251. On Razi as a
crypto-Manichean, see the contemporary perspectives of Nasr, *Three Muslim Sages*,
17; Corbin, *La Philosophie islamique*, 197; and Monnot, *Penseurs Musulmans*, 136.

For present purposes, it is especially important to note that Abu Hatim responds to Razi's allegedly Manichean antibiblical diatribe with classic Isma'ili ta'wil—that is, he argues that such biblical details must be properly understood in their esoteric, figurative meanings. The Tabernacle and the Ark, the burnt fat and the carved altar—all these details are *metaphors* for inner realities. "And if these are not metaphors . . . then [the Bible] is the work of madmen, of those who do not understand their own statements. . . . And we seek protection in God from the one who thinks this of Moses!"[51]

What, then, was the source of true authority? For Abu Hatim, ta'wil was the employment of metaphoric exegesis as the legitimation of an in-group. For his opponent, Razi, raciocination was the delegitimizing aggression of an out-group. Both strove for the truly authoritative reading. The example of the ta'wil of blood sacrifices shows that quite disparate readers could use similar ta'wil of the same verses for utterly divergent purposes. Precisely such contrasts can be found in two ninth and tenth-century debates. The disputation of the Rabbanite Saadia Gaon versus the dissident Jew Hiwi al-Balkhi can be instructively compared with the debate between the Isma'ili Abu Hatim al-Razi and the radical philosopher al-Razi in this regard.

The Jewish disputation between Saadia and Hiwi plays on motifs familiar from antiquity. Hiwi asked how God could accept fat and blood "as sweet savor."[52] Saadia responded that "like of all flesh is in the blood, therefore God has given it to us to bring to the altar as an atonement that we may remember that we are but flesh and blood and thereby humbled and reproved."[53] Saadia's response follows midrashic lines, which likewise defended the book of Leviticus against such contemporaneous anti-Jewish accusations of Marcion and the author of the Pseudo-Clementines.[54] Marmorstein has shown that the rabbis of the Amoraic period were "as well aware as the author of the Pseudo-Clementine works, or in later centuries Maimonides, or nowadays any student of the history of religions, that sacrifices were a temporary measure adapted to the needs of Moses' pupils."[55]

---

[51] See below, for my translation of this passage in its full context.

[52] Davidson, *Saadia's Polemic*, 52–55. See also Zucker, *Torah Translation*, 14. Georges Vajda. See "À propos de l'attitude religieuse," 81–91, at 88: Hiwi "was in no sense a crypto-Christian or crypto-Manichean Jew, but rather a representative within Judaism of *zandaqa* [radical freethought]" (my translation). Baron follows Vajda in this regard (*Social and Religious History* 6:482 n. 96). Guttmann, *Philosophies of Judaism*, asserts that the "decisive influence" on Hiwi was Manicheanism (57–58). On the other hand, Zucker, *Torah Translation,* has argued vigorously that the influence was that of indigenous radicalism of the freethinking sort, "extreme rationalism [leading to] complete religious nihilism" (31). This is not the place to review the slowly growing literature on Hiwi, Bible critique, and the relations he had to al-Razi and Ibn al-Rewandi. But see, for example, van Ess, "Ibn al-Rewandi," 5–27, esp. 14, to the effect that he "associated himself with his Jewish colleague Hiwi from Balkh."

[53] Saadia, *Book of Beliefs*, 55.

[54] Marmorstein, *Studies in Jewish Theology*, 39–42.

[55] Ibid., 41.

Both Saadia and Abu Hatim resort to ta'wil in defense of commonly recognized holy books. Saadia employs a Judaized Muʿtazilite ta'wil; Abu Hatim utilizes Ismaʿili Batini (esoteric) ta'wil. The individual authority of "rational" interpretations on the question of biblical sacrifices posed by the challengers Hiwi and Razi threatened the collective authority of ta'wil in Saadia's rabbinism and Abu Hatim's Ismaʿilism. In other words, they exemplify, respectively, the ethical and the mystical forms of allegorical defense. These were the two poles of ta'wil. The first is metaphoric: the rational reading of metaphor designed to extract "safe" ethical referents. The other pole was Batini, "interior": the familiarly mystical violence done to the scriptural figure.

These polarized positions of the Kulturkampf over the meaning of scripture were not new. The problem of sacrifices—the apparently counter-rational nature of revealed ritual—inexorably drew Manicheans and Brahmins, heretics and philosophers, into this many-sided debate, as it had in late antiquity. This thematic continuity led some scholars, such as Marmorstein, to consider Hiwi as a kind of Marcionite. Altmann likewise spoke of Jews with "strong leanings towards the Manicheaen religion. It seems that Hiwi al-Balkhi was the spokesman of this group. This strange and mysterious figure, the Jewish Marcion of the age . . . sharply criticized the Bible from a Gnostic point of view."[56] While we do read that Marcionites were still around in tenth-century Khurasan, and so-called Marcionite sectarians were known to Muslim heresiographers, this does not constitute a sufficiently compelling reason to prove this case one way or another.[57]

Marcionite or not, antirabbinic "Gnosticizing" objections to the Bible were passed on from antiquity to the tenth century. A catalog of topoi was already organized in antiquity, which linked tabernacles, sacrifices, and light in a critique of the notion the "needs" of God. Elkesaites and Ebionites found sacrifices abhorrent to God.[58] The Clementine Homilies state flatly that "He is not pleased with sacrifices," and Epiphanius relates that the Ebionites reject sacrifices, using the Hebrew Bible to render New Testament meanings.[59] Another Jewish-Christian sect, the so-called Nasaraioi, "refused to offer or to eat the flesh of animals."[60]

But the rejection of sacrifices was in fact neither reserved as an antiquarian fetish nor as a topos lacking a contemporary historical referent. The Jewish

---

[56] Introduction to Saadia's *Book of Beliefs*, 14. Marmorstein suggested (less apodictically but more tendentiously) that "dark corners of the East may have preserved Marcionite doctrines and writings, especially in Hiwi's native place or country" (*Studies in Jewish Theology*, 19).

[57] Ibn al-Nadim does say that in his day there were "many Marcionists in Khurasan, their cause being openly known" (The Fihrist of Ibn al-Nadim 2:807). For the heresiographical treatment, see, for example, Shahrastani, *Livre des religions* 1:669–70.

[58] Koch, *Critical Investigation*, 303–4, stresses that the Ebionites reject sacrifices, using Torah verses to make New Testament meanings.

[59] *Clementine Homilies*, homily 3.

[60] See, for example, M. Simon, *Jewish Sects*, 104.

'Isawiyya explicitly rejected the act of making sacrifices.[61] Moreover, if Manicheans were still active in the tenth century, then they also were asserting this position, for it was long a doctrine of theirs.[62] The Karaites developed a position of their own in this regard. They were well aware of the positions in the air. Qirqisani explicitly refutes "the problems involved in biblical passages of ambiguous and seemingly contradictory nature, which are pointed out by dissenters and deviators, such as the Mannaniya sect (Manicheans) and others."[63] Qirqisani also explicitly defends biblical sacrifices in his extended refutation of the doctrines of the 'Isawiyya—another indication, incidentally, that they too were still threateningly apparent on the scene.[64]

Abu Hatim thus defends revelations as metaphors, while Razi attacks them as philosophically puerile and logically inconsistent. In fact, Razi finds prophetic religions plainly repugnant. Elsewhere, Razi cites a poet to make this latter point:

I wonder at Chosroes and his people,
washing their faces in the urine of cows;
I wonder at the Byzantine Caesar who adores
what human hands have wrought.
How strange are the Jews with their God
Who rejoices in spilling blood and smelling incense.

Corbin is surely accurate: Razi was possessed by an "egalitarian furor."[65] His compulsion to level off all revelations veers almost imperceptibly into a doctrinaire positing of the relative equivalence of all religions. Serious comparison, classification, and typology became possible at precisely this transition point from comparative exegesis to comparative religion.

As is well known, the counter-rational character of ritual tends to elicit such allegorizing and historicizing explanations in every age of criticism.[66] The Islamicate Renaissance was no exception in this regard. What made it exceptional, if not entirely novel, was the extent to which it went beyond piecemeal and self-interested critiques to produce a seriously generalizing and encyclopedic discourse on religion as such. Under conditions of such potentially unmanageable complexity, what were the criteria utilized to establish agreement and difference between religions? One answer is that both official leaders and unofficial challengers, rationalists and mystics, exploited ta'wil.

[61] Pines, "Jewish Christians," 28.
[62] I deal with this question in chapter 2 above. Pines "Jewish-Christians," (280) also makes this connection.
[63] Cited in Nemoy, *Karaite Anthology*, 53. See also the paragraph on p. 336 (from *Kitab al-Anwar* 3:251) on the Manicheans.
[64] This is a leitmotif of his attack on the 'Isawiyya. See *Kitab al-Anwar* vol. 2 and 3:283–301, particularly the discussion of *naskh* (abrogation).
[65] Poem cited in Perlmann, "Medieval Polemics," 107; Corbin "La philosophie islamique," 200.
[66] Grant, *Letter and the Spirit*; Dawson, *Allegorical Readers*.

Indeed, the respectively dissident and establishment members of the comparativist discourse both favored allegorical interpretation, thereby setting the limits of this discourse. Allegorical interpretation, then, was not only a discourse on the borders; it also emanated from the center. It could function in an apologetic or a mystifying mode. In its apologetic, moralizing thrust it was mobilized primarily by a rationalist leadership who opposed the perceived threat of anthropomorphism, of portraying God in corporeal imagery. This mode was purgatively metaphoric: "clean" ethical referents were extracted from metaphors. It was thus used by rationalists against literalists and mystics. The contrasting, mystical mode was employed by Shiʿites, for example, to imply a transcendent unity of world religions out of scriptural figuration. This mode, in fact, was put to the service of a charismatically legitimated sectarian vision, that of Shiʿism.

I now return to Massignon to conclude this stage of my discussion. He drew the apparently paradoxical conclusion: "The very special character of this Renaissance is its aspect of being simultaneously skeptic and gnostic." Yet more precisely for my purposes, Bernard Lewis observes, "For both the skeptic and the mystic, the differences between religions was of not great importance. For the one they were all equally true, for the other almost equally false."[67] At the extremes of this situation, in other words, philosophers rejected all revealed religion—while mystics purported to embrace them all. This meeting of extremes in the comparativist method, paradoxical as it appears, made comparative religion possible. Those who felt that "the differences between religions was not of great importance" thus helped stimulate a new science, comparative religion, which posited the master explanation for such relativized similarity and difference as its very raison d'être.

We have, then, an irony: the radical program (which could be skeptic or Gnostic) to level off all revelations now converges with the communal leaders' imperative to confute the official opposition (which could be Jewish or Muslim). Unofficial and offical comparativisms are extremes that now meet. This confluence of heretofore opposed assumptions and interests synthesizes a singular idea. There is now a broadly multilateral agreement that "religions" are generic. There is not only one True Religion, but rather a category, a species. Serious comparison, classification, and even typology become possible at precisely this transition point from comparative exegesis to comparative religion.

JEWISH STUDIES AND COMPARATIVE RELIGION

Because the major Muslim contribution to writing the history of Jewish life comes from the *milal wa nihal* literature, I shall consider this great corpus of scholarship. As I said at the outset, this literature does indeed contain much scholarship of lasting value: the encyclopedists of the eleventh and twelfth

[67] Massignon, *Passion*, 1:195; Lewis, *Jews of Islam*, 88.

centuries authored this Muslim comparative study of "religion," (strikingly) comprehensive and (sporadically) dispassionate overviews of world religions. This new scholarly study came to be known (retrospectively) as *al-milal wa'l-nihal*, "religions and sects."[68] Western scholarly approbation of this literature has been properly sustained and enthusiastic, based on the accurate observation that this historical science was pioneered by Muslims. Von Grunebaum notes that "in their books on sects, or comparative religion, the research acumen of the Muslims shows at its best." Goitein observes that "[Islam], which for the first time in the world history made lasting physical contacts with all contemporary cultures, created also a new science: Comparative Religion. . . . [The] science of *Milal wa-Nihal*, or comparative religion, as developed by . . . Islam, is still awaiting a worthy heir." Laoust says, "The comparative history of religions is a Muslim creation."[69]

Muslim comparative religion began as and remained a kind of blend of science and law, and not simply a dispassionate science. That is, most of these "scientists" were also lawyers, and their law, the *shari'a*, demanded objective information on non-Muslim communities so that those communities could be treated appropriately by law-enforcement officials. The vaunted scientific accuracy of much of the research, then, while indeed admirable, was never a plainly disinterested taxonomizing. Rather, it constituted a study designed to be applied practically to living communities at hand. For my purposes, I must note that Muslim scholars applied categories to Jews and Judaism not merely out of a scientific love of the subject.

As it turned out, the majority of those who undertook such work were motivated by extraneous motives, that is, motives often only tangentially theological—they had other axes to grind. In other words, the analysis and description of Judaism was taken up widely, and not only by theologians armed with a precise polemical program. In fact, jurisprudential, "mythological," and historical catgegories were applied to Jews by a surprising variety of scholars. Laoust makes this point forcefully in his major survey of Muslim heresiography: "All Muslim thinkers, whether they are included in the category of juriconsults, dogmatic theologians, traditionists or philosophers, in their own manner, and in varying degrees, also are heresiographers."[70]

The popular genre of categorizing into which Jews were so frequently found to fit, then, was that of *heresiography*, what might be called the science of the errors of others. Of course, it has long been recognized that the history of misbelief comprises an integral part of the history of belief.[71] It is due to the impulse to record, refute, and control perceived errors on the part of "the

[68] For the following, see Wasserstrom, "Islamicate History," some of which is reproduced with modifications here.
[69] Von Grunebaum, *Medieval Islam*, 336–37; Goitein, "Between Hellenism," 218–19; Laoust, "Comment définir," 4 (my translation).
[70] Laoust, "L'hérésiographie," 157 (my translation).
[71] G. Cohen, *Book of Tradition*, lix.

others" that so much of the basic data we possess for the study of the history of religions has survived. In the present context, I emphasize that the origins of comparative religion are simply inseparable from the study of Muslim heresiography. I therefore agree with Massignon: "it was the Muslim heresiographers writing in Arabic . . . who systematized the science of religions as an autonomous discipline."[72] This systematization was possible, as I have said, because the sources, the data, for comparative religions are adduced in heresiographies, and because most of the major Muslim thinkers were also, to one degree or another, heresiographers.

This heresiography originally derived from comparative exegesis, from the disputations and salons in which Jews, Muslims, Christians, and others met to discuss scriptures and other matter. Because Muslim comparative religion extended in scope far beyond that of the study of Judaism or even of monotheism—it encompassed Hinduism and Buddhism, Gnosticism and Zoroastrianism—comparative exegesis would appear to be only one factor in its origins. That point is of course accurate, but also misleading, for it was in the first instance—though I cannot argue out this point here—that is, the personal encounter with Jews and Christians, in the disputational, polemic, apologetic, and sectarian milieu of the eighth and ninth centuries that developed "comparativist language" and the category of "religion," and placed them into the mental armaments of the Muslim intelligentsia. The weapons tested in that formative encounter then could be applied with more surgical precision elsewhere.

Eventually, those interested in Judaism would also study other religions. Ibn Hazm, the eleventh-century Spanish author of one of the earliest and most complete works on "Religions and Sects" cites dozens of pages of the Hebrew Bible—and the New Testament.[73] Biruni (b. 973) learned not only Hebrew, but Syriac and even Sanskrit.[74] This incipient comparative religion culminated in the work of the twelfth-century Shahrastani, who was simply the greatest of all premodern historians of religions.[75] Interestingly enough, Shahrastani organized his study of non-Muslim religions according to proximity to Islam: the first of dozens of non-Muslim religions that he treated in sequence—and therefore in theological priority—was Judaism. From a Jewish starting point, as it were, he ranged through all religions known in his day.

The Study of Judaism

How did this Muslim scholarship regarding Jews and Judaism eventually operate? This question addresses the concern raised by Anawati: "Heresiology

---

[72] Massignon, "Language," 251.
[73] Ibn Hazm, *Kitab al-Fisal*; N. Roth, "Forgery"; Powers, "Reading/Misreading"; Adang, *Muslim Writers*.
[74] Baalabaki, "Early Arab Lexicographers," 120.
[75] Wasserstrom, "Islamicate History."

has to *classify* the doctrines which it has collected. It can do so in a material way, even according to the order of appearance of the heresies, but it must also try to reduce them to a certain number of types. It is therefore interesting to find out the method of classification."[76] In the context of the present discussion, it remains to analyze this "method of classification." Accordingly, I will now briefly unpack the generative propositions that underlie the Muslim analysis of Judaism.

How, then, did these Muslim historians of religion differentiate kinds of Jews and Judaism? What was their category "Jew"? Muslim heresiographers, first of all, classified Jewish groups by applying the criteria and categories formed by the jurisprudents and traditionists upon a Qur'anic and traditional basis. Their categorization of kinds of Jews, therefore, was determined by the legal categories governing non-Muslims.

But these categories were ultimately modeled upon the paradigmatic religion, Islam. As a result, the methods of classification in Muslim heresiography of the Jews were not different in substance from the normative methods of classification used in Muslim heresiography of Muslims. The structure of Shahrastani's presentation of the Jews is identical in structure to his presentation of the Muslims, and of all other groups. This structural similarity supports the supposition that these authors assumed an essential homology between religions, that Judaism was seen by this comparative religion as being essentially homologous with Islam in terms of its basic makeup. They both belonged to the common category of "religion."

Modes of Classification in Muslim Heresiography of the Jews

However self-evident and however significant this observation may appear, little scholarly study has been applied to analyze the Muslim construction of the category of religion and the assumptions underpinning it. How, then, were lists of kinds of Jews constructed following the blueprints of such assumptions? Following Wansborough's categories, one could schematize these modes of classification as: "(1) *numerical* (to make up the celebrated total of 'seventy-three sects'), (2) *ad hominem* ('schools' generated from the names of individuals by means of a *nisba* suffix), (3) *doctrinal* (divergent attitudes to specific problems)."[77] I will address the numerical, ad hominem, and doctrinal propositions in turn.

The remarkable Ignaz Goldziher produced what remains the *mise-au-point* on the *numerical* proposition, in his classic paper "Le dénombrement des sectes mohamétanes." He points out that the hadith (with its numerous variations) that reads "The Jews are divided into seventy-one sects, the Christians seventy-two: My community will be divided into seventy-three sects" constitutes the basic form of the proposition that underlies much of the operating

---

[76] Anawati, "Philosophy, Theology and Mysticism," 361.
[77] Wansborough, *Sectarian Milieu*, 116.

procedure for Muslim histories of religious communities. "This hadith, soon generally disseminated with quite light variations, comprises the basis for the history of religions and sects in Muslim literature . . . [and] consequently it is universally considered to be the point of departure for the interior religious history of Islam."[78]

I take the most celebrated such example first. Muhammad said, "The Jews are divided into seventy-one sects, the Christians seventy-two: My community will be divided into seventy-three sects." This tradition underlies much of the operating procedure for Muslim histories of all religious communities. It not only provides the paradigm of the Muslim perception of the essential homology between Islam and Judaism; it moreover serves as an exemplary instance of Muslim belief in what might be termed the provident plurality of religious communities. One of the most thorough Muslim scholars of Judaism thus begins his extensive discussion of Jewish sects by proclaiming, "Know that the Jews, whom God dispersed in the world . . ."[79] In other words, sectarianism is seen as a kind of divinely ordained complication. The Muslim heresiographers thus see the Jews in terms of sects (*firaq*), sects that God designed both as paradigm and as warning for the Muslim community. Indeed, this perception constitutes perhaps the fundamental doctrinal legitimation for the practice of Muslim comparative religion as such.

A second mode of categorization, *ad hominem*, is organized around ostensible "originators" of Jewish groups. This sometimes resulted in the thinly veiled personification of a doctrine, with no apparent motivation other than to "hang" the heresy around the neck of a purported founder figure. The best example of the application of this technique was in the case of Abu 'Isa al-Isfahani, who was usually little more in these accounts than the hypostasis of the idea that divine revelations were of a limited purview. Abu 'Isa, nevertheless, was indeed a historical figure.[80] The ad hominem proposition could even occasionally result in sects' being related to wholly spurious, concocted originators. This is the case with the comment made in the *Rasa'il Ikhwan al-Safa'* concerning what were cast as the seemingly legendary originators of the three major Jewish groupings, the Rabbanites, the Karaites, and the Samaritans. The three that were so named, "Jaluti," "Anani," and "Samiri," were none of them in fact actual people (though a certain 'Anan was).[81]

An interesting sidelight on the ad hominem proposition was the sustained and often ingenious efforts by Muslim scholars to derive "Islamic" heresies from what were represented as actual Jewish figures, who were then equipped with the rudiments of a biography. It would be difficult to find a Muslim heresy that was not at one time or another traced back to a Jewish originator.

---

[78] Goldziher, "Le dénombrement," 131.
[79] Maqrizi, *Al-Mawa'iz*, 2:476.
[80] See chapter 2 above.
[81] Wasserstrom, "Species of Misbelief," 115–19 reviews the literature and discusses this passage in more detail.

Thus, to cite only a few, the ghulat deification of ʿAli was assigned to ʿAbd Allah ibn Saba';[82] the origination of Ismaʿilism was ascribed to Maymun al-Qaddah;[83] the Fatimids were said to have been further inspired by Yaʿqub ibn Killis;[84] the idea of the "Created Qur'an" was ascribed to Labid;[85] and the heretic Jahm b. Safwan was said to have been taught by Aban b. Maymun, who was taught by Talut b. Aʿsam, "the Jew who bewitched Muhammad."[86]

A more generalizing, and inverted, variation on the ad hominem proposition were the traditions that read, "The *X* [a heretical group] are the Jews of this umma" (addressed more fully in chapter 3 above). Here again is a reflection of the assumption of the homology of the two communities. The Jews are the paradigm in this case of the religious community gone astray. They are thus held to be the model for various subversions of Islam, an accusation frequently made of the Rafida, the Murji'a, and the Mushabbiha.[87]

For the purposes at hand, the ad hominem proposition was used to organize lists that derived each sect from its named sectary founder. This could be easily done with the Karaites, founded by ʿAnan, and the ʿIsawiyya, founded by Abu ʿIsa. The Rabbanites, without any apparent founder, presented a problem for the heresiographer concerned with ad hominem symmetry. This problem was solved by some of the heresiographers by ascribing Rabbanite Judaism to a fictional Ashmaʿath, or Shamʿun.[88] Others resorted to even more strained derivations; Isfara'ini relates an involved legend concerning the origins of sectarianism in Judaism being derived from an ancient rabbi who hid the true text of the Torah in a horn around his neck, which led subsequent Jews to quarrel over the true text.[89]

The third and final method of classification, sometimes overlapping with one or the other of the first two, was *doctrinal*—that is, Jewish sects were listed according to their respective positions on a certain doctrine. Two doctrines were most frequently utilized for such a purpose. The first, that of the abrogation of divinely revealed laws by subsequent revelations (*naskh*), was frequently a point of departure.[90] The second, less-popular organizing principle within doctrinal discussion was to group the Jews according to their adherence to or divergence from anthropomorphism (*tajsim* or *tashbih*).[91]

Of these three categories, the doctrinal category was most clearly drawn from the data and observations of comparative exegesis. For example, the categorization of Jews according to anthropomorphism, often adduced with

[82] I. Friedlaender "ʿAbdallah b. Saba."
[83] Vladimir Ivanow, *Ibn al-Qaddah*.
[84] Lewis, *Origins of Ismailism*, 67–69.
[85] Baron, *Social and Religious History* 6:484 n. 104.
[86] Tritton, "Discords and Differences," 85.
[87] Wasserstrom, "Delay of *Maghrib*," 271–72.
[88] Wasserstrom, "Muslim Designation."
[89] Isfara'ini, *Al-Tabsir*, 132–33.
[90] Ashtor, "Methods of Muslim Polemics."
[91] Altmann, "Moses Narboni," 228–29.

reference to passages from the biblical Book of Daniel, remained a discernible vestige of the debates with Jews. Abu Hatim al-Razi, for example, adduces these biblical passages in this celebrated debates with the philosopher Razi.[92]

The propositions by which Muslim "Jewish studies" were organized were workably objective in theory, however subjectively distorted they may have been in application. As a result of this systematic approach, coupled with its occasional research acumen, it is possible to farm this literature, for example, to aid in writing Jewish history: this rarely undertaken procedure is itself important enough to warrant the present discussion.

The Prehistory of Muslim Heresiography of the Jews

Before discussing the history of Muslim heresiography of the Jews, it is necessary to mention a number of purportedly early Muslim classifications of Jews, some of which are indeed early and others of which are only spuriously so. The earliest Muslim classification of Jews is found in the Qur'an (61:14): "A faction (*ta'ifa*) of the Banu Isra'il believed, and a faction disbelieved" (cf. 43:65).[93] The study of the earliest Muslim contacts with the Jewish communities of Arabia may yet reveal the precise delineation of the pluralism of the communities to which the Qur'an alludes, but for the moment these remain uncertain.

A number of other early texts may be adduced. The Hanafite legist Shaybani, for example, describes the "Jews of Iraq," circa 184/800, as holding a doctrine that was commonly ascribed to the 'Isawiyya, whom, it is reasonable to assume, he is in fact describing.[94] The historian Baladhuri and the legist Abu Yusuf both discuss the Samaritans.[95] Auza'i, dealing with inheritance, and Shafi'i, addressing the problem of who is appropriately liable to pay the *jizya*, also apparently dealt with the question of the Samaritans in the context of their Jewishness within the legal frame of reference.[96]

Perhaps the most significant of these early mentions appears in the vexed context of the so-called 'Ahd 'Umar, the "Pact of 'Umar."[97] The problem with this allegedly early text, said to have been authored by the caliph 'Umar (ruled 634–44) himself in making a covenant with the newly subjugated communities, is that the surviving versions of the pact do not antedate the fourth/tenth century. This is certainly the case with all the best-known ver-

---

[92] Abu Hatim al-Razi, *A'lam al-Nubuwwa*, 52; Brion, "Philosophie"; Brion, "Le Temp, l'espace"; Daiber, "Abu Hatim al-Razi on Unity."

[93] Pines, "Notes on Islam," 135–45; Abbott, "Wahb b. Munabbih," 109.

[94] Goldziher, "Usages juifs," 91–92.

[95] Montgomery, *Samaritans*, 351.

[96] Yaqut, *Irshad al-Arib* 6:454–55; Ibn Qayyim al-Jauziyya, *Ahkam Ahl al-Dhimma* 2:90–92.

[97] Bosworth, "Concept of Dhimma"; Khadduri, *War and Peace*, 175–202; von Grunebaum, "Medieval Islam."

sions of the pact.[98] One of the purportedly earliest variants of the ʿAhd ʿUmar begins by addressing the known variety of Jews and Christians. The Jews are specified as the "Rabban, Qarran and Samira."[99] Since the Karaite schism did not occur until the mid-second/eighth century, this text could not have been written until at least ʿAbbasid times. It would likely be rather later, since the Arabic designation of the schismatics as Qarra'un did not come into currency for some time after their initial break from Rabbanism. Nevertheless, this text is particularly significant precisely for its anachronistic retrojection of the heresiographic list into the formative political confrontation between the Jewish and Muslim commmunities, the establishing of the pact of toleration. Here is the clearest example of the legal implications and political motivations for writing these lists.

The History of Muslim Heresiography of the Jews

Heresiography, as I am using the term, is not a genre in itself. Rather, it is an approach and an inquiry. As such, it can and was undertaken within all kinds of genres. As I have already noted, Laoust emphasized this point: "All Muslim thinkers, whether they are included in the category of juriconsults, dogmatic theologians, traditionists or philosophers, in their own manner, and in varying degrees, also are heresiographers."[100] In consideration of this scattering of context, it may be helpful to reiterate here the locations of heresiographic lists of kinds of Jews, as they are found in Arabic (and to a lesser extent, Persian) from the tenth through the twelfth century. While these citations can be expressed in the ninth century, and certainly continue beyond the thirteenth century, the influx of new data and novel treatment of that data are predominantly (though not exclusively) confined to the tenth through the twelfth centuries.

Before I review the history of Muslim heresiography of the Jews as such, I should first consider the earliest formative influences on it. Elsewhere I have argued that Christian influence was especially significant in this regard, and that that significance is somewhat neglected in modern scholarship. I argue that Christian influence can be perceived, for example, in Muslim heresiographical classifications of Samaritans.[101] I also suggest that one of the most common (and curious) epithets for the Rabbanites ("Ashma'ath") may have passed into Muslim usage through Christian intermediation.[102]

Muslim heresiography of the Jews as such begins with the Muʿtazilites in the ninth and tenth centuries. The Muʿtazilite involvement in this nascent technique was manifold. Jahiz, for example, touches on several of the themes,

[98] Ahmad, "Non-Muslims and the Umma."
[99] Bernhauer, "Mémoires," 57.
[100] Laoust, "L'hérésiographie," 157 (my translation). See also Madelung, "Häresiographie," 374–78.
[101] Wasserstrom, "Species of Misbelief," 35–80, 50–52.
[102] I discussed this in "Muslim Designation for Rabbanite Jews."

such as the motif of the exilarch, which was to recur throughout the history of Muslim heresiography of the Jews.[103] Encyclopedist-littérateurs such as Mas'udi and Maqdisi set forth the first lists, and provide some of the most tantalizing historical tidbits.[104] And Mu'tazilite theologians, writing qua theologians, also began to organize lists of Jews according to their respective divergence from certain Islamic doctrines.[105] Mu'tazilites were heavily involved in both disputations with the Jews and polemical writing against them, but their heresiographic works can be only indirectly linked with their explicitly controversial activities.[106]

In the fourth/tenth and fifth/eleventh centuries, a series of talented writers take up this heresiography of the Jews from quite varied perspectives. Khwarizmi subsumes his unique list in a chapter on the technical terms used by Mutakallimun. Biruni discusses these groups when he considers the calendars of "ancient peoples." Ibn Hazm writes a book-length monograph against the Jews, containing a great deal of heresiography, which he then includes as a single, albeit hypertrophied, chapter of his great work on world religions. Even such "Gnostic encyclopedists" as the Ikhwan al-Safa' bring up the Jewish sects several times.[107]

At the same time these various writers were beginning to use Jewish sects as "literary material," the major Mutakallimun of the fourth/tenth through fifth/eleventh centuries were developing their own scholastic heresiological discourse. The categories of sects and the arguments against them were unmistakably part of a Kalam discourse passed on in a direct line from Baqillani to Ghazali.[108] In later centuries Razi, Amidi, and others continued this highly specific rhetorical deployment of Jewish sects to prove the universality of the message of Muhammad and of the traditions concerning him, precisely as this usage had been standardized already in the beginning of the fifth/eleventh century.[109] Kalam provides the one consistent usage of these materials, and the regularization of the Kalam citations stands out from the otherwise irregular and unpredictable Muslim heresiographical usages.[110]

This rich variety is fully in evidence by the sixth/twelfth century, against a sustained backdrop of ongoing Kalam repetitions. The most distinguished

---

[103] Goldziher, "Renseignements," 122; Jahiz, *Kitab al-Hayawan* 1:234, 340, 375, 2:27, 5:107, 451, 6:71, 359, 7:25, 246.

[104] Maqdisi, *Kitab al-Bad'* 4:34–36; Mas'udi, *Kitab al-Tanbih*, 112–13, 219.

[105] 'Abd al-Jabbar, *Sharh al-Usul*, 576–77.

[106] Laoust, "L'hérésiographie," 160–61.

[107] Khwarizmi, *Liber Mafatih*, 34; Biruni, *Athar al-Baqiyya*, 15, 21, 58–59, 284–85; Ibn Hazm, *Kitab al-Fisal* 1:78–79, 90, 93; *Rasa'il* editions, Beirut II: 367; Cairo II: 308; Beirut III: 161; Cairo III: 167.

[108] Baqillani, *Tamhid*, 160, 170; Baghdadi, *Usul al-Din*, 325–26; Isfara'ini, *Al-Tabsir*, 132–34.

[109] Razi, *Kitab I'tiqadat*, 82–83; Amidi, *Ghayat al-Maram*, 341, 349–50; Amidi, *Ihkam al-Hukkam* 2:245.

[110] Wasserstrom, "Species of Misbelief," 153–221.

use of heresiography in this period was surely that of Shahrastani.[111] He uses his primary sources critically and sets forth his presentation of them with (for such studies) unparalleled objectivity.[112] By contrast, Samau'al al-Maghribi, a Jewish convert to Islam, writes a lengthy and viciously anti-Jewish polemic in which he turns his intimate confessional awareness against his former co-religionists. Several Kalamists wrote their by-now-standardized treatments in this century, one of which, that of Murtada, was in Persian. And Nashwan al-Himyari wrote an unusual updating of earlier lists, which presents several difficulties for the historian.[113]

Rabbanites, Karaites, and Other Denominations

Much if not most of recorded Muslim knowledge of Judaism and Jewish life concerns generic Jews (Yahud), is denominationally non-specific, and so should not be taken to refer to Rabbanites as a matter of course, as it often is. With regard specifically to Rabbanites, it is well known that Muslim treatment of rabbinic belief, practice, and history generally tended to be stereotyped, and polemically driven.

To some considerable extent, the same may be said of the treatment of Samaritans. We do, fortunately, possess miscellaneous, sometimes unparalleled details concerning the historical distribution and occasional activities of Samaritans, ranging from Baladhuri's early report on Samaritan cooperation during the Muslim conquest of Palestine, to the kind of oaths submitted by Samaritans in court, given on the authority of 'Umari and Qalqashandi.[114]

The history of early Karaism has certainly been enriched by Muslim sources. While we usually possess no corroborating evidence for some of the details, and so cannot confirm their historicity, it is nevertheless the case that these sources do provide important, unparalleled pieces of evidence with regard to Karaite origins. Most especially, we are told precious details regarding the still very obscure 'Anan ben David, the so-called founder of Karaism.[115] In this regard it is interesting to note that the lastest scholarship emphasizes the distinction between the 'Ananites and the subsequent Karaites. Early Muslim sources also attest to this distinction.

The disparity between the post-Islamic Jewish sects and the more ancient Samaritans and Rabbanites is of some significance. Of all the Jewish sects, the most frequently treated was the post-Islamic group most commonly known as the 'Isawiyya (discussed in chapter 2 above). This group was discussed for several reasons. The most important of these was that the 'Isawiyya were

---

[111] Shahrastani, *Kitab al-Milal*, 503–17.

[112] Wasserstrom, "Islamicate History."

[113] Samau'al al-Maghribi, *Ifham al-Yahud*, 79–82; Murtada, *Tabsirat*, 22–23; Nashwan al-Himyari, *al-Hur al-'Ayn*, 144–45.

[114] Montgomery, *Samaritans*, 351; 'Umari, *Al-Ta'rif*, 142–44; Qalqashandi, *Subh al-A'sha*, 13, 256, 268; Tzedaka, "History of the Samaritans."

[115] Nemoy, "'Anan ben David."

purportedly preaching the relativity of revelations, that is, that Muhammad was indeed a prophet of God, but that he was sent only to the Arabs and not to all peoples. The ʿIsawiyya were the most important Jewish sect (aside from the Karaites and the Samaritans) from the second century through the seventeenth century; insofar as they are attested almost exclusively by Muslim literature (aside from some Karaite reports), this is one of the most notable examples of Muslim knowledge of Jews and Jewish life that is not attested in Jewish literature.[116] Other sects, such as the Qarʿiyya, which was very little known, are also attested in Muslim heresiography.[117] Some, such as the so-called Jewish Christians, may be of considerable significance for the history of Jewish sectarianism, if they existed at all—for no consensus has emerged concerning their existence.[118]

Conclusion

> Yet is not Thy glory diminished by reason of those that adore aught beside Thee, for the intent of them all is to reach Thee.
>
> —Ibn Gabirol

These first critical studies of Judaism, as found in Muslim comparative religion, were revivifying variations on a dormant concept, now startlingly disseminated: the category of "religion" as such. As the Muslim Renaissance progressed, however, this maturation of the idea and category of religion also traced a process of abstraction, a certain falling off of living contact. The transition from concrete conversation to abstract category, from deeply felt disputation to dispassionate category, traced a shift from comparative exegesis to comparative religion. These dislocating origins of comparative religion are described in the sources with poignant complaints of cognitive dissonance. Such encyclopedism seems to have been experienced, in a sense, as both the cause of and the compensation for this stress. These Renaissance comparativists sought shelter under the totalizing umbrella of completeness, by encompassing all religious oppositions in a unifying discourse. This critical advance, however, could not assuage discontent. Loudly complaining of cultural confusion and uncertainty, the Islamicate historians of religions unsuccessfully neutralized the threat of their rivals when they pinned them on a grid of commonalities and differences.

The Jewish leaders Saadia and Qirqisani wrote Muʿtazilite defensive apologetics analogous to those of their official Muslim counterparts.[119] And they

---

[116] See chapter 2 above for details.
[117] Golb, "Topography of the Jews," 260; Suʿudi, *Disputatio*, 188–90; Wasserstrom, "Species of Misbelief," 279–83.
[118] See my brief overview of the problem, in chapter 1 above.
[119] Saadia Gaon, *Book of Beliefs*; Qirqisani, *Kitab al-Anwar*.

certainly complained with equal vehemence. But the crucial difference was that Jews never made the full transition from comparative exegesis to comparative religion. Jews wrote polemical and defensive exegeses but never took the ultimate step of naming erroneous others at length. The reason, I think, is that comparative religion is a prerogative of the dominant: it is the privilege of the submissive to be the object of inquiry. Thus Baron was led to observe:

> Certainly, by immersing oneself in a religious philosophy basically common to all three faiths, one unconsciously built a bridge to the understanding of the other creeds. Not without reason were such students of comparative religion as Shahrastani suspected of heresy. How much more dangerous must the scaling of interdenominational walls have appeared to members of an embattled minority, in any case subjected to endless conversionist pressures![120]

The category of "religion," then, allowed Muslims, but not Jews, to connect oppositions typologically under this one encompassing rubric. Viewed retrospectively, the irony in this situation was that such an overarching categorical boldness masked an underlying "failure of nerve"—if the spiritual crisis I sketched at the beginning of this chapter may be characterized aptly by such a phrase. Indeed, this complex of uncertainty and overcompensation demarcates the problem of misbelief in the tenth century.

In any event, the comparativist "blessed rage for order" and its radical quest for assurance did not hold the day. They futilely struggled with, in Wallace Stevens's words, "The maker's rage to order words of the sea / And of ourselves and of our origins, / In ghostlier demarcations, keener sounds,"[121] for the seriously critical study of religious difference lasted barely two hundred years, and even then was practiced by only a very few scholars.

[120] Baron, *Social and Religious History* 8:68.
[121] Stevens, *Poems of Wallace Stevens*, 56.

PART III

Intimacies

> Never has Judaism encountered such a close and fructuous symbiosis as that with the medieval civilization of Arab Islam.
>
> —S. D. Goitein, *Jews and Arabs*

CHAPTER FIVE

Origins and Angels: Popular and Esoteric Literature in Jewish-Muslim Symbiosis

> Rabbi: Now little Jesus, the carpenter's son,
> Let us see how Thy task is done;
> Canst thou thy letters say?
> Jesus: *Aleph.*
> Rabbi: What next? Do not stop yet!
> Go on with all the alphabet.
> Come, *Aleph, Beth*; dost thou forget?
> Cock's soul! Thou'dst rather play!
> Jesus: What *Aleph* means I fain would know
> Before I any farther go!
>
> —Longfellow, *The Golden Legend*

A PROPHET, as a young child, attends school for the first time. The teacher prompts him, "Say *A*!" to which the child-prophet responds "*A*." The teacher then proceeds, "Say *B*!" to which the wise child answers, "Tell me the meaning of *A* and I will tell you *B*!" The dumbfounded teacher faints. The child then recites the meaning of the entire alphabet, with a mystical meaning attached to each letter. The prophet-child's knowledge is a priori to education.

This story is told of the Buddha;[1] of Jesus;[2] of the Shi'ite Fifth Imam;[3]

---

[1] Some of the following reflects a revised version of Wasserstrom, "Jewish Pseudepigrapha." For the Buddha's first day of school and its relation to the Apocryphal Infancy Gospels, see Lillie, *Popular Life of the Buddha*, 30; Scott, *Buddhism and Christianity*, 162–64, on the Lalita Vistara and Christianity; Kuhn, "Buddhistisches in den apokryphen," 116–19; Buhler, *Indian Brahma Alphabet*, 29; Gray, "Indian Parallels," 398–440; Edmunds, *Buddhist and Christian Gospels* 2:243–44; Bauer, *Das Leben Jesu*, 96–97; Garbe, *Indien und das Christentum*, 70–80; Kennedy, "Gospel of the Infancy," 209–43, 469–540, esp. 520–23. For the carved depictions of the Buddhist Schulanekdote, see Krom, *Life of Buddha on the Stupa*, 44; Foucher, *Life of Buddha*, 55–56. Radhakrishnan provides yet more literature on this once "hot" topic in his *Eastern Religion and Western Thought*, 185 n. 1. One scholar who actively continues to pursue these parallels is Derrett; see "A Moses-Buddha Parallel," 310–17.

The textual question is reviewed in Klatt, *Literarische Beiträge*. For the best critique of the problems of theory and method involved in these "parallels" see J. Z. Smith, *Drudgery Divine*.
[2] The literature on the Apocryphal Infancy Gospels alone is vast. For early texts and

of the Jewish Ben Sira;[4] of the Sikh Guru Nanak;[5] and of the Bab of the Baha
'i.[6] It is told of each of them in a form that is structurally almost identical in
each tradition—a clear case of borrowing and influence. Or is it? While this
"Wise Child's Alphabet" does make for an interesting diffusion-of-motifs
study, such a point-by-point analysis would not tell us why such diverse religions needed this mytheme.

One could just as well argue, for example, that the Wise Child's Alphabet is
an imaginal argument for the priority of the new tradition: the prophet-
child's primordial wisdom represents the new commmunity's claim to an eternal truth. Of many such understandings of the remarkable diffusion of the
Wise Child's Alphabet, the analysis that tells us the least is that it is a "slavish
imitation" of a mytheme from an earlier tradition. In other words, for the
historian of religions, this common Wise Child's Alphabet suggests a self-
conscious innovation, more than it does something merely old. Whatever the
"source" of the image of the wise child, the new tradition recreates it as if it
were original.

translations see Thilo, *Codex Apocryphus Novi Testamenti*, esp. 122–23; and Hone, *The
Apocryphal New Testament*, 38, for more on the early literature. Most recently, a range
of versions of the "Alpha-Beta Logion" were compared by Gero in his work "Infancy
Gospel of Thomas," 46–80, at 71–73; see esp. p. 72: "One is immediately struck by
the fact that the core of the saying itself has been transmitted in a remarkably constant
form." The range of texts is translated and thoroughly annotated in Peeters, *Evangiles
Apocryphes* 2:58–62, 208–13, 302–05. Further literature can be found above, in n. 1.
The Muslim Arabic (as distinct from Christian Arabic sources, such as the Arabic
Infancy Gospel) sources on this mytheme are likewise vast. For a few of these, which
do not vary substantially in form (e.g., the teacher in some is called *mu'addib*, and in
other *mu'allim*), see Kulaini, *Al-Kafi* 6:192; Majlisi, *Bihar al-Anwar* 14:286; Abu
Nu'aim, *Hilyat al-Awliya'*, 7:251–52; Khoury, *Les Legendes*, 324–25; Tha'labi, *Qisas
al-Anbiya'*, 270; and the important translation and richly annotated text of *Futuh al-
Bahnasa*, by Galtier, 17–19. The only major difference in these versions is the contents of the meaning of each letter of the mystical alphabet revealed by the child Jesus.
[3] As found in the *Umm al-Kitab*: first annotated by Ivanow in "Notes sur l''Ummu'l-
Kitab,'" 419–81, esp. 438; see also the annotated Italian translation by Filippani-
Ronconi, *Ummu'l-Kitab*, and the abridged German translation by Heinz Halm, *Die
islamische Gnosis*, 113–99, esp. 128–32, "Baqir deutet das Alphabet"; the fullest commentary is that of Tijdens, *Der mythologisch-gnostische Hintergrund*, 276–99.
[4] See now the exhaustive *Tales of Ben Sira*, by Yassif, which surveys all the primary and
secondary literature. In English, his "Pseudo Ben Sira," 48–63, is relevant to the
present discussion. On its relation to the Indian Arabic fable literature, see Heller,
"Ginzberg's Legends," 413. See further, on its quotation by Peter the Venerable, Lieberman, *Shekiin*, 32–42; and the pioneering investigation of I. Levi, "La nativité de
Ben Sira," 197–205. For the text and discussion see Lachs, "Alphabet of Ben Sira,"
9–28, at 18. Bronzick, Stern and Mirsky translated the work in *Rabbinic Fantasies*,
167–203.
[5] Macaullife, *Sikh Religion*, 1, 3–15. Also see Cole, *Sikhism and Its Indian Context*,
172–73.
[6] Bahaullah, *The Dawn Breakers*, 72; Esslemont, *Baha'u'llah and the New Era*, 27 n. 1.

The Islamic use of the Wise Child's Alphabet is told in two distinct forms. The first version, widely repeated, is told of the child Jesus at school. It is found in all the so-called Isra'iliyyat, or Israelitish, collections, even the oldest known such collections.[7] It is frequently repeated in Sunni and Shi'i sources as well.[8] The second unique instance is told about Muhammad al-Baqir, the Fifth Imam. In this eighth-century version, which comprises the frame story for the proto-Shi'ite Gnostic apocalypse known as the *Umm al-Kitab*, al-Baqir is the child at school: his wise child's response to the unsuspecting teacher is a comprehensive review of not only the mystical meaning of the alphabet, but of all things, which are revealed subsequently and constitute the body of the book itself.[9]

I would suggest that this mytheme can be understood on at least three levels: it concerns new religions, it concerns popular traditions, and it concerns new religions' popular attitude to the preceding, learned tradition.

The Wise Child's Alphabet thus typifies a generative oxymoron of the history of religions: new tradition. In almost every known instance, the Wise Child's Alphabet is related by early sources in new religions deriving from the time of the origins of those religions. The wise child—the new religion—asserts its total mastery a priori. The wise child proves his (in this case, male) superiority over his predecessor in a child's ultimate fantasy: learning without work, smug knowledge that humbles the towering adult. An analogous archetypalization of the wisdom prior to education may be found in the image of the Prophet Muhammad as *ummi*, "illiterate."[10] A similar process may also be detected in the development of the Sar Torah (Prince of Torah) myth in the medieval Jewish mystical tradition. Here again the hunger for learning without the effort of education is depicted in quasi-miraculous imagery.[11]

A second feature of the Wise Child's Alphabet is that it derives primarily from popular traditions: the Christian apocryphal Acts; the Muslim Isra'iliyyat and *Umm al-Kitab*; and the Jewish *Alphabet of Ben Sira*. Usually consigned to what is inadequately termed "folklore," these are not quite unlearned

---

[7] For example, the early text of Wathima b. 'Umara, edited in Khoury, *Les legendes prophetiques*, 324–25.

[8] For Shi'i versions, see, for example, Kulaini, *Al-Kafi* 6:192; and Majlisi, *Bihar al-Anwar* 14:286. For Sunni versions see Abu Nu'aim, *Hilyat la-Awliya'*, 7:251–52; Tha'labi, *Qisas al-Anbiya'*, 230.

[9] The most recent and most reliable work done on *Umm al-Kitab* has been done by Halm. Sections of *Umm al-Kitab* are translated there, and the section under discussion can be found on pp. 128–32 of *Die islamische Gnosis*.

[10] Goldfeld, "Illiterate Prophet," 58–67. I discuss this motif with regard to Abu 'Isa al-Isfahani and his ghulat contemporaries in chapter 2 above. For more on the motif of "innate" learning in the Muslim tradition, see Schimmel, *And Muhammad Is His Messenger*, 72–73. She observes that "For the mystics, Muhammad the *ummi* became the exemplar of all those who, without bookish learnedness, have been inspired solely by Divine Grace" (73).

[11] Halperin, *Faces of the Chariot*, especially 376–85, 427–45, 518–22.

traditions, but neither do they derive from authoritative, normative, scholasticized traditions. Finally, these popular Wise Child images repeated by new religions suggest, more generally, a familiar child's fantasy. We know many forms of this fantasy. In folktales, it is that of the orphan who is secretly a prince. In the Gnostic texts, this secret prince has come from above with wisdom for humankind. We also know this fantasy in today's teenager starfighter movies: the suburban kid is "really" from another galaxy, where he is an extraordinary skywalker.

In terms of its *Sitz im Leben*, the Wise Child's Alphabet derives from new religions after their foundation, but before the creation of an inescapably authoritative school tradition. The yet-half-literate class favoring this mytheme fantasizes the cosmic potencies of the ABCs, onto which they project their hope to control the old tradition. As such, the Wise Child's Alphabet is the new-religion fantasy par excellence: the *coup de bouleversement* at school, in which the new religion displaces the old, represented by the hapless schoolteacher. This mytheme posits the a priori superiority of the new group, whose child-prophet virtually subsumes the dominant church—thus its frequently parodistic, satirical, sometimes vicious edge. This edge is particularly sharp in the Jewish *Alphabet of Ben Sira*.

And finally, the mystical knowledge itself: it constitutes the comprehensive mysteries inherent in the seemingly neutral tool of the alphabet. I refer to the divine neutrality of the alphabet. In such traditions, the alphabet is the "nature" of language, "the natural state" of language, and as such is virtually elemental. The new religion's reach is thus total: it reaches even into this very nature of things. The most apposite implication of this totalism is that the new religion has nothing to learn from the old: it knows it all already.

But this hubristic implication of the Wise Child's Alphabet is simultaneously subverted by a curious fact. Most commonly, the alphabet taught in the mytheme is not the alphabet of the language in which the story is recounted. The famous carved depictions of this school anecdote featuring the child-Buddha include letters from the sixty-four alphabets of which he claimed knowledge, including Aramaic.[12] The most common Greek-language apocryphal Acts of Jesus tell the story with Jesus learning Hebrew.[13] And the Muslim tales utilize the *abjad* alphabet, the Arabic alphabet in the order of Hebrew and Aramaic (and Greek).[14]

This linguistic lag brings the new religion full circle, for the use of an older alphabet implies the superiority of the old tradition. In the tightly paratactic compass of this little mytheme, the old and the new collide, and they simultaneously resolve: the new religion speaks the old language, in familiar but

[12] See especially the works of Krom, *Life of Buddha on the Stupa*, and Foucher, *Life of Buddha*, 55–56.
[13] Gero, "Infancy Gospel."
[14] Galtier, "Memoires," 17–19.

novel formulations. This immediately accessible lesson is not the sterile truism that new religions are both continuous and discontinuous with the old. Rather, it is an imaginative proof of the wedding of debt and obsolescence that is new religion.

JEWISH "INFLUENCES" ON THE ORIGINS OF ISLAM: HISTORICIST THEORIES

Early academic students of the origins of Islam shared certain scholarly predispositions with contemporaneous students of the origins of Christianity. In both cases, the search for "influence and borrowing" was instrumental in depicting new religions as essentially derived from earlier religions. Thus, reading the older Islamicists, one gains the impression that the Prophet Muhammad was little more than an ignorant anthologist who misunderstood and thus corrupted the many Jewish and Christian materials he uncomprehendingly collected. Maxime Rodinson has analyzed the range of such arguments, most of which simply pluck names, phrases, images, and narratives from the Qur'an and point out a Jewish or Christian text as the alleged "source" from which the Qur'an "borrowed."[15] The operative reconstruction behind this ever-successful search for borrowings was that Muhammad listened to Jewish and Christian merchants and/or preachers at the annual trade fairs of his native Mecca. What he heard he later, crudely, stitched together into the Qur'an.

There has been a particularly vigorous enthusiasm among Jewish scholars to find rabbinic derivations for Qur'anic materials. This practice was inaugurated by Abraham Geiger, later the founder of the Reform movement, who wrote his dissertation in 1832 on Muhammad's borrowing from rabbinic literature. In the early years of this century, Josef Horovitz could still author a detailed analysis of Qur'anic nomenclature and figures along the same lines. After World War II, an American rabbi, Abraham Katsh, could even write an entire book comprising a line-by-line rabbinic gloss on the first 2—of 114!— suras of the Qur'an.[16]

Similar arguments were put forth, and continue to be put forth, which argue that the Jewish source from which Muhammad "borrowed" was not rabbinic Judaism but rather some form of sectarianism, Jewish, quasi-Jewish, or otherwise. Samaritan sources were found, and Jewish Christian, and Mandaean, and Manichean.[17] Perhaps because no one could ever make a convincing argument for exclusively Jewish or exclusively Christian borrowings, a

[15] Rodinson, "Critical Survey."
[16] Geiger, *Judaism and Islam*; Horovitz, "Jewish Proper Names"; Katsh, *Judaism and the Koran*.
[17] Rodinson, "A Critical Survey of Modern Studies."

particularly popular hypothetical "influence peddling" was said to be that of the Jewish Christian sects, Jewish groups who acknowledged Jesus as a prophet but not as a Messiah: a fair-sized and still-growing literature exists in this connection.[18]

Such arguments were extended to the nature of the Islamic cultus. Mittwoch and others detailed the ways that Islamic ritual arguably was derived from Jewish rite. The creedal proclamation "there is no god but God and Muhammad is the Prophet of God" was said to come from Samaritanism.[19] The list could be extended. Similar arguments were adduced "to explain" the entire range of formative Islamic religious literature.

My criticism of these efforts is not to suggest that the new Islamicate civilization did not in fact put into use what it took over from antiquity. The early Islamic conquests subsumed ancient civilizations—Egyptian, Persian, Arab, Eastern Christian, and the bulk of world Jewry at that time. The conquerors were certainly aware, often sensitively aware, of the "foreign" narratives, administrative traditions, and architectural techniques that they incorporated into building the superstructure of their new community. It would be absurd to suggest that early Muslims were not themselves conscious of their utilization of the old, in religion as in anything else.

Jewish Sources in Islamic Self-Definition: Isra'iliyyat

This intra-Islamic awareness is sharply silhouetted in the so-called Isra'iliyyat traditions. Generally speaking, Isra'iliyyat are the manifold and miscellaneous traditions that the early Muslim community received, through various channels, from the Banu Isra'il, the "Children of Israel." These so-called inheritances from Judaism and, to a lesser extent, from Christianity, were occasionally branded as suspect and were sometimes proscribed.[20] But the prevalent form of canonical tradition in this regard is the frequently found statement of the Prophet Muhammad: "narrate [traditions] from the Children of Israel and there is nothing objectionable in that."[21]

Isra'iliyyat were more than merely superstitions, popular legends, and the like. It is true that some scholarly characterizations of Isra'iliyyat have tended to restrict Isra'iliyyat to a species of folklore.[22] But C. E. Bosworth correctly specifies that

[18] Pines, "Jewish Christians"; idem, "Notes on Islam" Roncaglia, "Eléments Ébionites"; Crone, "Islam, Judeo-Christianity."

[19] Mittwoch, *Enstehungsgeschichte*; Gaster, *Samaritans.*

[20] Kister, "Haddithu"; Newby, "Tafsir Israiliyyat." Abu Shuhbah, *al-Isra'iliyyat*, provides an extensive treatment of these materials in the *tafsir* literature.

[21] Kister, "Haddithu."

[22] Goldziher, *Gesammelte Schriften* 2:156

the term Isra'iliyyat is actually used in classical and more recent Islamic terminology not merely for the specifically Jewish elements which entered the science of
Qur'anic *tafsir* but [also] for the Christian and other non-Muslim extraneous elements. The use of the Isra'iliyyat for elucidating certain aspects of Qur'anic and
hadith texts, or for amplifying vaguenesses in them, was regarded as legitimate;
hence Ibn Taymiyya . . . classifies Isra'iliyyat under the headings of *sahih* (sound),
kadhib (unsound) and *maskut 'anhu* (those about which it is not possible to validate
or invalidate).[23]

More generally, stories, narratives, tales, and salvation history were not only
accepted as Isra'iliyyat, but such materials served as the basis for much of the
Islamicate view of pre-Islamic history. By the tenth century, the major histories
and the collections of narratives concerning pre-Islamic communities and their
prophets to some substantial extent comprise Isra'iliyyat. I am using the term
Isra'iliyyat, therefore, in this general sense, with special reference to the Umayyad and early 'Abbasid periods, before the term Isra'iliyyat developed a rather
more limited and admittedly much more abusive connotation.

Obviously, as the range of debates in the traditions so well record, there were
many opinions concerning this practice, but the objectors seemed to have been
in the minority, particularly in the early period. From either side of that debate,
those who dealt with Isra'iliyyat were obviously, explicitly, self-consciously
aware that these stories were taken from a foreign source. Foreign scriptures
are commonly cited.[24] Two of the most popular tradents of Isra'iliyyat were
Jewish converts, who were well remembered as such in later traditions.[25]

I stress this awareness because Isra'iliyyat provides us with a case of open,
acknowledged, and religiously condoned borrowing. Islam's openly acknowledged indebtedness to Judaism reminds us that religions can validly perceive
each other as "religious," and that their interactions therefore may be considered, as in the case of the Wise Child's Alphabet, as religious events. This is
perhaps most acutely evident in the origins of new traditions. That the new
tradition self-consciously employs materials from the old must imply some
living religious charge in the old that remains meaningful and relevant to the
new community. My surmise is that this process usually has been more
self-aware and more positively valuated by new traditions than earlier generations of scholars—constricted by mechanical models of "influence and
borrowing"—were willing to recognize.

[23] Bosworth, "Concept of *Dhimma*," 8.
[24] Khoury, *Les Legendes*. And see Lazarus-Yafeh, *Intertwined Worlds*: "exact literal Biblical quotations are extremely rare [and so one makes] the assumption of oral tradition." (112, 114).
[25] Ka'b al-Ahbar and Wahb ibn Munabbih. See Abbott, "Wahb b. Munabbih";
Khoury, *Les Legendes*; Hirschfeld, "Historical and Legendary Controversies"; Leveen,
"Mohammed"; Mann, "Early Theologico-Polemical Work"; Perlmann, "Legendary
Story." I trace the subsequent fate of the convert 'Abdallah ibn Salam below.

What I want to emphasize, then, is the specific twist, the novel torsion, that the early Muslims introduced in their reimagining of ancient traditions. This novelty, naturally, was the prophethood of Muhammad and his revelation. This is more than an obvious truism, for it was not only true, it was overwhelmingly, blindingly apparent to new Muslims. Muhammad overwhelmed the old in every imaginable sense. Such was the appropriately imperious confidence of new Islam that it did not merely condone but may have (at times) even encouraged the collecting of Isra'iliyyat.

In this early period, then, I believe that the attitude of those traditionists collecting Isra'iliyyat is as follows: Judaism had to attest to the truth of Islam. Jewish traditions were not intrinsically a serious threat, because they had already been overcome. Jewish and Christian (and other non-Muslim) traditions could therefore be collected as Isra'iliyyat because—in fact, and necessarily—they attested to the truth of Islam.

Isra'iliyyat was an outside witness brought in to testify to the veracity of the new religion. The older religion is called to the witness box to speak on behalf of the new. That Muslim traditions seem to bulge with talmudic, halakhic, aggadic, midrashic, and other Jewish materials cannot therefore be due to the naïveté or sheer credulity of the early Muslim tradents who were responsible for the transmission of traditional reports. These tradents were not merely mouthing old wives' tales they had heard from Jewish converts. Such a reconstruction is universally insulting, and obviously inadequate.

Rather, I would argue that the popularity of these various Islamic rereadings of Jewish traditions imply respect for the witness. I say this not to gloss over the castigations of Jews by Muslims from Muhammad on down.[26] But I would counterpoint the notable absence of respect accorded Isra'iliyyat both by later Muslims and by modern scholars of all stripes with the obvious respect implicit in the act itself.

The pre-Islamic (*jahiliyya*) component of Tabari's great history, for example, or the Tales of the Prophets (*qisas al-anbiya'*) collections made edifying reading (or listening) for all levels of culture, but were much more. They presented a view of history that was almost unanimously accepted into the historical worldview of Islamicate civilization. This was part of the real history of the world. Such acceptance is significant enough: even more theologically significant was the manifold purposes to which Isra'iliyyat was put in Qur'an commentary (*tafsir*), though the details of that exegetical usage lie outside my purview here.

To this exegetical principle was added the theory of *tahrif*, the purportedly willful corruption by Jews and Christians of their own scriptures (Qur'an 2:75, 4:46, 5:13, 5:41).[27] A fundamental principle for Muslim scholars dealing with biblical materials, the accusation of tahrif acted as a kind of universal

[26] Steinschneider, "Polemische"; Perlmann, "Medieval Polemics."
[27] Perlmann, "Medieval Polemics." For more, see now Lazarus-Yafeh, *Intertwined Worlds*, esp. 26–29, 58–72.

solvent, resolving every exegetical contradiction in favor of the Muslim reading. The Jews had possessed God's word, but only the Muslim version of the Jews' revelation was the accurate version. This is the catch: if Muslim tradition accepted it, it was true.

The content of Jewish traditions thereby testified to the truth of Islam, but only through what one might call Muslim tahrif, the pious fraud applied to Isra'iliyyat. This is not to say that individual Jews themselves, and some few Jewish sects, did not acknowledge the prophethood of Muhammad.[28] But what I want to do at this point is to discuss a different form of the Jewish response to Muslim claims that Judaism acknowledges Islam. This mythically "Jewish" response allows a rounded, more fully dialectical reading of the history of Isra'iliyyat.

TALES OF ʿABDALLAH IBN SALAM

Muslim scholars found many ways, in addition to Isra'iliyyat, to demonstrate that Jews and Judaism acknowledged the prophethood of Muhammad; Jews in turn found ways to turn those demonstrations on their heads. In the connection it is worthwhile to consider Muslim legends concerning the Jewish follower of Muhammad, ʿAbdallah b. Salam, as well as the dialectical transformations of these legends by Jewish authors.[29] This figure was used by Muslims to give voice to purportedly Jewish age-old traditions that had prophesied the coming of Muhammad. But subsequent Jews in turn retold these same tales to create a Jewish legend of Muhammad, namely, that ʿAbdallah converted only for "the purpose of saving God's people so that he [Muhammad] should not harm them by his false charges."[30]

The historical ʿAbdallah b. Salam (d. 43/663–64) was a member of the famous Jewish Arab tribe of Qaynuqaʾ.[31] His conversion at the hand of Muhammad, like all matters pertaining to the life of Muhammad, was eventually subjected to a sustained mythological deepening—deep, that is, when compared with the rather thin reports on ʿAbdallah in early Muslim traditions.[32] In other words, ʿAbdallah was a real Jewish convert mouthing identi-

---

[28] See for example the data gathered in my "Mutual Acknowledgments," 56–75.

[29] Horovitz has written the entries on ʿAbdallah in *Encyclopedia of Islam*, 2d ed., 1:52, and *Encyclopedia Judaica* 1:53–54; see also Steinschneider, *Polemische und apologetische*, 110 15.

[30] Mann, "Early Theologico-Polemical Work," 411–59, at 421. The text treated by Mann, as well as other variants, are ably analyzed by Shimon Shtober in "Muhammad and the Beginning of Islam," 319–52.

[31] Lecker, "Muhammad at Medina," 37–38.

[32] I have not seen Pijper, *Het Boek*, but Horovitz's review suggests its (limited) importance in this regard. Another late version is the sixteenth-century Turkish work of Mevla Furati. See the edition of Zenker, *Quarante Questions*, and the German translation thereof by Hein, *Das Buch der Vierzig fragen*. Vajda called attention to the Shiʿi

fiably Jewish material, but material not necessarily his own: he functioned as a symbol of the Islamization of the Jews. As Horovitz said concerning the Jewish materials taken from ʿAbdallah, "if they do not really come from ʿAbd Allah himself, they certainly come from Jewish renagade circles."[33]

There is no reason, historical, spiritual, or otherwise, to dispute the essential historicity or the original Jewishness of ʿAbdallah b. Salam. But the words put into his mouth in his encounter with the new prophet, like the Isra'iliyyat to which they are closely related, are not simply borrowings from Jews; they are Muslim reimaginings of the primordial confrontation with Judaism. Retrojections into the mouth of ʿAbdallah, these myths must be seen in the context of a general tendency toward a primordialization of Isra'iliyyat. They may be seen as part of the larger cycles of tales in which non-Muslims prophesy Muhammad, such as the section in the *Sira*, "Arab Soothsayers (*Kuhhan*), Jewish Rabbis (*Ahbar*) and Christian Monks foretell his Coming."[34]

It may be that this primordialization is responsible for the longevity of the ʿAbdallah b. Salam tales. By the tenth century his family had come to be seen as a kind of dynasty of Jewish converts transmitting miscellaneous holy books. Thus, Thaʿlabi attributes the apocalypse of "Buluqiyya" to him;[35] Biruni attributes the transmission of the *Gospel of the Seventy* to Salam ibn ʿAbdallah ibn Salam;[36] and Ibn al-Nadim begins one of the first disquisitions of his *Fihrist* with a translation of the gospels he attributes to Ahmad ibn ʿAbdallah ibn Salam.[37] In short, ʿAbdallah and his family became personifications of the Isra'iliyyat process, a dynasty of intellectual middlemen.

This sustained Muslim mythicizing of a primordial Jewish convert to Islam also, eventually, did elicit a response from Jews. ʿAbdallah b. Salam was reappropriated, re-Judaized in Jewish legends concerning Muhammad.[38] Isra'iliy-

---

versions of such legitimating interviews, in which a quizzical Jew queries an ominiscient ʿAli. See the references in "Juifs et musulmans," 99 n. 1. No single study yet exists that surveys the full range of ʿAbdallah's persistent survival in Muslim (traditional), Jewish (Geniza), and Christian (Syriac and European) literature. While the aforementioned studies are useful, nothing on the scale of Wolfensohn's treatment of Kaʿb exists with regard to ʿAbdallah; see *Kaʿb al-Ahbar*. I thank Camilla Adang of Nijmegen for copying this rare work for me.

[33] Horowitz, "Abdallah ibn Salam," *Encyclopedia of Islam*, 2d ed., 1:52.
[34] Discussed by Lazarus-Yafeh, *Intertwined Worlds*, 77 and 78 n. 6.
[35] Translated and discussed by Galtier, "Memoires," 156–69. An English synopsis of this version is provided in Dalley, "Gilgamesh in *The Arabian Nights*," 7.
[36] *Chronology*, 27. See also Hennecke, *New Testament Apocrypha*, 269–70. See also the unlikely suggestions of Pines, "Jewish Christians," 308–09. Lazarus-Yafeh comments: "He did not distinguish between Hebrew and Aramaic (?) and knew very little of either!" (*Intertwined Worlds*, 120–21).
[37] Ibn al-Nadim, *The Fihrist of al-Nadim* 1:41–43.
[38] Hirschfeld, "Historical and Legendary Controversies," 100–116; Chapira, "Legendes bibliques attribuées a Kaʿb el-Ahbar," 86–107; Leveen, "Mohammed and His Jewish Companions," 399–406; Mann, "Early Theologico-Polemical Work," 419–22; and, most recently and most fully, Shtober, "Muhammed and the Beginning." To

yat fed back into Jewish traditions. In the Jewish-Muslim mythomachia, arguments were as often put forth in the form of counter narratives as in the form of directly disputational denials of historicity. ʿAbdallah's encounter with Muhammad was consciously rewritten by Jewish writers, who polemically invert its valuation in tales concerning the Jewish companions of Muhammad.

As I have tried to show, ʿAbdallah's encounter with Muhammad in early Muslim traditions—which Shtober terms "the sophisticated legend"—seems to have been designed to support the Muslim assertion of a Jewish prophesying and recognizing of the coming of Muhammad.[39] Moreover, ʿAbdallah played this role even in Christian versions of this legend, which were later made much of in Europe.[40] Likewise, a parallel re-Christianization of legends about the monk Bahira thus took place in Christian circles: Bahira, like the Jew ʿAbdallah, acknowledges Muhammad's prophethood.[41] Even so, Isra-ʾiliyyat remained more a "Jewish" than a "Christian" problematic. This can be seen in the Christian legends, where, as Griffith puts it, this "misuse of Islamic history in this matter is simply for the purpose of blaming Islam on the Jews. . . . The point of the story for the Syriac writers is that Islam, religiously speaking, amounts to Judaism."[42]

That being said, both Jewish and Christian "antibiographies" of Muhammad shared a common purpose. They were designed to deflect the authority of canonical Muslim biography (Sira) of Muhammad, as well as other hagiographic tales of Muhammad. Vajda could thus refer justifiably to countersiras, or antibiographies.[43] In such cases, however, Jews and Christians could not and did not seriously try to refute the fact that their own communities were in fact insinuated into the earliest origins of Islam. What Mann says about the Jewish case hold true, mutatis mutandis, concerning the Christian case: "All

---

these may be added the Shiʿi parallel literature. Vajda has noted that the *Kitab al-Ihtijaj* of al-Tabarsi (d. 548/1153) is comparable to the "Difficulties" of Hiwi al-Balkhi (discussed in chapter 4 above). In particular, he points to questions which the so-called *zindiq* lobs to Jaʿfar al-Sadiq, the Sixth Imam. See "Àpropos de l'attitude," 81–91, esp. at 88. The encounter between the *zindiq* and the Sixth Imam (as found in the *K. al-Ihtijaj* of Tabarsi) is translated in a popular, contemporary Shiʿi paperback, *The Biography of Jaʿfar-e-Sadiq*, 42–90.

[39] Shtober, "Muhammed and the Beginning," 347 n. 1.

[40] See Kritzeck, *Peter the Venerable*, 33 and 89–96.

[41] I wish to thank Professor Sidney Griffith for sharing with me his unpublished study, now available as "Jews and Muslims in Christian Syriac and Arabic Texts," 65–94, esp. 80–82 and corresponding nn. 86–94. See also Abel, "L'Apocalypse de Bahira," 1–12. In one version of a related Jewish tale of Kaʿb al-Ahbar, the Jewish convert encounters a monk named Bulukhya, who reveals the secrets of the coming of Muhammad to him. See Perlmann, "Legendary Story," 85–99, at 88 (English synopsis) and 95 (of the text). See also Shtober, "Muhammed and the Beginning," 338–40.

[42] Griffith, "Jews and Muslims," 29.

[43] Vajda, "Un Vestige oriental," 177–80.

such stories are apparently the reflection of a vague notion current in Jewish circles concerning the Jewish share in the evolution of the new religion."[44] The Muslim biography of Muhammad, with its encounter with ʿAbdallah, was enough of a compelling presence for the Jews and Christians to retell this encounter with their own revalutions.

In addition to its re-Judaization and re-Christianization, Isra'iliyyat also continued dialectically to metamorphose in other Muslim guises. ʿAbdallah ibn Salam remained a common denominator in the later cycle of tales, in which he starred as an interrogator of Muhammad. Eventually these tales developed into the later *Masa'il* literature, a question-and-answer genre in which Muhammad answers dozens of questions put to him by ʿAbdallah.[45] The content of their dialogue came to comprise a popular mini-encyclopedia of Islamic cosmology and doxology.

To recapitulate: the Jewish convert ʿAbdallah ibn Salam's briefly described encounters with Muhammad in the early Muslim traditions were amplified dramatically in the later *Masa'il* literature. Simultaneously, ʿAbdallah's encounter also was reformulated by Jews and Christians precisely in order to refute the explicitly prefigurative implications of its Muslim formulation.

FULL CIRCLE: BULUQIYYA

A late, attenuated form this dialectic took was the tale of Buluqiyya. ʿAbdallah ibn Salam was ascribed the telling of the tale of Buluqiyya by Thaʿlabi (d. 1030) in his popular *Tales of the Prophets*.[46] The tale of Buluqiyya— an Israelite prince's series of visionary adventures—may have originated as a Jewish apocalypse. In addition to the matters of internal content he uses in his analysis, Horovitz argues that the world spanning hero Buluqiyya would seem to have originally been modeled after, or named after, the obscure Hilqiyahu mentioned in the biblical Book of Kings, who discovered a "Book of the Law" at the time of the Josianic reform: Dalley now

---

[44] Mann, "Early Theologico-Polemical Work," 422.

[45] Examples of this literature are analyzed by Pijper, *Het Boek*; Kritzeck, *Peter the Venerable*; and Hirshfeld, "Historical and Legendary Controversies." Tellingly, ʿAbdallah ibn Salam's review of knowledge found its way into glosses on the *mirʿaj*, that prototypical review of the cosmic phenomena. See "Le voyage de Mahomet: Au paradis et en enfer: une version persane du *miʿraj*," in Kappler *Apocalypses*, 293–318, at 312.

[46] Galtier, "Memoires," translates into French this story from Thaʿlabi. William Brinner is presently translating this text. For a literary history of this story, see Bencheikh, *Les Mille et une nuits*, 176–94. The core of the story was already cited by Tabari (d. 373/974); ibid., 181. Wolfensohn deals with Buluqiyya only in passing (*Kaʿb al-Ahbar*, 19 and 86), but his work is invaluable for tracing the historical dialectics of this narrative in the context of Jewish-Muslim symbiosis. For another version, in which Bulukhya is a prophesying monk, see Perlmann, "Legendary Story."

suggests that the name Buluqiyya is a transformation of none other than Gilgamesh.[47]

Whatever its genesis, by the tenth century or so, the tale of Buluqiyya had become a popular Muslim story. Eventually it came to form several dozen nights of *The Thousand and One Nights*.[48] Most importantly, all the intercontinental visionary journeying of Buluqiyya in the *The Thousand and One Nights* is precisely to find the prophet who has been prophesied— Muhammad. The "Jewish" material in the tale of Buluqiyya is thereby all Islamically refocused. Thus, the tale, earlier ascribed to the prototypical Jewish convert, ʿAbdallah, retains the classic point of Israʾiliyyat: to create a veritable myth of prefigurations of Muhammad. Foreign materials, in other words, could retain their power for this purpose precisely by remaining "foreign." Buluqiyya is an ancient prince of the Banu Israʾil: thus even pre-Islamic religions attest to the truth of Islam.[49]

But the shape of the Buluqiyya trajectory is circular in more than one sense. The content of the *Masaʾil ʿAbdallah ibn Salam*, in fact, contain a variety of traditions that recur in the Buluqiyya narratives. For example, in the *Masaʾil*, ʿAbdallah asks Muhammad questions concerning cosmological mysteries, including "what is beneath the seven worlds." Muhammad's answer includes a description of an angel, rock, bull, fish ("with its head pointed towards the East"), and an ocean. This detail, and others like it, occur in the version of ʿAbdallah's questions translated into Latin by Herman of Dalmatia; in a popular pamphlet of the *Masaʾil*, published in Cairo in 1897; and in *The Thousand and One Nights*.[50] The antiquity and the consistency of this mytheme is

---

[47] Horovitz's is the consensual position, first suggested by V. Chauvin (see Galtier, "Memoires," 169, for his approval, with a rejection of Burton's theory of Persian origins), but established by the clever if not fully persuasive arguments of Horovitz; see "Buluqya," 519–25. Summarized also in Idem., "Origins of the 'Arabian Nights,'" 53. Its Jewishness is accepted by both Jewish and Muslim scholars. See al-Qalamawi, *Alf Laylah wa Laylah*, 43–45, 170 (originally cited in an earlier edition by Perlmann, "Legendary Story of Kaʿb al-Ahbar's Conversion to Islam," 85–99 at 89 n. 9); Ben-Zeev, "Jewish Sources," 494–95. Vladimir Vikentiev suggests that the tale derives from Gilgamesh, by way of an ancient Egyptian folktale. See "Boulouqiya-Gilgamish-Naufragé," 1–54 (cited by Ritter, *Das Meer der Seele*, 115). Dalley misses the work of Vikentiev in this connection in her otherwise interesting attempt to link Buluqiyya to Gilgamesh: "Gilgamesh in *The Arabian Nights*," 1–17. For a perceived similarity between Buluqiyya and certain tales in their European versions, see Palacios, *La Escatología Musulmana en la Divina Comedia*, 312–328. For an analysis of Buluqiyya in terms of apocalypse see Abel, "L'Apocalypse de Buluqiya," 189–98.

[48] In the Bulaq edition of *Alf Layla wa Layla*, this tale is found on 4:281–331.

[49] Goitein, "Concept of Mankind in Islam," 72–91.

[50] Herman of Dalmatia is translated and analyzed by Kritzeck, *Peter the Venerable*, 94. The Cairo *Masaʾil* is translated by Hirschfeld, "Historical and Legendary Controversies." In the Payne translation of *The Book of the Thousand and One Nights*, the "fish facing East" motif is found on 5:77–78; in the Mardrus and Mathers version, (Alf Layla Wa Layla 4:67–84) this detail is missing.

thus clear enough: others can likely be proven to be so as well.[51] Remarkably, this mytheme is found also in the eighth-century Gnosticizing *Umm al-Kitab*, a extremist-Shi'i revelation dialogue with close affinities to works of Jewish gnosis.[52]

The convergence of content between the 'Abdallah-*Masa'il* and the tale of Buluqiyya, which was said to be recounted originally by 'Abdallah ibn Salam, brings the interpreter of Jewish-Muslim symbiosis full circle.[53] That is to say, this encyclopedic cosmology, a folkloristic version of the encyclopedic revelation of worldly secrets familiar from apocalyptic literature, was long understood by generations of Muslims to be *mythically* Jewish. In other words, both the historical Jewish figure, 'Abdallah ibn Salam, and the legendary Israelite figure, Buluqiyya, bear witness to the world-spanning sapience of the Prophet of Islam. The questions and adventures associated with their names amount to varieties of a *Muslim myth of Judaism*: a myth which stubbornly demonstrated that Jews, whether historical figures or legendary worthies, are persuaded perpetually of the irrefutable prophethood of Muhammad.

FEEDBACK EFFECTS IN FOUNDATION MYTH

Origin is the goal.

—Karl Kraus

What might be called *mythomachia* and *logomachia*—the contest of myth and the contest of reason—were interpenetrated in the millennial commingling of Judaism and Islam. Whether the foreign materials being used in a domesticated Muslim form were rational arguments, biblical texts, heavenly ascents, quasi-scientific heresiographical reports, or tales of the rosh golah, their foreignness was intentionally retained in order for it to serve as outside witness. In this way all manner of things was made to testify to the truth of Islam. The manifold Muslim uses of Judaism constituted different languages stating the same thing: There is no god but God, and Muhammad is the Apostle of God.

Isra'iliyyat represents a significantly self-conscious and self-referential in-

[51] For example, the specified identification of Mt. Qaf in both the *Qisas al-Anbiya'* (Tha'labi) version, and in the *Nights*.

[52] For this motif in *Umm al-Kitab*, see Ivanow, "Notes," 470, question 21.

[53] While the early attribution of the Buluqiyya story to 'Abdallah (by Tha'labi) has long been known, to my knowledge it has not been recognized heretofore that the 'Abdallah cycle and the Buluqiyya cycle bear substantial similarities of *content* as well as *intent*. I would point out that a comparatively little-known Jewish tale, *The Tale of the Jerusalemite*, bears substantive similarities to certain aspects of the narratives of 'Abdallah and Buluqiyya. See Zlotnick, *Maaseh Yerushalmi*, and the English translation by Stern and Weinstein in Stern and Mirsky, *Rabbinic Fantasies*. I thank David Stern for bringing this story to my attention.

stance of this process. In the case of Isra'iliyyat, a new religion overcomes its "anxiety of influence" by re-creating its own sacred histories. This rewritten history, without question, draws from preexisting histories. But it is nonetheless created by a new person, and therefore cannot usefully be reduced to "the derivative." And so it follows that we must treat a new religion as a new adult and not merely as a product of its parents. The history of religions can no longer be content to merely point to the family background of a new religion as "sufficient explanation" of that new religion. Rather, through detailed historical analysis, we should elucidate the dynamics by which religions incorporate, idealize, repress, deny, and otherwise remake their inheritance, as that inheritance is re-created into the adult personality of the new religion.

Finally, it makes no sense to talk about new representation of older materials without simultaneously showing that that new rereading is reciprocally returned to the chronologically prior tradition. I have tried to make this point in tracing the dialectic of Isra'iliyyat. As Goitein and others have shown, there was no unidirectional flow of influences into formative Islam. There was, rather, a synergy, a two-way street: certainly in the case of Judaism, we know that it was altered, root and branch, in its growth in the soil of Islamicate civilisations. In one of his last published statements, Goitein began his remarks with these unequivocal observations: "Every aspect of what we regard today as Judaism—the synagogue service and prayer book, law and ritual, theology and ethics, the text of the Bible, the grammar and vocabulary of the Hebrew language—was consolidated, formulated and canonized in [the first centuries of Islamicate civilization]."[54]

At the least, this common development of Judaism and Islam in the first centuries of Islamicate civilization provides historians of religions with another instance of the positive synergy between religious traditions. With W. C. Smith I would ask, "Shall we not say that once again the history of one tradition is in part a function of the history of another?"[55]

METATRON AFTER MUHAMMAD

The esoteric interpenetration of Judaism and Islam provides another example of a history which is "a function of the history of another."[56] "Metatron," despite the technocratic resonance of the name, is not a postmodern electronics corporation. He is an ancient corporate entity, the supreme Rabbinic angel, the ultimate achievement of the Jewish angelological imagination. This Jewish right-hand man of God was reimagined by Muslim visionaries. Such Muslim reception of Jewish esoteric imaginings is the final historical subject of the present project. Toward that end, I will review the biography of this

[54] Goitein, "Political Conflict," 169–81, at 169.
[55] W. C. Smith, "Traditions," 22.
[56] Ibid.

Jewish angel, starting with his youth in late antiquity. Two new phases in the biography of Metatron will then be introduced, one concerning Metatron's role in the magical texts of the Cairo Geniza, and the other in the esoteric traditions of Islam. I hope to show that Metatron's life after Muhammad constitutes a particularly subtle example of the esoteric symbiosis of Judaism and Islam.

Incarnation and Demiurge

Incarnation was an interreligiously distributed religious problem in late antiquity; the incarnation of Jesus Christ was but the most complete and dramatic institutionalization of such a common myth. In the last two decades, scholars have elucidated the impact of Jewish speculation concerning principal angels and other divine "chief agents."[57]

Without entering into details, I note that at some point rather late in this development, perhaps after the third century, Metatron was enthroned as *the* Jewish "principal angel."[58] This Jewish privileging of a principal angel paralleled and interpenetrated the mythic concerns of contemporaneous Christians, as well as those of Gnostics and Samaritans.[59] We now know, in short, that Jewish imaginings of divine intermediaries intensified in a dimly understood imaginative synergy with Christology, Gnosticism, and some forms of sectarianism.

Since it is not my intention to provide a systematic biography of Metatron, I shall not cite all of his varied features. Suffice to say that it would be difficult to exaggerate the extent to which he was impressively depicted: thus Metatron proudly proclaims, "[God] fashioned for me a kingly crown in which 49 refulgent stones were placed, each like the sun's orb . . . [and God] set it upon my head and he called me 'the lesser YHWH'."[60]

Jewish leadership understandably was disturbed by this phenomenon. The rabbis thus warned against belief in "two powers in heaven" (*shtey reshuyyot*), and, indirectly, against deifying the angel Metatron.[61] In this way they successfully warded off all such perceived threats to the purity of monotheism. This story is quite well known, having been ensconced in the Talmud and reexamined by the scholars of late antiquity mentioned above.[62]

What is far less well known is what happens to this problem after the "blackout" of antiquity. The blackout, as conventional historiography has it, was the Arab Conquests, the subsequent dark age for Jewish history, in fact

[57] Segal, *Two Powers in Heaven*; Hurtado, *One God, One Lord*; Fossum, *Name of God*.
[58] The standard overview of the sources is that of Margulies, *Mal'akhe 'Elyon*, 28–73.
[59] See n. 57 above.
[60] "The Book of Enoch, by Ishmael the High Priest," trans. Philip Alexander, in Charlesworth, *Old Testament Pseudepigrapha*, 265.
[61] A. Segal, *Two Powers in Heaven*.
[62] For recent studies, see Fauth, "Tatrosjah-Totrosjah," and Morray-Jones, "Transformational Mysticism."

"the most obscure in Jewish history," in the judgment of S. D. Goitein.[63] I restrict myself to the Gaonic period, conventionally dated from the seventh through the thirteenth centuries, a time when many of the most significant texts concerning Metatron are written. These relatively well studied texts (*Pirke Rebbe Elizer*; *Nistarot de Shimon bar Yochai*; *Alphabet of R. Akiva*, *Shi'ur Qomah*; and most especially *3 Enoch*), however, are not my primary concern. Rather, I shall discuss some lesser-known chapters in the biography of Metatron after Muhammad.

Metatron's Fame

The earliest suggested example of Metatron in an Islamic work is that of the still-mysterious 'Uzair mentioned in the Qur'an (9:30–31).[64] Gordon Newby argues that 'Uzair may be equated with Enoch, who was identified with Metatron in the Merkaba texts.[65] Newby has in the connection pointed to the work by David Halperin, which suggests the knowledge of Enoch/Metatron Merkaba texts among the Jews of Arabia in Muhammad's day.[66] Although not directly bearing on the Islamicate Metatron, I would extend the suggestions of Halperin and Newby at the same time as I would revive a nearly forgotten theory: that is, in 1924, Paul Casanova suggested that 'Uzair may derive from Azazel, who was one of the "children of God" (*b'nai elohim*).[67]

Concomitantly, a second argument for the early appearance of Metatron concerns the teaching of *tafwid* (relegation) among the eighth-century proto-Shi'i *ghulat* (extremists). Some ghulat, according the heresiographers, taught that God himself did not create the universe but rather relegated (*fauwwida*) the act of Creation to a lesser divinity.[68] The clearest instance of this association with Metatron is found in the *Umm al-Kitab*, a Persian-language Gnostic apocalypse that Heinz Halm has shown to be representative of eighth-

---

[63] Goitein, *Jews and Arabs*, 95.

[64] Lazarus-Yafeh, "Ezra-'Uzayr," 359–79.

[65] Newby, *History of the Jews of Arabia*, 60–61.

[66] Halperin, *Faces of the Chariot*, 467–90.

[67] This suggestion, supported by Bernard Lewis, has several features to commend it. It links this Qur'anic verse with a well-known Jewish tradition concerning the "children of God." It is not entirely unreasonable on philological grounds. And, it creates a trajectory into a subsequent Islamic tradition playing on Metatron-related myths, that of the eighth-century *Umm al-Kitab*. This is in support of the theory of Casanova, "Idris et 'Ouzair," 356–60.

[68] Friedlaender considered *tafwid* as one of the fifteen "Shiitic elements" that he isolated among the Jewish sects of early Islam; see "Jewish-Arabic Studies" 254–58. See also, van Ess, *Anfänge*, 126, on the *ashab al-tafwid*; Ash'ari, *Maqalat*, 564–65, on the Mufawwida and their relation to Christian and Jewish doctrine (see Brentjes, *Die Imamats Lehren*, 29); For Halm's more recent overview of the sources, see *Die islamische Gnosis*, 230–32.

century, partially Jewish-inspired ghulat teachings.[69] Most strikingly, Salman al-Farisi becomes a demiurgic divine potency in the *Umm al-Kitab*. That Salman may be in some way a reflex of Metatron is suggested by a reference to the "lesser Salman," a phrase reminiscent of Metatron as "the lesser Lord."[70] The archaic tradition expressed here thus may be related to the Qur'anic depiction of 'Uzair as a Jewish divine figure.

The mature Metatron remained quite famous after the eighth century. One indication of his impact is the fact that Karaites, Muslims, Christians, and even Zoroastrians routinely characterized rabbinic Judaism by its anthropomorphism, angel worship, and/or belief in an angel-creator. This common accusation was characteristic of all four fronts in the polemical war against rabbinic Jews under early Islam. In other words, the Jewish theory and practice of Metatron was notoriously and almost universally misunderstood by the neighbors of the Jews.

Muslim heresiography of the Jews confounded three polemically inspired motifs that bear on the history of the Islamicate Metatron: the interrelated assertions that Jews worshiped God-as-old-man, God-as-youth, or God's Angel-Demiurge. However, it would require a separate investigation to fully and adequately disengage these reports. Therefore, in what follows, I will concentrate on the claims that (1) specifically name Metatron and (2) specify the worship of a angelic "lesser Lord."

Ascribing an Angel-Creator as the defining characteristic of Judaism had long been both broadly and deeply embedded in Christian heresiography of the Jews. The hypothesis of Christian priority is made the more likely when one examines the several Islamicate-era heresiographies that either pair *Ashma'ath* and the doctrine of an Angel-Creator or cite the two separately but link them both with the majority, rabbinic party. The earliest author who thus might be adduced, Mas'udi, in the tenth century, brings up the so-called *Ashma'ath*, specifying that they were the majority of the "Isra'iliyyun." Elsewhere, he polemicizes against the Jewish adoration of a "little Lord" (*al-rabb al-saghir*). But he does not explicitly pair the two. Significantly, however, evidence of an originally Christian provenance exists for both of these passages. In the case of the former, Mas'udi mentions the group in the middle of a chronography of the Greek kings, as in the closely related Nestorian chronography or its Muslim counterpart, the chronography of a certain Ibn al-Munajjim. In the case of his passage concerning a Jewish Angel-Creator, Mas'udi places the polemic against the "little Lord" doctrine in the mouth of a Jacobite Coptic disputant.[71] This would also seem to imply a Christian connection in the transmission to him of this motif.

---

[69] I deal at length with this question in chapter 5 above.

[70] See below for Muslim polemical attacks on Jewish *mujassima* (anthropomorphizers), whom they accuse of worshiping a divine "chief agent." I have analyzed some aspects of these reports in "Magical Texts," 160–66 (parts of which are utilized herein).

[71] Mas'udi, *Muruj al-Dhahab* 2:389–91. This passage has been discussed by Moore, "Metatron," 62–85, at 73.

Roughly contemporary with Mas'udi, Maqdisi also mentions an Ash-ma'ath, considering this term to refer to a man. As with Mas'udi, Maqdisi also pairs Ashma'ath with 'Anan: "and the majority of Jews follows the positions of one or the other of these two men (*hadhayn al-rajulayn*)." In another passage, addressing the ritual of the Jews, Maqdisi again summarizes a ritual variation as being dichotomized between these two leaders, just as Mas'udi discussed them as the two dominant Israelite parties.[72]

Similarly, Ibn Hazm mentions the Ash'aniyya after the 'Ananiyya in his list by identifying the former as Rabbanites "who hold to the teachings of the learned [i.e., rabbis] and their practices [and who] constitute the majority of the Jews." Precisely as did Mas'udi, Ibn Hazm elsewhere criticizes the Jewish worship of the *rabb al-saghir*, little Lord, which he explicitly associates with the Rabbanites.[73]

Finally, in a Muslim list repeated by several later authors (Khazraji, Su'udi), but which is closely related, textually, to these earlier citations (and especially to Christian sources) not only are the Ashma'iyya ascribed the demiurgic doctrine, but so are two other Jewish sects. This version, most fully presented by Su'udi in the sixteenth century, says of the Ashma'iyya that they assert "that their Creator has the form of an old man with white hair and a beard. They assert that He has a deputy in the Third Heaven whom they call the 'Littler God' (*allah al-asghar*): they assert that he is the Ruler (or 'Organizer') of the World (*mudabbir al-'alam*)." Here I are reminded of Alan Segal's caveat that, as far back as the Gospel of John, "references to the Ruler of this World appear in highly charged contexts where the targets of hostililty are specifically mentioned as Jews. . . . We should therefore expect that the 'Lord of the World' and the 'God of the Jews' should be linked somehow."[74] It seem significant, then, that this Christian linkage of motifs recurs in Muslim sources.

Yet more significant for the present investigation are the two Islamicate-era Christian authors of works that declare such demiurgic doctrines to be centrally Jewish. The author of the Syriac compendium known as the *Gannat Bussame* (ca. 1000?) attacks the worship of foreign gods. When he arrives at a discussion of the Jews, he exclaims, "I will recall only one thing here, *Adonai Qaton* (Little Lord), general of *Adonai Gadol* (Great Lord), scandalous error, cult of the Israelites."[75] Here again, the "Lesser God" doctrine, and this doctrine alone, is identified as being centrally Jewish.

[72] See pp. 33, 34 of Maqdisi, *Kitab al-Bad'*.
[73] For a recent translation and analysis of this passage, with reference to the earlier literature, see Saperstein, *Decoding the Rabbis*, 1–3. Saul Lieberman also discussed Ibn Hazm's treatment of these (and other) materials in *Shekiin*, 11–18. Perlmann believes that this passage may have been based on Christian sources: "Eleventh-Century Andalusian Authors," 269–90, at 278. Lazarus-Yafeh notices that Ibn Hazm also cited the important Jewish angel Sandalphon (*Intertwined Worlds*, 31–32, and especially 32 n. 38).
[74] Su'udi, *Disputatio pro religione*, 188; see also Alan Segal, "Ruler of This World," 252.
[75] First noted and cited by Bidez and Cumont in *Les Mages Hellénisés* 2:115, where they dated it to the eighth century. Baron and Scholem both noticed this text and commented on its significance, assuming its early dating: see 8:16; and *Major Trends*

The final and most important heresiography to be adduced as evidence for the Christian influence on the origins of Muslim heresiography of the Jews is that of the tenth century Severus (Sawirus) ibn al-Muqaffaʿ, Jacobite Coptic bishop of al-Ashmunain in Egypt. In no less than three of his works, Severus attacked Jewish demiurgism, which he assigned both to "Ashmaʿath al-Yahud" and to the "ʿAnaiyya" (*sic*).[76] He shares the same tradition as the compiler of the aforementioned *Gannat Bussame* concerning this demiurgism (which fact shows that the early Coptic and Syriac usages are interconnected). Like his contemporaries Maqdisi and Masʿudi and (possibly) like Tabari before them, Severus uses the term Ashmaʿath to refer to the majority party of the Rabbanites. And like these Muslim writers, he mentions Ashmaʿath in juxtaposition to the ʿAnanites.

The evidence militates against a conclusion that this mid-tenth-century usage derived from Karaites. It is important to note that Maqdisi and Masʿudi, like Severus, were writing circa 950, and that all possessed sources on these Jewish sects independent of any knowledge of Qirqisani's *Anwar*, written in 927. This can be established for several reasons. First, throughout the *Anwar*, and specifically when he is discussing "the Lesser Lord," Qirqisani refers to his opponent party as Rabbanites.[77] Indeed, Qirqisani's own knowledge of these matters is probably indirect, for when he claims that the passage concerning "the Lesser YHWH" is found in the Talmud, he errs—it is in the *Alphabet of Rabbi Akiba*.[78] Finally, as is well known, Qirqisani himself drew on Christian material for the form and some of the substance of his masterwork.[79]

Conversely, there is little reason to suggest that Severus drew his information from Qirqisani. True, the Coptic bishop does attack the Angel-Creator

---

in Jewish Mysticism, 336 n. 106. Reinink now places it around the tenth century (*Studien zur Quellen*).

[76] This bishop, the earliest Arabic-using Coptic theologian, was an active controversialist who inveighed against rival Christian denominations, against philosophers, and against Muslims. He also apparently authored at least two refutations of the Jews, and is noted for having debated a "clever Jew," the record of which meeting survives. "Ibn al-Mukaffaʿ," *Encyclopedia of Islam*, 2d ed. 3:885–86; Severus ibn al-Muqaffaʿ, *Histoire des Conciles* and *Lamp of the Intellect*. Lewis has identified the Jew with whom Severus debated in "Paltiel," 180–81. In *Histoire des Conciles*, 524, 527, 529; and in *Lamp*, text p. 16, trans. p. 15. A common tradition with Gannat Bussame can be posited for three reasons. First, both use the term, Adonai Qaton." Second, both specify that this Lesser Lord is subordinate to a High God. Finally, both criticisms come in the context of a methodical critique of the wrong beliefs of foreign religions concerning the godhead, in which the beliefs of Mani, Bardaisan, and Marcion are also specified. Since the roughly contemporary Gannat derives from Syriac circles, one may reasonably suggest that in the tenth century there was already well established a Christian literary tradition on this question.

[77] Qirqisani, *Yaʿqub al-Qirqisani*, index, s.v. "Rabbanites."

[78] Ibid., 174 n. 70.

[79] For a review of the literature concerning Christian influence on early Karaite theology, see my "Species of Misbelief," 47–50.

doctrine of the Karaite Benjamin al-Nihawandi, but he could have obtained this material from any number of literary or oral sources on this important Karaite theologian.[80] Moreover, Qirqisani speaks of "the lesser YHWH" while Severus specifies "the Lesser Lord." Furthermore, Severus uses the term Ashma'ath, while Qirqisani uses Rabbanites. Finally, Severus corrupts and conflates the very name of Qirqisani's Karaites as "'Anaiyya," while Qirqisani himself, of course, is always careful to distinguish Karaites from 'Ananites.

From the preceding evidence, I would draw a few tentative conclusions. First, "Ashma'ath," though misunderstood as a meaningful term, was always associated with one doctrine in particular, the Jewish belief in a Creator-Angel. This polemical characterization of a Jewish Demiurge had a long Christian pre-Islamic literary history. Second, the most plausible etymology of the name Ashma'ath—"tradition"—as well as its defining characteristic, the doctrine of the Creator-Angel, may ultimately have some attenuated historical basis in rabbinic fact. However, the weight of the evidence, especially the detailed coincidence between the Christian and the earliest Muslim reports, and the disparity between those reports and the Jewish material suggest that these motifs reached Muslim authors through Christian and not Karaite intermediation.

In addition to these scholastic caricatures, a second arena of Metatron's fame was found in *aggada*, a ramified body of homily, folk narratives, and other Jewish narrative genres. In this regard, Séd is thus almost correct: "in the texts of the Genizah, the work of [magical] purification economizes on the name of Metatron, probably because at this late epoch of Merkava Mysticism the secret name of [Metatron] was widely distributed in midrashic literature and had practically no esoteric connotation".[81] In other words, by the high Geniza period more than a few initiates knew about these theories and practices. But that is *not* to say that Metatron did not retain some esoteric significance; as I shall argue more fully, his being both esoteric *and* accessible comprised a key element in his success.

Metatron grew notoriously familiar after Muhammad. This archangel's maturation implies a transformation of Jewish theory and practice. To recreate the little-known story of Metatron's development, I have reconnoitered two bodies of literature, the Cairo Geniza and the magical texts of medieval Islam, for Metatron was a superstar in both realms.

Metatron in Geniza Magic

S. D. Goitein was the modern master of Judeo-Arabica, and most especially of the Cairo Geniza, the vast repository of manuscripts dating primarily from the ninth through the twelfth centuries, discovered in a Cairo synogogue in 1897. Goitein's magisterial five-volume synthesis, *A Mediterranean Society*, is

---

[80] Qirqisani, *Ya'qub al-Qirqisani*, 140 and 144, where he cites 'Ananites and Karaites in the same phrase.

[81] Séd, *La Mystique*, 142 (my translation).

based on the documentary evidence of the Geniza, primarily business letters.[82] As magnificent an achievement as it is for social history, any extrapolations from this monumental "sociography" for the history of religions must
proceed with caution. To take an apt example, Goitein emphasizes the "absence of angels" in the texts he studied. He goes so far as to say that "the
direct appeal to God, so prevalent in the Geniza, is emphasized by the total
absence of intermediaries."[83]

Metatron's surprising success therefore highlights a central scholarly
mystery concerning the Geniza discoveries as such. That is, we have yet to
correlate the Geniza's extensive esoteric materials—upon which I am
drawing—with its much more massive documentary evidence, upon which
Goitein worked. We simply do not know how the esoteric practices are to be
set into his general social description of this Mediterranean society.

Goitein describes the religion of the Geniza people as "a stern, straightforward, Talmudic type of piety, concerned with the strict fulfillment of the
commandments and with the pursuit of the study required for their knowledge."[84] He repeatedly characterized this religiosity as "bourgeois" and "jejune," as very much this-worldly and outer directed.[85]

The esoteric literature of the Geniza, amply represented in Cambridge's
Taylor-Schechter collection, and which simply lay beyond Goitein's legitimate
purview, tells another story. By striking contrast to Goitein's description of
the religiosity of the Geniza folk, this evidence includes an exotic variety of
still-little-understood mystical and magical texts and practices. I shall now
describe two of these: invocations to Metatron as an intercessor and invocations to Metatron as the Prince of Torah.

Metatron as Intercessor

By the dawn of the Geniza period, in the ninth and tenth centuries, Metatron
was widely regarded as the ultimate angel by both elite and popular mystics.
His attraction was the same at the elite and popular ends of the community:
not only did he possess the closest access to God but, concomitantly, a Jew
could have access to Metatron. This mediating, prime-ministerial function is
most succinctly expressed in a text of the period, *3 Enoch*, also known as *Sefer
Hekhalot*: "If any angel or prince has a matter to bring before Me, he should
bring it to [Metatron]. You must observe and do all that [Metatron] enjoins
you in My name."[86] In a variety of Geniza texts, the Tetragrammaton, the

---

[82] I review the fifth volume in my review essay, "Recent Works on the 'Creative
Symbiosis.'"
[83] Goitein, *A Mediterranean Society* 5:336–37.
[84] Goitein, "Religion in Everyday Life," 8.
[85] "matter-of-factness and sobriety of a middle class consisting mainly of skilled arti-
sans and merchants" (ibid., 15); "sober, straightforward, even jejune" (p. 16).
[86] Ginzberg, *Legends of the Jews* 1:139, gives a different translation.

great four-letter name of God, is invoked by the practitioner to engage the services of the intermediary Metatron.[87]

These invocations to an intercessor begin by invoking the name of the High God in order to coerce Metatron into acting on the client's behalf. Hai Gaon, (939–1028) was aware of this function: "Amulets are written, and divine names are spoken, in order that angels may help." Hai apparently recognized a formula for obtaining this help, which in fact is found in both Jewish and Muslim texts: "In the name of God I abjure you O Metatron."[88]

Thus, Metatron as intercessor is found in a Geniza charm:

> In the Name of YHWH may we do and prosper! According to the word of YHWH may it bring to me the Prince of the princes, Akh! Mitatron! . . . I adjure you by the Name YHWH Sebhaoth the God of Israel, seated above the Cherubim! and by the Ineffable Name![89]

Metatron as Sar Torah

Why did Jews call upon the name of God to force Metatron to help them? What kind of help did they need? A second type of Geniza magic, the theurgically induced "Revelation of the Sar Torah" provides one answer to this question. What these unidentified Jews wanted to have was the ultimate status of a Jew. Their perennially Jewish need was the need to learn Torah, to memorize Torah, and to be rewarded for doing so. The esoteric answer, then, was a practice: invoking an angel called the Prince of Torah (Sar Torah), to magically secure one's desire for Torah mastery: to have it all and have it now.

Scholem, the first in all fields of Jewish mysticism, defined the Sar Torah phenomenon and argued for the antiquity of this praxis. Gruenwald succinctly described this practice as a "secret magical method of studying the Torah and memorizing that study."[90] In the past decade, scholarship has corroborated the significance of the Sar Torah in medieval Jewish esoteric practice. Most recently, Yosef Dan has gone so far as to argue that "the Revelation of the Sar Torah" constitutes, in fact, the third of three major types of ancient Jewish mysticism.[91]

I would emphasize that Dan's point precisely pertains to the ultimate goal

---

[87] For example, TS K 1.70, edited and translated in Naveh and Shaked, *Amulets and Magic Bowls*, with this reference at 226–27. Here Metatron is abjured along with Sandalphon.

[88] On Hai and his responsum, Halperin, "A New Edition." For more on Hai's responsum, see nn. 139–40 below.

[89] Metatron is found as an intercessor in Muslim texts as well. Thus Ibn al-Hajj calls upon Metatron this way: "Be our intercessor, O Lord Metatron, and give orders to the angelic spirit." I translate from the French translation of Doutté, *Magie et Religion*, 134. See also Buni, *Manba' al-Hikma*, 185.

[90] Gruenwald, *Apocalyptic and Merkabah*, 169.

[91] Dan, *Three Types of Ancient Jewish Mysticism*.

of a traditional Jewish life, the learning of Torah. Thus, one Geniza incantation conjures Metatron:

> [I, so-and-so], so that I learn Torah and cleave to wisdom so that I learn Torah and do not forget Your Name, I recite:
>
> Mittatron Sar ha-Panim who is Sar Shel Torah AMY'L is your name KNYNYA is your name MIHOM 'ITIMON PISKON STRGRON is your name, your name that is like that of your Lord's.[92]

Elsewhere a mystical text states of the invocation of Sar Torah, "he who is worthy is answered when using it."[93] These names were to be invoked daily.

This enacted fantasy of theurgic empowerment purported to affect a kind of private revelation to the individual. Following elaborate conjurations of Metatron by his secret names, the author of the Geniza-era magical book *Sword of Moses* addresses the Angel of the Presence this way: "Reveal all the secret mysteries to me from above and beneath . . . just as a man speaks to his neighbor."[94]

I detect in this latter tone of familiarity—"just as a man speaks to his neighbor"—a clue to Metatron's function. A typical Geniza amulet calls on "Metatron Sar haPanim" to ward off demons and diseases from the owner of the amulet, one Eliyahu ben Esther.[95] This common, everyday magical recourse to Metatron—"just as a man speaks to his neighbor"—would seem to indicate that Metatron was not only the most exalted minister of God, the Prince of Torah; he was also, simultaneously, a familiar enough presence to be domesticated as a spirit warding off the most common infirmities and fears. He was so accessible, in fact, that he could be purchased commercially: the most esoteric materials, such as the conjuration of Metatron, could be bought and sold on the magical marketplace.

This, then, may be the central paradox of Metatron's personality after Muhammad: The "highest" divine powers were precisely the most popular forces for use in the everyday. This paradox held true not only in Judaism under early Islam but in early Islam itself. In fact, this dialectic of the foreign and the familiar may be characteristic of monotheistic myth in general. In order to further explore this possibility, I turn now to the Islamicate chapter of Metatron's life story.

Islamicate Metatron

As I have noted, a far-reaching recent scholarship establishes Metatron as the most important of postbiblical Jewish angels. This scholarship shows that Metatron, particularly influential in the period between the Talmud and the

---

[92] TS K-1 #19 which resembles the appendix to the *Sword of Moses*, ed. Gaster, in *Studies and Texts* 1:330–36.

[93] *Hekhalot Rabbati*, cited in Gruenwald, *Apocalyptic and Merkabah Mysticism*, 172.

[94] Gaster, *Studies and Texts* 1:334.

[95] Mosseri S. 4a, edited by Mann, *Texts and Studies* 2:93.

Zohar, rose to such eminence in the imagination of some Jews that he could even be conceived as a "Lesser Lord."[96] Metatron was the chief of the angels, "whose name was like that of his Lord's."

But it remains little known that Metatron was revered outside of Jewish circles. McCullough, following the *Jewish Encyclopedia* of 1904, believed that his Mandaic bowl was the first known instance of Metatron in a non-Jewish source.[97] Alexander, in an otherwise entirely admirable article, could assert that "'Metatron' is not found in any extant non-Jewish text."[98] And Pingree could make the argument that a magical invocation should not be ascribed to al-Kindi on the grounds that Metatron is mentioned in it.[99]

It is therefore all the more necessary to survey here the range and variety of the Islamic reverence of the angel Metatron. To do this I shall begin by suggesting several possible early instances of an awareness of Metatron on the part of Muslims, including one suggested instance in the Qur'an. I have already traced this motif in Muslim heresiography of the Jews, a literature that fulminated against the Jews for their alleged exaltation of an Angel-Demiurge. This accusation, as I have said, had already gained prominence in Muslim scholarly circles of the tenth century. It remained a polemical set piece for many centuries, and can be found in a broad range of Muslim literatures, Shi'i, Sunni, Mu'tazilite, Kalam (scholastic theology), and *adab* (belle lettres). At this point, I shall examine instances of Metatron mentioned by name in Islamicate magical texts. I will conclude with some consideration of an apparent paradox: Muslim scholars attack the Jews for revering an angel that itself had gained a permanant, elevated niche in Muslim angelology.

The Spread of the Islamicate Metatron

In the foregoing I have shown that a number of Muslim scholars from the tenth century onward portrayed the Jews as worshipers of an Angel-Creator.

---

[96] See this chapter, nn. 71–81 above.

[97] Ironically, Greenfield has since demonstrated that this bowl must have been written by a Jew, although Metatron in this instance was apparently hallowed by a Mandean (Greenfield, "Aramaic and Mandaic Magic Bowls," 149–56, esp. 154–55).

[98] Alexander, "Historical Setting," 180. But, in point of fact, in addition to the many examples of Metatron in Islamicate works, Metatron remained alive in Mandean magic for perhaps over a millennium. For an important discussion of Metatron in the Mandaic incantation bowls, see Greenfield, "Aramaic and Mandaic Magic Bowls," 149–56, esp. 154–55. An Arabic-script Mandean magical text (Lady Drower's collection, Bodleian Library, Oxford University, roll no. 43, on the back; dated colophon 1274/1854; spell no. 14), includes a corrupt instance of Metatron—"Titrun." Professor Juan E. Campo generously shared his description and translation of this text with me. I am grateful to him for his help.

[99] David Pingree noticed the citation but denied its attribution to al-Kindi (Pingree, "Some Sources" 5 n. 28). The text is found in Veccia and Celentano, "Trois Epitres d'al-Kindi," 523–62, at xviia of the text, p. 560 of the translation.

This depiction was more than a set-piece of the polemic against the Rabbanites. Indeed, it evolved from the very origins of Muslim heresiography of
the Jews as a purportedly essential characterization of Judaism itself. It is thus
all the more striking to find that in the same years as the critique "Rabbinists
= Demiurgists" was elaborated, the angel Metatron was itself spreading into
Islamic cosmology and magic.

In this section I shall look at several instances of Metatron in Islamic
sources. These are not the earliest instances: those of Kindi and Mas'udi are
the first such examples. In the following section I shall discuss the numerous
instances of Metatron in Islamicate magical texts. For the moment, I shall
consider the occurrence of Metatron outside of its widespread popularity in
Muslim heresiography and magic.

Already in the mid-nineteenth century de Sacy translated a Druze cosmological text that depicted Metatron as one of the "Throne Bearers" (*hamalat
al-'arsh*).[100] The others were Gabriel, Michael, Israfel, and Azareel. This pentad of the throne brings to mind the Metatron of the Muslim magical tradition recorded by the twelfth century magician al-Buni, who lists Metatron in
a pentad, one other of which is Israfil.[101] Another Muslim magician, Ibn al-
Hajj, wrote an invocation to Metatron in which he describes Metatron as a
scribe at the right side of the Throne of God.[102]

All of these associations of Metatron and the Throne scene bear a close
family relationship to similar Jewish depictions. The name Metatron could be
derived from its position as "one who sits beside the throne."[103] This aspect
of Jewish angelology strikingly was reprised in the Islamic reimagining of
Metatron.

Another important Jewish image of Metatron which was reimagined by
Muslim mythologists was that of Metatron as "the angel serving before the
curtain." This association is made in Midrash and in the Hebrew book of
Enoch.[104] It had already been made in a Mandaic-language incantation bowl,
which calls upon "the name of Metatron HLDH who serves before the
curtain." Greenfield has shown that this bowl must have been authored
by a Jewish magician.[105] Thus already in pre-Islamic times the association
of Metatron and the veils was available to non-Jewish patrons of Jewish
magic.

However this motif entered into Islamicate literature, it was eventually ensconced in Islamicate cosmology. Thus, the fifteenth-century Egyptian poly-

[100] de Sacy, *Exposé de la religion des Druzes* 2:67–68.

[101] Winkler, *Siegel und Charaktere*, 77.

[102] Doutté, *Magie et religion*, 133–34.

[103] These Jewish traditions have been analyzed by Bar-Ilan in his article "Throne of
God," 21–35.

[104] Greenfield, "Aramaic and Mandaic Magic Bowls," 149–56, at 154. The literature
on the veils is extensive, cosmological commonplace in Jewish, Muslim, and other
texts. See, for example, Jeffrey, *Qur'an as Scripture*, 62, n. 34.

[105] Greenfield, "Aramaic and Mandaic Magic Bowls."

math al-Suyuti, in two of his works on cosmology, describes the following transmundane cosmography:

> The heaven of this world (*al-dunya*) is a wave held back; the second is white marble; the third is iron; the fourth is copper; the fifth is silver; the sixth is gold; the seventh is ruby; above that are the deserts of light (*sahara min nur*); no one knows what is above that except God Most High and the angel in charge of the veils, called *Mitatrush*.[106]

Although Jewish and Muslim parallels to this cosmography are not hard to find, they do not reveal—and at this stage of understanding cannot yield to us—the pathways by which Muslim cosmological schematizers came upon and eventually remade the angel Metatron. True, Hekhalot traditions describe numerous heavens above the seventh heaven, and other Muslim texts specify the "deserts of light."[107] It is also true that the occurrence of the motifs of water and marble may indicate an association with the Hekhalot traditions.[108] But it is also possible that Suyuti's tradition may have had an origin in magic, for the metals iron and copper were standard motifs of these magical traditions. Moreover, the only other possible instance of the form of Metatron as "Mitatrush" occurs in Muslim magic, where the nominal ending *ush* for angelic appellations likewise was a commonplace.[109]

Before moving on to discuss Metatron in Islamicate magic, I should note other occurrences of Metatron in nonmagical Muslim texts. The twelfth-century author of the Persian language *Deha'iq al-Haqa'iq*, for example, equated Metatron with the angel Samhourash. Moreover, this author asserts that Samhourash is to Khidr as Metatron is to Elijah.[110] In the absence of more evidence for a clear understanding of these apparently facile equations, I might simply point out Winkler's eytomology for the angel Samhourash. Winkler suggested that this angel's name should be derived from the Hebrew Shem ha-meforash, "the Hidden Name of God." This form of the Hebrew "Greatest Name" itself achieved some popularity in Muslim traditions, and may itself have at some point been hypostatized as an angel.[111]

In contrast to Muslim heresiographical usages of Metatron, the foregoing occurrences are rather obscure. Perhaps the most significant aspect of these various usages is that such a variety of sources all depict Metatron as a divine potency of some importance. That a Persian-language philosopher, a Druze scripture, and an Egyptian cosmographer can equate Metatron with the great

---

[106] Heinen, *Islamic Cosmology*, 141; al-Suyuti, *Al-Haba'ik fi Akhbar al-Mala'ik*, 47.

[107] Tritton, "Discords and Differences," 100, "Above the seventh heaven are deserts of light." "Deserts of light" are also mentioned by Lahiji: Corbin, *Man of Light*, 112.

[108] See the remarks of Halperin concerning the "water-test" (*Faces of the Chariot*, 487–90).

[109] For Mitatrush, see Buni, *Manba'*, 110.

[110] Blochet, "Études sur le gnosticisme musulmane," 717–56, at 724.

[111] This is argued by Winkler, *Siegel und Charaktere*, 142. *Shamhouras* was contemporaneously available to Jews in such Geniza texts as T-S K 1.68.

Khidr, or even place him near the Throne of God, at least indicates the wide-spread reverence accorded this angel by a range of Muslim religious writers.

Metatron in Islamicate Magic

The magical tradition absorbed Metatron into Islamicate spirituality. Two aspects of the Jewish traditions concerning Metatron are relevant in this regard. First, there was a wavering, but undoubtedly strong, relationship between the Metatron traditions and the Jewish magical tradition. And second, the Jewish magical traditions had always been, like most magical traditions, interconfessional in orientation. Both these aspects of the Jewish Metatron are reflected in the evolution of the Islamic Metatron. Therefore, I must now address these points in order to set the occurrences of Metatron in Islamicate magical traditions into context.

Those two intertwined traditions, while not offically approved, were at least tolerated in practice,[112] as was magic in general. Naveh and Shaked have recently restated the concensus that "contemporary Jewish sources, notably the Talmudic and Midrashic literatures, are notoriously ambiguous about magic."[113] From the point of view of law, then, magical and mystical practices were not encouraged but neither were they vigorously nor uniformly suppressed.

In other words, the symbiotic interplay between these two aspects of spiritual enterprise survived in an atmosphere of commonly benign neglect. These two streams of active spiritual praxis fed into each other, fed on each other, in almost indistinguishable motions of simulation and dissimulation. Surrounding this interplay was the aura of the numinous and the diffusely pious in which these texts were shrouded. Contemporaries, like observers today, could therefore render them emotional respect, even if they might not lend them intellectual credence. Scholem's emphasis on this interplay, and his stress on its ultimately acceptable halakhic status, are reflected in Cohen's conclusions concerning the *Shi'ur Qomah*: "The user of the *Shi'ur Qomah* was able to pronounce his magic formulae and acquire the rewards stored up for him precisely because he worked his magic in the context of the longing all religious men feel towards their gods, a longing that is legitimate, noble and ancient."[114]

A similar concensus holds, moreover, that Jewish magic, like all magic, tends to be interconfessional in orientation. This commonplace observation, however, does not yet tell us how or why certain magicians found certain names and specific images particularly powerful. At the least, a comparison of

---

[112] Scholem's conclusions in his "Halakhic Caracter of Hekhaloth Mysticism" have been widely accepted (*Jewish Gnosticism*, 9–14).
[113] Naveh and Shaked, *Amulets and Magic Bowls*, 36.
[114] Martin Cohen, *The Shi'ur Qomah*, 71.

Jewish magic under Islam with contemporary Islamicate magic is certainly a desideratum. One question that should be asked in such an inquiry concerns the role of professional Jewish magicians. As Naveh and Shaked have recently said, "magic may have been considered to some extent a Jewish specialization and pagans and Zoroastrians often turned to Jewish practitioners when they sought an effective remedy, protection or curse."[115] Only further research will tell whether Muslims may not have had similar recourse to Jewish professional magicians.

The interconfessionalism of magic, to be sure, should not lead us to see Islamic magic as a mere function of Jewish magic. The two traditions developed together, with some awareness of each other and with sporadic if apparently continual cross fertilization. That Islamic magic influenced Jews can be seen in Jewish magical texts of the Geniza. One Jewish amulet even acknowledges Muhammad as a prophet, while another begins with the Islamic formula "In the name of God," Bismillah.[116] As S. D. Goitein emphasized in his characterization of Jewish-Muslim symbiosis, magic was very much a two-way street.[117]

In what follows I shall cite seven instances of Metatron found in Islamicate magical texts dating from the ninth century to the present day. In all of these instances, other "Jewish" motifs—magical or other motifs familiar from Jewish sources—can be found alongside Metatron. The intertextuality of magic, it would seem, is nearly total. As a self-referential and seamlessly self-sustaining system of ready references, magic moves on, oblivious of credit, plagiarism, or blame. The following examples reveal the chief of Jewish angels demoted to a prestigious retirement. His name lived on, however, as an efficacious epithet meant to evoke his once-divine powers.

The earliest datable occurrence of Metatron in Islamicate magic is a "Letter on the Invocation of the Spirits" attributed to Abu Ya'qub b. Ishaq al-Kindi (d. ca. 252/866).[118] Stating that he is borrowing his invocation from Hipparque, the son of Efrete the Greek, al-Kindi begins by calling upon twenty-four spirits. The first twelve are the "servants of the day," one of whom is Metatron. If this invocation is indeed to be attributed to al-Kindi, this occurrence is interesting for the comparative insignificance accorded Metatron as early as the ninth century. In this letter, that is, Metatron occurs merely as one of dozens of magical names. Other names in this invocation familiar from Jewish and Christian sources include Immanuel and Elohim. The attribution of this "Invocation" to al-Kindi has been questioned. If it is indeed correctly attributed, it is unusual not only for its being so early, but also for its being (purportedly) authored by a great philosopher. The rest of the examples of

---

[115] Naveh and Shaked, *Amulets and Magic Bowls*, 18.
[116] Friedlaender, "Muhammadan Book," 84–103. Lazarus-Yafeh also cites a Hebrew Qur'an which cites evokes the Basmallah, in *Intertwined Worlds*, 154–60.
[117] See my introduction to this book, above.
[118] See n. 99 above.

Metatron in Islamicate magic, by contrast, derive from popular culture, even when the names of the magicians are known.

The best description of the social setting of the following examples can be found in the excellent study by C. E. Bosworth, "Jewish Elements in the Banu Sasan."[119] Bosworth details the extent to which Jewish magical motifs were a standard feature of Egyptian popular culture of the thirteenth and fourteenth centuries. I would just add that Bosworth's rich documentation could be supplemented in a fully comparative study of Jewish and Muslim magic of medieval Egypt. Such a study would necessarily take into account the Greek magical papyri, *Sefer ha-Razim*, the numerous other magical texts found in the Geniza, and the massive works of magicians such as al-Tilimsani and al-Buni. Only with such a work in hand shall we properly comprehend the intricate intertwinings constituting this Jewish-Muslim popular culture.

It is in this context that one must understand the invocation of the "jinni" Metatron in the *ʿAjib wa-Gharib* of Ibn Danyal, a medieval Egyptian shadow play. The fact that the chief of Jewish angels had been downgraded into a mere jinni is less important than the fact of Metatron's tenacious survival. The value of this occurrence of Metatron is that it apparently highlights the continuing *popularity* of Metatron in popular magic. Ibn Danyal chose to have his protagonist invoke the name of Metatron. The playwright presumably made this artistic decision in order representatively to illustrate the magical practices in an Egyptian marketplace.

One such text describes a magician in the marketplace, conjuring Metatron and al-Shaisaban (from the Hebrew *ha-shoshbin* "friend," "companion," "best man at a wedding"). This Muslim sorcerer drives out demons by "the Hebrew formula '*eheyh asher eheyh*' if the spirits are Jews; by the Greek formula 'In the beginning was the Word' if they are Christians; and [by] the invocation of fire and light, darkness and heat, if they are Magians."[120] The verisimilitude of this description may be guaranteed by the presence of just such formulas in the work of al-Buni and in several Geniza magical texts.[121] It is also possible that the Jewish and Muslim uses of this formula have a common ancestry, for such formulas are also found in the Aramaic incantation bowls and the Greek magical papyri of late antiquity.[122]

I may cite just one other piece of corroborating evidence concerning the popular context of Geniza magic. Like al-Buni, a member of the Banu Sasan

---

[119] Bosworth, "Jewish Elements," 1–17.

[120] Ibn Daniyal, *Khayal al-Zill wa-Tamthiliyyat Ibn Daniyal*. For Metatron ("Mitatrun") see p. 193; for the formula, pp. 213–14.

[121] In the Muslim magic of al-Suyuti, *Al-Rahmah fi al-tibb wa-al-Hikmah*, 120; in the Muslim magic of Buni, *Manba*, 162; and Jewish, Christian, and Muslim examples in Shaked, "On Jewish Magical Literature," 20–21.

[122] For examples of this formula on an Aramaic incantation bowl see Gordon, *Adventures in the Nearest East*, 163 (see further on this text in Shaked, "On Jewish Magical Literature," 19 n. 28); on the Leiden magical papyrus, Scholem, *Jewish Gnosticism*, 81; Goodenough, *Jewish Symbols* 2:294.

claimed to write out charms in Hebrew and Syriac called *qalafturiyya*.[123] This term, denoting "magical characters" is also utilized in Geniza texts.[124]

Metatron's Egyptian marketplace popularity would seem to be confirmed by the recurring use of his name in magical collections of the thirteenth and fourteenth century. Three such collections, the *Shams al-Maʿarif* and *Manbaʿ al-Hikma* of Ahmad al-Buni (d. 1225) and the *Shumus al-Anwar wa Kunuz al-Asrar* of al-Tilimsani (sixteenth century), have been known for some years to contain references to Metatron.[125] However, these hitherto iolated citations have not been reexamined, nor have they been studied in the light of a continuum of usages of Metatron by Muslims. I shall therefore concern myself here largely with setting these citations into the general context of the Islamicate Metatron.

The invocation cited by Ibn Hajj al-Tilimsani uses the Qur'anic sura "The Sun" as its framework. In this invocation, Metatron himself is invoked and ascribed the highest of attributes:

> notre intercesseur . . . vous avez la connaissance et la science des mysteres, puisque vous savez cela des esprits, et que les esprits le tiennent de vos chefs (communs), et que ceux-ci le tiennent de *Miṭʾaṭʾroun*, lequel voit toutes les choses qui passent à la droite du trône divin, et entend le grincement de la plume avec laquelle la destinee s'ecrit sur la "table conservée," et peut copier le tout à course de son rang et de son poste élevé qui sont près de la Seigneurie unique de l'ange Mikail, sur lui soit le salut![126]

> [our intercessor . . . you have the knowledge of mysteries, since you know these spirits, and these spirits are controlled by your [delegated] chiefs, and that they in turn are controlled by Metatron, who sees all things that pass to the right of the divine throne, and who understands that scratching of the [Divine] Pen with which fate is written on the "safely preserved tablet" [*lauh mahfuz*: Qur'an 75:22], and who can copy down all things in their place, and whose exulted post is near that of the lordship of the angel Michael, peace be upon him.]

This text bears so many resemblances to Jewish texts that it reads almost like a translation of a Jewish original. Here, as in Jewish texts, Metatron is

[123] Bosworth, "Jewish Elements," 16 n. 20.
[124] Naveh, "A Good Subduing," 377, edited T.S. K. 1. 15, which contains this term. On p. 377 n. 11, Naveh provides rich documentation on other instances of the use of this term.
[125] *Kitab Shumus al-Anwar* by Ibn al-Hajj al-Tilimsani (d. 930 H.) contains numerous instances of the angel Metatron. See pp. 42, 49, 50. For other examples of Metatron in Islamicate magic see Buni, *Manbaʿ*, 76, 88, 110, 162, 265, 270, 285. And see next note.
[126] Doutté, *Magie et religion*, 133–35, which contains the following Jewish elements (which he does not discuss as being originally Jewish): Metatron is depicted as (1) intercessor; (2) chief of the divine powers; (3) one who knows the great mysteries; (4) one who sits at the right hand of the divine throne; (5) a celestial scribe; and (6) one who is associated with the angel Michael. The original text was unavailable to me.

presented as the chief of the angels; is positioned at the right of the Divine
Throne; is pictured holding the pen that inscribes the fates of all persons; and
is explicitly associated with the angel Michael.[127] In this text, as in certain
Jewish Merkabah and magical traditions, the status of Metatron is greatly
elevated. By contrast, most of the Muslim magical texts merely picture Metatron as one of many quasi-divine potencies.

This demotion of Metatron similarly is evident in the incantations recorded by the prolific Egyptian al-Buni. As Vajda noticed, Buni speaks repeatedly of Metatron.[128] But neither the citations noticed by Vajda, (Metatron's crown and lance) nor those noticed by Winkler (Metatron as one in a
pentad of angels) particularly elevate this angel. However, the lance wielded
by Metatron must be understood in the light of Fodor's study, "The Rod of
Moses in Arabic Magic." Fodor points out, for example, that one of the
angelic names that Buni elsewhere ascribes to the inscription on the rod of
Moses is also one of the names of Metatron.[129]

Metatron's wielding of a lance, cited by al-Buni, must also be compared
with a talisman adduced by Blochet. This *Kitab ʿazim fi ʿilm al-hikma wa-ma
yatarataba ʿalaih* (Great book concerning the knowledge of wisdom and what
derives therefrom) is unavailable for perusal, but is described by Blochet as
being based on "la gnose juive." In this talisman Metatron is said to be holding a whip of seventy-three lashes.[130]

I have found a number of other examples of the variety and the perceived
power of the magical Metatron in Buni's *Manbaʿ Usul al-Hikma*. Most of
these usages are found in invocations that include "Maitatrun" among numerous other divine potencies whose names are invoked.[131] In one of these,
concerning the thousands of times certain specified letters of the "Greatest
Name of God" are to be repeated during a nighttime ritual, an invocation is

[127] On the relation to Michael, see Alexander, "Historical Setting," 162–63; and
Alexander's commentary, "3Enoch." See especially Séd, *La Mystique*, chap. 6, devoted
to Michael and Metatron.
[128] Vajda, "Sur quelques éléments juifs," 387–92.
[129] Fodor, "Rod of Moses," 1–21, at 10.
[130] Blochet, "Études sur le gnosticisme musulmane," 295. Although I have not found
this particular motif in Jewish texts, it is sufficient to read "3Enoch" (*Sefer Hekhalot*)
to feel the terrifying aspect of Metatron in his Merkabah depiction, which may per-
ahps have some bearing on this whip-wielding Metatron.
[131] "Maitatrun" is found in Buni, *Manbaʿ*, on pp. 76, 88, 110, 162, 265, 270, 285.
Note that in these usages, he usually is vocalized as "M*ai*tatrun/M*ee*tatrun": in any
case, the name is spelled with a *ya* after the initial *mim*, which leads one to recall the
observation of Scholem, that "It is interesting, by the way, that the spelling in the
oldest quotations and manuscripts would seem to suggest that the word was pronounced Meetatron rather than Metatron" (*Major Trends*, 70). Note too that Buni
says: "Know that the writing (of these magical names) can be accomplished in Arabic
and Hebrew alike" (in Fodor, "Rod of Moses in Arabic Magic," 8). Also compare TS
K-1 58, which has Arabic glosses on Hebrew and Aramaic text, including the name of
Metatron.

given that includes calling upon "Mitatrush." Several of these invocations clearly include Metatron among the most powerful angels, three of them referring to him in the unusual form of Sayyid Maitatrun, "Lord Metatron." In several of these invocations, moreover, Metatron is associated with the names of God, the Shahadah, and the Bismillah. Most importantly, Metatron is even called upon as being the chief of angels residing under the Throne (ʿarsh) of God.

The last portrayal of Metatron I have found in Islamicate magical texts is that of a contemporary Shiʿi amulet. Because of its significant bearing on the present discussion, I translate it here in full (altering and completing the anonymous, inadequate, and incomplete English translation provided with the amulet):

> [Title (given in English)]: "*TAVIZ*, Protection from Magic," (Taken from *Sahifa-e-Alaviya*) [title is followed by, in Arabic: "This is taken from an invocation (*daʿwa*) against weapons (ʿala al-silah) as a magical protective charm, written to fortify the aiding of faith," followed in Urdu (?): "_____"]
>
> Aya Kanush Arkanush Arahush ʿAtbitquinkh ya Mitatrun Qaryalisiyun Ma wama Sumalsuma Titsalus Khabzus Mafqis Ma Maʿush Ifritiʿush Latifkish Latifush!
>
> You were not on the Western side (of Mt. Sinai) when we imposed the Law on Moses! Nor were you one of the (Children of Israel) who were witnesses (to that Law-giving)!
>
> By the Power of God, be gone from (this place), O accursed one! By the _____ of God, Lord of the Worlds, be gone from this (place), lest you become one of the imprisoned ones! Be gone from this (place), for you should not swagger here! Be gone, O you of the lowly ones! Be gone from this (place)!
>
> _____, banished and cursed, just as we cursed the People of Sabbath, for the Decree of God is ever executed.
>
> Be gone, O Keeper-of-secrets (*dhawa al-makhzuna*), be gone O wall! O wall, be illuminated by the Secret Name (*munawwar bi al-ism al-makhzun*), O *Tatatrun Tarʿun Maraʿun*, Blessed be God, the best of the Creators, *Ya haya ya haya sharahaiya*, Living and Everlasting, by the Name written on the brow of Israfil, be gone from the wearer of this amulet, whether you be jinn, male or female, demon, male or female, familiar spirit, male or female, sorcerer, male or female, sprite, male or female, maker-of-mischief against man or woman!
>
> There is no might and no power but with God the Exalted and Majestic. May God bless Muhammad and his all of his delightful, pure and infallible progeny.
>
> [Concluding, in the Arabic, with magical letters and words; concluding, in the English: "This should be recited thrice in each ear of the person haunted by evil spirit, ALI QUL MOKHAL KHAL MOSHALSHAL"].[132]

[132] This amulet is found as an appendix to a popular anonymous Shiʿi work, *Biographies of the Faithful*, published in Karachi in 1973. The amulet itself is printed twice, once on the paper in which the book is printed, and again on onionskin, with a perforated left-hand edge. This second version is intended to be torn out and used as a phalactery, as the reader is instructed in the English-language superscription: "This

The amulet begins with a series of names of angels, one of which is Metatron. Metatron is the fifth angel named, and is the first to be directly addressed by the apostrophe "Ya!" (O!). The text proper of the amulet then begins with the voice of God, in a quasi-Qur'anic diction, invoking the revelation in phrases also reminiscent of the Voice out of the Whirlwind (Job 38:4–39:30.). Thereafter the protection-exclamations are written, their hortatory intention being to expel evil spirits.

At the structural center of the amulet the name of God is invoked in two telling forms. God is first invoked by permutations of the name Metatron. These three permutations of the name Metatron are not known from the Jewish mystical traditions' lists of the seventy names of Metatron, nor did the Jewish magical tradition commonly permutate the name of Metatron.[133]

Following these names in the Shi'i amulet are the well-known Arabic magical variations of the Hebrew "Ehyeh asher Ehyeh" (I am that I am). The translator did not seem to understand this phrase, for he hypostatized the "Ehyeh" and simply left out the "name" Sharahia. At the least, it is clear that this hoarily numinous phrase as well as the permutations of the name Metatron were used at a central point in the incantation as appellations of particular power. Indeed, they are clearly associated with the Secret Name of God: this would seem to be the name "written on the brow of Israfil."

Metatron and the Problem of Symbiosis

Even without looking far, one can see that these motifs would have been available to Muslims by Jews in Egypt. For example, the angel Shamhouras of Muslim magic seems to have been derived from the Hebrew Shem ha-Meforash.[134] Likewise, "Mitatron" was known in a number of Geniza magic texts. However, the fact of a pooling of resources for Jewish-Egyptian magic does not help explain the unresolved complexities of the earlier era. For example, Qirqisani does not cite Metatron in a setting of magic, but rather of

---

invocation taught by Hazrat Ali (A.S.) is like a fortress for protection—write it and tie it as an emulet [*sic*] on the right arm."

[133] Permutation (Heb., *tzeruf*; Arab., *tasrif*) was indeed an aspect of the mystical and magical practices of the Jews under Islam, but invocatory chanting of permutated syllables—*Tatrun, Tar'un, Mara'un*—was more commonly a feature of Muslim practice. Shi'ur Qomah traditions do include apparent permutations of Metatron, such as *itmon, mitan*, and *miton* (Martin Cohen, *Shi'ur Qomah*, 128), as well as traditions that the name Metatron can be spelled with six, seven, or twenty-four letters. A more striking example is contained in the invocation personally given to E. W. Lane by a magician in Cairo. This charm invoked the magician's two "familiar spirits," "Tarsh" and "Taryush." See Lane, *Manners and Customs*, 269. These names appear to be corruptions of the form "Mitatrush," found, for example, in the works of al-Suyuti and al-Buni, as described above.

[134] This is argued by Winkler, *Siegel und Charaktere*, 142. Shamhouras was contemporaneously available to Jews in such Geniza texts as T-S K 1.68.

rabbinic ritual.[135] Nor did the polemics of the Geonim seem to specify an abuse of Metatron-devotionalism. The problem is that the Karaite and the rabbinite leaderships of the tenth century knew of Metatron and knew of their magic but did not associate Metatron with the magical traditions of their opponents.

Who used these magical texts? The same merchants studied so exhaustively by Goitein? The people in the numerous marriage contracts (*ketubbot*)? The same pietists who retained the Damascus Document, the Testament of Levi, and other ancient texts discovered in the Geniza? What was the social role of magic? What was the social role of interconfessionalism? Only when we have answered such questions will we be able to say what the relationship was between the Jewish and the Islamic Metatrons. While the interconfessionalism of magic had been so well known as to be a cliché of the literature, lost are the motivations, the impetus for a conjurer to teach or to learn from an outsider. At the least, this vast terra incognita of traditional magic awaits colonization.

Metatron has been in continuous use in Muslim magic since its first (purported) occurrence in an incantation written by none other than the celebrated mid-ninth-century philosopher al-Kindi. And Metatron remains in use in recent decades on Shi'ite amulets in Karachi Pakistan. This Muslim depiction usually positions Metatron in the same location as do Jewish cosmologies: that is, beyond location. Metatron is neither in the world nor in the heavens, but just at the lip of the perceptible, above the heavens and just below God.[136] In Islamicate monotheistic myth, then, as in Jewish monotheistic myth, Metatron stars as a divine potency of *almost* unimaginable elevation; so too in Muslim magic. But he was also an ordinary spirit.

Magic is stubbornly conservative and interconfessional. Motifs from antiquity are used in the twelfth and thirteenth centuries, shared across group boundaries, and passed on intact. Thus the ultimate Islamicate instance of Metatron that I have found occurs in an incantation written down by the magician Ibn Hajj al-Tilimsani in the sixteenth century. Resilient as any of the greatest mythological creatures, the indomitable Metatron, in fact, even found his way into the Ottoman Empire of the eighteenth and nineteenth centuries.[137] Thus scholarship has missed a full millennium of Islamicate

---

[135] Qirqisani, *Ya'qub al-Qirqisani*, 124, 128.

[136] On this point, see Séd, that Metatron, in certain depictions, resides neither in the seven heavens nor by the throne, "mais dans une région plus élevée que ce trône" (but rather in a region higher than the throne; *La Mystique*, 287–88).

[137] Demonslabon, "Notes sur deux vêtements talismaniques," 234. Here "Mitrun" is sewn into a late-Ottoman war tunic. On the magical "putting-on" of the Name, see 2 MC 12:40, that Jewish soldiers kept amulets under their tunics. See more fully the remarks of Scholem, in *On Kabbalah and Its Symbolism*, 136–37 (*malbush*). Gaster has also discussed this practice in connection with his study *Wisdom of the Chaldaeans*. He described the accoutrement as "the divine garment with which, if a man is covered, he becomes raised to the status of an angel" (*Studies and Texts in Folklore* 1:445 n. 9).

magical Metatron. The Islamicate Metatron clearly was no merely marginal curiosity; a Persian-language philosopher, a Druze scripture, and an Egyptian cosmographer, among others, commonly place him near the Throne of God or in charge of the curtain before God himself.

This angel was exalted by a tellingly diverse chronological, geographical, and ideological range of Muslim religious writers. Nevertheless, Metatron was an *angel*, who never could "officially" rival the normative role of the revealing angel Gabriel in orthodox Islamic tradition. As I tried to show in the case of the Geniza evidence, moreover, the problem of symbiosis is not yet coordinated with that of social history; and so we cannot yet establish accurate proportions for the full role of Metatron within either Jewish or Islamic practice. But until we can locate such images and practices in their setting, with regard to their proper proportions, we simply will not know how the monotheistic imagination operated within history.

Merely redressing the scholarly neglect of Metatron's impressively varied survival after Muhammad was not, however, the impetus for the foregoing study. To be sure, once a demiurge always a demiurge: world creators are not easily forgotten. But this point alone is still trivial. Mere tenacity is insignificant in itself. How, then, does the additional evidence, Geniza and Islamicate, help us understand the meaningfully symbiotic trajectory of his angelic life?

Metatron dissolved social distance, but not as a secret reserved for an elite. Nor was he a merely compensatory expression of social deprivation. Rather, he seems to have served both functions. What Goitein noted about the related phenomenon of astrology holds true for angelology as well: "Astrology was either a high art, destined for the courts of the kings and the computations of the physicians, or a poor technique providing solace or false hopes to lower-class people."[138] Metatron's theurgic allure, concomitantly, was both popular and elite, esoteric and accessible, foreign and familiar.

Geniza Magic in Its Social Context

Magic in this Mediterranean society, then, was familiar at both the elite and popular ends of the cultural scale. For the period under consideration, we

---

Other examples of late usages of Metatron in Muslim magic exist. When Baron Carra de Vaux collected examples of charms in the marketplaces, he came on several such examples. See Carra de Vaux, "Charms and Amulets," 257–61. The examples he cites are Paris Ar. 2630, which cites "Seven great angels by the throne of God who have names inscribed on their foreheads, hands and feet; the knowledge of these names gives great power in conjurations." The baron observes that "Metatron is assigned sometimes to Jupiter and sometimes to Mercury, although he sometimes appears independently, and is identified with the archangel Michael." He adds a personal experience: "Some years ago the present writer had an amulet prepared by a dervish of Constantinople," which concluded with "Metatron." Finally, see the testimony of Jacob, concerning Metatron in North African magic in the early Twentieth Century, "Ein ägyptischer market," 8–9.

[138] Goitein, "Religion in Everyday Life," 15.

know that magic and its texts were available to a considerable variety of elite readers. A range of contemporaneous elites—Geonim, as well as some of their Karaite and even Muslim counterparts—were directly familiar with Jewish magical practices and texts. These elite readers could cite several titles of these books and could even accurately copy passages from them.

Hai Gaon is an instructive case in point. His famous description of an apparent trance induction in his responsum to Kairouan was cribbed from the theurgic *Hekhalot Zuttarti*, as Halperin has shown.[139] Hai speaks of magical texts "such as they are found among us in large numbers."[140] Indeed, though he was disapproving, Hai wrote of magic and mysticism in such detail that the mid-thirteenth-century Kabbalists believed him to be a great master of mysteries.[141] Karaite scholars also attacked Rabbanite magic from a position of well-prepared research. Daniel al-Qumisi accused the Rabbanites of using *Sefer ha-Yashar*, *Sefer ha-Razim*, *Sefer Adam*, *Raza Rabba*, and "many [other] magic books, whether one wanted to arouse a man's love for a woman or make them hate each other, or else one wished to leap across great distances."[142] Qirqisani speaks of Rabbanite amulets in the same breath as he does the Rabbanite books *Sefer ha-Yashar*, *Metatron,* and *Sefer ha-Razim.*[143]

The Muslim elite also knew of Jewish magic in some detail. Al-Mas'udi and Ibn Hazm both recount the details of invocations to Metatron on the eve of Yom Kippur.[144] These Muslim polymaths may have been aware of such esoteric rituals as the *Sidre Shimmusha Rabba.*[145]

My second point is that contemporaneous Muslim evidence also helps establish a social context for Geniza magic on the popular level. I take as just one instance of this context the Jewish elements contained in the popular Egyptian magic documented throughout this period. The celebrated twelfth century Egyptian magician al-Buni's magical encyclopedia is larded with Jewish materials that surpass the merely nominally Jewish, as Georges Vajda recognized forty years ago.[146] I would add to Vajda's observations that al-Buni,

[139] Halperin, "New Edition," 543–51, esp. 551.
[140] This oft-cited responsum was published by Lewin in *Osar ha-Geonim*, 4, 20–21. Halperin, "New Edition," provides a fresh interpretation of it. For another reading see now Idel, chapter 5 of his *Kabbalah: New Perspectives.*
[141] Scholem, *Origins*, 322 n. 253.
[142] Mann, *Texts and Studies* 2:80–81, 82–83. See also Scholem, *Origins*, 106–7. The responsa are already analyzed in Hildesheimer, "Mystik und Agada," 259–86, esp. 276–86.
[143] Vajda, "Études sur Qirqisani," 87–123; Robinson, "Jacob al-Kirkisani on the Reality of Magic," 41–55.
[144] For Ibn Hazm on Jews and Judaism, see Wasserstrom, "Species of Misbelief," 131–40, 368–71. For al-Mas'udi, ibid., 86–94, 350–52. For a discussion of Ibn Hazm's text, see Saperstein, *Decoding the Rabbis*, 1–2, with accompanying nn. on 213–15; al-Mas'udi, *Muruj al-Dhahab*, 2:390–91.
[145] For this ritual see the text edited by Scholem, in *Tarbis* 16:196–209.
[146] Vajda, "Sur quelques éléments juifs," 387–92.

like his later successor al-Tilimsani, describes some of the details of Metatron's celestial characteristics in terms unmistakably drawn from Jewish mystical and magical traditions.[147]

Muslim and Jewish evidence, finally, suggests that in this Mediterranean society elite and popular magical traditions were not isolated, polar opposites. Rather, the elite and the popular operated in a dialectic with each other. A Muslim example of this dynamic from our period of concern can be cited from *The Thousand and One Nights*. Here hitherto elite magical and hermetic literary motifs are popularized in tales. Such a tale, relevant to the magic of the Geniza period, is that of Buluqiyya. Buluqiyya is a heroic, questing prince of the Children of Israel, Banu Isra'il, whose lengthy tale is narrated with identifiably Jewish magical contents.[148] A similar Jewish dialectic that confounds the elite and popular is found in the Geniza texts, contemporaneous with the development of *The Thousand and One Nights*. In one such text, the sublime Metatron is invoked to help find some gold pieces.[149] Numerous secret names of Metatron, known from the Hekhalot literature, are also cataloged in common apotropaic charms.[150]

All this evidence concerning the social context for Geniza magic leads me to the final, inevitable question. This question must be stated directly even though it is presently unanswerable: Who, in fact, were the practitioners of this Jewish magic? The only possible answer at this stage of research is: the Jew who was not there. The Geniza does reveal the names of some of the customers of the magicians—and indeed these names must be cross-indexed in a comprehensive Geniza onomasticon, to see if we can identify these figures.[151] But the Geniza does not seem to have preserved the names of the magicians themselves.

Trachtenberg argued that there never were Jewish professional magicians; Joseph Dan claims that "many Jews, especially in the East, usually consulted non-Jewish magicians rather than Jewish magicians"; Shaked and Naveh suggest, by contrast, that magic was a Jewish specialization.[152] What has thus far been learned from the Geniza evidence tells us little to resolve this question. For example, it does tell us that *soferim* (scribes) sometimes wrote out

---

[147] Buni seems to have been involved in the Sufi tradition of Ibn 'Arabi. See Chodkiewicz, *An Ocean without Shore*, 9.

[148] I have reviewed the literature on Jewish elements in the Buluqiyya tale in the present chapter, above.

[149] Gottheil and Worrell, *Fragments from the Cairo Genizah* 15:76–81. Gottheil and Worrell edit one other magical text, their no. 24, pp. 106–7. Two letters (texts no. 3 and 27) in their collection shed some interesting light on the social context of Genizah magic.

[150] For example the following texts found in the Taylor-Schechter Collection of the University of Cambridge: T-S K1.19; T-S K1.58; T-S K1.36; T-S K1.70.

[151] See the discussion in Wasserstrom, "Magical Texts," 166 no. 44.

[152] Trachtenberg, *Jewish Magic*, 11–24; Dan, "Magic," in *Encyclopedia Judaica*, vol. 11, col. 714; Naveh and Shaked, *Amulets and Magic Bowls*, 18.

amulets as a sideline.[153] Still, at this stage of research the question remains open.

This much seems reasonably clear. In the Jewish-Muslim symbiosis under early Islam, numerous kinds of magic, in varying attitudes of employment, were accessible practices. These magical practices, like myths of religious origins, were textually and commercially available, through unidentified channels, to both the popular and elite members of this mobile society who desired to somehow acquire and utilize them. Between Muslim and Jew, angels and origins were traded on the marketplace. Such imaginary figures as Buluqiyya and Metatron belonged equally to both communities, and both communities used their foreignness to articulate local visions of another world.

[153] ENA N.S. 18, f.7, cited by Goitein, *Mediterranean Society* 3:226.

CHAPTER SIX

Conclusion

REFLECTIONS ON THE HISTORY AND PHILOSOPHY
OF SYMBIOSIS

AT THE BEGINNING of this book I surveyed scholarly opinion concerning the obscurity of the early Islamic period in the historical study of Judaism. Having now investigated several dimensions of the symbiosis between Muslim and Jew, I find it remains remarkable how few personalities emerged from this study. It is not only that the preponderance of figures studied here (necessarily) remain anonymous. The impossibility of ascertaining the social location, much less the specific identity, of many of the actors in the social drama of symbiosis should not, however, incapacitate the student of symbiosis—for the symbiosis, on my conception, constituted more than the economic, political, and otherwise sociological interaction of identifiable, datable, and historically biographical individuals.[1] In any event, we rarely can identify the names of authors of apocalypses, or the membership lists of sectarian groups, or the customers of marketplace magicians. Nonetheless, we can and do interpret the phenomena of apocalypticism, sectarianism, and magic.

The data, as I have shown, are scattered throughout all manner of Jewish and Muslim letters. The anonymous and pseudonymous literature of storytellers, magicians, and other socially marginal intellectuals has proven particularly important in the quest for evidence concerning covert intimacy cultivated between Muslim and Jew. So has the literature of celebrated critical intellectuals seeking theologically to classify and typologize other religions. But beyond the recovery and explication of this primary data, the present effort has been devoted to an *interpretation* of symbiosis that concentrates on the *products of mutuality*. My concern accordingly has centered on the modes of acknowledgment between Muslim and Jew: perception, reception, construction, interiorization. I have suggested that, beyond the pieties of official, doctrinal acceptance of the other religion, additional dynamics of mutual recognition persisted. For an understanding of these dynamics I have turned to the concept of the imaginary. The ways in which one religion made the image of the other into an image of themselves, which image was then used to redefine and continuously legitimate themselves, constituted an interreligious imaginary that is perceptible to us today only from certain hermeneutical angles. It is these angles that I explore in what follows.

[1] My concern, therefore, has not been to study intermarriage, conversion, occupational patterns, demography, or other sociological indicators as such, aside from the brief overview undertaken in the first chapter above.

In the first place, to sharpen my focus on the social setting of the early symbiosis, I turned to the study of apocalypticism and apocalyptic literature. Now, at the present juncture, a new angle emerges—for, at the end of this project, it appears that the discrete studies incorporated here are framed by *apocalypse* in several senses. First, the trajectories of Jewish and Muslim Messiahs, with which I began, unmistakably were themselves species of apocalyptic phenomena. At the other end of the volume's frame, my studies conclude with such apocalyptic texts as the narrative cycles dramatizing the prophesying and recognizing of the new prophet. Whether linked to the name of ʿAbdallah ibn Salam or the legendary Buluqiyya, these latter stories appropriately may be termed "Muhammad apocalypses." The angel Metatron, likewise, enters my purview through such Jewish apocalypses as the *Nistarot de-Shimon bar Yochai* and *3Enoch*.

This apocalyptic frame provides a new angle on other aspects of this study. At the center of my book I have studied the development of various Muslim forms of Jewish studies, so to speak. While this phenomenon admittedly seems rather removed from the more obvious forms of apocalyptic, I see it as an outgrowth of the comprehensivist drive, the felt necessity to encompass other denominations and practices into a global overview; so too had the authors of "panoramic" apocalypses demonstrated their desire to englobe the known universe in the singular compass of a text. But more direct is the biographical connection. Comparativist literature was first the product of a context, an interconfessionalism at once profound and rare. The meetings, correspondences, friendships, and cooperations between intellectuals marginal to their own communities formed a common cause and so stimulated an interest in religious commonality as such. The resultant development of the critical study of other religions, while remaining as strange and rare as its pioneers, demonstrates the extent to which they sustained a critical stance with respect to the existing religious situation. Here, then, I locate an additional link between the apocalyptic writers and the intellectuals who engendered the comparative-religions literature, for both groups constituted a kind of countertradition-as-critique of existing institutional arrangements.

In the following, then, I elaborate this interpretation of symbiosis. I set out the terms of this reading, in sequence, as *imaginary worldmaking*, *apocalyptic social settings of symbiosis*, and *countertradition as critique*.

IMAGINARY WORLDMAKING

> Poets are the legislators of the unacknowledged world.
>
> —George Oppen

Jewish and Muslim worlds mingled in the imaginary. The concept of the imaginary (*l'imaginaire*) has been used to advantage in Islamic studies, and its usefulness in the study of religion is to be encouraged.[2] While the neologism of Henry Corbin's *imaginal* has gained limited currency, his innovation in fact carries no improvement on the concept of the imaginary.[3] The imaginary, unlike the imaginal, possesses the advantage of retaining its connection with the social life-world. That is, the imaginary, like the apocalypses under discussion here, is a system of symbols rarely disengaged from the social reality it criticizes and subverts.[4] Unlike Corbin's transcendental *mundus imaginalis*, the imaginary is mundane: it has a history, and indeed is itself an operant factor in historical change.

I use imaginary to refer to the symbolic systems in which the creative conflict between mythos and logos is enacted. As Paul Ricoeur suggests, it is in the imaginary that ideology finds its narrative coherence, its story.[5] This *capital pensé* (Ali Bouamama) has been said to found the self-image of society: "Beyond the conscious activity of institutionalization, institutions have drawn their source from the *social imaginary*. This imaginary must be interwoven with the symbolic, otherwise society could not have 'come together', and have linked up with the economic-functional component; otherwise it could not have survived."[6]

The life and the afterlife of images—the life of the "Messiah" Abu 'Isa, and his afterlife in *milal wa nihal*; the Jewish life of Metatron and his magical Muslim afterlife—comprises one theme of the present project, for, in its routine rebirths and commonly dynamic reassertion, the imaginary rarely respects confessional boundaries. This, in fact, constitutes its special value for the study of symbiotic relations. This tenacity may be psychologically explicable. David J. Halperin has argued in psychoanalytic terms that implications latent in Jewish stories may be made manifest on Muslim rereading of those narratives.[7] The imaginary, ever freely renovated in new confessional guises,

---

[2] Among those who have used it are Bencheikh, *Le Voyage nocturne de Mahomet*; Bouamama, "L'imaginaire dans le Coran," 90–99; Gilliot, *Aspects de l'imaginaire islamique*; Arkoun, *Pour une critique*; idem., "Notion of Revelation," 62–89. For an informed history of the concept, see Kearney, *Wake of Imagination*, 251–96. A prolix but sometimes insightful treatment is found in Castoriadis, *Imaginary Institution*.

L'imaginaire, thus, has proved fruitful in the analyses of Islamicists (Arkoun) and Marxists (Althusser, Castoriadis), psychologists (Lacan), philosophers (Ricoeur, Sartre). It is also presently providing new insights in feminist philosophy: Le Doeuff, *Philosophical Imaginary*.

[3] Corbin trumpeted his terminology in numerous forums. A typical discussion is "Toward a Chart of the Imaginal," 23–37.

[4] Sefer Yesira is a notable exception. In general, the hermetic style of scientistic Gnosis is the most purely removed from its context; hence, the difficulties of locating a *Sitz im Leben* (see Wasserstrom, "*Sefer Yesira*").

[5] Here I loosely follow remarks made by Stanislas Breton and Paul Ricoeur in conversations with Richard Kearney: *Dialogues with Contemporary Continental Thinkers*, 28–29 (Ricoeur), and 102 (Breton).

[6] Castoriadis, *Imaginary Institution*, 131, his emphasis.

[7] Halperin, "Hidden Made Manifest," forthcoming in the *Festschrift* for Jacob Milgrom. I am grateful to Professor Halperin for the conversations and correspondence

thus provided an arena in which the foreign content remained operative and accessible to reimagining. In this sense, the imaginary could regularly reassert itself, could make the social world cohere again. As Jürgen Habermas suggests, "Social process is the generation of radically different patterns, a demiurge setting itself to work, the continuous creation of new types, embodied in ever different exemplary ways—in short, the self-positing and ontological genesis of ever new worlds."[8]

The social impact of imaginary worldmaking fortunately is coming to be recognized in the study of religion. Kurt Rudolph, for example, has observed that inasmuch as "symbols open for humankind an approach to the cosmos (symbolization is equivalent to making a cosmos!), they give us meaning and free us from pure objectivity."[9] This idea, of course, has its heritage in the social scientific study of religion:

> From a sociological point of view, religion is the product of that "world-forming" action of human beings through which they constitute a sphere of the sacred, which is at the same time a realm of superior power . . . For Max Weber . . . religion requires the construction of a world behind or above the world, which is populated by demons and gods. Ordering the relationship of demons and gods to human beings constitutes "the realm of religious action."[10]

In the study of interreligious symbiosis, several features of the theory of a worldmaking imaginary must be differentiated. First, the religions themselves posited multiple worlds: this imaginary in itself frequently provided an arena of interreligiously shared "worlds."[11] Second, the imaginary provided psychic and social cohesion for the institutions of both religions. Third, the process of worldmaking was creative; the circumstances of society changed, and the imaginary accounted for these changes by positing "ever new worlds." Fourth, the process of imaginary worldmaking articulates what Tambiah calls "multiple orderings of reality."[12] For all these reasons, then, the dialectical reception and construction of other social worlds made symbiosis

---

we have had concerning this and related matters. I would add that psychoanalytic interpretation of the apocalyptic has found intelligent articulation in Ostow's "Archetypes of Apocalypse," 307–34. See also the Jungian reading of a portentious apocalyptic dream published by Reb Hile Wechsler in 1881; see Kirsch, *Reluctant Prophet*.

[8] Habermas, *Philosophical Discourse of Modernity*, 329.

[9] Rudolph, "Mircea Eliade" 19:101–27, at 112.

[10] Schluchter, *Rationalism, Religion and Domination*, 252. The idea of multiple objective worlds in anthropology is elaborated by Shweder, "Post-Nietzschian Anthropology," 99–140. In philosophy, the most influential statement has been Goodman, *Ways of Worldmaking*.

[11] For an excellent short overview of sources for the "worlds" at issue here, see Vajda, *Juda ben Nissim ibn Malka*, 95–99. See also "Alam," in *Encyclopedia of Islam*, 2d ed., 1:349–50.

[12] Tambiah, *Magic, Science, Religion*, chapter 5, "Multiple Orderings of Reality: The debate Initiated by Lévy-Bruhl," 84–111.

function effectively. Jews had to construct "the Muslim" and Muslims necessarily constructed "the Jew." This is the problem of symbiosis at its heart: the
existence of other worlds was always social and imaginary.

Perhaps nowhere was this social imaginary more keenly realized than in its
solution to the problem of religious diversity. Rarely at home in a monotheistic
universe dominated by the Divine Oneness, the notion of divinely ordained
religious multiplicity nevertheless was inescapable. As a response to this cognitive dissonance, apocalyptic comprehensivism subversively and sometimes successfully countered the tradition of monistic unicity, by swallowing it.
Countertraditional apocalyptic, in this sense, did not come at the singularity of
monotheistic tradition head-on. Rather, it adroitly relocated an exclusive purview within a new frame. Thus, countertradition presumed, subsumed, incorporated, allegorized, displaced, co-opted religious authority.[13] One profound
means of this refunctioning was the very notion of new tradition, that generative oxymoron of young religions. This retrojection of primordiality, this colonization of origins, typically makes novelty possible in religion.[14] Antiquity is
purchased, and purchased again, at the price of an achieved newness.

One implication of this apparent paradox is that this reframing of the past
necessarily also requires the framing of the other religion. That is, the incorporation of the history of other religions into one's own salvation-history requires a
certain accommodation to the realities being encompassed. This intertextuality,
if I may be permitted a term currently in vogue, often operates by means of the
importation and reframing of ancient content.[15] The nested apocalypse, most
strikingly, embedded older sectarian content in a new nomian frame. This is most
apparent in Gnostic works that operated within a framework narrative rendering lip service to the nomocentricity of Judaism and Islam. Such reframing exemplified in a stark form the intertwined worlds evoked by Hava Lazarus-Yafeh.[16]

Apocalyptic Social Settings of Symbiosis

The otherwise rigorous and far-reaching studies undertaken on the genre
apocalypse in recent years have ignored the Muslim case.[17] Thus, the land-

[13] N. O. Brown, *Apocalypse and/or Metamorphosis*.
[14] Much of chapter 3 (especially on the Shiʿi tales of the rosh golah) is relevant to this
point.
[15] The idea of intertextuality, like that of reception criticism, may present promising
avenues of interpretation for a field sorely in need of them. See Bernstein, "Stories of
the Prophets," 27–34. Note his conclusion: "These stories about biblical figures held
to be prophets by both Judaism and Islam are one fruit of this symbiotic relationship"
(134). Bencheikh has produced a nuanced and important discussion in "l'aventure de
la parole", the concluding segment of *Le Voyage*, 231–91, especially the section "Mi-
ʿradj et intertextualité," 280–86.
[16] Islamicate apocalypses could be adduced. "Qissat Islam Kaʿb al-Ahbar," for example,
comprises a pietistic Sufi opening, followed by the "nested" tale of the Islamization of
the Jewish "rabbi" Kaʿb al-Ahbar. See Perlmann, "Legendary Story," 85–99.
[17] Muslim texts considered to be apocalypses have been suggested by Abel, "L'Apoca-

mark publication *Apocalypse: The Morphology of a Genre* includes Jewish, early Christian, Gnostic, Greek and Latin, rabbinic, and Persian apocalypses, but no Islamic instances.[18] The subsequent, massive Uppsala symposium, *Apocalypticism in the Mediterranean World and the Near East*, had at least three shots at it: the original symposium, the expanded second edition of the proceedings, and a recent follow-up volume. Islamic apocalypses are treated nowhere here.[19]

In fact, the sources for the ghulat (proto-Shiʿite extremist) utilization of apocalyptic, especially the biographical sources on such figures as Jabir al-Juʿfi and others around him, arguably provide both broader and deeper social context than for any other period of apocalypticism.[20] In this period, moreover, we have strong evidence for both the reception of ancient apocalypses and the active fabrication of new ones. This almost uniquely documented situation is remarkably underutilized when one considers the paucity of sources for the ancient social setting of the genre apocalypse.[21] I follow the theory which suggests that the dislocated function of the unemployed scribe originally stimulated the apocalyptic mentality. Jonathan Z. Smith and others argue, for example, that apocalypses originally derive in part from scribal circles, which also produced Wisdom literature.[22] "Scribes without a king,"

---

lypse de Bahira," 1–12; idem, "L'Apocalypse de Baluqiya," 189–98; "An Apocalypse Concerning the Heavenly Status of al-Husayn and the Future Deliverer, the Qa'im," in the translation of Crow, "Death of al-Husayn," 71–117, at 114–16; numerous works that include in their title *kashf* (revealing), which may sometimes legitimately be translated as apocalypse, as for example Ibn Mansur's *Kitab al-Kashf*; sura 18 of the Qur'an, or even the whole of the Qur'an: "Massignon calls Sura 18 the apocalypse of Islam. But Sura 18 is a résumé, epitome of the whole Koran. The Koran is not like the Bible, historical, running from Genesis to Apocalypse. The Koran is altogether apocalyptic" (Brown, "Apocalypse of Islam," 69–95, at 86).

Leaving aside the validity of these speculations by Massignon and Brown, few have studied Islamicate apocalyptic in a synoptic way. One who has is Armand Abel; see "Changements politiques"; and "La signification."

[18] Collins, *Apocalypse*.

[19] Hellholm, *Apocalypticism in the Mediterranean World*. The Uppsala follow-up is Collins and Charlesworth, *Mysteries and Revelations*. For a short, up-to-date bibliography of bibliographies on apocalypticism, see Charlesworth's contribution to the latter volume, "Folk Traditions," 91–113, at 91 n. 1.

[20] The biographical and *adab* literature, in particular, is vast and largely unexploited, despite the fact that, as Franz Rosenthal puts it, "nearly every page of this literature provides details on all sorts of topics of sometimes major, usually, of course, minor, importance for social and intellectual historians" ("Muslim Intellectual and Social History," 5). I would add that Funkenstein's assertion that apocalypticism is reserved to two centuries in antiquity is confounded by the Islamicate evidence. He himself acknowledges that this may be the case: "A Schedule for the End of the World," 44–60, at 57.

[21] I review this question in Wasserstrom, "Jewish Pseudepigrapha in Muslim Literature," especially 109–10 nn. 36–43.

[22] J. Smith, "Wisdom and Apocalyptic," 131–56. See also idem., *Imagining Religion*, 94.

on this reading, produced the early apocalyptic literature. I suggest, by extension, that functionaries without a function provided the social base for the apocalypses that I have studied here.

My hypothesis concerning the social setting of the kinds of apocalypses is predicated on a growing sociological literature regarding semi-erudite intellectuals operating as marginal elites.[23] Theda Skocpol, for example, defines marginal elites as "groups which have an upper class education and access to national debates over political and social issues; however, they are restricted . . . from any prospect of active participation in the highest levels of government and society."[24] I would note that the marginal elite as the avant-garde bearer of intellectual syntheses is well known in the history and sociology of religions.[25] Norman Cohn, for example, observes the following concerning the *prophetae* of medieval European chiliasm: "more usually they were intellectuals or half-intellectuals—the former priest turned freelance preacher was the commonest type of all."[26] Joseph Weiss similarly theorized that the social origins of Hasidism may be located in peregrinations of *maggidim* (wandering preachers); again, we are dealing with intellectuals lacking a fixed role in society.[27] In his scathing but frequently penetrating study of the sociology of astrology, Adorno similarly argues that "the climate of semi-erudition is the fertile breeding-ground for astrology."[28] And the theory that apocalyptic literature was produced by intelligentsia lacking a stable role in society may converge with the hypothesis of David J. Halperin concerning the social setting of Merkaba mysticism in the apparently marginalized classes of the *amme ha-arez*.[29]

In general, to state the case in abstract terms, I presume that marginal elites

[23] The literature is of course predicated on the work of Max Weber. On "relatively nonprivileged intellectuals" as agents of change see Weber, *Sociology of Religion*, chaps. 7–8. On "proletarian intellectualism," self-taught intellectuals, and lay intellectuals see ibid., 125, 126, 129. Weber concludes that "lay intellectualism is involved in every complex soteriology which develops abstractions" (129).

[24] Skocpol, "When Do Vanguards Try to Remake the World?" (forthcoming, cited by Goldstone, in "Cultural Orthodoxy," 129). Much of interest can be found in the contributions of Shmuel Eisenstadt to the sociological theory of the Axial Age, especially with regard to the role of intellectuals therein: see "Heterodoxies, Sectarianism and the Dynamics," 1–21; "Transcendental Visions," 1–17; "Cultural Traditions," 155–81; and, as editor, *Origins and Diversity*.

[25] The classic older account is that of Mannheim, *Ideology and Utopia*, esp. chapter 4, "The Utopian Mentality," 192–264. For somewhat more recent theoretical studies and case studies, see Rieff, *On Intellectuals*. Recent reflections on the problem may be found in Bauman, "Love in Adversity," 81–105; and Rorty, "Intellectuals at the End of Socialism," 1–17.

[26] Cohn, *Pursuit of the Millennium*, 280.

[27] Ettinger, "The Hassidic Movement," 253–254, where he dissents from this view of Weiss.

[28] Adorno, "The Stars Come Down to Earth," 23.

[29] Halperin, *Faces in the Chariot*, 437–39.

comprised of semi-erudite intellectuals drove the machinery of symbiotic interactions, especially at those moments when epistemological crises engendered the renovation of cosmology and eschatology. The tension between
epistemological crisis and dramatic narrative gives rise to foundational alter-
nations in the history of science.[30] But so too do new theosophical narratives,
new cosmological accounts, new myths alter the course of religious history.
In the case at hand, such a reinvention of lost communal integrity by means
of renarrativization seems to have been authored by institutionally dislocated
intellectuals driven by what Peter Gay called "wholeness-hunger."[31]

Does this hypothesis suggest that the symbiosis which produced the ʿAbdallah and Buluqiyya cycles, for example, was a "popular" or "folk" expression?[32] Or was it in fact high culture and low culture at once? The great angel
Metatron, thought to be exclusively Jewish, and long hidden in esoteric traditions, turns up in the marketplace, by means of legerdemain, written out in
charms for a price. To consider this appearance as a mere degeneration of a
previously "high" cultural expression is to miss the richness of symbiotic dialectics, for the "high" and "low" can be confounded when the system of symbols is available to be reconfigured. From the point of view of the
apocalypticist, then, such variable revision of the imaginary is perennially
possible, if not mandatory.[33]

I have found that such an interpenetration of esoteric and exoteric is typical
of the symbiosis of Muslim and Jew. A particularly stunning example of this
synergy is the ways that so-called folk literature, especially *Qisas al-anbiya'*,
Isra'iliyyat, and *The Thousand and One Nights*, refunctioned heavenly ascen-
sions into exciting popular tales of world-spanning adventurers. The scenario
of the quest to find a treasure, and the surprise revelation of a divine revealer
seated on a throne, for example, are motifs both of the "secret" hermetic
traditions and of the "popular" tales.[34] It is important to note, then, that the
imaginary, in contrast to Corbin's imaginal, thus retained from the outset a
social implication, derived from its social setting. But it is equally important

---

[30] MacIntyre, "Epistemological Crises," 453–72. I thank Professor Rogers Blood
Miles for bringing this article to my attention. For a comparative account of the role
played by dramatic narrative in theosophical Gnosis, see Corbin, "Élément dramatique commun."
[31] Cuddihy, *No Offense*, 181.
[32] Massignon, "Le Folklore"; Charlesworth, "Folk Traditions," 91–113.
[33] On the concept of real possiblity in Ernst Bloch, see Hudson, *Marxist Philossophy of
Ernst Bloch*, 132–36. For Bloch, this perennial possibility holds utopian promise. This
poetics of the endtime is elaborated in his magniloquent apocalypse of modernism,
The Principle of Hope. While this exemplar of (what George Steiner calls) the Pythag-
orean Genre may be understood to be an apocalypse as a whole, it also deals explicitly
with the question of apocalypse. Such was his preoccupation since the conclusion to
Geist der Utopie entitled, "Karl Marx, Death and the Apocalypse." For Bloch in the
context of apocalyptic, see Rabinbach, "Between Messianism and Apocalyptic," 34.
[34] See Fodor, "Metamorphosis of Imhotep," 155–81.

to bear in mind that such a social implication was not one that resulted linearly in direct criticism of the status quo. Still, this critique function seems to have been a significant reflex of such global, if imaginary, revisionism.

Countertradition as Critique

Symbiosis may have functioned both as the cause and as the effect of social critique, sometimes in radical, even extreme modes. Scholem, it should be kept in mind, never ceased to argue that the mystic's impact on society is at once reinforcing of tradition and revolutionary in its impact.[35] I would add that the same polarity holds true for apocalyptic and its congeners. And the aspect of apocalyptic that I most emphasize here accordingly is also the most paradoxical. The apocalyptic often is understood to be a polemical articulation of in-group interests, the sect's self-legitimation writ large, stretched to cover globally the cosmos, extended to the end of time.[36] While this may not be strictly inaccurate as a general characterization, if left at that, it would, in the present context, incur an error in method, for students of apocalyptic, like those of mysticism, tend too often to truncate Scholem's binocular dialectic.

Scholem, however, wisely recognized that mysticism—to which phenomena apocalyptic often runs parallel—ideologically could cut both ways. Symbiosis, on this interpretation, would lose its constituent, creative inner tension if reduced to some blandly interconfessional sentiment, as in the frequently misread verses of Ibn al-ʿArabi, often claimed to be paeans to a universal ecumenicism.[37] In fact, the modes of mutual acknowledgments were subtly multiple. The lineaments of interreligious recognition, as the present work is designed to show, could take the form of borrowing; acknowledged reception; generous inclusivity; clandestine esoteric burrowing; incorporation through comparison; colonization of older narrative; reframing of the content of received cosmology; and so forth.

Perhaps most significantly for present purposes, late apocalyptic may be

[35] Scholem, "Religious Authority and Mysticism," in *On Kabbalah and Its Symbolism*, 5–32, at 9: "For the same experience, which in one case makes for a conservative attitude, can in another case foster a diametrically opposite attitude. . . . This accounts for the revolutionary character of certain mystics."

[36] Abel, "Les eschatologies," in *Eschatologie et cosmologie*, 9–38: "Enfin, l'acquis le plus important, semble-t-il, que cette étude réserve, et celui qui résulte de l'analyse des représéntations que les apocalypses impliquent, du rapport entre les coreligionnaires des auteurs d'apocalypses, et les étrangers à cette collectivité de fidèles" (In short, it would seem that the most important lesson that this study affords is one which results from analysis of the representations implied by the apocalypses, concerning the relationship between the coreligionists of the author of apocalypses and the strangers to that group of believers [37–38]).

[37] "My heart has become capable of every form; it is a pasture for gazelles and a convent for Christian monks, / And a temple for idols, and the pilgrims' Kaʿba and the tables of the Tora and the book of the Koran" (Nicholson, *Mystics of Islam*, 105).

seen to have functioned as "paraprophecy," (in Gruenwald's phrase). On this reading, apocalyptic literature retained and extended the earlier prophetic function of critique, the righteous condemnation of unjust circumstance. Apocalyptic eschatology, thus, has been characterized as "the idiom of those who are oppressed and powerless and whose hopes appear impossible of realization within existing order. Apocalypses are a form of resistance literature of a type found in other national settings in the Near East."[38] The apocalypse, again, is seen here as an expression of critique on the part of semilearned and socially unmoored intellectuals.

What is too often forgotten, if it was ever known, is that this ancient paraprophetic critique rearticulated in apocalyptic literature continued to flourish during the first centuries of Islam.[39] As the differentiation of society progressed—with the growth, that is, of urbanization, Mediterranean trade, advances in agricultural techniques, and the expansion of an assertive bourgeoisie—so too, for a time, did Jews and Muslims expand their varieties both of social oppression and of textual sophistication. To be sure, I would not want to be misunderstood as suggesting that this paraprophetic critique function amounted to any expression whatsoever—free thought, liberalism, or revolution *avant la lettre*.[40] Even so, an occasionally radical transcendence of confessional boundaries, as I have tried to show, could transpire interconfessionally.[41] The subversive and the contrary, the challenging and the dissenting, the provocative and the disturbing, no less than the entertaining *merveilleux* and the easily marginalized "folklore"—all these countertraditions bolstered the symbiosis between Muslim and Jew, just as Jewish texts were used to strengthen the revelation given to Muhammad.[42] A Muslim thinker today properly argues the significance of such Jewish countertexts (some of which were apocalypses, properly speaking) as support for the Qur'anic text itself:

> The numerous narrations in the *Qisas al-anbiya'* (narrations on the prophets), especially those collected by the two converted Jews, Ka'b al-Ahbar and Wahb ibn Munabbih, provide the mythological background that explains the circumstances in which each verse or piece of the *Qur'an* was revealed. These narratives show the

[38] Aune, *Prophecy in Early Christianity*, 110.
[39] Alexander, "Late Hebrew Apocalyptic."
[40] The Mu'tazila were once taken for Freidenker, but no more. See Goldziher's rejection of Steiner's characterization, in Hamori and Hamori, *Introduction to Islamic Theology and Law*, 86–87, and esp. 86, note d, for more recent literature. Some have sought radicalism. See the uneven but always simulating foray by Bloch, *Avicenna*.
[41] This phenomenon is treated at length in chapter 4 above. See Niewohner's tracking of the parable of the three rings, and its implications for the development of the Enlightenment, in *Veritas sive Varietas*.
[42] The term *folklore* works at best uncomfortably in my analysis. See Charlesworth, "Folk Traditions," 91–113.

strong relationship between the religious *imaginaire* which prevailed during the first three centuries of the Hijra and the interpretations of the *Qur'an*. The sense of the marvellous, as a psychocultural category, is displayed in all the narrations and projected on the Qur'anic discourse itself. Until today, the perception of Revelation has been dominated by this sense of the marvelous as a basic element of mythical knowledge.[43]

The countertraditional thrust of apocalyptic thus need not present itself in directly oppositional terms. To expect it to be so, in fact, is to reduce multi-directional social process to a few mechanically bipolar forces. The unpredictable adaptability of comprehensivism, the cunning of the imaginary's drive to encompass, finds surprising means to surmount apparent defeat. Examples of the cunning, countering effect of apocalypse come readily to hand from recent scholarship. The Dantean countertext of the *Inferno* and *Paradiso* is said to vary Muslim tours of heaven and hell.[44] The apocalyptic imagination could repeatedly rewrite the biography (Sira) of Muhammad, each time with a new implication, but each decidedly still a counter-Sira.[45] And, perhaps most relevant here, Gershom Scholem's historiography of Kabbalah has been considered by David Biale as a kind of counterhistory. That is,

> the belief that true history lies in a subterranean tradition that must be brought to light, much as the apocalyptic thinker decodes an ancient prophecy or as Walter Benjamin spoke of "brushing history against the grain." Counter-history is a type of revisionist historiography, but where the revisionist proposes a new theory or finds new facts, the counter-historian transvalues old ones.[46]

It will be noted that Biale reverts to the metaphor of the apocalyptic writer. Biale's teacher, Amos Funkenstein, instructively, suggests elsewhere that the apocalyptic "schedule for the end" could articulate an entire counterhistory.[47]

Between Muslim and Jew: The History of Symbiosis

The *trajectories*, *constructions*, and *intimacies* with which this study are organized are perhaps somewhat misleadingly set out in roughly chronological order, for they can be understood equally well as occurring simultaneously,

[43] Arkoun, "Notion of Revelation,"62–89, at 69. See also Arkoun, "Peut-on parler," 87–144.
[44] Fischer, "Is Islam the Odd-Civilization Out?" 56: "Not only was troubadour poetry modeled on Arabic forms, but also Dante's *Divine Comedy* might well be seen as a countertext by a Christian nativist to the *mi'raj* (mystical journey to heaven and hell) traditions of Muhammad." I note that the traditions of women in the Bible recently have been termed *countertraditions*: Pardes, *Countertraditions*.
[45] Vajda, "Un vestige oriental," 177–80.
[46] Biale, *Gershom Scholem*, 7.
[47] Funkenstein, "A Schedule for the End of the World" and "History, Counterhistory, and Narrative."

insofar as they each possesses some elements of the other. The messiahs of early Islam; the apocalyptic outbreaks that they stimulated; the rise of Shiʿi Gnosis; the Jewish-Shiʿi ʿIsawiyya; the eventual development of discourse designed to encompass difference in religion; the continuing transformations of apocalyptic depictions of pre-Islamic prophethood *ad majorum Dei gloriam*— these phenomena also coexist in a nonsynchronous history.[48] In short, "apocalyptic," "Gnosis," and "encyclopedism" are not coordinated in some direct or mechanical linkage to a monolithic chronological progression. To make this point more clearly, and to draw toward a close, I will now reconsider the categories of trajectories, constructions, and intimacies in turn.

Trajectories present a first-order phenomenon. The usage "apocalyptic" is fairly apposite in the case of the chiliastic prophets of the second Islamic century, whose Messianism was the concern of the first part of the book in hand. Here the apocalyptic sect is (insofar as it was presented in the early Islamicate sources) a historical actuality. There is, I suspect, little dispute that those millenarian meltdowns, and certain of the texts that emanated from their debacles, accurately may be labeled apocalyptic. The Jewish Messiahs of early Islam, first of all, then, may be seen as trajectories of the rise and function of the holy man in late antiquity.[49] Jonathan Z. Smith has characterized the general social shift that produced this development:

> Rather than a sacred place, the new center and chief means of access to divinity will be a divine man, a magician, who will be, by and large, related to "protean deities" of relatively unfixed form whose major characteristic is their sudden and dramatic autophanies. Rather then celebration, purification and pilgrimage, the new rituals will be those of conversion, of initiation into the secret society or identification with the divine man. As part of this fundamental shift, the archaic language and ideology of the cult will be revalorized—only those elements which contribute to this new, anthropological and highly mobile understanding of religion will be retained.[50]

These Jewish and Muslim holy men and women involved in the milieu surrounding the rise of Shiʿism were in contact with Gnostics, as I have shown above. The social status and social setting of Gnosis before and after Muhammad therefore directly is relevant to the present discussion. Max Weber, followed more recently by Kurt Rudolph and Carsten Colpe, articulated

[48] Bloch, "Nonsynchronism," 22–38.
[49] I am of course thinking, in the first instance, of the classic paper by Brown, "Rise and Function of the Holy Man," 80–101. See also his "Saint as Exemplar in Late Antiquity." Brown's work stimulated and coincided with much of interest on this subject. See for example, Fowden, "Pagan Holy Man," 33–59; Frankfurter, "Stylites and Phallobates," 168–99; Cox, *Biography in Late Antiquity*; and Harvey, *Asceticism and Society in Crisis*. It should be emphasized that women also served as holy leaders among both the Eastern Christian ascetics and among the ghulat. See Harvey and Brock, *Holy Women*, for the situation in late antiquity.
[50] Smith, "The Temple and the Magician," 233–47, at 238.

the sociologically ambidextrous facility of gnosis in late antiquity. It is perhaps Carsten Colpe who most closely has analyzed this characteristic doubleness.[51]

The lines running from apocalypticism to, variously, Gnosis, apocalyptic sectarianism, and radical intellectuality, are decidedly not linear. What I have argued, instead, is that the interaction between those movements and the coeval imagery of the "Messianic" imamate traced a trajectory of the Messianic deriving from late antiquity and leading forward into the encyclopedic constructions of early comparativist students of "religion."

Constructions, within this process, appear historically as a second-order abstraction. The totality of "Jews," indeed of all known varieties of religious groupings, were reviewed by Muslim scholars as species of misbelief (to vary the phrase of Aquinas). This shift from first-order actuality to second-order abstraction passed through a common filter, that of allegory, especially the variant of symbolic interpretation known to Arabophone Jews and Muslims as ta'wil. This hermeneutical encoding device provided a reading in which the rational classification of religions (milal wa-nihal) and the Gnostic reduction of reality to symbols or to universal elements valorized their respective schemes of reality as the imaginary. The imaginary is, in this sense, a certain collective representation of social reality. Mohammed Arkoun, following Castoriadis, points out that the imaginary in fact becomes "more real than real": it founds, constructs, and thus heightens a coherent sense of the "real" social world.[52]

In the case of constructions of Jews and Judaism and of an eventual comparative religion, the social role of the critics, the transconfessional intellectuals, gave rise to a category of "religion" as such. Individual rewriting of religious history, exemplified in critical milal wa-nihal, was articulated in a voice finally breaking through the pseudepigraphy with which it long had been disguised. In the classic cases of the genre apocalypse in antiquity, the autobiographical form predominated, alongside the pseudepigraphic conceit.[53] This distinctive foregrounding of a stylized voice, a ventriloquism calling attention to its very theatricality, provides support for the assertion of Derrida to the effect that "as soon as we no longer know very well who speaks or who writes, the text becomes apocalyptic."[54] Analogously, Bencheikh notes, that this was the case in the Islamicate apocalyptic *miʿaj*.[55]

---

[51] Rudolph, "Zur Soziologie," 19–29; Colpe, "Die gnostische Anthropologie," 31–44.

[52] "Ainsi se forge une fausse conscience collective, un imaginaire social qui est 'plus réel que le réel' puisqu'il commande, en définitive, le destin des sociétés" (Thus a false social consciousness is created, a social imaginary that is "more real than real" inasmuch as it definitively dictates the destiny of societies [Arkoun, *Pour une critique*, 367]).

[53] The point is made by Aune, "Apocalypse of John," 65–97, at 86–87.

[54] Derrida, "Of an Apocalyptic Tone," 63–97, at 87.

[55] Bencheikh, *Le Voyage*, 260.

The pseudepigraphic voice paradoxically heightens the individuality of the author's autobiographical self-presentation. The imaginary thereby liberates the author, whose "true" identity we may never know—but whose personality may be divulged nonetheless intimately.[56]

Moreover, constructions of religion, like Gnostic revelations, could be cast in terms of a questionnaire. Rationalist challenges to scriptural authority, such as those of Hiwi al-Balkhi, took this form. In these rationalizing critiques, the *angelus interpretes*, the classical revealer-figure in the apocalypses of antiquity, was replaced by a differently omniscient narrator. To be sure, ancient apocalypses were known (in some form) to the collectors of Isra'iliyyat and *qisas al-anbiya'*. Jabir al-Ju'fi seems to have known a world-spanning apocalypse associated with the patriarch Abraham; Tha'labi apparently knew a version of the *Apocalypse of Abraham*; and such teachings in turn seem to be reflected in the 'Abdallah ibn Salam questionnaires, as well as in other pious, legendary interrogations of Muhammad, 'Ali and the imams. Eventually the Buluqiyya story in *The Thousand and One Nights* incorporates some of this material: here, coming full circle, an angel again acts as interlocutor.

This global meaning also could be framed in an encyclopedic overview. Such overview frequently took the form of a cosmic tour, in which phenomena of creation are surveyed from a great height.[57] Recent researches, especially of Michael Stone, have investigated the historical background to such overviews. He has concluded, with much critical support, that the widely read Enochic astronomical sections, in fact, partly emerged from a context embedded in Babylonian protoscience.[58] In short, this "scientizing" thrust is marked in the earliest forms of apocalyptic. However, the continuation of that tendency within late apocalypticism, especially in the Muslim world, tends to be overlooked.[59] This comprehensivism even extended the world-spanning sweep of apocalyptic vision from the arrogation of charismatic

---

[56] Daniel Matt vivaciously evokes the self-reflexive effects of pseudepigraphy on Moshe de León: "The pseudepigraphic venture has succeeded. By surrendering his identity to Rabbi Shim'on and company, by adopting a talmudic alter ego, Moses de León has been liberated. Relieved of the burden of self-consciousness, he is free to plumb the depths of his soul and soar to timeless dimensions. Released from the constraints of acknowledged authorship, he can record his own ecstasy and pathos. The personality of Rabbi Shim'on makes him immune from criticism and enables him to publish all secrets. He expounds mythology and mysticism; revels in anthropomorphic imagery" (*The Zohar*, 27).

[57] Himmelfarb, *Tours of Hell*. Northrop Frye, in literary-critical terms, refers to this as the "panoramic apocalypse" (*Great Code*, 136–37).

[58] Stone, *Scriptures, Sects and Visions*, 37–49. Funkenstein also emphasizes that an "apocalyptic science" eventually develops within the Abrahamic traditions, as a kind of extension of the apocalyptic mentality: "Schedule for the End of the World," 44–60, at 57.

[59] For now, I might suggest the following heuristic shorthand: encyclopedism follows apocalyptic as apocalyptic follows prophecy.

revolutionaries to that of urban intellectuals. No longer was comprehensive generalization, in other words, necessarily dependent on supernatural validation. By contrast to the apocalyptic sectarian, who understood himself or herself to be the event as such, now an observer was perched above the event. The distanced observer still retained a pretense to cognition of cosmic totality, though no longer in the sense of personally revealed mysteries. Now phenomena could be observed and described from afar, from an intellectual distance.

When these two tendencies—distantiation and immediacy—converge, the psychological ground is prepared for gnosis. Adorno makes this point for astrology, in negative terms. "It may be reiterated that the climate of semierudition is the fertile breeding-ground for astrology because here primary naïveté, the unreflecting acceptance of the existent, has been lost whereas at the same time neither the power of thinking nor positive knowledge has been developed sufficiently."[60] Put in sociological terms, when a social group was torn between relative deprivation and cascading expectations, their perception of failure intensified a preexistent world-rejection. Gnosis in this way eventuated as a latter-day reaction to the failure of apocalyptic activism; rational distanciation from a plurality of religious phenomena likewise could signify a parallel sense of defeat.[61]

What resignation in the face of the disconfirmation of prophecy holds in, the missionary Gnostic surmounts, to teach the news again. This Gnostic gospel comes as a shock to the monotheistic believer. Revelation, binding law, and nomocentric cohesion are diminished, even dwarfed, by the enormities of Gnostic imagination. So too did the rationalist maker of constructions subject "religions" (milal wa nihal) to abstraction, categorization, and distancing. In both cases, the monotheistic world is shrunken and pinned onto a chart of multiple worlds; both rational and Gnostic constructions of religious reality thus transcend the parochial claims of the little, local apocalyptic sect.

Finally, the apocalyptic heritage of comparativism and Gnosis also is evident in the rare interreligious openness of both. The demonstrated inclination to appropriate traditions from others betrays a kind of subterranean *intimacy*. Esoteric intimacies allowed (among others) sectarians and storytellers actively to reorganize all knowledge, as it were. In both cases, to say the least, this open attitude did not come in the form of a public pronouncement: they certainly did not preach some transcendental unity of world religions, for the author of the milal wa nihal treatise, like the gnostic theosophist, always operated within confessional bounds on the basis of a strict and even severe in-group centeredness. And yet they shared these features: a pretense to categorical totality in matters of religion; a purportedly privileged access to the understanding of foreign traditions, which were domesticated and trans

---

[60] Adorno, "The Stars Come Down to Earth," 13–90, at 23.
[61] I explore the dialectic of Gnostic and rationalist critiques in chapter 4 above.

posed into the terms of the writer; a critical attitude to the doctrine of the singularity of revelation; and an emphasis on contention contained within a controlled framework.

The fabric of apocalyptic representation thus comprised a tension of warp and woof. The contention of Jews and Muslims thereby was reimagined within another reality, nesting the opposition of religions in an ascension narrative; embedding a variety of legal systems in some encompassing, classificatory discourse; and so forth. Apocalyptic mentality, in this process, understandably tended toward a necessary intertextuality, for in striving to posit a reality transcending that of contentious history, the apocalypticist necessarily subsumed thesis and antithesis into a synthesis of multireligious sources. *Apocalypse* (etymologically) denotes *revelation*—indeed, by definition, the revealing of a total explanation. And the social marginality of intellectuals intensified this innate drive for totality.

Apocalyptic, then, was a total revelation of sorts. The symbiosis of Muslim and Jew unfolded under this sign of apocalypse—that is, under the shadow of revelation.[62] I have studied here, however, neither revelation as such, nor the great powers of political life or religious law. The counterworld of the symbiotic imaginary otherwise comprised a dialectic of historical and counterhistorical forces; realistic and fanstastic literatures; rationalizing and remythologizing discourses; distancing and intimate gestures; familiarization and defamiliarization. Perhaps to call this a shared tradition is to go too far. But there were shared tendencies, shared cultural products, and, therefore, shared implications for the reader today. Perhaps Ernst Bloch was correct that apocalypse is the "*a priori* of all politics and culture."[63] It may well be, on the other hand, that we have exhausted the potentialities of apocalypse.[64] In any case, it is not untoward to suggest a certain continuity in mentality between the counterhistory of the apocalypses and that of certain modernist thinkers. Modern reflections on apocalypse, for example, have taken up and refunctioned apocalyptic thinking itself.[65] Indeed, Scholem goes so far as to speak in this connection of a "theology of revolution."[66] Scholem himself, while a mighty

[62] See chapter 2 above.
[63] Cited in Rabinbach, "Between Messianism and Apocalypse," 78–124, at 69.
[64] Derrida calls for an "end of the metalanguage concerning eschatological language" ("Of an Apocalyptic Tone," 63–97, at 81).
[65] For studies of this context, see Rabinbach, "Between Enlightenment and Apocalypse," 78–124; Mendes-Flohr, "'To Brush History against the Grain,'" 631–50 (especially "Negative Dialectics, the Apocalypse and the Frankfurt School," 633–36); Löwy, "Jewish Messianism and Libertarian Utopia," 105–15; Wolin, "Reflections on Jewish Secular Messianism," 186–96. See also Münster, *Utopie, Messianismus und Apokalypse*.
[66] "That is the attitude behind the writings of most important ideologists of revolutionary messianism, such as Ernst Bloch, Walter Benjamin, Theodor Adorno and Herbert Marcuse, whose acknowledged or unacknowledged ties to their Jewish heritage are evident" (Scholem, "Jews and Germans," 286–87).

pioneer in the study of Jewish mysticism already in the Weimar period—and eventually one of the sharpest observers of apocalyptic thinking—hardly was alone in his championing of counterhistory after the war. The felt necessity to erect a comprehensive counterhistory within the history of religions in fact virtually defined the history of religions in the postwar period.[67] Today, this high modernist period, epitomized (ironically) by the antimodernist Eranos group, has come to an end. Our new starting point as students of religious history, I conclude, presumes history and tradition, but only if in constant tension with counterhistory and countertradition. The Jewish-Muslim symbiotic prehistory of that dialectic, especially in its mode of radical critique and its equally radical conservatism, accordingly is one to which we now must return if we are properly to represent the foundational history and apocalyptic counterhistory of monotheism.

The "Problem" of Symbiosis

> The Jewish people incurred a debt of deep gratitude to Arabian culture. This people, for whom gratitude is a commandment from God, must never forget this. Then and there these people experienced, as once in the good days of Persia, of Hellas, and of Rome—and most certainly they felt it deeply—how portals were opened before them, through which they could enter and through which one came in to them. . . . In this cultural encounter, the existence of this people, this constant, ancient existence, was newly determined.
>
> —Leo Baeck, *This People Israel*

The problem of symbiosis is more than the problem of mutual influence and borrowing. Nor have I conceived of this usage only in the sense of *das Problem*, a research agenda that delineates a field of scientific inquiry. Nor is it, furthermore, simply a difficulty faced by modern scholars attempting to discern what belonged to whom. All of these senses necessarily played some part in the present study. However, there is yet another, reflexive sense in which I have cast the problem of symbiosis. This shared problem, that is, transcended the need for Muslims and Jews to borrow from each other, or to distinguish themselves from each other. Self-definition in this latter sense constituted a project that could prove challenging intellectually, no doubt, but that was for the most part rather straightforward (when it was not downright trivial). But during the first centuries of Islam, the problem of symbiosis itself developed

[67] The Weimar context produced among certain intellectuals the imperative *épater les bourgeois*, as well as to brush history "against the grain." See Mendes-Flohr, "'To Brush History against the Grain,'" 631–50.

as a stimulant of critical thinking, transcending the problematic sheer existence of the other in any immediately concrete sense.

After the arrival of Islam as an irresistible force, after its confrontation with Judaism as an immovable object, both parties devised means of coexistence. These means worked well enough (despite the occasional breakdown) until their ultimate collapse. But it was encounter itself that may have posed the most pointed intellectual challenge   the idea that ideas could emanate from outside one's group and could not be wished away. This multicultural situation had long existed for Jews in antiquity, without question. But the advent of Islamic hegemony, insofar as it reconfigured existing power relationships, revivified the largely moribund challenges of pluralism and multiplicity in late antiquity, and brought them to a new pitch of intensity. And this requestioning of interreligious relations was most intense between Muslims and Jews— as opposed to Muslim relations with other minorities—because of the obvious, unavoidable, and therefore quickly recognized commonalities in the form and content of Judaism and Islam.

Their remarkable sibling resemblance, that is, complicated their joint effort to establish separate identities. In emphasizing the significant differences between the German Jewish and Muslim Jewish "symbiosis," Goitein correctly stresses that, unlike German Jews who wrote in German,

> most of the Jewish authors of the Middle Ages who wrote in Arabic never had the slightest doubt about the absolute superiority of Judaism. I emphasize this fact not because I believe that such an attitude should be adopted in our times, but simply as an indication that Judaism inside Islam was an autonomous culture sure of itself despite, *and possibly because of*, its intimate connection with its environment.[68]

In this light, the theory of the other formulated by Jonathan Z. Smith, reminiscent of what Freud called "the narcissism of minor difference," begins to make a certain analytical sense.

> While the "other" may be perceived as being either LIKE-US or NOT-LIKE-US, he is in fact, most problematic when he is TOO-MUCH-LIKE-US, or when he claims to BE-US. It is here that the real urgency of a "theory of the other" emerges. This urgency is called forth not by the requirement to place the "other," but rather to situate ourselves. It is here, to invoke the language of a theory of ritual, that we are not so much concerned with the drama of "expulsion," but with the more mundane and persistent processes of "micro-adjustment." This is not a matter of the "far," but, preeminently, of the "near." The problem is not alterity, but similarity—at times, even identity. A "theory of the other" is but another way of phrasing a "theory of the self."[69]

In other words, the problem of symbiosis per se acted as a potentially radicalizing catalyst in the interaction of Muslim and Jew, insofar as it was always

[68] Goitein, *Jews and Arabs*, 130, emphasis added.
[69] J. Smith, "What a Difference a Difference Makes," 3–49, at 47.

there to reinforce powers ostensibly outside one's group that could be construed as one's own. As such it acted as a kind of conceptual irritant.[70] It prodded Muslims and Jews to new heights and depths of subterfuge, diatribe, submerged transaction, and profound coalition. The irritating aspect of this uncomfortable version of social exchange was characteristic of the problem of symbiosis. By means of (usually unacknowledged) commonalities—self-legitimation, delegitimation of the other, distanced constructions of the other, esoteric intimacies—otherness could be implemented as an agent of self-construction. The irritant could be interiorized; opposition could be domesticated; the other could be used to present the self. By such means, the problem of symbiosis long was reconstrued in the historical trajectories, ideological constructions, and esoteric intimacies sketched above.

S. D. Goitein, it will be recalled, considered the symbiosis between Muslim and Jew (in the years roughly between 500 and 1300) to be *creative*. For my part, I have tried to explicate this creativity in terms of *worldmaking*, the *apocalyptic*, the *imaginary*, and *self-definition*. While I have not undertaken my inquiry by means of Goitein's comprehensive sociographic overview, it is nevertheless the case that, even given my more limited investigation, our interpretations are complementary—for I have tried to interpret symbiosis as a creative means of making novelty, as the cultural machinery of newness, as worldmaking. My conclusion, in short, is that in these senses, as well as in the more general sense expressed by Goitein, the symbiosis *was* creative. My limited studies on selected aspects of symbiosis—as opposed to the general study of creative symbiosis undertaken by Goitein—accordingly have been concerned with the implicit and explicit ways in which Jews and Muslims newly made their own worlds with reference to the other.

Goitein was not a critical student of religions, but rather a humanistic Orientalist. There is little reason to doubt that Goitein's cultural and personal predispositions sustained his enduring—and almost universally accepted—emphasis on the idea of symbiosis. With the tenacious faith of a true believer, Goitein believed—unwaveringly, from Frankfurt to Jerusalem, and then to Philadelphia and eventually Princeton—in the potential of humanism to improve history. In some of his last published words, after sixty productive years, he still stated this conviction as his Orientalist articles of faith:

> In this time of general confusion, a final warning may be in order. . . . our humanistic, scientific, technological civilization is unique. Only if we firmly believe in the validity and worthiness of our own humanistic, scientific, and technological civilization, will we possess that Archimedean point from which we shall be able to observe Islam, learn to esteem it and to be edified by its creations. By the term "our

[70] With regard to Muslim-Jewish relations, von Grunebaum notes that "a great deal of irritation on both sides must have been the rule under the Muslim system" ("Medieval Islam," 168–86, at 182).

own" civilization, I mean that of the worldwide republic of good, sensible, and knowledgeable modern men and women.[71]

In the unshakable fidelity with which he conceptualized and applied his Orientalist humanism, Goitein represents a bridge sturdily grounded in another century. His career, in fact, does overlap that of those Orientalists who stimulated the first flowering of modern Judeo-Arabic scholarship. The greatest of them, another liberal Jewish Central European Orientalist, Ignaz Goldziher, died in 1921, when Goitein was an advanced graduate student. We are presently perched at the other, postmodern, end of Goitein's century-spanning career. And the critical study of religions has yet to reexamine this construct, much less its institutionalization. Is fin de siècle religious studies finally ready to reexamine "creative symbiosis," this article of faith, this humanism-as-theory so entrenched in "our own" civilization?

INTERCONFESSIONAL PHILOSOPHY AND THE END OF SYMBIOSIS

The present volume is neither philosophy nor the history of philosophy: I have not set out to study Judeo-Arabic philosophy as such.[72] That being said, it is difficult to avoid positing Jewish-Muslim philosophy as the intellectual end product of symbiosis; most historians of the period agree that the period of and the content of "creative symbiosis" coincides with the flourishing of philosophy among Muslims and Jews. Characterizations of this era also tend to emphasize its efflorescence of freethinking, its interreligious tolerance, the enlightened character of its interfaith relations. Goitein, as always, set (or reflected) the dominant tone: "We are also able to confirm Warner [*sic*] Jaeger's assumption that a truly international fellowship of science existed in the days of the Intermediate civilization. Both literary sources . . . and documentary sources . . . prove that in general a spirit of tolerance and mutual esteem prevailed between the students of Greek sciences of different races and religions."[73] According to this conventional understanding, then, the time, content and setting of symbiosis coincided with that of the flourishing of philosophy.

Goitein was a social historian, and, as such, keenly was aware that this "spirit of tolerance and mutual esteem" emerged from the needs of the new bourgeoisie.[74] Shlomo Pines, perhaps the greatest student of Jewish-Muslim philosophy in this century, joined Goitein in embedding the newly critical Jewish thinkers in their social setting.

[71] Goitein, "The Humanistic Aspects of Oriental Studies," 11–12.
[72] I address this history more directly in "Social and Cultural Context."
[73] Goitein, "Between Hellenism and Renaissance," 215–33, at 230.
[74] Goitein, "Rise of Near Eastern Bourgeoisie," 583–604.

In the ninth and tenth centuries, after a very long hiatus, systematic philosophy and ideology reappeared among Jews, a phenomenon indicative of their accession to Islamic civilization. There is undoubtedly a correlation between this rebirth of philosophy and theology and the social trends of that period, which produced Jewish financiers—some of whom were patrons of learning and who, in fact, although perhaps not in theory, were members of the ruling class of the Islamic state—and Jewish physicians who associated on equal terms with Muslim and Christian intellectuals.[75]

In addition to the needs of commerce to cross cultural barriers, other factors in the rise of a Jewish-Muslim philosophy have been adduced. Another reason for sharing on the part of philosophers was a common pagan adversary. The seriousness of this joint effort is a leitmotif of the scholarship on symbiosis. In her overview of Judeo-Arabic culture, Hava Lazarus-Yafeh thus reminds the readers of the *Encyclopedia Judaica* that there was

> a profound religious-cultural alliance among these three positive religions in their common confrontation with the pagan cultural legacy, which, in its philosophical Arabic guise, threatened equally the existence of the three revelational religions. The extent and depth of their spiritual collaboration is highly astonishing and probably has no parallel in any other period of human history.[76]

Scholarship on this "spiritual collaboration" has tended to emphasize the sympathy of Jews for Arabic philosophy. Already in 1922, Étienne Gilson could express this sympathy in vigorous terms.

> Sans aller jusqu'à soutenir avec Renan que la philosophie arabe n'a réellement été prise bien au sérieux que par les Juifs, on doit accorder que la culture musulmane a poussé dans la culture juive du moyen âge un rejeton extrêmement vivace et presque aussi vigoureux que la souche dont il sortait.[77]

> [Without going so far as to agree with [Ernst] Renan that Arab philosophy was only really taken seriously by Jews, one can agree that Muslim culture sprouted an extremely vital shoot in the Jewish culture of the Middle Ages, one almost as vigorous as the source from which it emerged.]

This influential formulation readily found repetition: in fact it is reflected, in various intensities, throughout the standard textbook and encyclopedia

---

[75] Pines, "Jewish Philosophy," 261–77, at 262–63.
[76] Lazarus-Yafeh, "Judeo-Arabic Culture," 101–10, at 102.
[77] Gilson, *La Philosophie au moyen âge* 1:368. While I accept Gilson's characterization, I reject his explanation: "Ce phénomène s'explique non seulement par le contact intime et prolongé des civilisations juives et arabes, mais encore, et peut-être surtout, par leur étroit parenté de race et la similitude de leur génies" (This phenomenon is explained not only by the intimate and prolonged contact between Jewish and Arab civilizations, but also, and perhaps principally, by their narrow racial parentage and the similarity of their genius).

entries on this subject. No less a successor than Pines would come to make an analogous point.

> Approximately from the ninth to the thirteenth centuries, Jewish philosophical and theological thought participated in the evolution of Islamic philosophy and theology and manifested only in a limited sense a continuity of its own. Jewish philosophers showed no particular preference for philosophic texts written by Jewish authors over those composed by Muslims, and in many cases the significant works of Jewish thinkers constitute a reply or reaction to the ideas of a non-Jewish predecessor. Arabic was the language of Jewish philosophic and scientific writings.[78]

Historians of philosophy thus consistently have seen the Jewish-Muslim "alliance" as a truly collective effort in the cultivation of philosophy, but one in which Jews were drawn to the dominant discourse controlled by the Muslim majority.

Finally, historians of philosophy have concluded that the "failure" of the Jewish-Muslim social contract in the twelfth and thirteenth centuries in turn foreclosed the philosophical mortgage. On this reading, the end of the symbiosis simultaneously concluded a joint philosophical tradition, one at least as much Jewish as Muslim.

> The famous altarpiece by Francesco Traini, in St. Catarina at Pisa, and many similar paintings depict the triumph of Thomas over Averroës, who lies prostrate before the Christian philosopher. Characteristically enough, Averroës wears the Jewish badge upon each shoulder. There is poetic truth in his presentation as a Jew, seeing that Jewish commentators and translators had a large share in making Averroës known to Latin Christianity. As has been pointed out by Steinschneider, the preservation of Averroës's *Commentaries on Aristotle* is due almost entirely to Jewish activity.[79]

From the vantage point of its "conclusion," symbiosis could now be viewed in its purest form. On the one hand, early Muslims had provided the Jewish community with the social and cultural means to keep on keeping on. As Goitein bluntly declared in another context, "It was Islam which saved the Jewish People." Leo Baeck could not put this case in more direct terms, nor with more direct implications: "The Jewish people incurred a debt of deep gratitude to Arabian culture. This people, for whom gratitude is a commandment from God, must never forget this."[80] And, from the other side of the bargain, the intellectual fruits of Islamic philosophy—Ibn Bajja, al-Farabi, Ibn Tufayl, Ibn Rushd, and many more—were preserved, translated, transmitted, and reverently studied by Jews.

One consequence of this philosophical symbiosis was its ultimate reception in modern educational systems. The collective Muslim-Jewish transmission of

[78] Pines, "Jewish Philosophy," 261–77, at 262–63.
[79] Altmann, "Judaism and World Philosophy," 65–116, at 86.
[80] Goitein, "Muhammad's Inspiration," 162; Baeck, *This People Israel*, 264.

Aristotelian sciences from antiquity into early modernity, and eventually into the university, simply cannot be gainsaid.[81] A properly dialectical study of this transmission and reception therefore should sensitize the reader to attend a shock of recognition—a recognition that we, in our turn, received ways of seeing creative symbiosis from the symbiosis itself. In this sense, the philosophical accomplishments of this interconfessional "Judeo-Arabic culture" could be said to provide the philosophical warrant for the present investigation. Alfred North Whitehead put this case in old-fashioned but accessible terms, rather like those of Goitein—those of "our own civilization."

> The record of the Middle Ages, during the brilliant period of Mahometan ascendency, affords evidence of joint association of Mahometan and Jewish activity in the promotion of civilization. The culmination of the Middle Ages was largely dependent on that association. . . . The association of Jews with the Mahometan world is one of the great facts of history from which modern civilization is derived.[82]

In these terms, the philosophical products of this epochal encounter constitute a vital element of "our own" heritage—however problematic one presently might consider that heritage to be.

Axiomatic Truths of Symbiosis

> I am only too well aware of the reasons for the uneasiness I felt on coming
> into contact with Islam: I rediscovered in Islam the world I myself had
> come from.
>
> —Claude Lévi-Strauss, *Tristes Tropiques*

While I would not want to be misconstrued as suggesting that *philosophia*, this high-cultural and masculinist "adventure of the mind," translates into *the* essence or *the* meaning of the Jewish-Muslim symbiosis, I also would not care to deny the paternity and maternity of our intellectual parentage. However much effort we must undertake to overcome the inadequacies of our heritage, one would hope that our goal, at least the goal of scholars of Jewish-Muslim relations, remains that of reimagining and not of parenticide. For one, I prefer to retain, so far as I can,

> the feeling every more or less conscious writer has, that he should write in such a way as to be understood by his ancestors. . . . We do not choose our parents: it is they who choose us by giving us life. They determine the way we look, and they often determine our material circumstances by bequeathing us their fortune—every

[81] Makdisi, *Rise of Colleges*.
[82] Whitehead, "An Appeal to Sanity," 61–83, at 79.

kind of fortune, including the literal one. Whatever we think of ourselves, we are they, and they must be able to understand us if we want to understand ourselves.[83]

In reassessing the history of philosophy during the era of Islamicate symbiosis, I therefore strive to keep the following considerations in mind. Islamic and Jewish readers received Greek thought in strikingly parallel fashions not due to influence and borrowing (though this factor obviously contributed), nor because they coexisted in a "common milieu." Rather, I assume that these sibling monotheistic civilizations constituted scripture-based interpretive communities that familially shared analogous and characteristic scripturalist dilemmas, problems of defending the supernatural status of revelation. Revelation-based readerships thus commonly responded in the first instance to the challenge of Aristotelian Reason by exclusion and by domestication. Logic, that is, was first forbidden outright, and then tamed for righteous purposes. Aristotle, in other words, confronted Abrahamic readerships, initially sending shudders down the backs of his disciples and his opponents alike, for he was recognized to pose a most fearsome threat and, eventually, immense intellectual promise. Jewish and Muslim interpretive communities thus each responded to philosophia with crucially different yet importantly analogous responses. And these responses, I am suggesting, derived precisely from the hermeneutical necessities inherent in such scriptural reading communities.

These variant Jewish and Muslim receptions of Aristotelianism would appear to epitomize the Latin Aristotelian maxim, "Quidquid recipitur ad modum recipentis recipitur" (What is received is received after the mode of the recepient)."[84] But the Jewish-Muslim symbiosis in fact propagated its own analogous aphorism, the meaning of which comprises an elegant epitome of the concept of reception, and the history of which neatly summarizes the routes of the symbiosis itself. This saying, "The first in thought is the last in action," which entered Islamicate discourse in the second half of the eighth century, was repeated in the works of the early convert Ibn al-Muqaffaʿ, the alchemical Pseudo-Jabir, the early Ismaʿili writers, and then the Jewish writers, including Abraham bar Hiyya, Judah Halevi, Abraham ibn Dawud, Jacob ben Anatoli, and eventually in the great synagogue hymn, *Lekha Dodi*.[85] "The first in thought is the last in action" encapsulates the consequentiality of thought, that thought is conclusive, necessarily, only in its eventuation. This idea clearly possessed a sustained appeal, particularly among a

---

[83] Brodsky, "Poetry as a Form of Resistance," 220–25, at 222. In this sense, then, I am concerned here with the intergenerational dialectics of incomprehension and reconciliation (and not with any "master narrative," or any such thing).

[84] Jauss, "Theory of Reception," 53–74, esp. 56–57, for the origins of medieval *receptio*.

[85] See the magisterial review of this history by Stern, "'The First in Thought Is the Last in Action.'" That this saying may have come into Jewish usage through Ismaʿili intermediation is one more confirmation of the vitality of Jewish-Ismaʿili symbiosis.

number of key players in the symbiosis. The self-reflexive implication of this notion—that its "meaning" resides not only in its initial utterance but in its subsequent rearticulations—makes its reception history particularly instructive for present purposes.

Aristotle, the master philosopher for medieval Jews and Muslims alike, thus was embodied in the saga of one maxim: a text comprises the sum of its responses.[86] Each book, we know, suffers its own fate. But the maxim, "habent sua fata libelli," should not, in fact, imply a mere linear accumulation of readings that simply stratify atop an initial authorship. For the case at hand, and insofar as the symbiotic development of Judaism and Islam may be construed as a common civilizational project, the metaphor of a collective book-in-progress perhaps better suits the situation. Hava Lazarus-Yafeh speaks to this metaphor.

> One should not think in terms of influences and cultural borrowing only, however. It has been said that the Near East resembles a palimpsest, layer upon layer, tradition upon tradition, intertwined to the extent that one cannot grasp one without the other, certainly not the later without the earlier, but often also not the earlier without considering the shapes it took later.[87]

The reader-response view implies that the distinctive fate of philosophers (and angels) is read in an accumulating truth, their eventual biography, just as an account of their production could describe their births, but not their lives. On this view, we can come to our philosopher (or angel) outside the history of responses to them—but only if we are prepared to live with the excisions and elisions an ahistorical stance mandates.

The Islamicate Aristotle (like the Islamicate Metatron) was a palimpsest long in progress, laboriously written and rewritten by Muslims and Jews. The analogies between the responses of Muslims and Jews to Aristotle during the brief period of Aristotle's intellectual celebrity of course are not coincidental.[88] However, a purely contextualist historicism describing filiations between Jewish and Muslim Aristotelians will not yield the results I hope to accomplish here. I cannot, in other words, responsibly conclude that the Jewish Aristotle should be understood straightforwardly as a function of the Islamic Aristotle. Even were this demonstrably the case, such an explanation yields a rather thin result: the conclusion that something went from point *A*

---

[86] See chapter 5 for a study of the Islamicate afterlife of the "Jewish" Metatron.

[87] *Intertwined Worlds*, 4. In her use of the metaphor palimpsest, she acknowledges the specialists in the ancient Near East, E. A. Speiser and Moshe Greenberg. Their view of the interreligiosity of the ancient Near East is expressed succinctly by Jacob Milgrom: "Presumed is that the ancient Near East was a cultural continuum where forms and ideas were exchanged without resistance unless they clashed with the value system of the borrowing culture" ("The Concept of Ma'al," 241). For the metaphor of palimpsest, see also *Meddeb*, "Le palimpseste du bilingue."

[88] As is well known, we would not know Averroës if not for the Jewish transmission of his texts. See n. 12 above.

to point *B*. For this reason, the purported "parallels" between the Muslim and Jewish Aristotles, from the perspective of reception criticism, are not to be "explained" reductively in terms of influence and borrowing. Such terminology suggests a quasi-physicalist scenario of material motion or, worse, a distortingly moralizing perspective of debtor and creditor.

A solution to this dilemma is that the philosophical tradition itself may be understood to be a religious tradition.[89] For Muslims as well as Jews, certainly, the study of philosophy was (for a time) considered to be a religious imperative.[90] In the always aphoristic Jewish-Muslim tradition, another maxim succinctly articulated the goal of this imperative: "The purpose of philosophy is the imitation of God." Like the path taken by the saying attributed to Aristotle, "The first in thought is the last in action," the maxim ascribed to Plato, "The purpose of philosophy is the imitation of God," traversed numerous reiterations, Jew to Muslim, Muslim to Jew. Lawrence Berman's conclusion to his tracing of the literary history of this latter maxim by now should not be surprising: "This is just another instance of the influence of the philosophical tradition which al-Farabi represents on Maimonides and that medieval 'symbiosis' of ideas among the professed members of different religions."[91]

It clearly lies beyond the purview of the present monograph to assess the philosophical truth of this symbiosis—even if I were qualified to do so. Still, it is important to note, at least, that contemporary German Jews, colleagues of Goitein's, were certainly determined to do so. In this effort, they pointed, for example, to the notion of a singular religious truth.[92] A favorite exemplum in this regard was the parable of the three rings, best known from its dramatic resetting in Lessing's *Nathan the Wise*.[93] Once there was a king who possessed a magic ring, a ring that "possessed the secret power to make its owner loved of God and man." The king's dilemma: to which of his three equally beloved sons should he leave his ring? And the king's solution? He ordered his royal jeweler to create two perfect replicas. Upon his death, the three princes inherited three identical rings. No one prince could prove that

---

[89] Wolfson, *Religious Philosophy*, especially the thesis stated in the preface.

[90] For the Jewish case see Herbert Davidson, "The Study of Philosophy as a Religious Obligation." For the Muslim case see Endress, "Defense of Reason."

[91] Berman, "Political Interpretation of the Maxim," 53–61, at 54 and 60.

[92] Guttmann, "Religion and Science," 281–343 : "Islam's direct contact, not only with the Judaism and Christianity which preceded it in time, but also with the Persian and Indian religions, creates a climate of enlightenment at a very early date, leading to significant beginnings in the scientific study of comparative religion and, in the sphere of religion, to a critical attitude with respect to one's own faith" (306). For more on the development of an idea of religion as such, and of the accompanying development of comparative studies in religion, see chap. 4 above.

[93] "This formulation of the idea of a universal religious truth, grown out of the concept of revelation, might perhaps be also considered as the latent source of the tale of the three precious stones" (Guttmann, "Religion and Science," 312).

he had received the original ring itself. Medieval Jewish, Christian, and Muslim literature transmitted variants of this "parable of the three rings."[94] Its message would seem to have been nothing less than the divine identity of Judaism, Christianity, and Islam. The three traditions thereby depicted themselves as divinely identical heirs of God's original revelation. In recounting this parable, three sibling traditions in effect admitted that none of them definitively could prove a superior claim to being "the one true religion."

Not only does this parable both derive from and speak to the problematic at hand, it also was to become (understandably) a long-standing favorite of German Jews.[95] The Jews of Germany, who saw the Jewish-Muslim symbiosis as the best model for (what they idealized as) their own cultural situation, reconstructed a history of thought that ran from the one to the other in an empoweringly genetic descent.[96] Schorsch recently has analyzed the German Jewish myth of Sephardic supremacy with regard to liturgy, synagogue architecture, literature, and scholarship. He summarizes "the historical myth" this way:

> As construed by Ashkenazic intellectuals, the Sephardic image facilitated a religious posture marked by cultural openness, philosophic thinking, and an appreciation for the aesthetic. Like many an historical myth, it evoked a partial glimpse of a bygone age determined and coloured by social need.[97]

But it was not only German Jews who adhered to this "golden age" historiography. The implications of Jewish-Muslim creative symbiosis remain, for most students of history, as Lazarus-Yafeh emphatically expresses it, "profound," "highly astonishing," and "without parallel."[98] And yet these implications persist almost unknown to the student of religion, not to speak of the general reader. The present volume, rising from the ashes of the myth of Sephardic supremacy, seeks, in a small way, to amplify that astonishment and to redress that ignorance.

THE ROAD TO SERAPHIC REASON

> The supernatural becomes an awareness of the individual's own potentiality,
> salvaged by being raised above the ambiguities and illusions of the natural
> world. Angels wither away in the mind and art of the twelfth century—

[94] A complete treatment of sources has now been published by Niewohner, *Veritas sive Varietas*.

[95] "With muffled sarcasm, Rosenzweig also reflects how odd it is that only Jews still take Lessing seriously" (Mendes-Flohr, "Mendelssohn and Rosenzwieg," 213–23, at 216).

[96] Schorsch, "Myth of Sephardic Supremacy," 47–66.

[97] Ibid., 47.

[98] Lazarus-Yafeh, "Judeo-Arabic Culture," 102.

ancient symbols of the non-human, they are rapidly replaced by symbols of
the idealized human.

—Peter Brown, "Society and the Supernatural"

It would be myopic to conclude that the symbiosis purely was Aristotelian
in its ultimate destiny. This would again fall victim to what might be called
the Aufklärung wish-fulfillment of Sephardic supremacy. Other cultural successes, however, could and should be claimed. Some have sought, for example, to derive a harmonistic ecumenical utopia from early Jewish-Muslim
exemplars. Such an interpretation is not without its primary sources. It would
seem to be partially confirmed in the joint mystical tradition of Jewish Sufism, only recently retrieved from the miraculous middenheap that is the Cairo
Geniza. The Maimonidean dynasty, it turns out, fundamentally was imprinted by Sufi theory and practice.[99] Not surprisingly, reviews of the Paul
Fenton's fundamental study of this Jewish Sufism repeat a by-now-familiar
phrase: "Cette exploration minutieuse est d'autant plus opportune que la
riche symbiose culturelle et spirituelle dont ces documents portent la tém-
moinage est précaire: les lettrés juifs d'Orient perdront bientôt l'usage de
l'arabe classique" (This painstaking exploration is all the more opportune
inasmuch as the rich cultural and spiritual symbiosis to which these documents testify was precarious: the literate Jews of the Orient soon lost the use
of classical Arabic); "The phenomenon of Jewish Sufism as it was practised in
Egypt during the thirteenth through fifteenth centuries offers a striking instance of the medieval Judaeo-Islamic symbiosis."[100]

While students of Jewish Sufism, then, tend to agree on the construct of
symbiosis, it has only rarely been used in connection with a related if rather
more controversial phenomenon, that of so-called philosophical mysticism.
Spanish-born Jewish and Muslim thinkers together decocted a heady blend
of philosophy and mysticism, hermeticism and Aristotelianism, which sometimes went under the name of "Illuminationism" (Ishraqiyya). Leaving aside
the knotty difficulty of determining the status of Maimonides in this regard,
the full extent of Illuminationist interconfessionalism has not yet been analyzed adequately (which task also lies beyond my scope here). But I would
suggest that the context—intermediate transmission and subsequent reception of the philosophical mysticism of Ibn Tufayl and Ibn Sab'in, for
example—was profoundly interconfessional.[101] While I cannot substantiate
this assertion here, I make it in order to arrive at a subsidiary point. Their
fusion of mythos and logos, I would suggest, was not an incidental response
to their interconfessional setting, any more than the far-reaching work under-

[99] The most productive worker in this field is Paul Fenton. The fruits of his considerable labors to date are found in *Deux traités de mystique juive*.
[100] Chodkiewicz, review of *Deux traités*, 185; Frank, review of *Deux traités*, 273.
[101] For now, see my "Social and Cultural Context."

way today on multiple rationalities and relativism, myth and philosophy "accidentally" addresses the challenging richness of our own multicultural context.[102] Clearly, the Illuminationists' interreligious cooperation arose to answer a social need.

Next to the development of this Iluminationist discourse may be placed the transformation of angels into intelligences. Jewish thinkers, near the end of the symbiosis, identified Metatron with the Active Intellect.[103] It seems to me that, in terms of the imaginary, the full historical significance of this identification has never properly been recognized. In a related context, Schwarzschild refers to Avicenna's theory of an intermediary holy spirit (*ruh al-quds*) "which in most ways completely parallels what I have been pointing to in Judaism and thus, again, illustrates the commonality of what I am inclined to call 'Semitic religion.'"[104] The road to seraphic reason found a way, that is, to unify mythos and logos. That this particular achievement actively was undertaken by Jews and Muslims together, once again, was no accident.

Finally, this seraphic reason anticipated the angels invoked by such modern Jewish philosophers as Hermann Cohen (1842–1918), Walter Benjamin (1892–1940), Emmanuel Lévinas (1906–   ). Already Abraham ibn Ezra (1092–1167) held that the "angel between man and his God is his reason."[105] From here we would seem to be near the spirit of the neo-Kantian Hermann Cohen: "God endowed man with reason, which he could not have attained for himself, for reason is the hallmark of divine creation. Through reason man becomes the image of God."[106] Cohen's erstwhile critic, Walter Benjamin, however, conjured up the destruction wrought by reason, in the image of a melancholy if still Messianic Angel of History.[107] And when

[102] See Tambiah, *Magic, Science, Religion*; and Reynolds and Tracy, *Myth and Philosophy*.
[103] Vajda, "Pour le dossier de Metatron," 345–54.
[104] Schwarzschild, *The Pursuit of the Ideal*, 375 n. 98. Schwarzschild relied on his Arabist colleague Peter Heath for this information. Heath subsequently published this study: "Creative Hermeneutics," 173–210, at 190–210. Heath then expanded his results in *Allegory and Philosophy in Avicenna*.
[105] Cited by U. Simon, "The Religious Significance of the *Peshat*," 41–63, at 53.
[106] H. Cohen, *Reason and Hope,* 132.
[107] Alter, *Necessary Angels*: "This is a most monotheistic angel, turning against the assumption of mythology (in which angels originate) that reality can be represented as a network of images and stories conveying coherent meaning," 120. In addition to Alter's work, Benjamin's Angel has received an extraordinary degree of recent attention, usually placed in a larger philosophical context: Cacciari, *L'ange nécessaire*; Mosès, *L'ange de l'histoire*; Handelman, *Fragments of Redemption;* Boyarin, *Storm from Paradise*; Niethammer, *Posthistoire*, 101–35.
  For more on this central text, see Tiedemann, "Historical Materialism or Political Messianism?" 71–105; Löwy, "Religion, Utopia and Counter-Modernity," 95–104; Werckmeister, "Walter Benjamin, Paul Klee," 16–40; Jay, *Permanant Exiles*, 78; idem, *The Dialectical Imagination,* 262; Adorno, "Commitment," 300–18, at 318; Wohlfarth, "Hibernation," 956–87, at 971. In her presidential address to the Ameri-

Lévinas elicited modern Jewish struggles with the Angel of Reason, he noted that "this sublime ambiguity remains: is one trying to preserve oneself within the modern world, or to drown one's eternity in it?"[108] In this last respect, perhaps, the modern Jewish struggle with Reason also recapitulates the Jewish-Muslim philosophical symbiosis—a civilizational assertion that, alas, collapsed.

CONCLUSION

> There is a new world waiting to be born, stretched along the eastern shores of the Mediterranean and the western shores of the Indian ocean. The condition for its life is the fusion of Mahometan and Jewish populations, each with its own skills and their own memories, and their own ideals.
>
> —Alfred North Whitehead, "An Appeal to Sanity"

Two types of imaginary worldmaking, the categorizing of other religions and the imagining of other worlds, blended into the creative symbiosis between Muslim and Jew. And this dialectical interaction was doubly reflective; the other world was vivified by a figure from the other religion, who was used to make one's own world new. This is the case with Abu 'Isa al-Isfahani's recognition of the Prophet Muhammad; Shi'i tales of the rosh golah; the foundational legends of 'Abdallah ibn Salam; and the marvelous peregrinations of Buluqiyya. These constructions of the self by means of imagining the other paradigmatically were symbiotic. Again, this was doubly so, for both parties did so in a shared process of worldmakings, and in a revitalizing mode of self-creation impossible to imagine without the other.

Thus, it is true that Jews presented a counterworld to that of Muslims; that the countertraditional critique shared by both generated a common philosophy; and that both enjoyed mutual imaginings of another world. Viewed in the round, symbiosis accurately may be said to have achieved a valiant laisser-faire, insofar as it allowed these shared orderings of reality to operate more or less routinely. To the extent that it succeeded, Muslim-Jewish symbiosis understood and implemented *imaginaries* that could order and reorder millions of Jewish and Muslim social worlds.

Nevertheless, in the end, it stopped working. Some have been inclined, perhaps inevitably, to liken the failure of the Jewish-Muslim symbiosis to the

---

can Historical Association, Natalie Davis concluded with reflections on this parable: "History's Two Bodies," 1–30, at 29–30. Scholem, who was responsible for the dissemination of this text, said of it that "with good reason did an open-minded reader like Jürgen Habermas describe these theses . . . as 'one of the most moving testimonies of the Jewish spirit'" (*Jews and Judaism in Crisis*, 231).
[108] Levinas, "Judaism and the Present," 252–59, at 255.

collapse of the German-Jewish symbiosis.[109] Indeed, a sanguine defense of
any Jewish historical symbiosis may seem absurd after the Holocaust. Claude
Lévi-Strauss, less than a decade after the end of the Shoah, once despaired
that his enterprise was not anthropology but entropology, not the study of
humanity but of entropy.[110] Even such despair, however, was not foreign to
the world of the Jewish-Muslim symbiosis. When they did not give in to a
world-denying Gnosis, however, ordinary Jews and Muslims could resist
world rejection by means of a seemingly limitless belief in the coming redeemer of this world. The Jewish and Muslim faith in a Messiah or Mahdi, in
other words, should not be dismissed from an assessment of the success and
failure of symbiosis.

To revert to my discussion in Part I of this book, I recall that Rabbanite and
Karaite Jews, Shi'i and Sunni Muslims expected the eventual savior to emerge
from a range of possible genealogies. E. I. J. Rosenthal aptly noticed that, in
the end, this difference in origination did not matter:

> This is, however, not relevant to our contention that basically the Jewish and the
> Muslim concept of Messianism is the same. It is immaterial that the Messiah is of
> the house of David and not a descendent of Moses. What matters is that the ideal of
> the kingdom of God on earth in justice, righteousness and peace for all mankind is
> united in the belief of the one and only God. This is the common ground both
> faiths share and their common hope and expectation.[111]

The study of Jewish-Muslim symbiosis is the study of historical change,
particularly of the generation of novelty in religion. The historical newness
that characterizes the Jewish-Muslim symbiosis manifested itself creatively in
philosophy and apocalyptic, mysticism and propositional logic, crisis cult and
Gnosis, hope and hope against hope. But the development of a common
Messianic perspective—"their common hope and expectation"—which end-
lessly justifies social lives of justice and reason as perpetual preparations for

[109] Most recently Faur, *In the Shadow of History*, chapters 2 and 3. Leaving aside the
question of the eventual failure of both, Goitein otherwise addressed this comparison
directly, demurring from the positive identification of the two cases as being "of equal
importance" made by the doyen of the German-Jewish Science of Judaism, Moritz
Steinschneider: "Here, however, I venture to disagree with the great master. Despite
their great relative importance, none of the creations of the Jewish authors writing in
German or conceived under the impact of modern Western civilization has reached all
parts of the Jewish people or has influenced the personal inner life of every Jew to the
profound degree as did the great Jewish writers who belonged to the medieval civilization of Arab Islam" (*Jews and Arabs*, 130).
[110] Lévi-Strauss, *Tristes Tropiques*, 472: "Anthropology could with advantage be
changed into 'entropology,' as the name of the discipline concerned with the study of
the highest manifestations of this process of disintegration." For some insight into
Lévi-Strauss's idiosyncratic response to Islam, see Wasserstein, "Greek Science in Islam," 57–72, at 57–58.
[111] E. Rosenthal, *Judaism and Islam*, 12.

the divinely enacted endtime, may be the most hidden, most obvious change of all.

Today, in the study of Jewish-Muslim symbiosis, as in the historical study of religions more generally, we search out unchanging inner principles within changing relations. Only in historical change can we properly seek the *concordia mundi*, the rational harmony hidden maddeningly inside a radically pluralistic world.[112] "The reassurance is / that through change / continuities sinuously work."[113]

[112] For the notion of *concordia mundi*, see Bouwsma, *Concordia Mundi*. Postel translated and commented on *Sefer haBahir*: Simmonnet, "La gloire de Dieu est de cacher la Parole," 247–66, 435–47.
[113] Ammons, "Saliences," 47–50, at 49.

Abbott, Nabia. "Wahb b. Munabbih: A Review Article." *Journal of Near Eastern Studies* 36 (1977): 103–12.

'Abd al-Jabbar b. Ahmad al-Asadabadi. "Mukhtasar fi Usul al-Din." In *Rasa'il fi al-'Adl wa al-Tauhid*, edited by Sayf al-Din al-Katib. Beirut, n.d., 315–91.

———. *Sharh al-Usul al-Khamsa*. Edited by 'Abd al-Qarim Uthman. Cairo, 1965.

Abel, Armand. "Changements politiques et littérature eschatologique dans le monde musulman." *Studia Islamica* 2 (1954): 23–43.

———. "Dù'l Qarnayn: Prophète de l'universalité." In *Annuaire de l'Institut de philologie et d'histoire orientales (et slaves)* 11 (1951): 6–18.

———. "L'Apocalypse de Bahira et la notion islamique de Mahdi." *Annuaire de l'Institut de philologie et d'histoire orientales (et slaves)* 3 (1935): 1–12.

———. "L'Apocalypse de Buluqiyya." In *Eschatologie et cosmologie*. Brussels, 1969, 189–98.

———. "La signification apologétique et politique des apocalypses islamo-chrétiennes au Moyen Age." In *Proceedings of the 22nd Congress of Orientalists,* edited by Zeki Togan. Leiden, 1957, 533–35.

Abitol, Michel. "Juifs Maghrébins et commerce Transsaharien du VIIIe au XVe siècle." *Revue française d'histoire d'outre-mer* 66 (1979): 177–93.

Abrahams, Israel. *Jewish Life in the Middle Ages*. 1896. Reprint, New York, 1973.

Abu al-Fida. *Mukhtasar Ta'rikh al-Bashar*. Edited by H. O. Fleischer. Leipzig, 1831.

Abu al-Ma'ali, Muhammad ibn 'Ubaydallah ibn 'Ali. *Bayan al-Adyan*. Edited by Abbas Iqbal. Teheran, 1933.

Abul-Husain al-Farrá. *Tabaqat al-Hanabila*. Edited by Muhammad Hamid al-Fiqi. 2 vols. Cairo, 1371/1952.

Abu-Lughod, Janet. *Before European Hegemony: The World System, A.D. 1250–1350*. New York, 1989.

Abu Nu'aim al-Isfahani. *Dhikr Akhbar Isfahan*. Edited by Sven Dedering. Leiden, 1931.

———. *Hilyat al-Awliya' wa Tabaqat al-Asfiya'*. 10 vols. Cairo 1932–38.

Abu Shuhbah, Muhammed ibn Muhammed. *Al-Isra'iliyyat wa al-mawdu'at fi Kutub al-tasfir*. Cairo, 1393/1973.

Abu Ya'la b. al-Farra'. *Kitab al-Mu'tamad fi usul al-Din*. Edited by Wadi Haddad. Beirut, 1974.

Adams, Charles. "The Hermeneutics of Henry Corbin." In *Approaches to Islam in Religious Studies,* edited by Richard C. Martin. Tucson, Ariz. 1985, 129–51.

Adang, Camilla. *Muslim Writers on Judaism and the Hebrew Bible from Ibn Rabban to Ibn Hazam*. Ph.D. dissertation, Nijmegen, 1993.

Adorno, Theodor W. "Commitment." In *The Essential Frankfurt School Reader*, edited by A. Arato and E. Gebhart. New York, 1988, 300–319.

———. *Minima Moralia: Reflections From Damaged Life*. London, 1974.

———. "Sociology and Empirical Research." In *Critical Sociology*, edited by Paul Connerton. Middlesex, 1978, 237–58.

———. "The Stars Come Down to Earth: The *Los Angeles Times* Astrology Column." *Telos* 19 (1974): 13–90.

Aeshcoly, A. *Messianic Movements in Israel* (in Hebrew) Jerusalem, 1956.

Aguadé, D. Jorge. "La importancia del 'Kitab al-Fitan' de Nu'aym b. Hammad para el estudio del mesianismo musulman." *Actas de las jornades de cultura arabe e Islamica* (1981): 349–52.

Ahmad, Syed Barakat. "Non-Muslims and the Umma." *Studies in Islam* 17 (1980): 80–119.

Ahroni, Reuben. "From *Bustan al-'uqul* to *Qisat al-batul*: Some Aspects of Jewish Muslim Religious Polemics in Yemen." *Hebrew Union College Annual* 52 (1981): 311–60.

———. *Yemenite Jewry*. Bloomington, Ind., 1987.

Alexander, P. S. "The Historical Setting of the Hebrew Book of Enoch." *Journal of Jewish Studies* 28 (1977): 156–80.

———. "Late Hebrew Apocalyptic: A Preliminary Survey." *Apocrypha: Le Champ des Apocryphes* 1 (1990): 197–217.

———. Translation and Commentary of "3 (Hebrew Apocalypse) Enoch (Fifth to Sixth Century A.D.). In *The Old Testament Pseudepigrapha*, edited by James H. Charlesworth. 2 vols. New York, 1983–85, 1:223–317.

Alter, Robert. *Necessary Angels: Tradition and Modernity in Kafka, Benjamin, and Scholem*. Cambridge, Mass., 1991.

Altmann, Alexander. "The Bible: Allegorical Interpretations." *Encyclopedia Judaica* 4:895–99.

———. "The God of Religion, The God of Metaphysics, and Wittgenstein's 'Language-Games.'" *Zeitschrift für Religions und Geistsgeschichte* 39 (1987): 289–306.

———. "Judaism and World Philosophy: From Philo to Spinoza." In *The Jews: Their Role in Civilization*, edited by Louis Finkelstein. 4th ed., New York, 1974, 65–116.

———. "Moses Narboni's 'Epistle on Shi'ur Qoma.'" In *Jewish Medieval and Renaissance Studies*. Cambridge, Mass., 1967, 225–64.

———. "The Religion of the Thinkers: Free Will and Predestination in Saadia, Bahya and Maimonides." In *Religion in a Religious Age*, edited by S. D. Goitein. Cambridge, Mass., 1974, 25–53.

———. "Saadia Gaon." In *Three Jewish Philosophers*. New York, 1973.

———. "Saadya's Theory of Revelation: Its Origin and Background." In *Studies in Religious Philosophy and Mysticism*. Ithaca, 1969, 140–60.

Amidi, 'Ali b. 'Ali b. Muhammad al-Taghlabi, Sayf al-Din al-. *Ghayat al-Maram fi 'Ilm al-Kalam*. Edited by Hasan Mahmud 'Abd al-Latif. Cairo, 1971.

———. *Ihkam al-Hukkam fi Usul al-Ahkam*. Cairo, 1929.

Amin, Ahmad. *Duha' al-Islam*. 3 vols. Cairo, 1961–62.

Ammons, A. R. "Saliences." In *The Selected Poems*. Exp. ed. New York and London, 1986, 47–50.

———. *Sumerian Vistas*. New York and London, 1987.

Anawati, George. "Fakhr al-Din al-Razi: Eléments de biographie." In *Mélanges d'orientalisme offerts à H. Massé*. Teheran, 1963, 1–10.

———. "Polémique, apologie et dialogue islamochrétien: Positions classiques médiévales et positions contemporaines." *Euntes docete* 22 (1969): 375–451.

———. "Philosophy, Theology and Mysticism." In *The Legacy of Islam*, 2d ed., edited by J. Schacht and C. E. Bosworth. New York, 1979, 350–92.

Anawati, George, and Louis Gardet. *Introduction à la théologie musulmane*. Paris, 1948.

Andrae, Tor. *Der Ursprung des Islams und das Christentum.* Uppsala-Stockholm, 1926.

Ankori, Tzvi. *Karaites in Byzantium.* New York, 1959.

ʿArid, ʿAli Hasan, al-. *Fath al-Mannan fi Naskh al-Qurʾan.* Cairo, 1973.

Arkoun, Mohammed. "New Perspectives for a Jewish-Christian-Muslim Dialogue." *Journal of Ecumenical Studies* 26 (1989): 523–29.

———. "The Notion of Revelation: From *Ahl al-Kitab* to the Societies of the Book." *Die Welt des Islams* 28 (1988):62–89.

———. "Peut-on parler de merveilleux dans le Coran?" In *Lectures du Coran.* Paris, 1988.

———. *Pour une critique de la raison islamique.* Paris, 1984.

Arnaldez, Roger. "Controverse d'Ibn Hazm contre ibn Nagrila le juif." *Revue de l'occident Musulman et de la Méditerranée* 13–14 (1973): 41–48.

———. *Grammaire et théologie chez Ibn Hazm de Cordoue.* Paris, 1956.

———. "Ibn Hazm," *Encyclopedia of Islam.* 2d ed. 3:813–22.

Arnold, T. W. *The Preaching of Islam: A History of the Propagation of the Muslim Faith.* New York, 1913.

Ashʿari, Abu- al-Hasan, al-. *Maqalat al-Islamiyyin.* Edited by H. Ritter. 2 vols., cont. pagination. Istanbul, 1929–30.

Ashtor, Eliyahu (Strauss). "Aperçus sur les Radhanites." *Revue suisse d'histoire* 27 (1977): 245–75.

———. "Methods of Muslim Polemics" (in Hebrew). In *Memorial Volume for the Rabbinical Seminary of Vienna.* Jerusalem, 1946.

———. *History of the Jews in Egypt and Syria under the Rule of the Mamluks* (in Hebrew). 3 vols. Jerusalem, 1944–70.

———. "The Number of Jews in Mediaeval Egypt." *Journal of Jewish Studies* 18 (1967): 9–42; 19 (1968): 1–22.

———. "Prolegomena to the Medieval History of Oriental Jewry." *Jewish Quarterly Review* 50 (1959): 55–68, 145–66.

———. *A Social and Economic History of the Near East in the Middle Ages.* London, 1976.

———. "The Social Isolation of the Ahl al-Dhimma." In *P. Hirschler Memorial Volume,* edited by O. Komlos. Budapest, 1950, 73–94.

Asmussen, Jes. *Studies in Judeo-Persian Literature.* Leiden, 1973.

Aune, David. "The Apocalypse of John and the Problem of Genre." In *Early Christian Apocalypticism. Genre and Social Setting,* edited by Adela Yarbro Collins. Chico, Calif., 1986, 65–97.

———. *Prophecy in Early Christianity and the Ancient Mediterranean World.* Grand Rapids, Mich., 1983.

Azmeh, Aziz al-. *Ibn Khaldun. An Essay in Reinterpretation.* Totowa, N.J., 1982.

Azmi, A. A. *Studies in Early Hadith Literature.* Beirut, 1968.

Baalabaki, Ramzi. "Early Arab Lexicographers and the Use of Semitic Languages." *Berytus* 31 (1983): 117–27.

Bacher, W. *Tradition und Tradenten in den Schulen Palästinas und Babyloniens.* Leipzig, 1914.

Badawi, ʿAbd al-Rahman al-. *Histoire de la Philosophie en Islam.* 2 vols. Paris, 1972.

Baeck, Leo. *This People Israel: The Meaning of Jewish Existence.* New York, 1964.

Baghdadi, Abu Mansur ʿAbd al-Qahir b. Tahir al-. *Al-Farq bayn al-Firaq.* Edited by Muhammad Badr. Cairo, 1911. Published in English as *Moslem Schisms and Sects,* pt. 1, trans. K. Seelye (New York, 1919) and *Moslem Schisms and Sects*, pt. 2, trans. A. Halkin (Tel Aviv, 1935).

———. *Al-Milal wa al-Nihal*. Edited by A. Nader. Beirut, 1970.

———. *Usul al-Din*. Istanbul, 1928.

Bahaullah. *The Dawn Breakers*. Translated by Shoghi Effendi. Wilmette, Ill., 1976.

Bamberger, Bernard J. "A Messianic Document of the Seventh Century." *Hebrew Union College Annual* 15 (1940): 425–31.

Bammel, Ernst. "Hohlenmenschen." *Zeitschrift für die neutestamentliche Wissenschaft* 49 (1958): 77–88.

Baqillani, Abu Bakr b. ʿAli b. al-Tayyib al-. *Tamhid fi al-Radd ʿAla al-Muʿattila wa al-Rafida wa al-Khawarij wa al-Muʿtazila*. Edited by R. J. McCarthy. Beirut, 1957.

Bar-Ilan, Meir. "The Throne of God: What Is Under It, What Is Opposite It, What Is Near It?" (in Hebrew). *Daat* 15 (1985): 21–35.

Bar-Khonai, Theodore. *Livre des scholies (recension de Seert)*. 2 vols. Translated by R. Hespel and R. Draguet. Louvain, 1982.

Barnard, L. W. *The Graeco-Roman and Oriental Background of the Iconoclastic Controversy*. Leiden, 1974.

Baron, Solo W. *A Social and Religious History of the Jews*. 18 vols. New York and Philadelphia, 1958– .

Bartal, Israel. "Messianic Expectations and their Place in History." In *Vision and Conflict in the Holy Land*, edited by Richard I. Cohen. New York and Jerusalem, 1985, 171–181.

Barth, J. "Midraschische Elemente in der muslimischen Tradition." *Festschrift Abraham Berliner*. Berlin, 1903, 33–40.

Barthélemy, D., and J. T. Milik. *Discoveries in the Judaean Desert of Jordon*. vol. 1, *Qumran Cave*. Oxford, 1955.

Barthold, W., and P. B. Golden. "Khazar." *Encyclopedia of Islam*. 2d ed. 4:1172–81.

Bashear, Suliman. "Apocalyptic and Other Materials on Early Muslim-Byzantine Wars: A Review of Arabic Sources." *Journal of the Royal Asiatic Society*, n.s., 1–2 (1991): 173–207.

Basri, Abu al-Husayn Muhammad b. ʿAli b. al-Tayyib. *Al-Muʿtamad fi Usul al-Din*. Edited by Muhammad Hamidullah. 2 vols. Damascus, 1964–65.

Bateson, Gregory. *Angels Fear: Steps Toward an Epistemology of the Sacred*. New York, 1988.

Bauer, Walter. *Das Leben Jesu*. Tübingen, 1909.

Bauman, Zygmunt. "Love in Adversity: On the State and the Intellectuals, and the State of Intellectuals." *Thesis Eleven* 31 (1992): 81–105.

Bausani, Alessandro. *L'enciclopedia dei Fratelli della Purità*. Naples, 1978.

Becker, C. H. "Christliche Polemik und islamische Dogmenbildung." *Zeitschrift für Assyriologie* 26 (1911): 175–95.

Beckwith, R. T. "The Essene Calendar and the Moon: A Reconsideration." *Revue de Qumran* 59 (1992): 447–66.

Beer, B. "Welchen Aufschluss geben jüdische Quellen über den 'Zweihörnigen' des Koran?" *Zeitschrift der Deutschen Morgenländischen Gesellschaft* 9 (1855): 785–94.

Bein, Alex. "The Jewish Parasite." *Yearbook of the Leo Baeck Institute* 9 (1964): 3–40.

Bellah, Robert. *Beyond Belief: Essays on Relgions in a Post-Traditional World*. New York, 1970.

Bencheikh, Jamel Eddine. *Les Mille et une nuits ou la parole prisonnière*. Paris, 1991.

———. *Le Voyage nocturne de Mahomet*. Paris, 1988.

Benjamin of Tudela. *The Itinerary of R. Benjamin of Tudela*. Translated by A. Asher. London, 1840–41.

Ben-Sasson, H. H. "The First of the Karaites: The Trend of Their Social Conceptions" (in Hebrew). *Zion* 15 (1950): 42–55.

Ben-Shammai, Haggai. "The Attitudes of Some Early Karaites Towards Islam." In *Studies in Medieval Jewish History and Literature*, edited by Isidore Twersky. Cambridge, 1984, 2:3–41.

———. "Between Ananites and Karaites: Observations on Early Medieval Jewish Sectarianism." *Studies in Muslim-Jewish Relations* 1 (1993): 19–31.

———. "A Note on Some Karaite Copies of Mu'tazilite Writings." *Bulletin of the School of Oriental and African Studies* 37 (1974): 295–304.

Bentzen, Aage. *King and Messiah*. London, 1948.

Ben-Zeev, Israel. "Jewish Sources in the *Thousand and One Nights*" (in Hebrew). *Moznayim* 6 (1937–38): 55–59, 489–96.

Berger, David. "Three Typological Themes in Early Jewish Messianism: Messiah Son of Joseph, Rabbinic Calculations, and the Figure of Armilus." *Association for Jewish Studies Review* 10 (1985): 141–65.

Berlin, Isaiah. "Historical Inevitability." In *The Philosophy of History in Our Time*, edited by Hans Meyerhoff. Garden City, N.Y. 1959, 249–71.

Berman, Lawrence. "The Political Interpretation of the Maxim: The Purpose of Philosophy Is the Imitation of God." *Studia Islamica* 15 (1961): 53–61.

Bernhauer, A. W. "Mémoires sur les instituts de police chez les arabes, les persans, et les turcs," *Journal asiatique*, 5th ser., 15 (1860): 461–508; 16 (1860): 114–90, 347–92; 17 (1861): 5–76.

Bernstein, Marc Steven. "The Stories of the Prophets: Intertextuality in Judaism and Islam." *Journal of the Association of Graduate Students in Near Eastern Studies* 1 (1990): 27–36.

Biale, David. *Gershom Scholem: Kabbalah and Counter-History*. 2d ed. Cambridge, Mass., 1982.

———. *Power and Powerlessness in Jewish History*. New York, 1986.

Bickerman, Elias. "Symbolism in the Dura Synagogue." *Harvard Theological Review* 58 (1965): 127–51.

Bidez, Joseph, and Franz Cumont,. eds. *Les Mages hellénisés*. Paris, 1938.

Biruni, Abu al-Rayham Muhammad al-. *Athar al-Baqiyya 'an al-Qur'an al-Khaliyya*. Edited by C. E. Sachau. Leipzig, 1878.

———. *Kitab al-Athar al-Baqiya* (The chronology of ancient nations). Translated by E. Sachau. London, 1879.

Björkman, Walther. *Beiträge zur Geschichte der StaatsKanzlei im islamischen Ägypten*. Hamburg, 1928.

Black, Matthew. "The Patristic Accounts of Jewish Sectarianism." *Bulletin of the John Rylands Library* 41 (1958–59): 285–303.

Blackman, Philip. *Mishnayoth*. New York, 1965.

Bland, Kalman. "An Islamic Theory of Jewish History: The Case of Ibn Khaldun." *Journal of Asian and African Studies* 18 (1983): 189–97.

Blichfeldt, Jan Olav. *Early Mahdism: Politics and religion in the formative period of Islam*. Leiden, 1985.

———. "*Khassa* and '*amma*: On Slogans, Concepts and Social Settings in Islamic History." *Orientalia Suecana* 38–39 (1989–90): 14–20.

Bloch, Ernst. *Avicenna und die Aristotelische Linke*. Berlin, 1952.

————. *Geist der Utopie*. Frankfurt, 1918.

————. "Nonsynchronism and the Obligation of Its Dialectics." *New German Critique* 11 (1977): 22–38.

————. *The Principle of Hope*. Translated by Neville Plaice, Stephen Plaice, and Paul Knight. 3 vols. Cambridge, Mass., 1986.

Blochet, Edgar. "Études sur le gnosticisme musulmane." *Rivista degli studi orientali* 3 (1908–9): 717–56; 4 (1909–10): 267–300.

Blumenthal, David. *The Commentary of R. Hoter ben Shelmo to the Thirteen Principles of Maimonides*. Leiden, 1974.

————. "An Example of Ismaili Influence in Post-Maimonidean Yemen." In *Studies in Judaism and Islam*, edited by Shelomo Morag, Issachar Ben-Ami, and Norman Stillman. Jerusalem, 1981, 155–75.

Bosworth, C. E. "Al-Ḫwarizmi on Theology and Sects: The Chapter on Kalam in the Mafatih al-ʿUlum." *Bulletin des études orientales* 29 (1977): 85–95.

————. "The Concept of *Dhimma* in Early Islam." In *Christians and Jews in the Ottoman Empire*, edited by B. Braude and B. Lewis. New York, 1982, 1:37–55.

————. "Jewish Elements in the Banu Sasan." *Bibliotheca Orientalis* 33 (1976): 1–17. Reprinted in *Medieval Arabic Culture and Administration* (London, 1982), art. 6.

Bouamama, Ali. "L'imaginaire dans le Coran." *Revue des sciences religieuses* 60 (1986): 90–99.

Bouwsma, William J. *Concordia Mundi: The Career and Thought of Guillaume Postel*. Cambridge, Mass., 1957.

Boyarin, Jonathan. *Storm from Paradise. The Politics of Jewish Memory*. Minneapolis, Minn., 1992.

Braun, O. "Ein Brief des katholikos Timotheos I über biblische Studien des 9 Jahrhunderts." *Oriens Christianus* 1 (1901): 299–313.

Brentjes, Helga. *Die Imamats Lehren im Islam nach der Darstellung des Aschʿari*. Berlin, 1964.

Breur, I. "Yudghanites." *Jewish Encyclopedia* 12:624–25.

Brinner, William M. and Stephen D. Ricks, eds. *Studies in Islamic and Judaic Traditions*. Vol. 1. Atlanta, 1986.

Brion, Fabienne. "Le Temps, l'espace et la genese du monde selon Abu Bakr al-Razi." *Revue philosophique de Louvain* 87 (1989): 139–64.

————. "Philosophie et révélation." *Bulletin de philosophie médiévale* 28 (1986): 134–62.

Brock, Sebastian. "A Letter Attributed to Cyril of Jerusalem on the Rebuilding of the Temple." *Bulletin of the School of Oriental and African Studies* 40 (1977): 267–86.

————. "Syriac Views of Emergent Islam." In *Studies on the First Century of Islamic Society*, edited by G. H. A. Juynboll. Carbondale and Edwardsville, Ill., 1982.

Brodsky, Joseph. "Poetry as a Form of Resistance to Reality." *PMLA* 107 (1992): 220–25.

Bronsen, David, ed. *Jews and Germans from 1860 to 1933: The Problematic Symbiosis*. Heidelberg, 1979.

Brooten, Bernadette. *Women Leaders in the Ancient Synagogue*. Chico, Calif., 1982.

Brown, Norman O. "The Apocalypse of Islam." In *Apocalypse and/or Metamorphosis*. Berkeley, Los Angeles and Oxford, 1991, 69–95.

————. "The Prophetic Tradition." *Studies in Romanticism* 21 (1982): 367–86.

Brown, Peter. "The Rise and Function of the Holy Man in Late Antiquity." *Journal of Roman Studies* 61 (1971): 80–101.

―――. "The Saint as Exemplar in Late Antiquity." In *Saints and Virtues*, edited by John Stratton Hawley. Los Angeles and London, 1987.

―――. "Society and the Supernatural: A Medieval Change." In *Society and the Holy in Late Antiquity*. Berkeley and Los Angeles, 1982, 302–33.

―――. *The World of Late Antiquity*. London, 1981.

Browne, E. G. "Account of a Rare Manuscript History of Isfahan." *Journal of the Royal Asiatic Society* (1901): 411–46, 661–704.

Brownlee, W. H. "The Anointed Ones of Aaron and Israel: Thesis, Antithesis, Synthesis." In *Mélanges bibliques et orientaux en l'honneur de M. Mathias Delcor*, edited by A. Caquot, S. Légasse, and M. Tardieu. Neukirchen-Vluyn, 1985, 37–45.

Brunschvig, Robert. "Métiers vils en Islam." *Studia Islamica* 16 (1962): 41–60.

―――. "Voeu ou serment? Droit comparé du Judaisme et de l'Islam." In *Hommage à Georges Vajda*, edited by G. Nahon and C. Touati. Louvain, 1980, 125–34.

Bryer, David. "The Origins of the Druze Religion." *Der Islam* 53 (1976): 5–28.

Buhler, A. *On the Origins of the Indian Brahma Alphabet*. Strasbourg, 1898.

Bundy, David. "Pseudepigrapha in Syriac Literature." In *Society of Biblical Literature 1991 Seminar Papers*, edited by Eugene H. Lovering, Jr. Atlanta, 1991, 745–776.

Buni, Muhyiddin al-. *Manba' Usul al-Hikma*. Cairo, n.d.

Burns, R. J. *Muslims, Christians and Jews in the Crusader Kingdom of Valencia: Societies in Symbiosis*. Cambridge, 1984.

Cacciari, Massimo. *L'Ange nécessaire*. Paris, 1988.

Cacquot, A. "Le Messianisme qumrànien." In *Qumran*, edited by M. Delcor. Paris and Leuven, 1978, 231–49.

Calmard, J. "Le chiisme inamite en iran à l'époque seljoukide, d'après le K. al-Naqd." *Le Monde Iranien et l'Islam* 1 (1971): 43–67.

Canard, Marius. "Les Expéditions des arabes contre Constantinople dans l'histoire et dans la légende." *Journal asiatique* 208 (1926): 61–121.

Carra de Vaux, Baron. "Charms and Amulets (Muhammaden)." *Encyclopedia of Religion and Ethics* 3:257–61.

Casanova, Paul. "Idris et 'Ouzair." *Journal asiatique* 205 (1924): 356–60.

Castoriadis, C. *The Imaginary Institution of Society*. Translated by Kathleen Blauney. Cambridge, Mass., 1987.

Chabot, J. B. "Trois épisodes concernant les Juifs." *Revue des études juives* 28 (1894): 291–94.

Chapira, B. "Legendes bibliques attribuées à Ka'b el-Ahbar." *Revue des etudes juives* 69 (1919): 86–101.

Charlesworth, James. "Folk Traditions in Jewish Apocalyptic Literature." In *Mysteries and Revelations: Apocalyptic studies since the Uppsala Colloquium*, edited by John J. Collins and James H. Charlesworth. Sheffield, 1991, 91–113.

―――. ed. *The Old Testament Pseudepigrapha*. 2 vols. New York, 1983–85.

Chiesa, Bruno. "Il Guidaismo Caraita." In *Correnti Culturali e Movimenti Religiosi de Guidaismo*, edited by Bruno Chiesa. Rome, 1987, 51–173.

Chitty, Derwas J. *The Desert a City: An Introduction to the Study of Egyptian and Palestinian Monasticism under the Christian Empire*. Crestwood, N.Y., 1966.

Chodkiewicz, Michel. *An Ocean without Shore: Ibn Arabi, the Book, and the Law*. Translated by David Streight. Albany, N.Y., 1993.

―――. Review of *Deux Traités*, by Paul Fenton. *Studia Islamica* 67 (1988): 184–86.

Cohen, Gerson. "Rabbinic Judaism (2d–18th Centuries)." *Encyclopedia Britannica*, 15th ed. 22:416–22.

———. "The Reconstruction of Gaonic History." In *Texts and Studies in Jewish History and Literature*, vol. 1, edited by Jacob Mann. 1931. New York, 1972, xiii–xcvii.

———. ed. and trans. *Sefer ha-Qabbalah: The Book of Tradition, by Abraham ibn Daud*. Philadelphia, 1967.

Cohen, Hermann. *Reason and Hope*. Translated and edited by Eva Jospe. New York, 1971.

Cohen, Mark R. "Islam and the Jews: Myth, Counter-Myth, History." *Jerusalem Quarterly* 38 (1986): 125–37.

Cohen, Mark R., and Sasson Somekh. "In the Court of Yaʿqub ibn Killis: A Fragment from the Cairo Genizah." *Jewish Quarterly Review* 80 (1990): 283–314.

Cohen, Martin. "ʿAnan ben David and Karaite Origins." *Jewish Quarterly Review* 68 (1977): 129–45, 224–34.

———. *The Shiʿur Qomah: Liturgy and Theurgy in Pre-Kabbalistic Jewish Mysticism*. Lanham, Md., New York, and London, 1983.

Cohen, N. G. "Jewish Names as Cultural Indicators in Antiquity." *Journal for the Study of Judaism* 7 (1976): 97–128.

Cohen, Shaye. "The Significance of Yavneh: Pharisees, Rabbis and the End of Jewish Sectarianism." *Hebrew Union College Annual* 55 (1984): 27–53.

Cohen, Stuart A. *The Three Crowns: Communal Politics in Early Rabbinic Judaism*. Cambridge, 1990.

Cohn, Norman. *The Pursuit of the Millennium*. 2d ed., rev. and exp. New York, 1970.

Cole, Owen W. *Sikhism and its Indian Context, 1469–1708*. London, 1984.

Collins, J., ed. *Apocalypse: Morphology of a Genre*. Missoula, Mont., 1979.

Collins, John J., and James H. Charlesworth, eds. *Mysteries and Revelations: Apocalyptic Studies since the Uppsala Colloquium*. Sheffield, 1991.

Colpe, Carsten. "Die gnostische Anthropologie Zwischen Intellektualismus und Volkstümlichkeit." In *Studien zum Menschenbild in Gnosis und Manichäismus*, edited by Peter Nagel. Halle/Saale, 1979, 31–44.

Cook, M. "Anan and Islam: The Origins of Karaite Scripturalism." *Jerusalem Studies in Arabic and Islam* 9 (1987): 161–83.

———. "Early Islamic Dietary Law." *Jerusalem Studies in Arabic and Islam* 7 (1986): 217–77.

Cook, M., and Patricia Crone. *Hagarism: The Making of the Muslim World*. Cambridge, 1980.

Corbin, Henry. *Avicenna and the Visionary Recital*. Translated by Willard Trask. New York, 1960.

———. *Histoire de la philosophie islamique*. Paris: Gallimard, 1964: English Translation = *History of Islamic Philosophy* (New York and London, 1993).

———. *L'élément dramatique commun aux cosmonogies gnostiques des religions du Livre.*" *Cahiers de l'Université St.-Jean de Jérusalem* 5 (1978): 141–73.

———. *The Man of Light in Iranian Sufism*. Boulder, Colo., and London, 1978.

———. "Theologoumena Iranica." *Studia Iranica* 5 (1976): 225–35.

———. "Toward a Chart of the Imaginal." *Temenos* 1 (1981): 23–37.

Cox, Patricia. *Biography in Late Antiquity: The Quest for the Holy Man*. Berkeley, Los Angeles and London, 1983.

Crone, Patricia. "Islam, Judeo-Christianity and Byzantine Iconoclasm." *Jerusalem Studies in Arabic and Islam* 2 (1980): 59–95.

Crow, Douglas. "The Teaching of Jaʿfar al-Sadiq." Master's thesis, McGill University, 1980.

————, trans. "The Death of al-Husayn ibn ʿAli and Early Shiʿi Views of the Imamate." *Alserat* 12 (1986): 71–117.

Crown, Alan. "Dositheans, Resurrection and a Messianic Joshua." *Antichthon* 1 (1967): 70–85.

Cuddihy, John Murray. *No Offense: Civil Religion and Protestant Taste.* New York, 1978.

Cutler, A. H. and H. E. Cutler. *The Jew as Ally of the Muslim.* Notre Dame, Ind., 1986.

Dabashi, Hamid. *Authority in Islam from the Rise of Muhammad to the Establishment of the Umayyads.* New Brunswick, N.J., and London, 1989.

Dagron, Gilbert. "Judaïser." *Travaux et mémoires* 11 (1991): 359–80.

Dagron, Gilbert, and Vincent Déroche. "Juifs et Chrétiens dans l'orient du VIIe Siècle." *Travaux et mémoires* 11 (1991): 17–46.

Daiber, Hans. "Abu Hatim al-Razi (10th century A.D.) on the Unity and Diversity of Religions." In *Dialogue and Syncretism. An Interdisciplinary Approach*, edited by J. D. Gort, V. M. Vroom, R. Fernhout, and A. Issels. Grand Rapids, Mich., and Amsterdam, 1989, 87–104.

————. "Masa'il wa'l-Adjwiba." *Encyclopedia of Islam.* 2d ed. 6:636–39.

Dalley, Stephanie. "Gilgamesh in *The Arabian Nights.*" *Journal of the Royal Asiatic Society*, 3d ser. 1 (1991): 1–17.

Dan, Josef. *The Hebrew Story in the Middle Ages* (in Hebrew). Jerusalem, 1974.

————. "Magic." *Encyclopedia Judaica.* Vol. 2, cols. 703–15.

————. *Three Types of Ancient Jewish Mysticism.* Cincinnati, 1984.

Daniel, Elton L. *The Political and Social History of Khurasan under Abbasid Rule, 747–820.* Minneapolis, Minn., and Chicago, 1979.

Danielou, Jean. "Christianity as a Jewish Sect." In *The Crucible of Christianity*, edited by Arnold Toynbee. London, 1969.

Davidson, Herbert. "The Study of Philosophy as a Religious Obligation." In *Religion in a Religious Age*, edited by S. D. Goiten. Cambridge, Mass., 1974, 53–69.

Davidson, Israel, ed. *Saadia's Polemic against Hiwi al-Balkhi.* New York, 1915.

Davis, Moshe, ed. *World Jewry and the Present State of Jewry.* New York, 1977.

Davis, Natalie Zemon. "History's Two Bodies." *American Historical Review* 99 (1988): 1–30.

Dawson, David. *Allegorical Readers and Cultural Revision in Ancient Alexandria.* Berkeley, Los Angeles, and Oxford, 1992.

De Felice, Renzo. *Jews in an Arab Land: Libya, 1835–1970.* Austin, 1985.

Déjeux, J. "La Kahina: De l'histoire à la fiction littéraire. Myth et épopée." *Studi Maghrebini* 15 (1983): 1–42.

Demonslaben, Philippe. "Notes sur deux vêtements talismaniques." *Arabica* 33 (1986): 216–50.

Déroche, Vincent, ed. "*Doctrina Jacobi Nuper Baptizati.*" *Travaux et Mémoires* 11 (1991): 47–275.

Derrett, J. and M. Duncan. "A Moses-Buddha Parallel and Its Meaning." *Archív Orientálni* 58 (1990):310–17.

Derrida, Jaques. "Of an Apocalyptic Tone Recently Adopted in Philosophy." In *Derrida and Biblical Studies*, edited by Robert Detweiller, (1982), 63–97.

Dexinger, F. "Der 'Prophet wie Mose' in Qumran und bei den Samaritanem." In *Mélanges bibliques et orienaux en l'honneur de M. Mathias Delcor*, edited by A. Caquot, S. Légasse, and M. Tardieu. Neukirchen and Vluyn, 1985, 97–113.

———. "Der Taheb: Ein 'messianischer' Heilsbringer der Samaritaner." *Kairos* 27 (1985): 1–173.

Dhahabi, Shams al-Din Muhammad. *Mizan al-I'tidal fi Naqd al-Rijal*. 4 vols. Cairo, 1963.

Dietrich, A. "Al-Hadjdjaj b. Yusuf." *Encyclopedia of Islam*. 2d ed. 3:39–43.

———, ed. *Akten des VII Congresses für Arabistik und Islamwissenschaft*. Göttingen, 1976.

Dimant, Devorah. "Qumran Sectarian Literature." In *Jewish Writings in the Second Temple Period: Apocrypha, Pseudepigrapha, Qumran Sectarian Writings, Philo, Josephus*, edited by Michael S. Stone. Assen and Philadelphia, 1984.

Dinur, B. Z. *Judaism in the Diaspora* (in Hebrew). 6 books in 2 vol. Tel Aviv and Jerusalem, 1958–72.

Diwald-Wilzer, S. *Arabische Philosophie und Wissenschaft in der Enzyklopädie Kitab Ihwan al-Safa'*. Vol. 3 of *Die Lehre von Seele und Intellekt*. Wiesbaden, 1975.

Djaït, Hichem. "Kufa." *Encyclopedia of Islam*, 2d ed. 5:345–51.

———"Les Yamanites à Kufa au 1er siécle de l'Hégire." *Journal of the Economic and Social History of the Orient* 19 (1976) 148–81.

Donaldson, D. M. *The Shi'ite Religion. A History of Islam in Persia and Irak*. London, 1933. Reprint, New York, n.d.

Donner, Fred M. "The Bakr b. Wa'il Tribes and Politics in Northwestern Arabia on the Eve of Islam." *Studia Islamica* 51 (1980): 5–38.

Doughty, Charles M. *Travels in Arabia Deserta* 2 vols. 1888. Reprint, New York, 1979.

Douglas, Mary. "The Effects of Modernization on Religious Change." *Daedalus* 111 (1982): 1–21.

———. *Implicit Meanings*. London, 1975.

———. *Natural Symbols: Exploitations in Cosmology*. New York, 1973.

Doutté, Edmond. *Magie and religion dans l'Afrique de Nord*. Algiers, 1908. Reprint Paris, 1984.

Dozy, R. Review of Ernst Renan *Averroës et l'Averroïsme. Journal asiatique* 5 (1852): 93.

Dunlop, D. M. *Arab Civilization to 1500*. Beirut, 1971.

———. *The History of The Jewish Khazars*. Princeton, 1954. Reprint, New York, 1967.

Dupont-Summer, Andre. "Le psaume CLI dans 11 QPsª et le probleme de son origin essenienne." *Semitica* 14 (1964): 25–62.

Dupuy, Bernard. "Les karaites sont-ils les descendents des esseniens?" *Istina* 29 (1984): 139–51.

Duri, A. A. *The Rise of Historical Writing among the Arabs*. Translated by L. I. Conrad. Princeton, 1983.

Duri, A. A. and A. J. al-Muttalibi, eds. *Akhbar al-Daula al-'Abbasiyya*. Beirut, 1971.

Eco, Umberto. *Foucault's Pendulum*. San Diego, New York, and London, 1989.

———. "Interpretation and Overinterpretation: World History Texts." In *The Tanner Lectures on Human Values*, vol. 12, edited by Grethe B. Peterson. Salt Lake City, Utah, 1991, 141–203.

Edmunds, Albert J. *Buddhist and Christian Gospels: Now First Compared from the Originals*. 2 vols. Philadelphia, 1908–9.

Eisenstadt, Shmuel. "Cultural Traditions and Political Dynamics: The Origins and Modes of Ideological Politics." *British Journal of Sociology* 32 (1981): 155–81.

————. "Heterodoxies, Sectarianism and the Dynamics of Civilization." *Diogenes* (1982): 1–21.

————. "Transformational Visions: Other Worldliness and Its Transformations." *Religion* (1983): 1–17.

————, ed. *The Origins and Diversity of Axial Age Civilizations*. Albany, N.Y., 1985.

Eliot, T. S. *Four Quartets*. New York, 1971.

Endress, Gerhard. "The Defense of Reason: The Plea for Philosophy in the Religious Community." *Zeitschrift für Geschichte der Arabisch-Islamischen Wissenchaften* 6 (1990): 1–49.

Ettinger, Shmuel. "The Hassidic Movement: Reality and Ideals." In *Jewish Society through the Ages*, edited by H. H. Ben-Sasson and S. Ettinger. New York, 1971, 253–54.

Fagnan, E. "Arabo-Judaica." *Revue des études juives* 59 (1910): 225–30.

Fakhry, Majid. *A History of Islamic Philosophy*. 2d ed. New York, 1983.

Faruqi, Nizar A. *Early Muslim Historiography*. New Delhi, 1979.

Faur, José. *Golden Doves with Silver Dots*. Bloomington, Ind., 1986.

————. *In the Shadow of History: Jews and Conversos at the Dawn of History*. Albany, N.Y., 1991.

Fauth, W. "Tatrosjah-Totrosjah und Metatron in der jüdischen Merkabah-Mystik." *Journal for the Study of Judaism* 22 (1991): 40–87.

Feki, Habib. *Les idées religieuses et philosophiques de l'ismaélisme Fatimide*. Tunis, 1978.

Fenton, Paul B. "The Arabic and Hebrew Versions of the *Theology of Aristotle*." In *Pseudo-Aristotle in the Middle Ages: "The Theology" and Other Texts*, edited by Jill Kraye, W. F. Ryan, and C. B. Schmitt. London, 1986, 241–64.

————. *Deux traités de mystique juive*. Paris, 1987.

————. *The Treatise of the Pool*. London, 1981.

Filippani-Ronconi, Pio. *Ummu'l-Kitab: Introduzione, traduzione e note*. Naples, 1966.

Finkel, Joshua. "Risala fi radd ʿala al-Nasara." In *Three Essays of Abu ʿOthman ʿAmr ibn Bahr al-Jahiz (d. 869)*, edited by Joshua Finkel. Cairo, 1926.

Fischel, Walter J. "The Beginnings of Judeo-Persian Literature." In *Mélanges d'orientalisme offerts a Henri Massé*. Teheran, 1963, 141–51.

————. "Ibn Khaldun and Josippon." In *Homenaje a Millas-Vallicrosa*. Barcelona, 1954, 1:587–98.

————. "Ibn Khaldun on the Bible, Judaism and the Jews." In *Ignace Goldziher Memorial Volume*, vol. 2, edited by S. Löwinger and J. de Somogyi. Budapest, 1948, 145–71.

————. "Isfahan: The Story of a Jewish Community in Persia." In *Joshua Starr Memorial Volume: Studies in History and Philology*. New York, 1953, 111–28.

————. "Israel in Iran." In *The Jews: Their History, Culture, and Religion*, edited by Louis Finkelstein, 2d ed. New York, 1955, 2:817–58.

————. "Jews and Judaism at the Court of the Moghul Emperors in Medieval India." *Proceedings of the American Academy for Jewish Research* 18 (1949): 137–77.

————. *The Jews in the Economic and Political Life of Medieval Islam*. London, 1937. Reprint, New York, 1969.

————. "The Jews of Central Asia (Khorasan) in Medieval Hebrew and Islamic Literature." *Historia Judaica* 7 (1945): 29–49.

————. "The 'Resch Galuta' in Arabic Literature" (in Hebrew). In *The Magnes Anniversary Book*, edited by F. I. Baer, F. J. Bodenheimer, J. N. Epstein, M. Fekete, A. Fodor, I. J. Kligler, and L. A. Mayer. Jerusalem, 1938, 181–87.

————. "Yahudiyya: On the Beginnings of Jewish Settlement in Persia" (in Hebrew). *Tarbis* 6 (1935): 523–26.

Fischer, Michael M. J. "Is Islam the Odd-Civilization Out?" *New Perspectives Quarterly* 9 (1992): 54–60.

Fitzmyer, J. "More about Elijah Coming First." *Journal of Biblical Literature* 104 (1985).

Fleischer, Ezra. "A Fragment from Hivi al-Balkhi's Criticism of the Bible" (in Hebrew). *Tarbis* 51 (1981): 50–57.

————. "Solving the Qiliri Riddle" (in Hebrew). *Tarbis* 54 (1985): 383–429.

Flusser, David, and Shmuel Safrai. "Nadab and Abihu in the Midrash and in Philo's Writings" (in Hebrew). *Milet* 2 (1985): 79–84.

Fodor, Alexander. "The Metamorphosis of Imhotep: A Study in Islamic Syncretism." In *Arabistik und Islamwissenschaft*, edited by A. Dietrich. Göttingen, 1976, 155–81.

————. "The Rod of Moses in Arabic Magic." *Acta Orientalia* 32 (1978): 1–17.

Fossum, Jarl. "The Magharians: A Pre-Christian Jewish Sect and Its Significance for the Study of Gnosticism and Christianity." *Henoch* 9 (1987): 303–43.

————. *The Name of God and the Angel of the Lord: The Origins of the Idea of Intermediation in Gnosticism*. Tübingen, 1985.

Foucher, A. *The Life of Buddha*. translated by S. B. Boas. Middleton, 1963.

Fowden, Garth. "The Pagan Holy Man in Late Antique Society." *Journal of Hellenic Studies* 102 (1982): 33–59.

Frank, Andre Gunder. "The Thirteenth-Century World System: A Review Essay." *Journal of World History* 1 (1990): 249–58.

Frank, Daniel. Review of *Deux traités*, by Paul Fenton. *Journal of Jewish Studies* 67 (1988): 184–86.

Frankfurter, D. T. M. "Styles and Phallobates: Pillar Religions in Late Antique Syria." *Vigiliae Christianae* 44 (1990): 168–99.

Friedlaender, Israel. "'Abdallah b. Saba', der Begründer der Šiʿa, und sein jüdischer Ursprung." *Zeitschrift für Assyriologie* 23 (1909): 296–327; 24 (1910): 1–46.

————. "The Heterodoxies of the Shiites in the Presentation of Ibn Hazm." *Journal of the American Oriental Society* 28 (1907): 1–81; 29 (1908): 1–184.

————. "Jewish-Arabic Studies." *Jewish Quarterly Review*, n.s., 1 (1910–11): 183–215; 2 (1911–12): 481–517; 3 (1912–13): 235–300.

————. "The Jews of Arabia and the Gaonate." *Jewish Quarterly Review*, n.s., 1 (1910–11): 249–52.

————. "A Muhammedan Book on Augury in Hebrew Characters." *Jewish Quarterly Review*, o.s., 19 (1907): 84–103.

Friedlaender, M. "L'Anti-Messie." *Revue des études juives* 38 (1899): 14–37.

Friedländer, Saul., ed. *Probing the Limits of Representation: Nazism and the "Final Solution."* Cambridge, Mass., 1992.

Friedman, Mordechai. "Menstrual Impurity and Sectarianism in the Writings of the Geonim and of Moses and Abraham Maimonides" (in Hebrew). In *Maimonidean Studies*, vol. 1, edited by Arthur Hyman. New York, 1990, 1–23.

Frye, Northrup. *The Great Code: The Bible and Literature*. Toronto, 1981.

Funkenstein, Amos. "History, Counterhistory, and Narrative." In *Probing the Limits of Representation: Nazism and the "Final Solution,"* edited by Saul Friedländer. Cambridge, Mass., and London, 1992, 66–82, 345–50.

————. "A Schedule for the End of the World: The Origins and Persistence of the

Apocalyptic Mentality." In *Visions of Apocalypse: End or Rebirth?* edited by Saul Friedländer. New York and London, 1985, 44–60.

Galtier, Emile. "Memoires et fragments inédits." *Memoires de l'Institut francais d'archeologie orientale* 27 (1912).

———, trans. "*Futuh al-Bahnasa.*" *Memoires publiés par les membres de l'Institut Francaise d'Archeologie Orientale du Caire* 22 (1909).

Garbe, Richard. *Indien und das Christentum.* Tübingen, 1914.

Gaster, Moses. *The Samaritans: Their History, Doctrine, and Literature.* London, 1925. Reprint, London, 1976.

———. *Studies and Texts in Folklore, Magic, Medieval Romance, Hebrew Apocrypha and Samaritan Archaeology.* 3 vols. New York, 1928. Reprint, New York, 1971.

Geiger, Abraham. *Judaism and Islam.* Translated by F. M. Young. 1896. Reprint, New York, 1970.

Gerber, Jane S. "Judaism in the Middle East and North Africa since 1492." *Encyclopedia of Religion* 8:157–64.

Gero, Stephen. "Infancy Gospel of Thomas." *Novum Testamentum* 13 (1971): 46–80.

Gil, Moshe. "The Babylonian Encounter" (in Hebrew). *Tarbis* 48 (1974), 35–74.

———. *A History of Palestine.* Translated by Ethel Broido. Cambridge, 1992.

———. "The Origin of the Jews of Yathrib." *Jerusalem Studies in Arabic and Islam* 4 (1984): 203–24.

———. "Religion and Realities in Islamic Taxation." *Israel Oriental Studies* 10 (1980): 21–33.

———. *The Tustaris, Family and Sect* (in Hebrew). Tel Aviv, 1981.

Gilliot, Claude. *Aspects de l'imaginaire commun dans le "Commentaire de Tabari."* Ph.D. dissertation, Paris, 1987.

Gilson, Étienne. *La Philosophie au moyen âge.* 1944. Reprint, 1976.

Gimaret, D., and G. Monnot, trans. *Livre des religions and des sectes.* Vol. 1. Paris, 1986.

Ginzberg, Louis. *The Legends of the Jews.* 7 vols. Philadelphia, 1909–28.

———. *An Unknown Jewish Sect.* New York, 1976.

———. "Allegorical Interpretation." *The Jewish Encyclopedia* 1:403–11.

Goitein, S. D. "Banu Isra'il." *Encyclopedia of Islam.* 2d ed.

———. "Between Hellenism and Renaissance: Islam, the Intermediate Civilization." *Islamic Studies* 2 (1963): 217–33.

———. "A Caliph's Decree in Favor of the Rabbanite Jews of Palestine." *Journal of Jewish Studies* 5 (1954): 118–25.

———. "The Concept of Mankind in Islam." In *History and the Idea of Mankind,* edited by W. Warren Wagar. Albuquerque, N.M. 1971, 72–91.

———. "The Humanistic Aspects of Oriental Studies." *Jerusalem Studies in Arabic and Islam* 9 (1987): 1–13.

———. "The Interplay of Jewish and Islamic Laws." In *Jewish Law in Legal History and the Modern World,* edited by Bernard Jackson. Leiden, 1980, 61–78.

———. "Isra'iliyyat." *Encyclopedia of Islam.* 2d ed. 4:211–12.

———. "Jerusalem in the Arab Period (638–1099)." *Jerusalem Cathedra* 2:168–96.

———. "Jewish Society and Institutions under Islam." In *Jewish Society through the Ages,* edited by H. Ben-Sasson and S. Ettinger. New York, 1975, 170–85.

———. *Jews and Arabs: Their Contacts through the Ages.* 3d ed. New York, 1974.

———. *A Mediterranean Society: The Jewish Communities of the Arab World as Portrayed in the Documents of the Cairo Geniza.* 5 vols. Los Angeles, 1967–88.

——. "'Meeting in Jerusalem': Messianic Expectations in the Letters of the Cairo Geniza." *Association for Jewish Studies Review* 4 (1979): 43–57.

——. "Minority Self-Rule and Government Control in Islam." *Studia Islamica* 31 (1970): 101–16.

——. "The Moses Maimonides-Ibn Sana' al-Mulk Circle (A Deathbed Declaration from March 1182)." In *Studies in Islamic History and Civilization in Honour of Professor David Ayalon*. Leiden, 1986, 399–405.

——. "Muhammad's Inspiration by Judaism." *Journal of Jewish Studies* 9 (1958): 144–62.

——. "Political Conflict and the Use of Power in the World of the Geniza." In *Kinship and Consent*, edited by Daniel J. Elazar. Washington, D.C., 1983, 169–81.

——. "Portrait of a Yemenite Weavers' Village." *Journal of Jewish Studies* 16 (1955): 3–26.

——. "Religion in Everyday Life as Reflected in the Documents of the Cairo Geniza." In *Religion in a Religious Age*, edited by S. D. Goitein. Cambridge, Mass., 1974, 3–17.

——. "The Rise of the Near Eastern Bourgeoisie in Early Islamic Times." *Journal of World History* 32 (1956–57): 583–604.

——. "A Turning Point in the History of the Muslim State." In *Studies in Islamic History and Institutions*. Leiden, 1966.

Golb, Norman. "The Dietary Laws of the Damascus Covenant in Relation to Those of the Karaites." *Journal of Jewish Studies* 7 (1957): 51–69.

——. "Literary and Doctrinal Aspects of the Damascus Covenant in the Light of Karaite Literature." *Jewish Quarterly Review* 48 (1956): 354–74.

——. "The Qumran Covenanters and the Later Jewish Sects." *Journal of Religion* 41 (1961): 38–50.

——. "The Topography of the Jews of Medieval Egypt." *Journal of Near Eastern Studies* 24 (1965): 251–70.

——. "Who Were the Magariya?" *Journal of the American Oriental Society* 80 (1960): 347–59.

Golb, Norman, and O. Pritsak. *Khazar Hebrew Documents of the Tenth Century*. Ithaca and London, 1982.

Goldberg, Percy. *Karaite Liturgy and Its Relation to Synagogue Worship*. Manchester, 1957.

Golden, P. B. *Khazar Studies: An Historical-Philological Inquiry into the Origins of the Khazars*. Budapest, 1980.

Goldfeld, Yeshayahu. "The Development of Theory on Qur'anic Exegesis in Islamic Scholarship." *Studia Islamica* 47 (1988): 5–27.

——. "The Illiterate Prophet (*Nabi Ummi*)." *Der Islam* 57 (1980): 58–67.

Goldstone, Jack. "Cultural Orthodoxy, Risk and Innovation: The Divergence of East and West in the Early Modern World." *Social Theory* 5 (1987): 119–35.

Goldziher, Ignaz. *Gesammelte Schriften*. Edited by J. de Somogyi. 6 vols. Hildesheim, 1967–73.

——. "Gesetzliche Bestimmungen uber Kunya-Namen im Islam." *Zeitschrift der Deutschen Morgenländischen Gesellschaft* 51 (1897): 256–66.

——. "Hebräische Elemente in muhammedanischen Zaubersprüchen." *Zeitschrift der Deutschen Morgenlandischen Gesellschaft* 48 (1894): 348–50.

——. *Introduction to Islamic Theology and Law*. Translated by Andras Hamori and

Ruth Hamori. Princeton, 1981. Originally published as *Vorlesungen über den Islam* (Heidelberg, 1910).

———. "Isra'iliyyat." *Revue des études juives* 44 (1902): 63–66.

———. "La Misasa." *Revue Africaine* 52 (1908): 23–28.

———."Le Dénombrement des sectes mohamétanes." *Revue de l'histoire des religions* 26 (1892): 129–37.

———. "Le Moutakallim Juif Abou-L-Kheyr." *Revue des études juives* 47 (1902): 41–46.

———. "Mélanges Judeo-Arabes." *Revue des études juives* 43 (1901): 263–76.

———. *Muslim Studies*. Edited by S. M. Stern, translated by C. R. Barber and S. M. Stern. 2 vols. London, 1971.

———. "Renseignements de source musulmane sur la dignité de Resch Galuta." *Revue des études juives* 8 (1884): 133–36.

———. "Usages juifs d'après la littérature religieuse des musulmans." *Revue des études juives* 28 (1894): 75–94.

Goodenough, Erwin. *Jewish Symbols in the Greco-Roman Period*. 13 vols. Princeton, 1953–68.

Goodman, Nelson. *Ways of Worldmaking*. Indianapolis, Ind., and Cambridge, Mass., 1978.

Goody, Jack. *The Domestication of the Savage Mind*. Cambridge, 1977.

Gordon, Cyrus H. *Adventures in the Nearest East*. London, 1957.

Goren, Asher. "As-Samau'al b. Adiya and the Poetry of the Jew of Ancient Arabia." *Ariel* 42 (1976): 55–66.

Goshen-Gottstein, M. M. "The Psalms Scroll (11 QPsa)." *Textus* 5 (1966): 22–33.

Gottheil, Richard, and W. H. Worrel. *Fragments from the Cairo Genizah in the Freer Collection*. Philadelphia, 1927.

Graetz, Heinrich. *Geschichte der Juden*. 11 vols. Magdeburg, 1860.

Grant, R. M. *Gods and the One God*. Philadelphia, 1986.

———. "Les êtres intermediares dans le judaisme tardif." In *Le Origini dello Gnosticismo*. Leiden, 1967, 141–57.

———. *The Letter and the Spirit*. London, 1957.

Gray, Louis. "Some Indian Parallels to the Apocryphal New Testament." *Journal of the American Oriental Society* 22 (1901): 398–440.

Green, William Scott. "Reading the Writing of Rabbinism: Toward an Interpretation of Rabbinic Literature." *Journal of the American Academy of Religion Society* 51 (1983): 191–207.

Greenfield, Jonas. "Notes on some Aramaic and Mandaic Magic Bowls." *Journal of the Ancient Near Eastern Society of Columbia University* 5 (1973): 149–56.

Greenstone, J. H. *The Messiah Idea in Jewish History*. Philadelphia, 1948.

Griffith, Sidney H. "Bashir/Beser: Boon Companion of the Byzantine Emperor Leo II. The Islamic Recension of His Story in *Leiden Oriental MS 951 (2)*" *Le Muséon* 104 (1990): 293–27.

———. "Jews and Muslims in Christian and Arabic Texts of the Ninth Century." *Jewish History* 3 (1988): 65–94.

Grossman, Avraham. "Aliya in the Seventh and Eighth Centuries." *Jerusalem Cathedra* 3:176–87.

———. *The Babylonian Exilarchate in the Gaonic Period* (in Hebrew). Jerusalem, 1984.

Gruenwald, Ithamar. *Apocalyptic and Merkabah Mysticism*. Leiden, 1980.

———. "Manichaeism and Judaism in Light of the Cologne Mani Codex." *Zeitschrift für Papyrologie und Epigraphik* 52 (1983): 29–45.

Guttmann, Julius. "On the Question of the Sources of Hiwi al-Balkhi." In *Alexander Marx Jubilee Volume*. New York, 1950, 95–103.

———. *Philosophies of Judaism*. New York, Chicago, and San Francisco, 1964.

———. "Religion and Science in Medieval and Modern Thought" In *Studies in Jewish Thought: An Anthology of German Jewish Scholarship*, edited by Alfred Jospe. Detroit, 1981, 281–343.

Habermas, Jürgen. *The Philosophical Discourse of Modernity*. Translated by Frederick Lawrence. Cambridge, 1987.

Hadassi, Yehuda. *Eshkol haKofer*. Eupatoria, 1836.

Halkin, A. S. "The Judeo-Islamic Age." In *Great Ages and Ideas of the Jewish People*, edited by Leo Schwarz. New York, 1956, 213–63.

Halm, Heinz. "Abu Hatem Razi." *Encyclopedia Persica* 1:315.

———. "Das 'Buch der Schatten': Die Mufaddal-Tradition der Gulat und die Ursprünge des Nusairiestums" *Der Islam* 55 (1978): 219–66; 58 (1981): 15–86.

———. *Die islamische Gnosis*. Zurich and Munich, 1982.

———. "Die Sieben und de Zwolf, Die isma'ilitsche Kosmogonie und das Mazdak-Fragment des Šahrastani." *18 Deutscher Orientalistentag*. Vortrage, 1972.

———. *Kosmologie und Heilslehre der frühen Ismailiya*. Wiesbaden, 1978.

Halperin, David J. *The Faces of the Chariot: Early Jewish Responses to Ezekiel's Vision*. Tübingen, 1988.

———. "The Hidden Made Manifest: Muslim Traditions and the 'Latent Content' of Biblical and Rabbinic Stories." In *Festschrift for Jacob Milgram*. Forthcoming.

———. "The Ibn Sayyad Traditions and the Legend of al-Dajjal." *Journal of the American Oriental Society* 96 (1976): 213–25.

———. "A New Edition of the Hekhalot Literature." *Journal of the American Oriental Society* 104 (1984): 543–51.

Handelman, Susan. *Fragments of Redemption: Jewish Thought and Literary Theory in Benjamin, Lévinas and Scholem*. Bloomington and Indianapolis, 1991.

Harkavy, Alexander "Anan ben David." *Jewish Encyclopedia* 1:553–56.

———. "Anan, der Stifter der Karäischen Secte." *Jahruch für jüdische Geschichte und Literatur* 2 (1899): 107–22.

Harnack, Adolf von. "Der Islam." In *Lehrbuch der Dogmengeschichte*. Darmstadt, 1964, 2:529–38.

Harvey, Susan Ashbrook. *Asceticism and Society in Crisis: John Ephesus and the Lives of the Eastern Saints*. Berkeley, Los Angeles, and London, 1990.

Harvey, Susan A., and Sebastian Brock, eds. *Holy Women of the Syrian Orient*. Berkeley, Los Angeles, and London, 1987.

Hayman, A. "The Image of the Jew in the Syriac Anti-Jewish Polemical Literature." In *To See Ourselves as Others See Us*, edited by J. Neusner and E. S. Frerichs. Chico, Calif., 1985, 423–43.

———. ed. and trans. *The Disputation of Sergius the Stylite against a Jew*. Louvain, 1973.

Heath, Peter. *Allegory and Philosophy in Avicenna (Ibn Sina. With a Translation of the Book of the Prophet Muhammad's Ascent to Heaven)*. Philadelphia, 1992.

———. "Creative Hermeneutics: A Comparative Analysis of Three Islamic Approaches." *Arabica* 36 (1989): 173–210.

Hedegard, D., trans. and ed. *Seder Rav Amran.* Lund, 1951.

Hein, Joachim. *Das Buch der Vierzig fragen.* Leiden, 1960.

Heineman, J. "The Messiah of Ephraim and the Premature Exodus of the Tribe of Ephraim." *Harvard Theological Review* 68 (1975): 1–17.

Heinen, Anton M. "The Notion of Taʾwil in Abu Yaʿqub al-Sijistani's *Book of the Sources (Kitab al-Yanabi)."* *Hamdard Islamicus* 2 (1979): 35–45.

———. ed. and trans. *Islamic Cosmology: A Study of As-Suyuti's al-Hayʾa as-saniya fi l-hayʾa as-sunniya.* Wiesbaden, 1982.

Heller, Bernhard. "Ginzberg's Legends of the Jews." *Jewish Quarterly Review* 24 (1933): 51–66, 165–90, 281–307, 393–418; 25 (1934): 29–52.

———. "La légende biblique dans l'Islam." *Revue des études juives* 98 (1934): 1–18.

———. "Muhammedanisches und Antimuhammedanisches in den Pirke Rabbi Elie-zer." *Monatsschrift für Geschichte und Wissenschaft des Judentums* 69 (1925): 47–54.

———. "Récits et personnages bibliques dans la légend mahometane." *Revue des études juives* 85 (1927): 113–36.

———. "Youschaʿ Al-Akbar et les Juifs de Kheybar dans le Roman d'Antar: Un mouvement messianique dans l'ancienne arabie." *Revue des études juives* 84 (1927): 113–37; and 85 (1927): 56–62. Original in Hebrew in *Festschrift zum 50 Jährigen Bestehen der Franz-Josef-Landesrabbiner Schule in Budapest,* ed. Ludwig Blau (Buda-pest, 1927), 1–14.

Heller-Wilensky, Sarah. "The Guide and the Gate: The Dialectical Influence of Mai-monides on Isaac ibn Latif and Early Spanish Kabbalah." In *A Straight Path: Studies in Medieval Philosophy and Culture,* edited by Ruth Link-Salinger. Washington, D.C., 1988. Original Hebrew version in *Jerusalem Studies in Jewish Thought* 7 (1988): 289–306.

———. "On the 'First Created Thing' in the Origins of Kabbalah and Its Philosophi-cal Sources" (in Hebrew). In *Studies in Jewish Thought,* edited by Sarah Heller-Wilensky and Moshe Idel. Jerusalem, 1989, 261–76.

Hellholm, D., ed. *Apocalypticism in the Mediterranean World and the Near East.* Tübingen, 1983.

Hennecke, E. *New Testament Apocrypha.* Edited by W. Schneemelcher, translated by R. McL. Wilson. 2 vols. Tübingen, 1973.

Henning, W. B. "The Inscriptions of Tang-i-Azao." *Bulletin of the School of Oriental and African Studies* 20 (1957): 335–42.

Henrichs, A. L., and L. Koenen. "Der Kölner Mani-Kodex." *Zeitschrift für Papyrologie und Epigraphik* 19:1–85; 32:87–199; 44:201–318; 48:1–59.

Heschel, A. J. *Maimonides.* Translated by Joachim Neugroschel. New York, 1982.

Hildesheimer, E. E. "Mystik und Agada im Urteile der Gaonen R. Scherira und R. Hai." *Festschrift für Jacob Rosenheim.* Frankfurt am Main, 1931, 259–86.

Himmelfarb, Martha. *Tours of Hell: An Apocalyptic Form in Jewish and Christian Litera-ture.* Philadelphia, 1983.

Hirschberg, H. J. Z. "The Footsteps of the Messiah in Arab Lands, in the Fifth and Sixth Centuries after the Second Temple" (in Hebrew). *Memorial Book of the Rab-binic Seminary of Vienna.* Jerusalem, 112–24.

———. *A History of the Jews in North Africa.* Jerusalem, 1965.

Hirschfeld, Hartwig. "Historical and Legendary Controversies between Mohammed and the Rabbis." *Jewish Quarterly Review,* o.s., 10 (1898): 100–116.

Hodgson, Marshall G. S. "Batiniyya." *Encyclopedia of Islam.* 2d ed. vol 1:1098–1100.

———. "Hemispheric Interregional History as an Approach to World History." *Cahiers d'histoire mondiale* 1 (1954): 715–23.

———. "How Did the Shi'a Become Sectarian?" *Journal of the American Oriental Society* 75 (1955): 1–13.

———. *The Venture of Islam*. 3 vols. Chicago, 1974.

Hoenig, Sidney. "Pre-Karaism and the Sectarian (Qumran) Scrolls." In *Jubilee Volume in Honor of Dr. Joshua Finkel*. New York, 1974, 71–93.

———. "Qumran Rules of Interpretation." *Revue de Qumran* 6 (1969): 559–67.

Holmberg, Bo. "The Public Debate as a Literary Genre in Arabic Literature." *Orientalia Suecana* 38–39 (1989–1990): 45–53.

Hone, William, trans. *The Apocryphal New Testament*. London, 1820.

Horovitz, Josef. "'Abdallah ibn Salam." *Encyclopedia of Islam*. 2d ed.

———. "Buluqya." *Zeitschrift der Deutschen Morgenländischen Gesellschaft* 55 (1901): 519–525.

———. "The Earliest Biographies of the Prophet and Their Authors." *Islamic Culture* 1 (1927) 535–59; 2 (1928) 22–50, 164–82, 495–526.

———. "Jewish Proper Names and Derivatives in the Koran." *Hebrew Union College Annual* 2 (1925): 145–227.

———. "The Origins of the 'Arabian Nights.'" *Islamic Culture* 1 (1927): 36–57.

———. Review of *Het Boek*, by G. F. Pijper. *Der Islam* 16 (1927): 296–98.

Hudson, Wayne. *The Marxist Philosophy of Ernst Bloch*. New York, 1982.

Humaydi, Abu 'Abdallah al-. *Jadwa al-Muqtabis fi Dhikr Wulat al-Andalus*. Edited by Muhammad Al-Tanji. Cairo, 1953.

Hurtado, Larry W. *One God One Lord: Early Christian Devotion and Ancient Jewish Monotheism*. Philadelphia, 1988.

Hurwitz, Siegmund. *Die Gestalt des Sterbenden Messias: Religionspsychologische Aspekte der judischen Apokalyptik*. Zurich, 1958.

Husik, Isaac. *A History of Mediaeval Jewish Philosophy*. 1916. New York, 1969.

Huxley, George. "Byzantinochazarika." *Hermathena* 148 (1990): 69–87.

Ibn 'Abd Rabbihi. *Kitab al-'Iqd al-Farid*. 7 vols. Cairo, 1375/1956.

Ibn Abi Usaibia. *'Uyun al-Anba fi Tabaqat al-Atibba*. Cairo, 1882.

Ibn al-Hajj al-Tilimsani. *Kitab Shumus al-Anwar wa Kunuz al-Asrar al-Kubra*. Cairo, 1911.

Ibn al-Jauzi, Abu al-Faraj. *Kitab al Maudu'at*. Cairo, 1983.

Ibn al-Qifti. *Ta'rikh al-Hukama'*. Edited by J. Lippert. Leipzig, 1903.

Ibn al-Nadim. *The Fihrist of al-Nadim*. Translated by Bayard Dodge. 2 vols. New York, 1970.

Ibn Babuya, Abu Ja'far Muhammad al-Qummi. *Kitab al-Tauhid*. Teheran, 1967.

———. *Man la Yahduruh al-Faqih*. Teheran, 1971.

Ibn Daniyal. *Khayal al-Zill wa-Tamthiliyyat Ibn Daniyal*. Edited by Ibrahim Hammada. Cairo, 1963.

Ibn Hajar al-Askalani. *Kitab al-Isaba fi tamyiz al-Sahabah*. 8 vols. Cairo, 1905–7.

Ibn Hazm, 'Ali ibn Ahmad. *Kitab al-Fisal fi al-Milal wa al-Nihal*. Cairo, 1963.

Ibn Hisham. *Life of Muhammed*. Translated by A. Guillaume. Oxford and Lahore, 1955.

Ibn Gabirol, Solomon. *The Selected Poems of Solomon Ibn Gabirol*. Edited and translated by Israel Davidson and Israel Zangwill. Philadelphia, 1923.

Ibn Mansur al-Yaman, Ja'far. *Kitab al-'Alim wal-Ghulam*. In *Sara'ir wa asrar al-nutaqa'*, edited by Mustafa Ghalib. Beirut, 1984.

————. *Kitab al-Kashf*. Beirut, 1984.

Ibn Qutayba, ʿAbdallah ibn Muslim. *Traité des divergences du hadit d'Ibn Qutayba*. Translated by Gérard Lecomte. Damascus, 1962.

Ibn Qayyim al-Jauziyya, Shams al-Din Abu Bakr Muhammad ibn Abu Bakr al-Zarʿi. *Ahkam Ahl al-Dhimma*. Edited by Subhi Salih. 2 vols. Damascus, 1381/1961.

————. *Ighathat al-Lahfan min Masayid al-Shaytan*. 2 vols. Cairo, 1357/1939.

Ibn Shadhan, Abu Muhammad al-Fadl. *Kitab al-Idah*. Beirut, 1982.

Ibn Taymiyya. *Al-Jawab al-Sahih li-man baddala Din al-Masih*. Cairo, 1905.

————. *Kitab Minhaj al-Sunna al-Nabawiyya fi Naqd al-Kalam al-Shiʿa wa 'l-Qadariyya*. Cairo, 1903.

Ibn Yeruham, Salmon. *Commentary on Lamentations I*. Edited by S. Feurstein. Cracow, 1892.

Idel, Moshe. *Kabbalah: New Perspectives*. New Haven, Conn., and London, 1988.

Isfaraʾini, Abu al-Muzaffar Shahbur b. Tahir al-. *Al-Tabsir fi al-Din wa Tamyiz al-firqa al-Najiyya ʿan al-Firaq al-Halikin*. Edited by Muhammad Zahid ibn al-Hasan al-Kauthari. Cairo, 1940.

Isser, Stanley. *The Dositheans*. Leiden, 1976.

Ivanow, Vladimir. *Ibn al-Qaddah: The Alleged Founder of Ismailism*. 2d ed. Bombay, 1957.

————. "Notes sur l' 'Umm' l-Kitab.'" *Revue des études islamiques* 6(1932):419–81.

Ivanov, V. V. "The Semiotic Theory of Carnival as the Inversion of Bipolar Opposites." In *Carnival*, edited by Thomas Sebeok. Berlin, New York, and Amsterdam, 1984, 11–34.

Ivry, Alfred L. "Islamic and Greek Influences on Maimodnies' Philosophy." In *Maimonides and Philosophy*, edited by Shlomo Pines and Yirmiyahu Yovel. Dordrecht, 1986, 139–56.

Jacob, C. "Ein ägyptischer market in 13. Jahrhundert." *Sitzungberichte der Königlich Bayaerlischen Akademie der Wissenschften, Philosophique-philologische und historische Klasse* 10 (1910).

Jafri, S. H. M. *The Origins and Early Development of Shiʿa Islam*. Beirut, 1979.

Jahiz, Abu ʿUthman ʿAmr ibn Bahr. *Kitab al-Hayawan*. Edited by ʿAbd al-Salam Muhammad Harun. 8 vols. Cairo, 1385–89/1965–69.

Jauss, Hans Robert. "The Theory of Reception: A Retrospective of Its Unrecognized Prehistory." In *Literary Theory Today*, edited by Peter Collier and Helga Geyer-Ryan. Ithaca, 1990, 53–74.

Jay, Martin. *The Dialectical Imagination*. New York, 1973.

————. *Permanent Exiles*. New York, 1985.

Jeffrey, Arthur. *Qurʾan as Scripture*. New York, 1980.

Jettmar, Karl. "Hebrew Inscriptions in the Western Himalayas." In *Orientalia Iosephi Tucci Memoriae Dicata*, edited by G. Gnoli and L. Lanciotti. Rome, 1987, 667–70.

Jospe, Raphael. "Early Philosophical Commentaries on the *Sefer Yesirah*: Some Comments." *Revue des études juives* 149 (1990): 364–415.

Kahle, Paul. *The Cairo Geniza*. 2d ed. Oxford, 1959.

Kaplan, C. H. "The Hidden Name." *Journal of the American Society for Oriental Research* 13 (1929): 181–84.

Kaplan, Mordechai Menehem. "Reconstructionism." In *Living Schools of Religion*, edited by Vergilus Ferm. New York, 1956, 431–37.

Kapplar, Claude, ed. *Apocalypses et voyages dans l'au-delà*. Paris, 1987.

Kashshi, Abu ʿAmr al-. *Rijal al-Kashshi*. Karbala, 1962.

Katsh, Abraham. *Judaism and the Koran*. New York, 1962.

Katz, Jacob. "Religion as a Uniting and Dividing Force in Modern Jewish History." In *The Role of Religion in Modern Jewish History*, edited by Jacob Katz. Cambridge, Mass., 1975, 1–19.

Kaufman, David. "Pseudo-Empedokles als Quelle Salomon ibn Gabirol." In *Studien über Salomon ibn Gabirol*. Budapest, 1899. Reprint, 1972.

Kearney, Richard. *Dialogues with Contemporary Continental Thinkers*. Manchester, 1984.

————. *Poetics of Imagining: From Husserl to Lyotard*. London, 1991.

————. *The Wake of Imagination: Toward a Postmodern Culture*. Minneapolis, 1988.

Kee, H. C., trans. "Testament of the Twelve Patriachs." In *The Old Testament Pseudepigrapha*, edited by James H. Charlesworth. 2 vols. New York, 1983–85, 1:775–828.

Kennedy, J. "The Gospel of the Infancy, the Lalita Vistara and the Vishnu Purana: Or the Transmission of Religious Legends between India and the West." *Journal of the Royal Asiatic Society* (1917): 209–43, 469–540.

Khadduri, Majid. *War and Peace in the Law of Islam*. Baltimore, 1955.

Khoury, R. J., ed. *Les Legendes prophetiques dans l'Islam*. Wiesbaden, 1978.

Khwarizmi, Muhammad ibn Ahmad al-. *Liber Mafatih al-Olum*. Edited by G. Van Vloten. Leiden, 1895.

Kiener, Ronald C. "Jewish Isma'ilism in Twelfth-Century Yemen: R. Nethanel Ben al-Fayyumi." *Jewish Quarterly Review* 74 (1984): 249–66.

Kippenberg, H. G. *Garizim und Synagoge: Traditionsgeschichliche untersuchungen zur Samaritanischen Religion der Aramäischen Periode*. Berlin, 1971.

————. "Name and Person in Ancient Judaism and Christianity." In *Concepts of Person in Religion and Thought*, edited by Hans G. Kippenberg, Yme b. Kuiper, and Andy T. Sanders. New York, Berlin, 1990, 103–25.

Kirsch, Hilde, ed. *The Well Tended Tree*. New York, 1971.

Kirsch, James. *The Reluctant Prophet*. Los Angeles, 1983.

Kisch, Guido. *The Jews of Medieval Germany*. Chicago, 1949.

Kister, M. J. "Haddithu 'an bani isra'ila wa-la haraja." *Israel Oriental Studies* 2 (1972): 215–39.

————. "Legends in *tafsir* and *hadith* Literature: The Creation of Adam and Related Stories." In *Approaches to the History of the Interpretation of the Qur'an*, edited by A. Rippin. Oxford, 1988: 82–114.

Kister, M. J., and Menahem Kister. "Do Not Assimilate Yourselves . . . La tashabbahu . . ." *Jerusalem Studies in Arabic and Islam* 12 (1989): 321–71.

Kister, Menahem. "Plucking the Grain on the Sabbath and the Jewish-Christian Debate" (in Hebrew). *Jerusalem Studies in Jewish Thought* 3 (1984): 349–66.

Klatt, Norbert. *Literarische Beiträge zum Problem Christlich-Buddhistischer Parallel*. Cologne, 1982.

Klausner, J. *The Messiah Idea in Israel*. New York, 1955.

Klein-Franke, Felix. *Iatromathematics in Islam*. Hildesheim, Zürich, and New York, 1984.

Klima, O. "Mazdak und die Juden." *Archív Orientálni* 24 (1956): 420–31.

Knox, Ronald A. *Enthusiasm: A Chapter in the History of Religion with Reference to the Seventeenth and Eighteenth Centuries*. Oxford and New York, 1961.

Kobler, Franz, trans. *Letters of Jews through the Ages*. 2 vols. New York, 1952.

Koch, Glenn Alan. "Critical Investigation of Epiphanius' Knowledge of the Ebionites." Ph.D. Dissertation, University of Pennsylvania, 1976.

Kohlberg, Etan. "From Imamiyya to Ithna-ʿAshariyya." *Bulletin of the School of Oriental and African Studies* 39 (1976): 521–34.

———. "Some Imami Shiʿi Views on the *Sahaba*." *Jerusalem Studies in Arabic and Islam* 5 (1984): 143–75.

———. "The Term 'Rafida' in Imami Shiʿi Usage." *Journal of the American Oriental Society* 99 (1979): 677–79.

Kopf, L. "Religious Influences on Medieval Arabic Philology." *Studia Islamica* 5 (1956): 33–61.

Kraemer, Joel L. "Apostates, Rebels and Brigands." *Israel Oriental Studies* 10 (1983): 34–74.

———. *Humanism in the Renaissance of Islam: The Cultural Revival during the Buyid Age*. Leiden, 1986.

Kraucauer, Siegfried. *History: The Last Things before the Last*. New York, 1969.

Kraus, Paul. "Hebräische und syrische Bibelzitate in Ismaʿilitischen Schriften." *Der Islam* 14 (1931): 243–63.

Kraus, Samuel. *Studien zur byzantinischen-jüdischen Geschichte*. Leipzig, 1914.

Kritzeck, J. *Peter the Venerable and Islam*. Princeton, 1964.

Krom, N. J. *The Life of Buddha on the Stupa of Barabudur According to the Lalitavistara Text*. The Hague, 1926.

Kuhn, E. "Buddhistisches in den apokryphen Evangelien." In *Gurupujakaumudi, Festgabe . . . Albrecht Weber*. Leipzig, 1896.

Labib, S. Y. "Ibn al-Mukaffaʿ." *Encyclopedia of Islam*. 2d ed., 3:885–86.

Lachs, Samuel T. "The Alphabet of Ben Sira: A Study in Folk Literature." *Gratz College Annual of Jewish Studies* (1973).

Lafargue, Michael, J. *Language and Gnosis*. Philadelphia, 1984.

Lammens, Henri. *Fatima et les filles de Mahomet*. Rome, 1912.

Lane, E. W. *An Account of the Manners and Customs of the Modern Egyptians*. 1836. Mew York, Reprint, 1973.

Laoust, Henri. "Comment définir le sunnisme et le chiisme." *Revue des études islamiques* 47 (1979): 1–17.

———. "L'hérésiographie musulmane sous les Abbassides." *Cahiers de civilisation medievale* 10 (1967): 157–78.

———. *Profession de Foi d'Ibn Batta*. Damascus, 1958.

Lasker, Daniel. "Rabbinism and Karaism: The Quest for Supremacy." In *Great Schisms in Jewish History*, edited by Raphael Jospe and Stanley M. Wagner. Denver and New York, 1981, 47–73.

Lauterbach, J. Z. "The Origin and Development of Two Sabbath Ceremonies." *Hebrew Union College Annual* 15 (1940): 367–424.

Lazard, G. "La Dialectologie de Judeo-Persan." *Studies in Bibliography and Booklore* 7 (1968): 77–99.

Lazarus-Yafeh, Hava. "Ezra-ʿUzayr: Metamorphosis of a Polemical Motif" (in Hebrew). *Tarbis* 55 (1986): 359–79. In English in William Brinner and Stephen Ricks, *Studies in Islamic and Judaic Tradition*, vol. 2 (Atlanta, 1989).

———. *Intertwined Worlds. Medieval Islam and Bible Criticism*. Princeton, 1992.

———. "Judeo-Arabic Culture." In *Encyclopaedia Judaica Yearbook 1977/1978*. Jerusalem, 1979, 101–10.

———. "Some Halakhic Differences between Judaism and Islam" (in Hebrew). *Tarbis* 51 (1982): 207–26. Translated as "Some Differences between Judaism and Islam as Two Religions of Law." *Religion* 14 (1985): 175–91.

Le Doeuff, Michèle. *The Philosophical Imaginary.* Translated by Colin Gordon. Stanford, Calif., 1989.

Lecker, Michael. "Muhammed at Medina: A Geographical Approach." *Jerusalem Studies in Arabic and Islam* 6 (1985): 29–63.

———. "A Note on Early Marriage Links between Qurashis and Jewish Women." *Jerusalem Studies in Arabic and Islam* 10 (1987): 17–40.

Leibman, Charles. *Deceptive Images: Toward a Redefinition of American Judaism.* New Brunswick, N.J., and Oxford, 1988.

Leveen, J. "Mohammed and His Jewish Companions." *Jewish Quarterly Review* 16 (1926): 399–406.

Levi, Israel. "La nativité de Ben Sira." *Revue des études juives* 29 (1894): 197–205.

———. "L'apocalypse de Zorobabel et le roi de Perse Siroes." *Revue des études juives* 69 (1919): 108–21.

Levi, Leo. "On the Astronomical Aspects of Twilight in Halakha." In *'Ateret Tzvi: Jubilee Volume for Rabbi Joseph Breur.* New York, 1962, 251–63.

Lévinas, Emmanuel. "Judaism and the Present." In *The Levinas Reader*, edited by Séan Hand. Cambridge and Oxford, 1989, 252–59.

Levine, David, trans. *The Bustan Al-Ukul.* New York, 1908. Reedited and translated by J. Qafih (Jerusalem, 1954).

Lévi-Strauss, Claude. *Tristes Tropiques.* Translated by John and Doreen Weightman. New York, 1977.

Lewin, B. *Osar ha-Geonim.* Jerusalem, 1931.

Lewis, Bernard. "An Apocalyptic Vision of Islamic History." *Bulletin of the School of Oriental and African Studies* 13 (1950): 305–38.

———. *The Jews of Islam.* Princeton, 1984.

———. "The Legend of the Jewish Origin of the Fatimid Caliphs" (in Hebrew). *Melilah* 3–4 (1950): 85–87.

———. *The Origins of Ismailism.* Cambridge, 1940.

———. "Paltiel: A Note." *Bulletin of the School of Oriental and African Studies* 30 (1967): 177–81.

———. "The Regnal Titles of the First 'Abbasid Caliphs." *Dr. Zakir Husain Presentation Volume.* New Delhi, 1968, 13–22.

———. *Semites and Anti-Semites.* New York, 1987.

Lieberman, Saul. *Shekiin* (in Hebrew). 2d ed. Jerusalem, 1939.

Liebes, Yehudah. "Who Makes the Horn of Jesus to Flourish" (in Hebrew). *Jerusalem Studies in Jewish Thought* 3 (1984): 313–48.

Lillie, Arthur. *The Popular Life of the Buddha.* London, 1883.

Loewenthal, E. "La storia del fiume Sambation: Alcune note sulla tradizione ebraica antica e medievale." In *Biblische und Judaistische Studien: Festschrift für Paolo Sacchi*, edited by Angelo Vivian. Frankfurt am Main, Bern, New York, and Paris, 1990, 651–63.

Löwy, Michael. "Jewish Messianism and Libertarian Utopia in Central Europe (1900–1933)" *New German Critique* 20 (1980): 105–15.

———. "Religion, Utopia and Counter-Modernity: The Allegory of the Angel of History in Walter Benjamin." *Social Compass* 36 (1989): 95–104.

Macaullife, Max A. *The Sikh Religion.* Vol. 1 of 6. Delhi, 1963.

MacDonald, D. B. *The Development of Muslim Theology.* New York, 1903.

———. "Sihr." *Encyclopedia of Islam.* 1st ed., 4:409–17.

MacIntyre, Alistair. "Epistemological Crises, Dramatic Narrative and the Philosophy of Science." *Monist* (1977): 453–72.

Mack, Burton. "Wisdom Make a Difference: Alternatives to Messianic Configurations." In *Judaisms and Their Messiahs at the Turn of the Christian Era*. Cambridge, 1987, 15–48.

Madelung, Wilferd. "Al-Mahdi." *Encyclopedia of Islam*. 2d ed. vol 5:1230–38.

———. *Der Imam al-Qasim ibn Ibrahim*. Berlin, 1965.

———. "Häresiographie." In *Grundriss der arabischen Philologie*, edited by Helmut Gätje. Wiesbaden, 1987.

———. *Religious Trends in Early Islamic Iran*. Albany, N.Y., 1988.

———. "Aba 'Isa al-Warraq über die Bardesaniten, Marcioniten und Kantaer." In *Studien zur Geschichte und Kultur des Vorderen Orients*, edited by H. R. Roemer and A. Noth. Leiden, 1981, 210–24.

Magne, J. "Recherches sur les psaumes 151, 154, et 155," *Revue de Qumran* (1975): 503–8.

Mahdi, Muhsin. "Islamic Theology and Philosophy." *Encyclopedia Britannica*. 15th ed., 1012–25.

Mahler, Raphael. *HaKaraim* (Hebrew translation of *Karaimer*). Merchavia, 1949.

———. *Karaimer*. New York, 1947.

Maimonides, Moses. *Iggeret Teiman*. Translated by Boaz Cohen. In *A Maimonides Reader*, edited by Isadore Twersky. New York, 1972, 437–63.

Maier, Johann. "Jüdische Literatur des Mittelalters im islamischen Bereich." In *Orientalisches Mittelalter*, edited by Wolfhart Heinrichs. Wiesbaden, 1990, 524–45.

Majlisi, Muhammad Baqir al-. *Bihar al-Anwar*. 110 volumes. Teheran, 1956–72.

Makdisi, George. *The Rise of Colleges*. Edinburgh, 1981.

Malti-Douglas, Fedwa. *Woman's Body, Woman's Word: Gender and Discourse in Arabo-Islamic Writing*. Princeton, 1991.

Mamorstein, A. *The Doctrine of Merits in Old Rabbinic Literature*. New York, 1968.

Mann, Jacob. "An Early Theologico-Polemical Work." In *The Collected Articles of Jacob Mann*. Gedara, 1971. 3:411–59.

———. "Geniza Fragments of the Palestinian Order of Service." *Hebrew Union College Annual* 2 (1925): 260–328.

———. "The Responsa of the Babylonian Geonim as a Source of Jewish History," *Jewish Quarterly Review* 7 (1916–17): 457–90.

———. *Texts and Studies in Jewish History and Literature*. 2 vols. 1931. Reprint, New York, 1972.

Mannheim, Karl. *Ideology and Utopia*. New York, 1946.

Maqdisi, Mutahhar ibn Tahir al-. *Kitab al-Bad' wa al-Ta'rikh*. 6 vols. In French as *Livre de la création et de l'histoire*, ed. and trans. C. Huart (Paris, 1899–19).

Maqrizi, Abu al-'Abbas Ahmad b. 'Abd al-Qadir al-Husaini Taqi al-Din al-. *Al-Mawa'iz wa al-I'tibar fi Dhikr al-Khitat wa al-Athar*. 2 vols. Cairo, 1892.

Marcus, J. and Z. Tar, eds. *Georg Lukács: Theory, Culture and Politics*. New Brunswick, N.J., 1989.

Marcus, Jacob, ed. *The Jew in the Medieval World: A Sourcebook*. New York, 1969.

Mardus, J. C., and E. Powys Mathers, trans. *Alf Layla Wa Layla* (The Book of the Thousand and One Nights). 8 vols. New York, 1930.

Margulies, Reuben. *Mal'akhe 'Elyon*. Jerusalem, 1964.

Marmorstein, Arthur. *Studies in Jewish Theology*. Oxford, 1950.

Marquet, Yves. *La Philosophie des Ihwan al-Safa'*. Algiers, 1975.

———. "Les Ikhwan al-Safa' et le christianisme." *Islamochristiana* 8 (1982): 129–58.

Martin, Richard C., ed. *Approaches to Islam in Religious Studies.* Tucson, 1985.

Massignon, Louis. "Language." In *Mid-East World-Center*, edited by Ruth Nanda Anshen. New York, 1956, 235–51.

———. "Le Folklore chez les Mystiques Musulmanes." *Opera Minora* 2 (1963): 345–52.

———. "Al-Muhassin ibn ʿAli." *Encyclopedia of Islam.* 2d ed. 7:468.

———. "Origines Shiʿites de la Famille viziral des Banu'l Furat." In *Melanges Gaudefroy-Denombynes* (Paris, 1935). Reprinted in *Opera Minora* 1 (1963): 484–85.

———. *The Passion of al-Hallaj.* 3 vols. Translated by Herbert Mason. Princeton, 1982.

———. *Salman Pak and the Spiritual Origins of Iranian Islam.* Bombay, 1955.

Masʿudi, Abu al-Hasan ʿAli ibn al-Hasan. *Ithbat al-wasiyya lil-imam ʿAli ibn Abi Talib alayhi al-salam.* Najaf, 1955.

———. *Kitab al-Tanbih wa al-Ishraf.* Edited by M. J. de Goeje. Leiden, 1894. In French, *Le Livre de l'Avertissement et de la Révision*, trans. Carra de Vaux. Paris, 1896.

———. *Muruj al Dhahab. Les Prairies d'Or.* Edited by C. Barbier de Meynard and Pavet de Courteille. 9 vols. Paris, 1861–77.

Matt, Daniel, trans. *The Zohar: The Book of Enlightenment.* New York, Ramsey, Toronto, 1983.

Maturidi, Muhammad ibn Muhammad al-. *Ta'wilat Ahl al-Sunna.* Baghdad, 1983.

Mayer, L. A. "The Status of Jews under the Mamluks" (in Hebrew). In *The Magnes Anniversary Book*, edited by F. I. Baer, F. S. Bodenheimer, J. N. Epstein, M. Fekete, A. Fodor, I. J. Kliyler, and L. A. Mayer. Jerusalem, 1938, 161–67.

Meddeb, Abd el Wahab. "Le palimpseste du bilingue Ibn ʿArabi et Dante." *Du bilinguisme* edited by Jalil Benani. Paris, 1985, 125–44.

Meier, Fritz. "Some Aspects of Inspiration by Demons in Islam." In *The Dream of Human Societies*, edited by G. Von Gruenbaum and Roger Caillois. Berkeley and L. A., 1966, 421–31.

Mendes-Flohr, Paul. "Mendelssohn and Rosenzweig." *Der Philosoph Franz Rosenzweig (1886–1929).* Vol. 1. Freiburg and Munich, 1988: 213–23.

———. "'To Brush History against the Grain': The Eschatology of the Frankfurt School and Ernst Bloch." *Journal of the American Academy of Religion Society* 51 (1983): 631–58.

Meron, Y. "Points de contact des droits juif et musulman." *Studia islamica* 60 (1984): 83–119.

Mez, Adam. *The Renaissance of Islam.* Patna, 1937.

Milgrom, Jacob. "The Concept of Maʿal in the Bible and the Ancient Near East." *Journal of the American Oriental Society* 96 (1976).

Milman, H. H. *The History of the Jews.* 3 vols. New York, 1831.

Mingana, Alphonse. "Syriac Influence on the Style of the Kur'an." *Bulletin of the John Rylands Library* 11 (1927): 77–99.

———. ed. *Apocalypse of Peter.* Woodbrooke Studies, vol. 3. Cambridge, 1931.

Mittwoch, Eugen. "Muslimische Fetwas über die Samaritaner." *Orientalistische Literaturzeitung* 29 (1926): cols. 845–49.

———. *Zur Entstehungsgeschichte des islamischen Gebets und Kultus.* Berlin, 1913.

Monnot, Guy. *Islam et religions.* Paris, 1986.

———. *Penseurs Musulmans et Religions Iraniennes.* Paris, 1974.

Montgomery, James. *Aramaic Incantation Texts*. Philadelphia, 1913.

——. *The Samaritans, the Earliest Jewish Sect: Their History, Theology and Literature*. Philadelphia, 1907.

Moore, G. M. "Metatron." *Harvard Theological Review* 15 (1922): 62–85.

Morabia, Albert. "Ibn Tamiyya, les juifs et la Tora." *Studia Islamica* 49 (1979): 91–123; and 50 (1980): 77–109.

——. "L'antéchrist (al-dajjal) s'est-il manifesté du vivant de la'envoyé d' Allah?" *Journal asiatique* 267 (1979): 81–99.

Morgenstern, Julian. "The Ark, the Ephod, and the Tent of Meeting." *Hebrew Union College Annual* 17 (1942): 153–267.

Morony, Michael. "Conquerers and Conquered: Iran." In *Studies on the First Century of Islamic History*, edited by G. H. A. Juynboll. Carbondale and Edwardsville, Ill., 1982, 73–89.

——. *Iraq after the Muslim Conquest*. Princeton, 1984.

Morray-Jones, C. R. A. "Transformational Mysticism in the Apocalyptic-Merkabah Tradition." *Journal of Jewish Studies* 43 (1992): 1–31.

Mosès, Stephane. *L'Ange de l'histoire: Benjamin, Scholem, Rosenzweig*. Paris, 1992.

Mufid, Shaykh al-. *Kitab al-Irshad: The Book of Guidance into the Lives of the Twelve Imams*. Translated by I. K. A. Howard. London, 1981.

Müller, Werner. "Mazdak and the Alphabet Mysticism of the East." *History of Religions* 3 (1963–64): 72–82.

Münster, Arno. *Utopie, Messianismus und Apokalypse in Frühwerk Ernst Bloch*. Frankfurt, 1982.

Murtada, 'Alam al-Huda al-. *Tabsirat al-'Awamm fi-Maqalat al-Anam*. Edited by Abbas Iqbal. Teheran, 1934.

Nagel, Tilman. *Alexander der Grosse in der Frühislamischen Volksliterateur*. Walldorf-Hessen, 1978.

Nashwan al-Himyari, Abu Sa'id al-Yamani. *Al-Hur al-'Ayn*. Edited by Kamal Mustafa'. Cairo, 1367/1948.

Nasr, Seyyed Hossein. *Three Muslim Sages*. Cambridge, Mass., 1964.

Naveh, Joseph. "A Good Subduing, There Is None Like It" (in Hebrew). *Tarbis* 57 (1985) 367–82.

Naveh, Joseph, and Shaul Shaked. *Amulets and Magic Bowls: Aramaic Incantations of Late Antiquity*. Jerusalem, 1985.

Nawbakhti, al-Hasan ibn Musa al-. *Firaq al-Shi'ah* Translated by M. J. Maskhur. *Revue de l'histoire des religions* 154 (1958), 153 (1957).

——. *Kitab Firaq al-Shi'a*. Edited by H. Ritter. Istanbul, 1931.

Nemoy, Leon. "'Anan ben David: A Re-appraisal of the Historical Data." In *Karaite Studies*, edited by Philip Birnbaum. New York, 1971, 309–18.

——. "Al-Qirqisani's Account of the Jewish Sect and Christianity." *Hebrew Union College Annual* 7 (1930): 317–97.

——. "The Attitude of the Early Karaites towards Christianity." In *Salo Wittmayer Baron Jubilee Volume on the Occasion of His Eightieth Birthday*, vol. 2, edited by Saul Lieberman and Arthur Hyman. Jerusalem and New York, 1974–75, 697–715.

——. "Elijah ben Abraham and his Tract against the Rabbanites." *Hebrew Union College Annual* 51 (1980): 63–87.

——. Review of *The Jews of Islam*, by Bernard Lewis. *Jewish Quarterly Review* 75 (1984): 186–88.

———. "Stroumsa's Edition of al-Muqammis's *'Ishrun Maqalah.*" *Jewish Quarterly Review* 82 (1991): 233–37.

———, ed. *Karaite Anthology*. New Haven, 1952.

Netton, Ian. *Muslim Neoplatonists*. London, 1982.

Neusner, Jacob. *A History of the Jews in Babylonia*. Vol. 5. Leiden, 1970.

Neusner, Jacob, W. S. Green, and E. Frerichs, eds. *Judaisms and Their Messiahs at the Turn of the Christian Era*. Cambridge, 1987.

Newby, Gordon D. *A History of the Jews of Arabia*. Columbia, S.C., 1988.

———. *The Making of the Last Prophet*. Columbia, S.C., 1989.

———. "Observations about an Early Judaeo-Arabic." *Jewish Quarterly Review* 61 (1971): 214–21.

———. "Tafsir Isra'iliyyat." *Journal of the American Academy of Religion*, thematic issue S (1980): 685–97.

Newsom, Carol. *Songs of the Sabbath Sacrifice: A Critical Edition*. Atlanta, 1985.

Nicholson, Reynold A. *The Mystics of Islam*. 1914. Reprint, New York, 1975.

Nickelsberg, George W. E., and Michael Stone. *Faith and Piety in Early Judaism*. Philadelphia, 1983.

Niebuhr, H. Richard. *Radical Monotheism and Western Culture*. New York, 1960.

Niethammer, Lutz. *Posthistoire: Has History Come to an End?* Translated by Patrick Camiller. London and New York, 1992.

Niewohner, Fredrich. *Veritas sive Varietas: Lessings Toleranzparabel und das Buch Von den drei Betrügen*. Heidelberg, 1988.

Nini, Yehuda. "A Writ of Protection for the Jews Attributed to the Prophet Muhammad" (in Hebrew). In *Studies in Aggada and Jewish Folklore Presented to Dov Noy on His Sixtieth Birthday*, edited by Issachar Ben-Ami and Joseph Dan. Jerusalem, 1983, 157–96.

Nizam Al-Mulk. *The Book of Government, or Rules for Kings*. Translated by Hubert Darke. London, Henley, and Boston, 1978.

Nock, Arthur Darby. *Conversion*. Cambridge, 1933.

Noja, S. "La Question se pose encore une fois: 'La pureté rituelle de l'islam dérive-t-elle ou non de celle du Judaïsme?'" *Jerusalem Studies in Arabic and Islam* 10 (1987): 183–95.

Noldeke, Theodore. *Sketches from Eastern History*. London, 1892.

Norris, H. T. *The Adventures of 'Antar*. Guildford and Surrey, 1980.

Noth, Albrecht. "Isphahan-Nihawand: Eine quellenkritische Studie zur Frühislamischen Historiographie." *Zeitschrift der Deutschen Morgenländischen Gesellschaft* 118 (1968): 274–96.

Nu'man ibn Muhammad Abu Hanifa, al-. *Daa'im al-Islam*. Edited by A. A. Fyzee. Cairo, 1951.

Nu'mani, Muhammad ibn Ibrahim. *Kitab al-Ghayba*. Beirut, 1964.

Odeberg, H. *3Enoch*. Cambridge, 1928. Reprint, New York, 1973.

Ostow, Mortimer. "Archetypes of Apocalypse in Dreams and Fantasies, and in Religious Scripture." *American Imago* 43 (1986): 307–34.

Palacios, Miguel Asin. *La Eschatologia Musulmana en la Divina Comedia*. 3d ed. Madrid, 1961.

Pardes, Ilana. *Countertraditions in the Bible: A Feminist Critique*. Cambridge, Mass., 1992.

Paret, R. "Contribution à l'étude des milieux culturels dans le Proche-Orient médiéval: L'Encyclopédisme arabo-musulman de 850 à 950." *Revue historique* 235 (1966): 47–100.

Parkes, James. *The Conflict of the Church and the Synagogue: A Study in the Origins of Anti-Semitism*. New York, 1974.

Paul, André. *Ecrits de Qumran et sectes juives aux premiers siècles de L'Islam*. Paris, 1969.

Pauliny, Jan. "Zur Rolle der Qussas bei der Entstehung und Überlieferung der populären Prophetenlegenden." *Asian and African Studies* 10 (1974): 125–41.

Payne, John, trans. *The Book of a Thousand and One Nights*. London, 1901.

Pearson, Birger A. *The Pneumatikos-Psychikos Terminology in I Corinthians*. Missoula, Mont., 1973.

Peeters, Paul. *Evangiles Apocryphes*. 2 vols. Paris, 1914.

Pellat, Charles. "Les encyclopédies dans le monde arabe." *Journal of World History* 9 (1966): 631–58.

Perlmann, Moshe. "Eleventh-Century Andalusian Authors on the Jews of Granada." *Proceedings of the American Academy for Jewish Research* 18 (1949): 269–90.

———. "A Legendary Story of Ka'b al-Ahbar's Conversion to Islam." In *The Joshua Starr Memorial Volume*. New York, 1953, 85–99.

———. "Medieval Polemics between Islam and Judaism." In *Religion in a Religious Age*, edited by S. D. Goitein. Cambridge, 1974, 103–139.

Peterson, Erik. "Urchristentum und Mandaismus." *Zeitschrift für neutestamentliche Wissenschaft und die Kunde der älteren Kirche* 27 (1928): 55–98.

Philonenko, Marc. "L'origine essenienne des 5 Ps. Syriaques de David." *Semitica* 9 (1959): 35–48.

Pijper, G. F. *Het Boek der Duizend Vragen*. Leiden, 1924.

Pines, Shlomo. "Fragment of a Jewish-Christian Composition from the Cairo Geniza." In *Studies in Islamic History and Civilization in Honour of Professor David Ayalon*. Jerusalem, 1986, 307–18.

———. "Gospel Quotations and Cognate Topics in 'Abd al-Jabbar's *Tathbit* in Relation to Early Christian and Judeo-Christian readings and traditions." *Jerusalem Studies in Arabic and Islam* 9 (1987): 195–279.

———. "Ibn Khaldun and Maimonides: A Comparison between Two Texts." *Studia Islamica* 32 (1970): 265–74.

———. "'Israel, My Firstborn' and the Sonship of Jesus." In *Studies in Mysticism and Religion*. Jerusalem, 1967, 177–90.

———. "The Jewish Christians of the Early Centuries of Christianity According to a New Source." *Proceedings of the Israel Academy of Sciences and Humanities* 2 (1968).

———. "Jewish Philosophy." In *The Encyclopedia of Philosophy*, edited by Paul Edwards. New York, 1967, 4:261–77.

———. "Judaeo-Christian Materials in an Arabic Jewish Treatise." *Proceedings of the American Academy for Jewish Research* 35 (1967): 187–217.

———. "Nathanaël ben al-Fayyûmî et la théologie ismaëlienne." *Revue de l'Histoire Juive en Egypte* 1 (1947): 5–22.

———. "Notes on Islam and on Arabic Christianity and Judaeo-Christianity." *Jerusalem Studies in Arabic and Islam* 4 (1984): 135–52.

———. "A Preliminary Note on the Relation Posited by Ibn Hazm between the Author of the *Book of Yosippon* and the 'Isawiyya Sect and on the Arabic Version of This Book." *Jerusalem Studies in Arabic and Islam* 6 (1985): 145–53.

———. "Shi'ite Terms and Conceptions in Judah Halevi's Kuzari." *Jerusalem Studies in Arabic and Islam* 2 (1980).

———. "Studies in Christianity and in Judaeo-Christianity Based on Arabic Sources." *Jerusalem Studies in Arabic and Islam* 6 (1985).

———. "Un Notice su les Resch Galuta chez un écrivan arabe du IXe siecle." *Revue des études juives* 100 (1936): 71–73.

Pines, S., and Y. Yovel, eds. *Maimonides and Philosophy: Papers Presented at the Sixth Jerusalem Philosophical Encounter, May 1985*. Dordrecht, Boston, and Lancaster, 1986.

Pingree, David. "Classical and Byzantine Astrology in Sassanian Persia." *Dumbarton Oaks Papers* 43 (1989): 227–39.

———. "Masha'allah: Some Sasanian and Syriac Sources." In *Essays on Islamic Philsosophy and Science*, edited by G. F. Hourani. Albany, N.Y., 1975, 5–13.

———. "Some Sources of the *Ghayat al-Hakim*." *Journal of the Warburg and Courtauld Institute* 43 (1980): 1–16.

Pingree, David and E. S. Kennedy, trans. *The Astrological History of Masha'allah*. Cambridge, 1971.

Pinsker, Simhah. *Likkute Kadmoniot*. Vienna, 1860.

Pirenne, Henri. *Mohammed and Charlemagne*. New York, n.d.

Plato. *The Republic*. Translated by G. M. A. Grube. Indianapolis, Ind., 1974.

Plessner, Martin (Meir). "Balinus." *Encyclopedia of Islam*. 2d ed. 1:994–95.

———. "Heresy and Rationalism in the First Centuries of Islam" (in Hebrew). In *The Ulama and Problems of Religion in the Muslim World: Studies in Memory of Professor Uriel Heyd*, edited by G. Baer. Jerusalem, 1971, 3–10.

———. "The Natural Sciences and Medicine." In *The Legacy of Islam*, edited by J. Schacht and C. E. Bosworth. New York and Oxford, 1979, 425–61.

Poonawala, Ismail K. "Isma'ili *ta'wil* of the Qur'an." In *Approaches to the History of the Interpretation of the Qur'an*, edited by A. Rippen. Oxford, 1988, 199–222.

Poznanski, Samuel. "Abu 'Isa al-Isfahani" (in Russian). *Evrenskaia entsiklopedia*. Mouton, 1969, vol. 1, cols. 171–74.

———. "Allegorische Gesetzauslegung bei den ältern Karäern." In *Studies in Jewish Literature in Honor of Professor Kaufmann Kohler*, edited by David Philipson, David Neumark, and Julian Morgenstern. Berlin, 1913. Reprint, New York, 1980.

———. "Anan et ses écrits." *Revue des études juives* 44 (1902): 161–87; 45 (1902): 50–69, 176–203.

———. Bibliographic additions to Heinrich Graetz. *Revue des études juives* 60:306–12.

———. "Founders of Sects in Judaism" (in Hebrew). *Reshumot* 1 (1917–18): 207–16.

———. "Karaites." *Encyclopedia of Religion and Ethics*. 7:662–72.

———. "Le nom de 'Isâ porté par les juifs." *Revue des études juives* 54 (1907): 276–79.

———. "Philon dans l'ancienne litterature judeo-arabe." *Revue des études juives* 50 (1905): 10–31.

Powers, David. "Reading/Misreading One Another's Scriptures: Ibn Hazm's Refutation of Ibn Nagrella al-Yahudi." In *Studies in Islamic and Judaic Traditions*, vol. 1, edited by William M. Brinner and Stephen D. Ricks. Atlanta, 1986, 109–23.

Pritsak, O. "The Khazar Kingdom's Conversion to Judaism." In *Harvard Ukrainian Studies* 2 (1980): 261–81.

———. "The Role of the Bosporus Kingdom and Late Hellenism as the Basis for the Medieval Cultures of the Territories North of the Black Sea." In *Mutual Effects of the Islamic and Judeo-Christian Worlds*, edited by A. Ascher, T. Halasi-Kun, and Bela Kiraly. Brooklyn, 1979, 3–21.

Puech, H. P. "Gnosis and Time." In *Man and Time: Papers From Eranos Yearbooks*, edited by Joseph Campbell. New York, 1957, 38–85.

Qadi, Wadad al-. "The Development of the Term Ghulat in Muslim Literature with Special Reference to the Kaysaniyya." In *Akten des VII Kongresses Fur Arabistik und Islamwissenschaften*, edited by A. Dietrich. Göttingen, 1976, 295–319.

———. *The Kaysaniyya in History and in the Arab Literature* (in Arabic). Beirut, 1974.

Qalamawi, Suhayr al-. *Alf Laylah wa Laylah*. Cairo, 1966.

Qalqashandi, Abu al-ʿAbbas Ahmad ibn ʿAli al-Shafiʿi al-. *Subh al-Aʿsha fi Sinaʿat al-Inshaʾ*. 14 vols. Cairo, 1963.

Qirqisani, Yaʿqub al-. *Kitab al-Anwar Wa al-Maraqib*. Edited by Leon Nemoy. 5 vols. in 4. New York, 1939–45.

———. *Yaʿqub al-Qirqisani on Jewish Sects and Christianity*. Translated by Wilfrid Lockwood. Frankfurt am Main, 1984.

Quispel, Gilles. "Jewish Gnosis and Mandaean Gnosticism." In *Les Textes de Nag Hammadi: Colloque sur la bibliotheque copte de Nag Hammadi*, edited by J. É. Menard. Leiden, 1975, 82–122.

———. "The Origins of the Gnostic Demiurge." In *Kyriakon: Festschrift Johannes Quasten*, edited by P. Granfield and J. A. Jungmann. Munster, 1970, 1:271–76.

Qummi, Sad ibn ʿAbdallah al-. *Kitab al-Maqalat wal Firaq*. Edited by M. G. Mashkur. 2 vols. Teheran, 1963.

Rabin, Chaim. *Qumran Studies*. New York, 1957. Reprint, 1975.

———. *The Scope of Semitic*. Princeton, 1986.

Rabinbach, Anson. "Between Messianism and Apocalypse: Benjamin, Bloch and Modern German Jewish Messianism." *New German Critique* 34 (1985): 78–124.

Radhakrishnan, Sarvepalli. *Eastern Religion and Western Thought*. Oxford, 1939. Reprint, New York, 1959.

Rajkowski, Withold. *Early Shiism in Iraq*. Ph.D. dissertation, University of London, 1955.

Rasaʾil Ikhwan al-Safaʾ. Edited by F. Dieterici. 4 vols. Leipzig, 1871–76 (subsequent editions include Cairo, 1928 and Beirut, 1957).

Razi, Abu Bakr Muhammad ibn Zakariyya al-. "The Book of the Philosophic Life." Translated by Charles E. Butterworth. *Interpretation* 20 (1993): 227–57.

Razi, Abu Hatim al-. *Aʿlam al-Nubuwwa*. Edited by Salah al-Sawy. Teheran, 1977.

Razi, Fakhr al-Din Abu ʿAbd Allah Muhammad b. ʿUmar b. al-Husayn al-. *Kitab Iʿtiqadat Firaq al-Muslim-n wa al-Mushrikin*. Edited by A. S. al-Nashshar. Cairo, 1938.

Reeves, John C. *Jewish Lore in Manichaean Cosmogony. Studies in the "Book of Giants" Traditions*. Cincinnati, 1992.

Reif, Stefan. "Liturgical Difficulties in Geniza Manuscripts." In *Studies in Judaism and Islam*, edited by S. Morag, I. Ben-Ami, and N. A. Stillman. Jerusalem, 1981, 99–123.

Reiff, Philip, ed. *On Intellectuals*. Garden City, N.Y., 1970.

Reinharz, J., and W. Schatzberg, eds. *The Jewish Response to German Culture*. Hanover and London, 1985.

Reinink, G. *Studien zur Quellen-und Traditionsgeschichte des Evangelion-Kommentars der Gannat Bussame*. Louvain, 1979.

Reynolds, Frank E., and David Tracy, eds. *Myth and Philosophy*. Albany, 1990.

Rippin, Andrew, ed. *Institute for Islamic-Judaic Studies Newsletter* 3 (1984): 1–5.

———. "Saʿadya Gaon and Genesis 22: Aspects of Jewish-Muslim Interaction and

Polemic." In *Studies in Islamic and Judaic Traditions*, edited by William M. Brinner and Stephen D. Ricks. Atlanta, 1986, 33–46.

Ritter, H. *Das Meer der Seele*. Leiden, 1955.

Robinson, Ira. "Jacob al-Kirkisani on the Reality of Magic and the Nature of the Miraculous: A Study in Tenth-Century Karaite Rationalism." In *Truth and Compassion*, edited by H. Joseph, J. N. Lightstone, and M. D. Oppenheim. Waterloo, Ontario, Canada, 1983, 41–55.

Rodinson, Maxime. "A Critical Survey of Modern Studies on Muhammad." In *Studies on Islam*, translated and edited by Merlin L. Swartz. New York and Oxford, 1981, 23–86.

Roncaglia, M. P. "Éléments Ébionites et Elkésaites dans le Coran: Notes and hypothèses." *Proche-orient chrétien* 21 (1971): 101–26.

Rorty, Richard. "The Intellectuals at the End of Socialism." *Yale Review* 80 (1992): 1–17.

Rosenberg, Shalom. "Link to the Land of Israel." In *World Jewry and the State of Israel*, edited by E. E. Urbach and Moshe Davis. New York, 1977.

Rosenblatt, Samuel. "Rabbinic Legends in Hadith." *Moslem World* 35 (1945): 237–52.

Rosenstiehl, J. M. "Le portrait de l'Antichrist." In *Pseudépigraphes de l'ancien testament et manuscrits de la Mer morte*. Paris, 1967, 45–60.

Rosenthal, Erwin I. J. *Judaism and Islam*. London and New York, 1961.

Rosenthal, Franz. "From the 'Unorthodox' Judaism of Medieval Yemen." In *Hommages à Georges Vajda*, edited by G. Nahon and C. Touati. Louvain, 1980, 279–90.

———. "A Jewish Philosopher of the Tenth Century." *Hebrew Union College Annual* 21 (1948): 155–75.

———. "The Study of Muslim Intellectual and Social History: Approaches and Methods." In *Muslim Intellectual and Social History*. London, 1990.

———. *The Technique and Approach of Muslim Scholarship*. Rome, 1947.

———, trans. *The History of al-Tabari*. Vol. 1, *General Introduction and From the Creation to the Flood*. Albany, N.Y., 1989.

Rosenthal, Judah. *Hiwi al-Balkhi. A Comparative Study*. Philadelphia, 1949.

———. "On the History of Heresy in the Era of Saadia" (in Hebrew). *Horeb* 9 (1946): 21–37.

Roth, Cecil. "Jewish Society in the Renaissance Environment." In *Jewish Society through the Ages*, edited by H. H. Ben-Sasson and S. Ettinger. New York, 1973, 239–51.

Roth, Norman. "Forgery and Abrogation of the Torah: A Theme in Muslim and Christian Polemic in Spain." *Proceedings of the American Academy of Jewish Research* 54 (1987): 203–36.

Rubin, Uri. "Morning and Evening Prayers in Early Islam." *Jerusalem Studies in Arabic and Islam* 10 (1987): 40–65.

———. "Prophets and Progenitors in the Early Shiʿa Tradition." *Jerusalem Studies in Arabic and Islam* 1 (1979): 41–65.

Rudolph, Kurt. *Gnosis: The Nature and History of Gnosticism*. San Francisco, 1983.

———. "Julius Wellhausen and His 'Prolegmena to the History of Israel.'" *Semeia* 24 (1983).

———. "Mircea Eliade and the 'History' of Religions." *Religion* 19 (1989): 101–27.

———. "Zur Soziologie, Sozialen 'Verortung' und Rolle der Gnosis in der Spatantike." In *Studien zum Menschenbild in Gnosis und Manichäismus*. Edited by P. Nagel. Halle/Saale, 1979, 19–29.

Russell, Jeffrey B. *Dissent and Reform in the Early Middle Ages*. Berkeley and Los Angeles, 1965.

Saadia Gaon. *The Book of Beliefs and Opinions*. Translated by S. Rosenblatt. New Haven, 1948.

de Sacy, Silvestre. *Exposé de la Religion des Druzes*. Paris, 1838.

Sachedina, Abdulaziz. "*Al-Khums*: The Fifth in the Imami Shi'i Legal System." *Journal of New Eastern Studies* 39 (1980).

———. *Islamic Messianism: the Idea of the Mahdi in Twelver Shi'ism*. Albany, N.Y., 1981.

———. *The Just Ruler (al-Sultan al-'adil) in Shi'ite Islam: The Comprehensive Authority of the Jurist in Imamite Jurisprudence*. New York and Oxford, 1988.

Sadan, J. "Genizah and Genizah-Like Practices in Islamic and Jewish Traditions." *Bibliotheca Orientalis* 43 (1986): 36–58.

———. "Some Literary Problems Concerning Judaism and Jewry in Medieval Arabic Sources." In *Studies in Islamic History and Civilization in Honour of David Ayalon*. Jerusalem and Leiden, 1986, 353–98.

Salem, E. A. *Political Theory and Institutions of the Khawarij*. Baltimore, 1956.

Salisbury, E. E. "Notice of the Book of Sulaiman's First Ripe Fruit." *Journal of the American Oriental Society* 8 (1866): 227–308.

Samau'al al-Maghribi. *Ifham al-Yahud. Proceedings of the American Academy for Jewish Research* 32 (1964) ed. and trans., M. Perlmann.

Sanders, E. P., A. I. Baumgarten, and Alan Mendelson. *Jewish and Christian Self-Definition*. 3 vols. Philadelphia, 1981.

Saperstein, Marc. *Decoding the Rabbis*. Cambridge, Mass., 1980.

Savage, Elizabeth. "Ibadi-Jewish Parallels in Early Medieval North Africa." *Al-Masaq* 5 (1992): 1–15.

Scheiber, Alexander. "Bernhard Heller." In *The Rabbinical Seminary of Budapest, 1877–1977*. New York, 1986, 198–200.

Schiffman, Lawrence. " The Recall of Rabbi Nehuniah ben haQanah from Ecstasy in the Hekhalot Rabbati." *Association for Jewish Studies Review* 1 (1976): 269–81.

Schimmel, Annemarie. *And Muhammad Is His Messenger: The Veneration of the Prophet in Islamic Piety*. Chapel Hill, N.C., 1985.

Schluchter, W. *Rationalism, Religion and Domination: A Weberian Perspective*. Berkeley and Los Angeles, 1989.

Schoeps, Hans Joachim. *Jewish Christianity*. Philadelphia, 1969.

Scholem, Gershom G. "A Candid Word about the True Motives of My Kabbalistic Studies: A Letter to Salman Schocken." In *Gershom Scholem: Kabbalah and Counter-History*, by David Biale. Cambridge, Mass., 1979, 31–32 (translation), 155–56 (text).

———. *Das Buch Bahir*. Leipzig, 1923.

———. *From Berlin to Jerusalem: Memoires of My Youth*. New York, 1980.

———. *Jewish Gnosticism, Merkabah Mysticism and Talmudic Tradition*. New York, 1960.

———. "Jews and Germans." In *On Jews and Judaism in Crisis*, edited by Werner J. Dannhauser. New York, 1976, 71–93.

———. *Major Trends in Jewish Mysticism*. New York, 1972.

———. *The Messianic Idea in Judaism*. New York, 1971.

————. *On Kabbalah and Its Symbolism.* New York, 1974.

————. *Origins of the Kabbalah.* Translated by Allan Arkush. Princeton 1987.

————. "Sidre Shimmusche Rabba." *Tarbis* 16 (1945): 196–209.

Schorsch, Ismar. "The Myth of Sephardic Supremacy." *Leo Baeck Institute Yearbook* 34 (1989): 47–66.

Schreiner, Martin. "Les Juifs dans al-Beruni." *Revue des études juives* 12 (1886): 258–66.

————. "Zur Geschichte Aussprache des Hebraische." In *Gesammelte Schriften*, edited by Moshe Perlmann. Hildesheim, 1983, 25–72.

Schwarz, Leo, trans. *Memoirs of My People.* 1943. Reprint, New York, 1963.

Schwarzbaum, Haim. *Biblical and Extra-Biblical Legends in Islamic Folk Literature.* Walldorf-Hessen, 1982.

————. "Prolegomenon." In *The Chronicles of Jerahmeel*, translated by M. Gaster. New York, 1971.

Schwarzschild, Steven S. "'Germanism and Judaism': Hermann Cohen's Normative Paradigm of the German-Jewish Symbiosis." In *Jews and Germans from 1860 to 1933: The Problematic Symbiosis*, edited by David Bronsen. Heidelberg, 1979, 129–72.

————. "On Jewish Eschatology." In *The Human Condition in the Jewish and Christian Traditions*, edited by F. Greenspahn. New York, 1986, 171–211.

————. *The Pursuit of the Ideal: Jewish Writings of Steven Schwarzschild.* Edited by Menachem Kellner. Albany, N.Y., 1990.

Scott, Archibald. *Buddhism and Christianity.* Edinburgh, 1890.

Séd, Nicolas. *La Mystique cosmologique juive.* Berlin, Paris, and New York, 1981.

Segal, Alan. "Ruler of This World: Attitudes about Mediator Figures and the Importance of Sociology for Self-Definition." In *Jewish and Christian Self-Definition*, edited by E. P. Sanders, A. I. Baumgarten, and Alan Mendelsohn. Philadelphia, 1981, 245–69.

————. *Two Powers in Heaven.* Leiden, 1978.

Segal, J. B. "The Jews of North Mesopotamia before the Rise of Islam." *Eres Israel* 17 (1964): 32–63.

Segal, M. Z. "The Descent of King Messsiah" (in Hebrew). *Tarbis* 21 (1950): 133–36.

Sells, Michael. "3 Enoch (Sefer Hekhalot) and the Miʿraj of Abu Yazid al-Bistami." Paper presented at the annual meeting of the American Academy of Religion (1989).

Serres, Michel. *Hermes: Literature, Science, Philosophy.* Translated by J. V. Harari and D. F. Bell. Baltimore and London, 1982.

————. *Le parasite.* Paris, 1980.

Severus ibn al-Muqaffaʿ. *Histoire des Conciles (Second Livre).* Edited and translated by L. Leroy. *Patrologia orientalis* 6 (1911).

————. *The Lamp of the Intellect of Severus ibn al-Muqaffaʿ, Bishop of Ashmunain.* Edited by R. Y. Ebied and M. J. L. Young. Louvain, 1975.

Sezgin, Fuat. *Geschichte des arabischen Schrifttums.* Vol. 1. Leiden, 1967.

Shahrastani, Abu Fath Muhammad b. ʿAbd al-Qarim b. Abu Bakr al-. *Kitab al-Milal wa al-Nihal.* Cairo, 1910.

Shaked, Shaul. "On the Early Heritage of the Jews of Persia" (in Hebrew). *Peʿamim* 23 (1985): 22–37.

————. "On Jewish Magical Literature in Muslim Countries—Notes and Examples" (in Hebrew). *Peʿamim* 15 (1983): 15–26.

———. "Persia and the Origins of the Karaite Movement." *Association for Jewish Studies Newsletter* 7–9.

Sharon, Moshe. *Black Banners from the East*. Jerusalem and Leiden, 1983.

Shboul, Ahmad M. *Al-Mas'udi and His World: A Muslim Humanist and His Interest in Non-Muslims*. London, 1979.

Shklovsky, V. "Art as Technique." In *Russian Formalist Criticism: Four Essays*, edited by L. T. Lemon and M. J. Reis. Lincoln, Neb., 1965.

Shtober, Shimon. "Muhammad and the Beginning of Islam in the Chronicle *Sefer Divrey Yosef*." In *Studies in Islamic History and Civilization in Honour of Professor David Ayalon*. Jerusalem and Leiden, 1986, 319–52.

Shweder, Richard. "Post-Nietzschian Anthropology: The Idea of Multiple Objective Worlds." In *Relativism in Interpretation and Confrontation*, edited by M. Krausz. South Bend, IN, 1989, 99–140.

Siddiqi, A. H., ed. *Sahih Muslim*. 4 vols. Lahore, 1975.

Silver, Daniel Jeremy. *Maimonidean Criticism and the Maimonidean Controversy, 1180–1240*. Leiden, 1965.

Simon, Ernst. "Martin Buber and German Jewry." *Leo Baeck Institute Yearbook* 3 (1958): 3–39.

Simon, Marcel. *Jewish Sects at the Time of Jesus*. Philadelphia, 1967.

———. *Verus Israel*. Translated by H. McKeating. Oxford, 1986.

Simon, Uriel. "The Religious Significance of the *Peshat*." *Tradition* 23 (1988): 41–63.

Simmonnet, Jacques. "Le gloire de Dieu est de cacher la Parole: La connaissance et sa séparation dans le commentaire de *Bahir* fait par Guillaume Postel à Venise." *Revue d'histoire et de philosophie religieuses* 63 (1983): 247–66, 435–47.

Sirat, Colette. *A History of Jewish Philosophy in the Middle Ages*. Cambridge and Paris, 1985.

Smith, Jonathan Z. *Drudgery Divine: On the Comparisons of Early Christianities and the Religions of Late Antiquity*. Chicago, 1990.

———. *Imagining Religion: From Babylon to Jonestown*. Chicago, 1982.

———. *Map Is Not Territory*. Leiden, 1978.

———. "Sacred Persistence: Toward a Redescription of Canon." In *Imagining Religion*. Chicago, 1982, 36–53.

———. "The Temple and the Magician." In *God's Christ and His People: Studies in Honour of Nils Alstrup Dahl*, edited by Jacob Jervell and Wayne A. Meeks. Oslo, 1977.

———. "What a Difference a Difference Makes." In *"To See Ourselves as Others See Us": Christians, Jews and "Others" in Late Antiquity*, edited by Jacob Neusner and Ernest S. Frerichs. Chico, Calif., 1985.

———. "Wisdom and Apocalyptic." In *Religious Syncretism in Antiquity: Essays in Conversation with Geo Widengren*, edited by Birger A. Pearson. Missoula, Mont., 1975, 131–57.

Smith, Wilfred Cartwell. "Traditions in Contact and Change: Toward a History of Religion in the Singular." In *Traditions in Contact and Change*, edited by Donald Wiebe and Peter Slater. Waterloo, Ont., 1983.

Solodukho, I. A. "The Mazdak Movement and the Rebellion of the Hebrew Population of Iraq in the First Half of the Sixth Century." In *Soviet Views of Talmudic Judaism*, edited by Jacob Neusner. Leiden, 1973, 67–86.

Spiegel, Shalom. On the interpretation of the polemics of Pirkoi ben Baboi. (In Hebrew) In *H. A. Wolfson Jubilee Volume*. Jerusalem, 1965, 243–74.

———. "On Medieval Hebrew Poetry." In *The Jewish Expression*, edited by Judah Goldin. New Haven and London, 1976, 174–217.

Starr, Joshua. "An Eastern Christian Sect: The Athniganoi." *Harvard Theological Review* 29 (1936): 93–106.

———. *Jews in the Byzantine Empire*. 1939. Reprint, New York, 1970.

———. "Le mouvement messianique au début du viiie siècle." *Revue des études juives* 102 (1937): 81–92.

Steiner, Heinrich. *Die Mutaziliten oder die Freidenker in Islam*. Leipzig, 1865.

Steinschneider, Moritz. "An Introduction to the Arabic Literature of the Jews." *Jewish Quarterly Review*, o.s., 9, 10, 12, and 13.

———. *Polemische und apologetische Literatur in arabische Sprache*. Frankfurt am Main, 1877.

Stern, David, and Mark J. Mirsky, eds. *Rabbinic Fantasies: Imaginative Narratives from Classical Hebrew Literature*. Philadelphia and New York, 1990.

Stern, Samuel M. *Fatimid Decrees*. London, 1964.

———. "'The First in Thought Is the Last in Action': The History of a Saying Attributed to Aristotle." In *Medieval Arabic and Hebrew Thought*, edited by F. Zimmerman. London, 1983.

———. "New Light on Judaeo-Christianity?" *Encounter* (May 1987): 53–57.

———. *Studies in Early Isma'ilism*. Jerusalem and Leiden, 1983.

Stetkevych, Jaroslav. "Arabic Hermeneutical Terminology: Paradox and the Production of Meaning." *Journal of New Eastern Studies* 48 (1989): 81–97.

Stevens, Elliot L., eds. *Rabbinic Authority. Papers Presented before the Ninety-First Annual Convention of the Central Conference of American Rabbis*. Vol. 90, pt. 2. New York, 1982.

Stevens, Wallace. *Poems by Wallace Stevens*. New York, 1959.

Stillman, Norman. *The Jews of Arab Lands*. Philadelphia, 1979.

———. *The Jews of Arab Lands in Modern Times*. Philadelphia, 1991.

Stillman, Yedida. "Libas." *Encyclopedia of Islam*. 2d ed. 5:732–42.

Stone, Michael. *Scriptures, Sects and Visions: A Profile of Judaism from Ezra to the Jewish Revolts*. Cleveland and New York, 1990.

Strothmann, Rudolf. *Festkalender der Nusairier*. Berlin, 1946.

Stroumsa, Gedaliahu. "Le couple de l'ange de de l'esprit: Traditions juives et chretiennes." *Revue biblique* 88 (1981): 42–61.

Stroumsa, Sarah. "From Muslim Heresy to Jewish-Muslim Polemics: Ibn al-Rawandi's *Kitab al-Damigh*." *Journal of the American Oriental Society* 107 (1987): 767–72.

———. "On Apostate Jewish Intellectuals in the Early Middle Ages under the Rule of Islam" (in Hebrew). *Pe'amim* 42 (1991): 61–76.

———. Review of *Creazione e caduta dell'uomo nell'esegesi qiudo-araba medievale*, by Bruno Chiesa. *Bulletin Critique des Annales Islamologiques* 7 (1990): 37–39.

Strugnell, John. "Notes on the Text and Transmission of the Apocryphal Ps. 151, 154 (= Syr 2) and 155 (= Syr 3)." *Harvard Theological Review* 59 (1966): 257–81.

Subhi, Ahmad Muhmud, al-. *Fi 'Ilm al-Kalam*. Cairo, 1978.

Sundermann, Werner. "Neue Erkenntnisse über die mazdakitische Soziallehre." *Das Altertum* 34 (1988): 183–88.

Su'udi, Abu al-Fadl al-Maliki al-. *Disputatio pro religione Muhammedanorum adversus*

Christianos (Al-Muntakhab al-Jalil min Takhjil man Harrafa al-Injil). Edited by F. J. Van Den Ham. Leiden, 1890.

Suyuti, Jalaluddin al-. *Al-Haba'ik fi Akhbar al-Mala'ik.* Cairo, n.d.

———. *Al-Rahmah Fi al-tibb wa-al-Hikmah.* Cairo, 1900.

———. *Ta'rikh al-Khulafa'.* Calcutta, 1857.

Szyzsman, Simon. "Compte rendu." *Bulletin des études karaites* 2 (1989): 103–6.

———. "La question des Khazars: Essai de mise au point." *Jewish Quarterly Review* 73 (1982–83): 189–202.

Tabari, Abu Ja'far Muhammad ibn Jarir al-. *Jami' al-Bayan 'an Ta'wil Ay al-Qur'an.* 16 vols. Cairo, 1954.

———. *Ta'rikh al-rusul wa'l-muluk.* Edited by M. J. de Goeje et al. 15 vols. Leiden, 1879–1901.

Tabarsi, Al-Fadl ibn al-Hasan al-. *Al-Ihtijaj.* 2 vols. Najaf, 1966.

———. *The Biography of Ja'far-e-Sadiq.* Karachi, n.d.

Tahanawi, Muhammad Ala ibn 'Ali. *Kashshaf fi Istilahat al-Funun.* Edited by 'Abd al-Haqq, Gholem Qadir, and A. Sprenger. Calcutta, 1853–55.

Talbi, Mohammed. "Al-Kahina." *Enciclopledia of Islam.* 2d ed. 4:422–23.

———. "Possibilities and Conditions for a Better Understanding between Islam and the West." *Journal of Ecumenical Studies* 25 (1988): 161–93.

———. "Un nouveau fragment de l'histoire de l'occident musulman (62–196/682–812), l'époque d'al-Kahina." *Cahiers de Tunisée* 73 (1971).

Talmadge, Frank. "Apples of Gold: The Inner Meaning of Sacred Texts in Medieval Judaism." In *Jewish Spirituality*, vol. 1, edited by Arthur Green. New York, 1986, 313–55.

Tambiah, Stanley Jeyarajam. *Magic, Science, Religion, and the Scope of Rationality.* Cambridge, 1990.

Tamir, 'Arif, ed. *Kitab al-Haft wa al-Azilla.* Beirut, 1981.

Tamir, Vicki. *Bulgaria and Her Jews: The History of a Dubious Symbiosis.* New York, 1979.

Taylor, W. R. "Al-Bukhari and the Aggada." *Moslem World* 33 (1943): 191–202.

Tchernowitz, Chaim. *Toldot haPoskim.* New York, 1946.

Téné, David. "The Earliest Comparisons of Hebrew with Aramaic and Arabic." In *Studies in the History of Linguistics*, vol. 20, *Progress in Linguistic Historiography*, edited by Konrad Koerner. Amsterdam, 1982, 355–77.

Tha'labi, Abu Ishaq Ahmad al-. *Qisas al-Anbiya'.* Cairo, 1347.

Thilo, J. C. *Codex Apocryphus Novi Testamenti.* London, 1832.

Thomas, David. "Two Muslim-Christian Debates from the Early Shi'ite Tradition" *Journal of Semitic Studies* 33 (1988): 53–80.

Tiedemann, Rolf. "Historical Materialism or Political Messianism? An Interpretation of the Theses 'On the Concept of History.'" *Philosophical Forum* 15 (1983–84): 71–105.

Tijdens, E. F. *Der Mythologische-gnostische Hintergrund des "Umm al-Kitab."* Leiden, 1977.

Trachtenberg, Joshua. *The Devil and the Jews.* 1943. Reprint, Philadelphia, 1983.

———. *Jewish Magic and Superstition.* New York, 1939.

Tritton, A. S. *The Caliphs and Their Non-Muslim Subjects: A Critical Study of the Covenant of 'Umar.* London, 1930.

———. "Discords and Differences in Islam." In *Essays in Honour of G. W. Thatcher*, edited by E. C. B. MacLaurin. Sydney, 1967, 85–102.

———. "Islam and Protected Religions." *Journal of the Royal Asiatic Society* (1927): 475–85; (1928): 485–508; (1931): 311–39.

———. "Muslim Thugs." *Journal of Indian History* 8 (1929): 41–44.

Tucker, William. "'Abd Allah ibn Mu'awiya and the Janahiyya: Rebels and Ideologues of the Late Umayyad Period." *Studia Islamica* 51 (1980): 39–58.

———. "Abu Mansur al-'Ijli and the Mansuriyya: A Study in Medieval Terrorism." *Der Islam* 54 (1977): 66–76.

———. "Rebels and Gnostics: Al-Mughira ibn Sa'id and the Mughiriyya." *Arabica* 22 (1975): 33–47.

Tusi, Muhammad Ibn al-Hasan al-. *Tahdhib al-Ahkam*. Najaf, 1378/1959.

Tustari, Muhammad Taqi al-. *Qamus al-Rijal*. Teheran, 1379.

Twersky, I., ed. *A Maimonides Reader*. New York, 1972.

Tzedaka, Binyamim. "History of the Samaritans under the Rule of Islam, 636–1099" (in Hebrew). Photocopy, Israel, n.d.

Udovitch, A. L. "The Jews and Islam in the High Middle Ages: A Case of the Muslim View of Differences." In *Settimane di Studio del Centro italiano di studi sull'alto medioevo*. Spoleto, 1980, 655–83.

Ullmann, Manfred. *Die Natur- und Geheimwissenschaften im Islam*. Leiden, 1972.

'Umari, Shihab al-din ibn Fadl Allah al-. *Al-Ta'rif bi-al-Mustalah al-Sharif*. Cairo, 1312.

Urbach, Ephraim. "Center and Periphery in Jewish Historic Consciousness: Contemporary Implications." In *World Civilization and the Present State of Jewry*, edited by Moshe Davis. New York, 1977, 217–37.

Utas, Bo. "The Jewish-Persian Fragment from Dandan-Uiliq." *Orientalia Suecana* 17 (1968): 123–37.

Vajda, Georges. "À propos de l'attitude religieuse de Hivi al-Balkhi." *Revue des études juives* 99 (1935): 81–91.

———. "Études sur Qirqisani." *Revue des études juives* 106 (1946): 87–123.

———. *Juda ben Nissim ibn Malka: Philosophe juif marocain*. Paris, 1954.

———. "Juifs et musulmans selon le *hadith*." *Journal asiatique* 229 (1937): 57–127.

———. "Les lettres et les sons de la langue arabe d'aprés Abu Hatim al-Razi." *Arabica* 8 (1961): 113–30.

———. "Les Zindiqs en pays d'Islam au début de la période abbaside." *Rivista degli studi orientali* 17 (1938): 173–229.

———. "Melchisédec dans la mythologie ismaélienne." *Journal asiatique* 234 (1943–47): 175–83.

———. "Mystique juive et mystique musulmane." *Les nouveaux cahiers* 7 (1966): 34–38.

———. "Pour le Dossier de Metatron." In *Studies in Jewish Religious and Intellectual History*, edited by S. Stein and R. Loewe. University, Ala. 1977, 345–54.

———. "Sur quelques éléments juifs et pseudo-juifs dans l'encyclopédie magique de Bûni." In *Ignace Goldziher Memorial Volume*, vol. 1, edited by S. Löwinger and J. de Somogyi. Budapest, 1948, 387–92.

———. "Un opuscule ismaélien en transmission judéo-arabe (*Risalat al-Jawharayn*)." *Journal asiatique* 246 (1957–58): 459–66.

———. "Un traité de polémique christiano-Arabe contre les Juifs attribué a 'Abraham de Tibériade.'" *Bulletin de l'Institut de recherches et d'histoire des textes* 15 (1969) 137–50.

————. "Un Vestige oriental de 'l'antibiographie' de Mohammed et un echo de la tragedie de Karbala." *Revue de l'histoire des religions* 189 (1975–76): 177–80.

van Ess, Josef. *Anfänge muslimischer Theologie: Zwei antiqadaritische Traktate aus dem ersten Jahrhundert der Higra*. Beirut, 1977.

————. "The Beginnings of Islamic Theology." In *The Cultural Context of Medieval Learning* edited by J. E. Murdoch and E. D. Sylla. Dordrecht and Boston, 1975, 87–111.

————. *Chiliastische Erwartungen und die Versuchung der Göttlichkeit: Der Kalif ul-Hakim (386–411 H.)*. Heidelberg, 1977.

————. "Das Kitab al-irǧa' des Hasan b. Muhammad al-Hanafiyya." *Arabica* 21 (1974): 20–52.

————. "Der Name Gottes im Islam." In *Der Name Gottes*, edited by H. von Stietencron. Dusseldorf, 1975.

————. "Dirar b. ʿAmr und de Čahmiya. Biographie einer Vergessenen Schule." *Der Islam* 43 (1967): 241–79; and 44 (1968): 1–70, 318–20.

————. "Disputationspraxis in der islamischen theologie." *Revue des études islamiques* 44 (1976): 233–60.

————. *Frühe muʿtazilitische Häresiographie*. Beirut, 1971.

————. "The Early Development of Kalam." *Studies on the First Century of Islamic Society*, edited by G. H. A. Juynboll. Carbondale and Edwardsville, Ill., 1982, 109–25.

————. "Ibn al-Rewandi, or The Making of an Image." *Al-Abhath* 28 (1978–79): 5–27.

————. "Yazid b. Unaisa und Abu ʿIsa al-Isfahani: Zur Konvergenz zweier sektierischer Bewegungen." In *Studi in onore di Francesco Gabrieli nel suo ottanesimo compleano*, edited by Renato Traini. Rome, 1984, 301–13.

————. "The Youthful God: Anthropomorphism in Early Islam." In *The University Lecture in Religion at Arizona State University*. Tempe, 1988.

VanderKam, James. "Jubilees and the Priestly Messiah of Qumran." *Revue de Qumran* 49–52 (1988): 353–65.

Vaudeville, Charlotte. *Kabir*. Vol. 1. Oxford, 1974.

Veccia Vaglieri, L., and G. Celentano. "Trois épîtres d'al-Kindi." *Annali: Istituto orientale di Napoli* 34, n.s. 24, (1974): 523–62.

Verlinden, Charles. "Les Radaniya et Verdun: A Propos de la traité des esclaves vers l'espagne musulmane aux IVe et Xe siecles." In *Estudios en Homenaje a Don Claudio Sánchez Albornoz en Sus 90 Años*, Buenos Aires, 1983, 2:105–35.

Vermes, Geza. "The Essenes and History." *Journal of Jewish Studies* 32 (1981): 18–32.

Vikentiev, Vladimir. "Boulouqiya-Gilgamish-Naufragé: Rapports folkloriques arabes, babyloniens et egyptiens." *Bulletin of the Faculty of Arts, Fouad I University* 10, no. 1 (May 1948): 1–54.

Vickers, Brian. "On the Function of Analogy in Occult." in *Hermeticism and the Renaissance*, edited by Ingrid Merkel and Allen B. Debus. Washington, D.C., London, and Toronto, 1988, 265–92.

Visotzky, Burton. "Rabbinic Randglossen to the Cologne Mani Codex." *Zeitschrift für Papyrologie und Epigraphik* 52 (1983): 295–300.

van Vloten, G., ed. *Liber Mafatih al-Olum (Mafatih al Ulum)*. Leiden, 1895.

Von Grunebaum, Gustave E. *Medieval Islam*. Chicago, 1969.

———— "Medieval Islam" (conversation with Norman Cantor). In *Perpectives on the European Past*. Edited by Norman Cantor. New York, 1971, 168–86.

————. *Modern Islam.* New York, 1962.

————. "Muslim World-View and Muslim Science." In *Islam: Essays in the Nature and Growth of Cultural Tradition.* London, 1961.

————. "The Sources of Islamic Civilization." *Der Islam* 46 (1970): 1–54.

Waardenburg, Jacques. "Jugements musulmans sur les religions non-islamiques à l'époque médiévale." In *La signification du Bas Moyen Age dans l'histoire et la culture du monde musulman.* Acts of the Eighth Congress of the European Union of Arabists and Islamists. Aix-en-Provence, 1976, 323–41.

————. "Muslim Studies of Other Religions: The Medieval Period." Paper presented at the International Symposium, Muslim Perceptions of Other Religions and Cultures Throughout History, Lausanne, 1991 (publication forthcoming).

————. "Quelques remarques sur l'étude de l'histoire des religions comme elle fut pratiquée dans l'islam à l'époque médiévale." *Actes du XXIXe congrès international des orientalistes.* Paris, 1975, 227–33.

————. "Tendances d'histoire des religions dans l'Islam médiévale." In *Akten des VII Kongresses für Arabistik und Islamwissenschaft.* 1976, 372–84.

————. "World Religions as Seen in the Light of Islam." In *Islam: Past Influence and Present Challenge,* edited by P. Cachia and A. Welch. Edinburgh, 1979, 245–75.

Waldrop, Rosemary. "Alarms and Excursions." In *The Politics of Poetic Form,* edited by Charles Bernstein. New York, 1990, 45–73.

Walker, Paul. "The Doctrine of Metempsychosis in Islam." In *Islamic Studies Presented to Charles J. Adams,* edited by Wael Halleq and Donald P. Little. Leiden, 1991.

Wansborough, John. Review of *The Jews of Islam,* by Bernard Lewis. *Bulletin of the School of Oriental and African Studies* 128 (1987): 28.

————. *The Sectarian Milieu.* Oxford, 1978.

Waqidi, al-. *Kitab al-Maghazi.* Vol 1. Edited by Marsden Jones. London, 1966.

Wasserstein, David, J. "Greek Science in Islam: Islamic Scholars as Successors to the Greeks." *Hermathena* 106 (1989): 57–72.

Wasserstrom, Steven M. "The Delay of *Maghrib*: A Study in Comparative Polemics." In *Logos Islamikos: Studia Islamica in Honorem Georgii Michaelis Wickens,* edited by Roger M. Savory and Dionisius A. Agius. Toronto, 1984, 269–87.

————. "The 'Isawiyya Revisited." *Studia Islamica* 75 (1992): 57–80.

————. "Islamicate History of Religions?" *History of Religions* 27 (1988): 405–11.

————. "Jewish Pseudepigrapha in Muslim Literature: A Bibliographical and Methodological Sketch." In *Tracing the Threads: The Vitality of Jewish Pseudepigrapha,* edited by John Reeves. Atlanta, 1994, 87–115.

————. "The Magical Texts in the Cairo Genizah." In *Genizah Research after Ninety Years: The Case of Judaeo-Arabic,* edited by Joshua Blau and Stefan Reif. Cambridge, Mass., 1992, 160–67.

————. "The Moving Finger Writes: Mughira ibn Sa'id's Islamic Gnosis and the Myths of Its Rejection." *History of Religions* 25 (1985): 1–29.

————. "A Muslim Designation for Rabbanite Jews and Its Significance." Paper presented to the Fifth International Congress of the Society for Judaeo-Arabic Studies, Princeton, 1991. Publication forthcoming.

————. "Mutual Acknowledgments: Modes of Recognition between Muslim and Jew." In *Islam and Judaism: 1400 Years of Shared Values,* edited by Steven M. Wasserstrom. Portland Ore., 1991, 56–75.

————. "Recent Works on the 'Creative Symbiosis' of Judaism and Islam." *Religious Studies Review* 16 (1990): 43–47.

———. "*Sefer Yesira* and Early Islam: A Reappraisal" *Journal of Jewish Thought and Philosophy* 3 (1993): 1–30.

———. "Social and Cultural Context: The Islamic Context." In *The Routledge History of Jewish Philosophy*, edited by Daniel Frank and Oliver Leaman. London and New York, forthcoming.

———. "Species of Misbelief: A History of Muslim Heresiography of the Jews." Ph.D. dissertation, University of Toronto, 1985.

Watt, W. M. *Formative Period of Islamic Thought.* Edinburgh, 1973.

———. "Shiʿism under the Umayyads." *Journal of the Royal Asiatic Society* (1960).

Weber, Max. *Ancient Judaism.* Glenco, 1952.

———. *Sociology of Religion.* London, 1965.

Wheeler, Brannon M. "Imagining the Sasanian Capture of Jerusalem: The 'Prophecy and Dream of Zerubabel' and Antiochus Strategos' Capture of Jerusalem," *Orientalia Christiana Periodica* 57 (1991): 69–85.

Werblowsky, R. J. Zwi. "The Common Roots of Judaism and Christianity." In *Jews and Christians in a Pluralistic World*, edited by Ernst-Wolfgang Böckenförde and Edward Shils. New York, 1991, 12–21.

Werckmeister, O. K. "Walter Benjamin, Paul Klee und 'Engel der Geschichte.'" *Neue Rundschau* (1976): 16–40.

Whitehead, Alfred North. "An Appeal to Sanity." In *Science and Philosophy.* New York, 1948, 61–83.

Whitman, Jon. *Allegory: The Dynamics of an Ancient and Medieval Technique.* Oxford, 1987.

Widengren, Geo. *Muhammad the Prophet of God and His Ascension.* Uppsala, 1955.

Wieder, Naphtali. "The Doctrine of the Two Messiahs among the Karaites." *Journal of Jewish Studies* 4 (1955): 14–25.

———. "Islamic Influences on the Hebrew Cultus" (in Hebrew). *Melila* 2 (1946): 37–120.

———. *The Judean Scrolls and Karaism.* London, 1962.

———. "The 'Law-Interpreter' of the Sect of the Dead Sea Scrolls: The Second Moses." *Journal of Jewish Studies* 4 (1953): 158–75.

Wilken, Robert D. "The Restoration of Israel in Biblical Prophecy: Christian and Jewish Responses in the Early Byzantine Period." In *"To See Ourselves as Others See Us": Christians, Jews, "Others" in Late Antiquity*, edited by Jacob Neusner and Ernest S. Frerichs. Chico, Calif., 1985, 443–73.

Williams, J. A., ed. *Islam.* New York, 1961.

Winkler, H. A. *Siegel und Charaktere in der Muhammedanische Zauberei.* Berlin and Leipzig, 1930.

Winkler, S. "Die Samariter in den Jahren 520–530." *Klio* 43–45 (1965): 435–57.

Wohlfarth, Irving. "Hibernation: On the Tenth Anniversary of Adorno's Death." *Modern Language Notes* 94 (1979): 956–87.

Wolin, Richard. "Reflections on Jewish Secular Messianism." *Studies in Contemporary Jewry* 3 (1991): 186–96.

Wolfson, H. A. "The Pre-Existent Angel of the Magharians and Al-Nahawandi." *Jewish Quarterly Review* 51 (1960): 89–106.

———. *Religious Philosophy: A Group of Essays.* Cambridge, Mass., 1960.

Wolfensohn, Israel. *Kaʿb al-Ahbar und seine Stellung im Hadit und in der islamischen Legendenliteratur.* Frankfurt am Main, 1933.

Wuthnow, Robert. "Religion and Politics." *Daedalus* 120, no. 1 (1991): 1–21.

Yahalom, Yosef. *Poetic Language in the Early Piyyut* (in Hebrew). Jerusalem, 1985.

Yadin, Yigael. *The Temple Scroll.* Edited by Yigael Yadin. Jerusalem, 1983. Reprint, London, 1985.

Yaqut ibn ʿAbdallah al-Hamawi, Abu ʿAbd Allah. *Irshad al-arib ila maʿrifat al-adib* (Dictionary of learned men). Edited by D. S. Margoliouth. 7 vols. Leiden and London, 1907–26.

Yassif, Eli. "Pseudo Ben Sira and the 'Wisdom Questions' Tradition in the Middle Ages." *Fabula* 23 (1982): 48–63.

———. *The Tales of Ben Sira in the Middle Ages* (in Hebrew). Jerusalem, 1984.

———. "The Transformation of Folktales into Literary Works in Hebrew Literature of the Middle Ages." *ARV*: 176–87.

Yerushalmi, Yosef Haim. *Zakhor.* Seattle, 1982.

Zafrani, Haim. "Judaisme d'occident musulman." *Studia Islamica* 64 (1986).

———. "Maïmonide, pèlerin de monde judéo-arabe." In *Les Africains,* edited by Charles-André Julien et al. Paris, 1977, 257–81.

Zand, Michael. "Bukhara." In *Encyclopaedia Judaica Yearbook, 1976,* 183–92.

———. "Jewish Settlements in Central Asia in Ancient Times and in the Early Middle Ages" (in Hebrew). *Peʿamim* 35 (1988): 4–23.

Zayd, Mustafa. *Al Naskh fi al-Qurʾan al-Karim.* 2 vols. Cairo, 1963.

Zayyat, Habib. "The Jews in the ʿAbbasid Caliphate" (in Arabic). *Al-Machriq* 36 (1938): 149–73.

———. "Sects, Innovation and the Salons of the Mutakallimun" (in Arabic). *Al-Machriq* 35 (1937): 37–40.

Zeitlin, Solomon. *The Zadokite Fragments.* Philadelphia, 1954.

Zenker, J. Th. *Quarante questions addressées par les Docteurs juifs au prophete Mahomet.* Vienna, 1851.

Zlotnick, Jehuda L., ed. *Maaseh Yerushalmi.* Jerusalem, 1946.

Zucker, Moshe. *Rav Saadya Gaon's Translation of the Torah; Exegesis, Halakha, and Polemics in R. Saadya's translation of the Torah* (in Hebrew). New York, 1959.

———. "Responses to the Karaite Movement in Rabbinic Literature" (in Hebrew). In *Volume in Honor of Rabbi Hanokh Albeck.* Jerusalem, 1963, 378–401.

Zuckerman, Arthur J. *A Jewish Princedom in Feudal France, 768–900.* New York, 1972.

Zurqani, Muhammad ʿAbd al-ʿAzim al-. *Manahil al-ʿIrfan fi ʿUlum al-Qurʾan.* 2 vols. Cairo, 1943.

———. *Sharh Muwattaʾ.* Cairo, 1310.

Shemoneh Esre, 'Isawiyya and, 85
Shi'ism, Isma'ili. *See* Isma'ilis/Isma'ilism
Shi'ism, Sevener. *See* Isma'ilis/Isma'ilism
Shi'ism, Twelver. *See* Imamiyya
Shi'ite Muslims/Shi'ism; amulets and, 199–
200, 201; beginnings of, 55, 124; in
common cause with Jews, 111; constitutional authority among, 67; evening
prayer timing and, 117–19; Gnosticism
and, 217–18; 'Isawiyya and, 47, 68, 85;
Judaic influences on, 13, 47–48, 66–67,
94–95, 124–27; Karaism and, 43;
Mansuriyya and, 82–84; Messianism and,
13, 47–48, 55–56, 63–64, 65, 70–71;
Saba'iyya and, 64–65; seen as "Jews" by
Sunni, 13, 55–56, 93, 96–108; tales of
rosh golah and, 108–16, 235; *ta'wil* and,
136–39, 153; treatment of Jews by, 93;
weavers and, 22; "Wise Child's Alphabet"
story and, 169; Yemenites and, 55, 56,
64, 124
Shi'ites, Sevener. *See* Isma'ilis/Isma'ilism
Shi'ites, Twelver. *See* Imamiyya
Shim'on, Rabbi, Moshe de León and,
219n.56
Shi'ur Qoomah, 125–26, 183, 194, 200n.133
Shklovsky, Viktor, 107
Shtober, Shimon, 177
Shubbayr (son of 'Ali), 95; Husain as
translation of, 66
Shumus al-Anwar wa Kunuz al-Asrar (al-
Tilimsani), 192
Sidre Shimmusha Rabba, 203
Sijistani, al-, Persian influences on, 131
Sikhs, prophet-child story told by, 168
silk route, Judaeo-Persian dialect on, 42
silk trade, 19
Simon, Marcel, 38
Sirach, Hebrew, 40n.101
Sirat, Colette, 134
Skocpol, Theda, on marginal elites, 212
Smith, Jonathan Z.: on apocalypticism, 211,
217; on "equation lists," 98, 99; on
theory of "other," 8, 223
Smith, W. C., on symbiosis, 181
social critique, symbiosis and, 214–16
"social imaginary," importance of, 208
social services, tenth century, 20
social settings, symbiosis and, 210–14, 217–
18, 220, 225–26
social theory: on religion and "world-
forming," 209; religious authority and,
121
"sociography," 6; Geniza materials and, 188

Spain: 'Isawiyya in, 88; Jewish philosophical
trends in, 128; philosophical mysticism in,
233–34
Speiser, E. A., 230n.87
"spiritual collaboration," 226–27
Steinschneider, Moritz, 73, 236n.109
Stern, S. M., 37; on Isma'ili missionaries,
129, 132; on Isma'ilism and tolerance,
123; on "Judeo-Isma'ili *ta'wil*," 143–44
Stevens, Wallace, 164
Stillman, Norman, 7n.18
Stone, Michael, 219
Stroumsa, G., 39n.99
Sufism, 86, 233
suftaja (letters of credit), 18
sumariyya, 19
Sumayr (Jewish minter), 19
Sunni Muslims: Banu Isra'il models and, 67;
contacts with other religions, 136; evening
prayer and, 116, 117; Messianism and,
13, 55; Mu'tazilite *ta'wil* used by, 142;
Shi'a seen as "Jews" by, 13, 55–56, 96–
108; treatment of Jews by, 93; "Wise
Child's Alphabet" story and, 169
Sus, Jewish/Isma'ili alliance at, 132
Su'udi, Abu al-Fadl al-Maliki al-: on
anthropomorphism in Judaism, 185; on
Jewish sects, 88
Suyuti, al-, Metatron and, 192–93
Sword of Moses, 190
symbiosis: apocalypticism and, 207, 210–14,
221–22; Aristotelian sciences and, 145,
227–28, 229–31; axiomatic truths of,
228–32; Buluqiyya narrative and, 180,
205, 207, 213, 235; chronology and,
216–17; cultural successes and, 233–35;
dialectics in, 213, 222; end of, 227–28;
of esoteric and exoteric, 213–14; Geniza
evidence on, 195, 196, 197, 200, 202–5;
German-Jewish, 3–4, 223, 235–36; Greek
thought and, 145, 227–28, 229–31;
imaginary worldmaking and, 209–10;
interconfessionalism and, 214, 215, 217,
218; Isra'iliyyat and, 180–81, 213;
Judaeo-Christian, 4n.5; of magical and
mystical practices, 194, 200–5; marginal
elites and, 212–13; Metatron and, 200–
202, 205, 207, 213; "negative," 9;
personalities and, 206; philosophical, 14,
225–28, 229–32; philosophical mysticism
and, 233–34; pluralism and, 33, 45–46,
210, 223–25, 236–37; "problem" of,
222–25; reason and, 145, 227–28, 229–
31; self- definition and, 11, 222–23;